Nigel Harris has spent nearly twenty years writing about and travelling in Asia, living in India, Japan and Malaysia. He worked as a journalist in South, East and South-East Asia and is the author of five previous books. A former editor of *International Socialism*, he now teaches at the University of London.

THE MANDATE OF HEAVEN

Marx and Mao in Modern China

𝛀_____

NIGEL HARRIS

QUARTET BOOKS
LONDON MELBOURNE NEW YORK

First published by Quartet Books Limited 1978
A member of the Namara Group
27 Goodge Street, London W1P 1FD

Copyright © 1978 by Nigel Harris

ISBN Hardcover 0 7043 2191 2
          Paperback 0 7043 3221 3
Photoset, printed and bound
in Great Britain by
REDWOOD BURN LIMITED
Trowbridge & Esher

CONTENTS

PREFACE

The Communist party of China claims that it is the leadership of the working class, and that the Chinese working class leads the peasantry in a State which exercises the dictatorship of the proletariat. This book is an appraisal of these claims in the light of present-day reality in China.

The first part is a brief résumé of the party's experience before coming to power in 1949. The second part describes the history of the new Chinese State and the problems it has faced in the period to 1977. Part three then examines the party's relationship to workers and peasants in the People's Republic. Part four appraises the degree of equality and democracy in China, and the ability of the new State to protect its hard-won national independence. Part five assesses the significance of China's foreign policy and the activities of the supporters of Mao Tse-tung thought abroad.

Throughout this account, a number of problems arise in relating the claims of the Chinese Communist party to the known record. Part six takes up these themes and attempts to offer an explanation of the past and the present, and so a suggestion as to the future course of events.

I am grateful for the discussions I have had with many people over the issues involved. Particular gratitude is due to Tony Cliff for his work in reading earlier drafts of the manuscript.

London, 1978

NOTES FOR THE READER

ABBREVIATIONS USED IN THE TEXT AND NOTES

ACFTU   All-China Federation of Trade Unions (before 1953, All-China Federation of Labour)

CB   *Current Background*, translation of official documents of the government or party, issued in translation by the United States Consulate General, Hong Kong

CC   Central Committee of the Chinese Communist party; when it occurs with a number (e.g. the Ninth), this refers to the Congress which elected it

CCP   Chinese Communist party

CI   Communist International (Comintern), 1919–43

CQ   *China Quarterly* (originally, Chungking; from 1960, London)

ECCM   *Extracts from China Mainland Magazines* (subsequently, *Extracts from People's Republic of China Magazines*), published by the United States Consulate General, Hong Kong

GAC   Government Administrative Council; from 1954, State Council, the council of ministers of the Government of the People's Republic

JMJP   *Jen-min Jih-pao* (*The People's Daily*, Peking); as officially now transliterated into Roman script, *Renmin Ribau*

JMP   Jen Min Piao or Yuan (or Chinese dollar), official currency of the People's Republic. Official transliteration now, Renminbau (RMB)

JP   *Jih-pao*, daily (of newspapers)

KMT   Kuomintang

NPC   National People's Congress

PLA   People's Liberation Army

PR   *Peking Review*, Peking, weekly (in English and other languages)

PRC   People's Republic of China

RMB   *See* JMP

SCMP   *Survey of China Mainland Press* (subsequently, *Survey of People's Republic of China Press*), translations from the Chinese Press, published by the United States Consulate General, Hong Kong

SCMM   *Survey of China Mainland Magazines* (subsequently, *Survey of People's Republic of China Magazines*), translations from Chinese weekly and monthly publications, published by the United States Consulate General, Hong Kong

SWB   *Survey of World Broadcasts*, monitoring service (of Chinese radio) by the British Broadcasting Corporation, London

Transliteration

Over the period concerned, different forms of transliteration from Chinese to Roman characters have been used. Where possible, these have been standardized on the first use in this book, without any regard to the relative merits of different forms. Where citations use different transliteration for the same term, no attempt has been made to standardize them.

Chinese measures

JMP/RMB: converted from old to new (10,000: 1) in 1955. Currently, 1 RMB equals 0·526 US dollars.

Mou: 0·067 hectares or 0·165 acres.

Catty: 500 grammes or 1·102 lbs.

NOTE ON SOURCES OF MAO'S WORKS

Statements before 1949

Selected Works of Mao Tse-tung, Vol. 1, Peking, 1965 (official translation of the second official Chinese edition, Peking, April 1960). Textual reference: *SW*I

Mao Tse-tung, Selected Works, 1926–1936, Vol. 1, New York, 1954 (official translation of the Chinese edition, Peking, 1951). Textual reference: *SW* I, New York, 1954

Selected Works of Mao Tse-tung, Vols II and III, Peking, 1956 (official translation of the second Chinese edition, Peking, 1960). Textual reference: *SW*II or III

Selected Works of Mao Tse-tung, Vol. IV, Peking, 1961 (official translation of the first Chinese edition, Peking, 1960). Textual reference, *SW* IV

Sources of citation from individual writings of Mao earlier than these editions are cited in the text. They include:

A Documentary History of Chinese Communism, edited by Conrad Brandt, Benjamin Schwartz and John H. Fairbank, New York, 1967. Textual reference: *A Documentary History*

Mao's China: Party Reform Documents, 1942–44, translated by Boyd Compton, London, 1952

Mao Tse-tung, *China: The March Towards Unity*, documents, Communist Party of the United States, New York, 1937

Speeches, writings and quotations after 1949

Official published sources – for example, *Mao Tse-tung on Art and Literature*, Peking, 1960; *Four Essays on Philosophy*, Peking, 1968; *Quotations from Chairman Mao Tse-tung*, Peking, 1966; and as cited in the text.

Internal party publications, as compiled in various sources, but particularly *Mao Tse-tung ssu-hsiang wan sui (Long Live Mao Tse-tung Thought)*, 1967/69, as translated in:

Miscellany of Mao Tse-tung Thought, 1949–68, Vols. I and II, Joint Publications Research Service, Arlington Virginia, n.d. (mimeo). Textual reference: *Miscellany*

Mao Tse-tung Unrehearsed, Talks and Letters, 1965–71, edited by Stuart R. Schram, London, 1974. Textual reference: *Mao Unrehearsed*

Mao Papers, Anthology and Bibliography, translated and edited by Jerome Ch'en, London, 1970. Textual reference: *Mao Papers*

The publication of *Selected Works of Mao Tse-tung*, Vol. V, Peking, 1977 (covering the period 1949 to 1957) occurred too late for the volume to be used here as a source.

For discussions of these documents, cf. the introduction to Schram, *op.cit.*; *CQ* 57, pp.156–65; John Gittings, *The World and China, 1922–72*, London, 1974, chs XI and XII; and *CQ* 60, pp.750–66; or Roderick McFarquhar, *The Times*, 5 Sept 1973.

References

Citations and notes to the text are given at the end of each part of the text.

PART I

THE LONG MARCH TO VICTORY

1

THE WORKERS' REVOLUTION

In 1921, when the Chinese Communist party was formed, China was in a state of grave crisis. The collapse of the old empire in 1911, the cumulative effects of foreign penetration (by Japan, Britain, France and the United States), the impact of the First World War and the Russian revolution, all posed severe problems and released new social forces. On the one hand, the old ruling order could not re-establish its power. Local warlords, petty gangsters and landlords filled the vacuum, dominating the countryside; foreigners controlled the great cities of the eastern seaboard. On the other, the nationalists – the Kuomintang, under their leader, Sun Yat-sen – could not mobilize sufficient military power to overcome local and foreign contenders for China's territory. The war had vastly expanded China's industry, which was heavily concentrated in the maritime cities.[1] By 1917, a new force was making its appearance – the Chinese working class.

In 1919, the Versailles treaty transferred Germany's holdings in China, not to the weak Peking government, but to the new imperialist power, Japan. The student agitation against the treaty – known as the May 4th Movement – rapidly drew into its ranks workers, merchants and businessmen, and spread to attack the privileged and dominating position of foreigners in China. It was the first anti-imperialist movement the country had seen.

The twelve founding members of the Communist party were active participants in the May 4th Movement. The Russian revolution was a powerful inspiration. Not only had the overthrow of the old Tsarist empire produced a régime confident and strong enough to defeat Russia's white 'warlords', the new Soviet government had repudiated the Tsar's claims on China's territory and promised to return all his thefts of the past. The Russians had also pledged their support to all oppressed peoples in the struggle for national independence.

The new Chinese Communist party set as its task the creation of a

3

mass working-class party which would champion the cause of China's national independence. To achieve victory, the party leadership acknowledged that it would have to displace the Kuomintang and give up the illusion that independence could be secured simply through military conspiracy. The party, though ambitious, was but a small group of intellectuals who lacked support among China's workers. Harried in the north by warlords and the satraps of foreign powers, the Communists were struggling for political identity against the currents of anarchy and bourgeois nationalism. In 1921, the party claimed fifty-seven members; and 432 in 1923.

Despite its small size, the party participated in the strike wave of the early 1920s which led to the first great Hong Kong strike of 1920–21. The party also experienced the sudden downturn of 1923, when employers and warlords inflicted massive repression to win back control of the workplace. Unused to the rise and fall of popular struggle, the party was plunged in gloom. Without military security and guaranteed civil rights, it seemed, the labour movement could not be built.

The strike wave had other effects. The success with which workers paralysed the British colony in Hong Kong impressed the Kuomintang leadership, who had their headquarters in neighbouring Canton. They contributed to strike funds, encouraged the workers to use Canton as their base of operations, and welcomed the labour leaders under the Kuomintang banners.

The strike wave and the Kuomintang response also impressed the local representatives of the Communist International, the international party set up by the Russian Bolsheviks in 1919. Maring (alias Sneevliet) visited Sun Yat-sen in Canton during the Hong Kong strike. His report to Moscow stressed that only a popular nationalist force was capable of standing up to the warlords and foreigners. The Kuomintang, already famous throughout China, was just such a force. It was, Maring said, the instrument not of a particular class, but a bloc of four classes – intellectuals, overseas Chinese capitalists, soldiers and workers. But it was a loose organization, and could be influenced by the Communist International from without and the Chinese Communists from within.

By August 1922, the Communist International seems to have been urging the Chinese Communist party to enter an alliance with the Kuomintang. But the alliance was not to be a tactical collaboration between two separate organizations; Communists were to *join* the Kuomintang as individual members, while the Soviet Union provided material assistance and advisers to the Kuomintang leadership. The Executive Committee of the International (ECCI) changed its evaluation of the Kuomintang. It was now a 'national revolutionary group', based 'partly on the liberal democratic bourgeoisie and petty bourgeoisie, partly on the intelligentsia and workers'. Nonetheless, the Chinese Communists were instructed to preserve their independence and build a mass party 'under its own colours'. China's revolution would not, the ECCI said, be proletarian, but bourgeois democratic, with the peasantry therefore playing the main role.

In fact, the Kuomintang was not much more than the personal following of Sun and his associates. Its declared aims were Sun's 'Three People's Principles' – Nationalism, Democracy (people's rights) and Socialism (people's livelihood). No concrete proposals gave content to these vague abstractions. The real aim was military power and it was the offer of Soviet military aid which attracted Sun towards the idea of an 'alliance'.

Chiang Kai-shek, one of the more energetic young leaders of the Kuomintang, was despatched to Moscow to study Russian military affairs, and a team of Russian advisers under Borodin arrived in Canton. Borodin set about a swift reorganization of the Kuomintang on the model of the Soviet Communist party.[2] This entirely changed the position of the Communists. At the first Kuomintang Congress in January 1924, the Communists pledged individual loyalty to the Three People's Principles and the Kuomintang leadership. In return, they secured three seats on the twenty-four-man Executive; one Communist became chief of the Kuomintang organization bureau.

Russian military assistance – the first arms shipments steamed up the Pearl river to Canton in October 1924 – brought the real rewards of the alliance. The Russians sponsored a new military academy at Whampoa and Chiang was made director. Sun's military forces were now substantial enough for him to propose a Northern Expedition in preparation for the conquest of China.

By late 1924, all the actors in the drama were in place. Already a mass peasant movement was under way. Through the winter of 1924–5, the agrarian movement spread with great rapidity in Kwantung, Hunan, Hopei and Shantung. The Russian advisers had transformed the Kuomintang from a civilian clique of aspirant politicians into a serious contender for national power, a centralized party with an increasingly professional army. As the Kuomintang grew in strength, so it attracted new support from those who feared for their property and calculated, rightly in retrospect, that the Kuomintang was their best hope for the future. The Kuomintang Right-wing grew.

The May 30th Movement
In 1925, Chinese workers returned to a phase of intense activity. Early

in the year, thirty to forty thousand workers in Japanese-owned mills struck in protest at sackings. A rash of strikes followed that spread from the Shanghai area to Wuhan and Canton in the south. On 15 May, a Japanese foreman killed a millworker. The Shanghai memorial meeting on 24 May was attended by some 5,000 people. On 30 May, a further protest demonstration was attacked by the police; ten demonstrators were killed and fifty wounded.

The May 30th Movement was born. Unlike the May 4th Movement, this was an overwhelmingly working-class reaction to foreign domination. On 1 June, a general strike against foreign capital was called by the newly founded General Labour Union (the leadership included a number of prominent Communists; in particular, Li Li-San and Liu Shao-ch'i). By the 13th, some 130,000 workers were out, and many of them remained on strike until July. The foreign authorities in Shanghai declared a state of martial law, and twenty-six gunboats were moved up the river to the city.

The movement spread. Three hundred thousand demonstrated in Peking, and other protests were launched in all the main cities. In Shanghai, the Communist–Kuomintang alliance led to the creation of a Shanghai Workers', Merchants' and Students' Federation. The Chinese Chamber of Commerce refused to join the Federation, but nevertheless, prominent businessmen and even warlords made donations to the strike fund and, where appropriate, provision for their workers to participate in the protests. It seemed that the political alliance of employers and workers against foreign capital fitted the mood of the moment.

However, even in June, Shanghai business opinion was becoming nervous. Workers in Chinese enterprises discovered, from talking on the streets with their brothers from foreign-owned factories, that their pay and conditions were frequently worse.[3] The Kuomintang leadership might stress that the Chinese workers had a quarrel only with foreign capitalists, but in battle, capitalism did not seem to wear different national faces.[4] On 25 June, the merchants withdrew from the Federation. On 6 July the foreign-controlled Municipality cut off the electricity supply to Chinese firms; the generators had been kept running by the workers so that Chinese capital would not suffer in the agitation.

By August, foreign and Chinese business had decided on a common front against 'anarchy'. On the 22nd, gangsters ransacked the headquarters of the General Labour Union. The strikes continued, but the workers tired as the tide of police, gangster and military violence rose. In mid-September, the military banned all trade union organization. In the factories, the employers had built up private armies to intimidate the

6

workforce.

The setback was temporary. The link between the first and the second waves of activity in Shanghai was the revolt in Hong Kong. There, on 19 June, the General Federation of Labour called a protest strike over the deaths in Shanghai. Seamen, telegraph workers and printers responded, and demonstrated in neighbouring Canton with the support of the Kuomintang. The demonstrators marched past the British and French concessions in Canton, Shameen Island, and the watching foreign police opened fire, killing fifty two and wounding over one hundred marchers. A general strike broke out in Shameen, and this spread into an overall boycott of Hong Kong and British goods. By July, 50,000 workers were on strike. The Hong Kong authorities reacted with violence, and the workers flocked out of the city to the sanctuary of Canton. By mid-July, some 80,000 had fled.

The strike and boycott lasted fifteen months. It was a disaster for the Hong Kong economy. As the historian E. H. Carr concludes, the boycott 'proved by far the most effective weapon wielded by the nationalists in their struggle against British imperialism; and the Kuomintang could hardly do other than applaud and support it'.[5]

The movement was extremely well organized. The strike was directed by a committee of thirteen, responsible to a delegate conference of 800 (in a ratio of one delegate to fifty strikers), meeting twice a week. The committee supervised the feeding, housing and entertainment of the strikers. It requisitioned gambling and opium dens in Canton as dormitories, rest rooms and education centres. It published a weekly newspaper. Strikers were organized to undertake voluntary work, which included building a road from Canton to Whampoa. By April, the strikers had set up a Workers' College with eight extra-mural schools for adult workers and eight primary schools for their children. These activities were financed by donations, fines and the sale of seized merchandise. To police the boycott, the committee maintained a force of several thousand uniformed and armed pickets and set up courts to deal with those breaking the regulations. It also maintained a fleet of twelve gunboats to apprehend river smugglers. Furthermore, strikers spread to the villages to raise support for the boycott and advance the movement for agrarian reform.

The strike committee was indeed – as it was called – a 'Government Number Two'. It maintained an administration apparently more powerful and of greater honesty, parallel to the Kuomintang régime of Canton. In essence, it was the first Chinese workers' soviet, one side of a system of 'dual power'

For the merchants and businessmen of Canton, however, the strike committee was a monster. They initially applauded its assault on British capital, no doubt calculating that what British capital lost, Chinese capital would gain. But as the committee's power grew, business was increasingly constrained. The strike caused a slump in both Hong Kong and Canton; armed pickets prevented Chinese businessmen reaping the reward. Taxes, fines for evading the regulations, confiscation of contraband, and the burden of dole payments weighed heavily on Chinese capitalists. In 1924, Cantonese businessmen, aping their Shanghai brethren and with British support, set up a paramilitary vigilante force to combat the pickets of the strike committee. The 'Merchant Volunteers', as they were called, demanded the government give them arms to maintain 'law and order'. The government dithered, but finally agreed. However, the Whampoa cadets refused to relinquish arms from the armoury. The Merchant Volunteers counter-attacked and, at one stage, the government was obliged to flee to the sanctuary of Whampoa, defended by the cadets, the worker pickets and Chiang's troops.

The alliance under strain
Businessmen were not alone in being compelled to reassess worker participation in the nationalist movement. In August 1924, Sun's political heir, a well-known member of the Kuomintang Left, was assassinated, apparently at the instigation of the Kuomintang Right. In November, a substantial section of the leadership, calling itself the Sun Yat-sen Society (Sun had died earlier), met outside Peking, proclaimed itself the Kuomintang Executive and expelled all Communists from the Kuomintang (but nonetheless affirmed the Kuomintang's undying 'friendship' with the Soviet Union and its arms supplies).

The International was also nervous that worker militancy might drive Chinese employers into the arms of foreign business. It instructed the Communist party to restrain the workers, to prevent 'excesses'. 'The Communist party leadership was equally alarmed, but its reaction was quite different; it proposed to end the alliance. However, Stalin – now supreme in the Russian party – was not prepared to jeopardize the considerable Russian investment in the Kuomintang and its future role in safeguarding the eastern flanks of the Soviet Union: certainly not for a wild gamble on the possibility of workers' power. The movement had to submit to the demands of the Kuomintang and its business allies.

Perhaps a policy of restraint would have worked, albeit with severe damage to the popular movement. But the Kuomintang's commitment to a Northern Expedition upset all calculations. While the Kuomintang felt it needed popular support, it needed the Communists, now heavily involved in the leadership of the worker and peasant movements. But as its military power expanded, it could afford to dispense with these allies, particularly if the allies appeared to threaten Kuomintang power itself. The Northern Expedition contained the threat of substituting military prowess for social revolution.

It was not surprising that the Communists and the Russian advisers viewed the Kuomintang's military ambitions with suspicion. The Northern Expedition, they argued, was premature; it required first, complete security in the south, and second, sufficient power to deter foreign military intervention. Not all were agreed – for example, the senior Russian military adviser, General Blücher, was an ardent supporter of the Expedition; it is said that Mao was also a supporter.[7]

Chiang Kai-shek, who had assumed great prominence, seemed likely to inherit supreme military command. This perhaps consoled the Russians, for he was seen as their nominee in the leadership. However, Chiang was wary of rising Communist influence in the Kuomintang. He was instrumental in securing, at the second Kuomintang Congress in January 1926, an obligation by the Communists to limit their membership of Kuomintang committees to one-third, and to submit a list of Communists in leading Kuomintang positions to the leadership.

If the Communists were worried, none of their fears were permitted public expression. The Soviet party's message to the Congress was all euphoria: 'To our Party has fallen the proud and historic role of leading the first victorious proletarian revolution of the world . . . We are convinced that the Kuomintang will succeed in playing the same role in the East.'[8]

On such an assessment, the Chinese Communist party had apparently no role.

The first coup

On 20 March 1926, Chiang Kai-shek took the first step to establish command. On the pretext of a Left-wing plot to kidnap him, he introduced martial law and arrested his Russian and Chinese Communist advisers and staff (including the fifty Communist delegates to his military units). The Communists were caught completely off guard, and Chiang swiftly ended all opposition to the Northern Expedition.

At the same time, Chiang arrested the strike committee, the 'Government Number Two', and eliminated the trade union movement in Canton. (The strike was officially called off on 10 October, without any of the original demands being won.) The Communists gave no lead in opposition, for they had been instructed to preserve the alliance.

9

Indeed, they retreated. They promised not to criticize the Three People's Principles, to divulge full membership lists to the Kuomintang Executive, to submit all Comintern instructions to the Kuomintang for permission to implement them, and to remove all Communists heading Kuomintang departments. Finally, on the instructions of the delegate from the Communist International they made a formal apology to Chiang for their 'misdemeanours'.

The weakness of the Russian advisers and the Chinese Communists was revealed. The Russians had only one card to play – the termination of military aid – and they were not prepared to play it. The power of the Communists lay in the worker and peasant movements. But to use it entailed breaking the alliance. The party proposed this to Stalin, but it was reproved as 'ultra-leftism'. Instead, Moscow despatched a new Communist International delegate, Voitinsky, to correct 'ultra-leftist', anti-Kuomintang tendencies in the party.

The Comintern banned any news suggesting a rift between Chiang and the Communists. The rumours that circulated in the Western press were denounced as imperialist fabrications, maliciously put about to wreck the 'revolutionary alliance'.[9] The Politburo of the Soviet party did not discuss Chiang's coup, nor was it mentioned in the long resolution considered by the Seventh ECCI in November. Secrecy had become vital, even though it disarmed the labour and peasant movements in China. It was not simply a result of the need to preserve the alliance in China. Indeed, it had little to do with China at all. To admit Chiang's coup was for Stalin to admit that the criticisms of the opposition in the Russian party, and above all the brilliant critique of policy by Trotsky, were correct.[10]

On 4 June, the Kuomintang leadership ratified the plans for the Northern Expedition and vested supreme power in the hands of Chiang. The coup had purged the Kuomintang and begun to roll back the workers' movement. It was a practice run for what was to happen a year later. It was also a signal to Chinese businessmen and landlords that Chiang was a man to be trusted. Kwantung's landlords now launched squads of armed men to dismember the peasant associations. The Communists appealed to Borodin for Russian arms to defend themselves. He refused, answering curtly but accurately that 'the present period is one in which the Communists should do coolie service for the Kuomintang'.

The Northern Expedition
Chiang might control the leadership of the popular revolt, but not the

10

revolt itself. Communists fanned out before his advancing troops, raising revolt in village and town to greet them. Workers in Hong Kong flocked to the army, to distribute propaganda, to assist in the creation of trade unions and peasants' associations. In Changsha, the trade unions seized the city. Railwaymen captured the Yueh–Han line to carry nationalist troops, and sabotaged the Hupeh section to block the movement of hostile forces. At the Wuchang arsenal, workers stopped production to prevent arms reaching the enemy.

A host of 'second governments' appeared in Hupeh and Hunan, with their own militia and administration. In January, spontaneous strikes behind the Kuomintang lines in Hankow and Kiukiang even forced the British to abandon their concessions there. The Kuomintang reproved the workers for 'excesses', but happily took credit for this defeat of British imperialism. The Communists reproved the workers also; they appealed to the peasants to ally with the 'good gentry', the landlords whose sons were now officers in the Kuomintang army.[11]

The ECCI affirmed that there was to be no confiscation of land except as a penalty for 'reactionaries, militarists and compradores and those landlords and gentry who are waging civil war against the Kuomintang National Government'. The Communist party leadership thus had the contradictory task of supporting the Kuomintang and its new officer class of landlord sons, and championing a peasant revolution against the landlords.

Shanghai
By the autumn of 1926, the labour movement was once more in the ascendant. The Communists prepared for the arrival of Chiang's armies. Forward military units reached Hangchow by February 1927, and then Kashing, only fifty miles from Shanghai. The General Labour Union launched a general strike to greet the army. Three hundred and fifty thousand workers joined in and there was street fighting. The Communists loyally persisted in looking to the 'revolutionary bourgeoisie' to lead the struggle, and proposed therefore the creation, not of workers' soviets, but of Citizens' Assemblies to represent all classes. Insurrection was proposed for 22 February to coincide with Chiang's arrival.

However, Chiang had been advised by the 'revolutionary bourgeoisie' to keep his troops out of the city lest they be infected by the Bolshevik virus. In the interim, warlord troops, police and sundry gangsters blunted the edge of worker militancy. For a whole month Chiang's troops delayed while warlord soldiers endeavoured to master the city. A foreign correspondent noted the paradox: 'Many people were arrested

11

because they carried handbills which read: "Welcome, Chiang Kai-shek, gallant commander of the Cantonese". They were found guilty and executed on the spot.'[12]

On 20 March, forward Kuomintang troops reached Lunghua on the edge of the city and halted to negotiate with the warlord troops in occupation. On 21 March, the General Labour Union again called a general strike. This time, between half and three-quarters of a million people responded, protected by a 5,000-man militia armed with only 150 pistols. Street-fighting broke out, but now the pickets seized the police stations and military posts and helped themselves to arms. The troops fled for protection to the foreign-controlled districts, the International Settlement. The General Labour Union set up a Provisional Municipal Corporation and, on the basis of this apparent victory, ordered the workers back to work.

On 26 March, Chiang entered the city. On the 27th, he imposed martial law, arrested Communists and Kuomintang Left-wingers, and banned trade union and student organizations. For the communists, it was not entirely unexpected, since Chiang had followed exactly the same procedure wherever his troops had taken over. In Kiangsi, his armies eliminated the labour and peasant movements as soon as they had secured control. But news of these events had been suppressed in the press lest they jeopardize the 'alliance'.

The General Labour Union was shut down and, on 12 April, Chiang launched his counter-attack, arresting, killing and disarming the pickets. The leadership of the Union again called a general strike, demanding the return of the arms and punishment for Chiang's underlings. Too late and too little. For the party still refrained from appealing to its known sympathizers in the Kuomintang armies, which would have blown the 'alliance' apart. One hundred thousand responded to the strike call, but Chiang's troops were now ready and machine-gunned the crowds. Some 5,000 were slaughtered, many of them publicly executed on street corners.

The leadership of the strongest centre of the Chinese working class had been decapitated. In Moscow, as in the first coup, rumours of the disaster were denied. Stalin insisted that the 'alliance' was still to be maintained: 'Chiang Kai-shek is submitting to discipline. The Kuomintang is a bloc, a sort of revolutionary parliament, with the Right, the Left, and the Communists. Why drive away the Right when we have a majority and when the Right listens to us? The peasant needs an old worn-out jade as long as she is necessary. He does not drive her away. So it is with us. When the Right is of no more use to us, we will drive it away ... Chiang Kai-shek has perhaps no sympathy for the revolution, but he is leading the army and cannot do otherwise than lead it against the imperialists . . . (the Right) have to be utilized to the end, squeezed out like a lemon and then flung away.'[13]

In Shanghai, it was not necessary to look far to see who had been 'squeezed out and flung away'.

Moscow did not give up so easily. A split occurred in the Kuomintang between the strong military centre (finally located under Chiang in Nanking) and the weak remnant of the civilian politicians (in Wuhan). The Communists were directed to 'ally' with the Wuhan government, but now on much weaker terms. It was a brief and ignominious episode, governed by the terror of 'excesses'. By July it was over, and the Communists were ejected.

Between 1926 and 1927, party membership fell from 57,900 to 10,000. Between April and December 1927, some 38,000 militants were killed, and 32,000 imprisoned. Trade union membership contracted sharply.

The alliance in retrospect

Events in China between 1925 and 1927 confirmed Lenin's estimate of the revolutionary capacity of a working class in a backward country. The labour movement developed with such speed because the later a backward country began industrialization, the more rapidly a new working class was concentrated in large-scale production, and the more rapidly the great cities grew. Workers were not snared in the conservative traditions of older working classes; the social structure contained relatively few of the middle classes, and so ideological control of the masses was weak. However, converting militant workers into political cadres depended upon the role of the small Communist party. In the China of the mid-twenties, as in Russia a decade earlier, both objective and subjective conditions for a workers' revolution briefly coincided.

Yet the workers' movement was disastrously defeated. Chinese workers never again played an important political role before the Communists came to power. The destruction of the workers' movement permitted a similar destruction of the peasant movement. It was not the balance of forces which determined the defeat, but the tactics and strategy of the Communist party – or rather, the tenacious loyalty of the Communist International to the Kuomintang, and of the Communist party to the International. The Comintern endlessly repeated the need for the Communists to be independent, yet rendered independence impossible by subordinating the party to the Kuomintang.

The very word 'alliance' became mystifying. In Russia, the alliance was between classes, not parties. The Bolsheviks did not organize the peasants, nor lead them in struggles against the landlords, nor even ally with the leading peasant party, the Social Revolutionaries. The alliance entailed that workers seize the State and so defend the spontaneous seizure of the land by the peasants; what Marx much earlier described in Germany as a 'peasant war'. *After* the October insurrection, the Bolsheviks adopted the agrarian programme of the Social Revolutionary party.[14]

In China, 'alliance' meant something different. It was not a relationship between social classes, nor was it an alliance of the parties of the exploited, the workers and peasants. There were no institutions to make possible such an alliance, no workers' soviets or national peasant federations. It was an agreement to subordinate a party which aspired to lead the working class to a party which aimed to lead Chinese capital and landlords. In 1925, these twin aspirations were transformed into reality – real social content, like a gale, filled the sails of the Communist craft. Compromise between the interests of the exploiters and those of the exploited became impossible.

Left to themselves, the Communists would almost certainly have ended the alliance. The Russian government, led by Stalin, decreed otherwise. It was the Russian government which transformed the Kuomintang into an organization which corresponded to the Russian Communist party in structure but without a Bolshevik programme. It supplied the arms and advice, which made it possible for Chiang Kai-shek to win the hegemony of China. Through the Comintern, it directed the Communist party to limit mass endeavours to what was acceptable to the Kuomintang. Finally, when it was obvious that the Kuomintang would sooner or later destroy the Communist party, it protected Chiang to the last by censoring all reports of what was happening.

Throughout, it invented labels to justify its strategy by describing the Kuomintang, in Stalin's words, as a 'workers' and peasants' party', which thereby rendered the Communist party obsolete.[15] The Kuomintang was whatever the tactics of Stalin required.

Stalin subordinated the Chinese Communists to the interests of the Soviet State and Russian foreign policy. To do so, he required a theoretical justification. The form this took was that China faced a 'bourgeois revolution' which must – contrary to Lenin's formulation in Russia – be led by the Chinese bourgeoisie. In Russia, in March 1917 when Stalin advanced a comparable formulation concerning the Provisional Government, it was described as Menshevism. But in China, no April Theses reversed the dominant party position. As a result, the party was compelled to accept the doctrine of 'stages' – first came the defeat of imperialism and feudalism, then the development of independent socialist forces. The task of the workers' movement could not be fulfilled until *after* the Kuomintang had won power. Until then workers must be 'restrained'. The act of popular self-emancipation was detached from the conquest of State power and indefinitely postponed. Yet in Russia in 1917, the act of seizing power *was* the seizure of the State, the workers seizing the factories and the peasants the land. The revolution was a mass action, not something undertaken by a special political or military group on behalf of the masses.

The Communists slipped further from the leadership of the popular movement as it developed. It was leadership by default, bending all its efforts to curb the militants. The leadership was obliged by the alliance not to champion the most advanced demands, but to fight against them, to reserve the right to decide what popular interests were tolerable. The party's verbal demands – for example, 'Land to the Tillers' – were rhetoric, not to be taken seriously; in practice it meant no more than a twenty-five per cent reduction in rent, and *government* confiscation of the land of 'wicked landlords'. Yet in conditions of revolution, it was the slogan which caught popular imagination, not the fine print. Then the slogan bounced back like a bomb into the middle of the alliance.

It could not be claimed that Stalin and the leadership of the International lacked adequate information. Trotsky had far poorer information than Stalin, yet he identified the impending catastrophe as flowing necessarily from the conjuncture of the 'alliance' and a popular revolution. The whole experience of 1917 stood as an object lesson of the need for the independence of the workers' movement and party. Stalin did not make an error. He pursued a strategy totally at variance with the declared aims of the International. As a result, what Lenin identified as the role of the Soviet Union in the world revolution – 'making the greatest national sacrifices for the overthrow of international capitalism'[16] – became reversed; the Chinese party was required to 'make the greatest international sacrifices for the preservation of Russia's national "socialism"'.[17]

2

FROM DEFEAT TO VICTORY

(i) The 'Third Period'
The defeat of 1927 was severe. For the Kuomintang the terror of revolution rang down the years, exaggerated by world economic crisis, Japanese invasion and the onset of a new World War. As Trotsky had predicted, the Kuomintang became an unstable coalition of warlords, capitalists and landlords, preserving its power by compromising with the imperialists. In the fight against Japan, Chiang substituted intrigue for defence. The 1933 T'ang-ku agreement was part of the continuing efforts by Chiang to accommodate Japanese depredations. Chiang formally recognized the Japanese puppet state, Manchukuo, in return for promised Japanese aid to consolidate Kuomintang power in China.

The victory of the Kuomintang in 1927–8 reversed all the gains made by workers in the preceding three years. Wage cuts followed the coup in Shanghai. Rising inflation robbed real wages, and unemployment rapidly increased in the wake of the world slump. With Chiang's patronage, gangsters created 'alternative trade unions'. They acted as employment agents, strike breakers, traders in child labour and opium, taking a cut from workers' pay and contributions from employers.[18]

However, workers continued to defend themselves. Even the corrupt unions, called 'yellow unions' by the Communists, were obliged to fight limited battles on behalf of their members. For example, there was a major post office strike in 1928, and 300,000 Kiangsi porcelain workers followed suit. In 1930, the number of workers who struck reached some sixty per cent of the 1926 level, and in 1935, the numbers were even higher.[19] Such action produced successive government 'reorganizations' of the unions.

The workers' actions were defensive, more often limiting defeat than making a positive advance. The tactics Communists should follow in such a situation had been outlined at the third Congress of the Communist International in 1921. The party should try to take up the limited material interests of workers through established trade unions, no matter how corrupt their leadership, to build a defensive 'united front' of all workers in order to restore their confidence in their capacity for collective action. In Tsarist Russia, the Bolsheviks had survived defeat by such methods.[20]

The Chinese Communist party could not follow suit, however, because the International did not permit it. The defeat of 1927 coincided with a premature rehearsal of what became known as the 'Third Period'. Stalin maintained that, in China, there had been no defeat. The movement might be temporarily checked, but the Chinese revolution was ascending. Armed insurrection, the very final point of revolution, was now on the 'order of the day'. Communists must therefore prepare for armed uprising. They must have no truck with the established unions, but form their own, Red, unions. Modest demands for the defence of basic conditions were 'reformist' obstacles to the revolution. Every strike movement must be converted into a mass strike and the conquest of State power.

Such a programme related in no way to the defensive tactics open to a defeated labour movement. Third Period slogans terrified the mass of workers, since they portrayed every defensive action as a challenge to the State, a provocation to the police. The Communists necessarily isolated themselves and demoralized their most loyal supporters. The party in the industrial cities shrank with great speed. What Chiang's police and soldiers could not accomplish, the International did for them. It rendered it impossible for the Chinese party to re-establish roots in the Chinese working class.

The party leadership committed itself wholeheartedly to implementing the tactics laid down by the International. When it failed, it was purged. As a result, not only did the party lose its social basis, its leadership was decimated.

In 1927, the men who had led the party from its formation were obliged to bear the responsibility for defeat and were sacked. The new leadership then launched itself upon a wave of insurrection. In every case, the party was defeated. The following year, the party leadership was dismissed by the International. The new leadership – the most prominent member of which was Li Li-san – had longer to prepare. But in the insurrection of July 1930, it achieved no more than the leadership it had replaced. In November, Li was dismissed, accused of a sensational list of crimes against the International. Those who succeeded him carried out yet another purge, but by now the party was so small, there was no possibility of an armed uprising.

The only force which survived intact was the partisans, operating in

17

areas remote from the cities. In the autumn of 1932, the Central Committee finally accepted the impossibility of reconciling Third Period slogans with the survival of the party. It fled from Shanghai to join the partisans, now based in a small republic in Kiangsi.

The Red Partisans

In origin the partisans were no more than the armed wing of a mass movement about to conquer power. The mass movement and the prospect of power disappeared. As a result, the partisans became the centre of the strategy, and the party came to argue that only *after* armed struggle would it become possible to create the mass movement of which the partisans were supposedly the instrument. As Mao put it in 1930: 'Only after wiping out comparatively large enemy units and occupying the cities can we arouse the masses on a large scale and build up a unified political power over a number of adjoining counties. Only thus can we arouse the attention of the people far and wide.'[21]

It followed that urban workers became no more than ancillary. The militants of the labour movement were now required to leave the cities as recruits for the partisans. The supposed vanguard became a rearguard.[22]

Rural guerilla warfare imposed its own constraints. It was not a form of struggle open to a settled working class. To participate, a worker was obliged to become a professional soldier. For guerilla warfare, secrecy and surprise were essential, not open political debate. The mode of struggle determined the type of contender. The party in the cities could advance Third Period slogans only at the cost of its survival. The partisans alone could advance those slogans with impunity where they possessed military power; but the slogans did not secure their power, only their arms did that. Thus, Third Period politics in China made necessary the partisans and so identified a different social stratum to propagate them, those who were socially rootless, members of the intelligentsia, workers who had abandoned their place of work and rural vagrants (*yu-min*).[23]

If China was, as Stalin argued, on the verge of revolution, there was no need for an agrarian programme that compromised with the most advanced demands. The elimination of landlords and rich peasants, and land nationalization were to be the immediate aims.

However, reality was as obdurate in the countryside as in the cities. The peasant revolution of 1925–7 had died away by the time the partisans arrived, as Mao discovered in contrast to his earlier Hunan experience: 'wherever the Red Army goes, it finds the masses cold and

18

reserved'.[24]

When the partisans were able to settle in one area, they discovered the severe limits imposed by circumstances on the implementation of their programme. Land, in the backward and impoverished areas where they operated, was extremely scarce. Collectivization required, for full peasant confidence, reasonably permanent military security which the partisans could not guarantee. Indeed, the presence of the partisans invited attack by the Kuomintang and warlord armies. Furthermore, they required feeding from the exiguous food surplus of the peasants, and they took peasant sons into the forces.[25]

The economic blockade of the Kuomintang imposed severe hardships upon the partisans. Indeed, at one stage, Mao had doubts as to the capacity of the soldiers to withstand the economic strain.[26] Necessarily, immediate survival took precedence over the programme, particularly when it was the better-off cultivators who produced the surplus product which fed the army and, when marketed, permitted the import of goods from the cities (salt, cloth and arms). Furthermore, the richer farmers supplied the bulk of fighters for the enemy. Mao and his associates solved the contradiction between the programme and the actual material circumstances in which they operated by not implementing the demands. As he later expressed it: 'Because the number of rich peasants was very small, we decided in principle to leave them alone and to make concessions to them. But the "leftists" did not agree. They advocated "giving the rich peasants bad land, and giving the landlords no land". As a result, the landlords had nothing to eat and some of them fled to the mountains and formed guerilla bands.'[27] Hypocrisy closed the gap – the party proclaimed radical agrarian transformation in the areas controlled by the partisans, but refrained from implementing the programme.[28]

Such a step implied that the interests of the landless labourers be restrained: 'Owing to the alliance with the rich peasants, the interests of the agricultural labourers were sacrificed ... We feared the counter-revolutionary turn of the rich peasants and consequently asked the agricultural labourers to lower their demands.'[29] It entailed also that the rich peasants continue to play a disproportionate role in the administrative organs of the Soviet districts.[30]

In the Kiangsi Soviet (created from six separate areas in November 1931), the partisans received their most promising chance to establish a stable administrative area. In power, the Red Army undertook a range of social reforms in education and welfare. It was an impressive military feat to survive against an enemy five to six times larger (the Kuomintang launched five massive assaults on the Kiangsi republic). The sheer

19

weight of arms, however, finally told. In 1934, the Kuomintang's Fifth Encirclement Campaign, employing half a million men, extinguished the Kiangsi republic. The party fled, setting out without clear destination on what became justly celebrated as the heroic exploit of the Long March. If 1927 had, to the party members, seemed to destroy the possibility of the urban working-class strategy, the destruction of the Kiangsi republic seemed to have destroyed the partisan alternative.

Between 1928 and 1935 Mao Tse-tung rose to a position of supreme leadership in the party. Retrospectively, it has been suggested that he fashioned an alternative strategy to that of the official party leadership which, after 1935, led to victory. However, this is not at all evident from the record. Most of his writing – for example, as editor of the Kuomintang journal *Political Weekly* – has disappeared or been heavily edited. As an individual, he clashed with the party leadership on numerous occasions (he was three times removed from office and eight times reprimanded), but never on the scale which afflicted his colleagues. On his later accounts, he apparently wholeheartedly supported the politics of the alliance with the Kuomintang up to 1927.[31] Whatever his private doubts, thereafter he acted as a loyal party member. None of the opposition factions in the party between 1928 and 1935 claimed Mao as member or inspiration.

Thus, if Mao had a separate political strategy, it cannot be detected in these years. His actions conformed to a combination of Comintern policy and the tactics of its implementation in small, isolated and backward districts of rural China. The result had some important features:

1. The party was obliged to assume that *it* was the proletariat of China. The peculiar circumstances of partisan warfare became the norm. As a result, the party implied it had no need of a continuing organic relationship to China's industrial workers.[32] The class struggle was not what workers did in the factories, but what the party, and in particular, the partisans, did. Thus, the essence of the class struggle became the contest to secure *military* dominance. Only after military victory did the old sort of 'class struggle', workers fighting employers, become possible.

2. Because military power became the decisive factor, the party programme was in practice relegated to winning support by propaganda work, rather than stimulating the independent initiative of the population. The slogans became part of the party's public relations work, and subordinate to the main questions of power and military strength. One aspect of this was the combination of radical slogans with relatively conservative practice. On the one hand, 'Land to the Tillers' and 'Down with Landlordism'; on the other, a limited administrative reform rather

20

than a popular seizure of the land.

These were not peculiarly Chinese Communist inventions. They reflected the changes impelled in the International by its Russian patron. The same points emerged in the writing and speeches of Stalin. But Stalin was not making a revolution; he was using the State to industrialize backward Russia. Material force backed his words. By contrast, the Chinese party was struggling for survival against extremely threatening forces. Its temporary foothold in Kiangsi was far too small to constitute a political alternative. For that, it needed a political case that simultaneously appealed to a mass audience but was not inconsistent with the imperatives of the International. After 1934, that became possible as the result of events quite outside the party's power.

(ii) The United Front
From 1932 to 1933, the Russian leadership became increasingly alarmed at the drift of the world powers to war, and at Russia's diplomatic isolation. Russian foreign policy became directed to securing alliances with leading powers against Nazi Germany, and in 1934 it entered the League of Nations, a body once described by Lenin as 'the League of Imperialist Bandits'.

In the Far East, policy became preoccupied with preventing an alliance between Kuomintang China and Japan. To this end, the Soviet Union recognized the Chiang government in Nanking and concluded a non-aggression pact. The International was similarly instructed to bend all efforts to securing Russia's safety. Communist parties in industrialized countries must now reverse the slogans of the Third Period, and enter Popular Fronts with the parties of the bourgeoisie against the threat of fascism. In Asia, the aim must be a united front with all patriotic forces against imperialism.

The change of line occasioned some embarrassment. The Chinese delegate to the Comintern, Wang Ming, baldly repeated the Third Period imperative in 1933: 'the overthrow of the Kuomintang as government of national betrayal and national disgrace is a condition of the successful prosecution of the national revolutionary war against the Japanese and other imperialists'.[33] But, by 1935, he was indignantly denouncing the idea that Communists call for the overthrow of the Kuomintang as 'an absolutely false and unfounded legend spread by pro-Japanese elements . . . a slander, a provocation'.[34] On the contrary, the Communists called for an alliance of *all* forces opposing the Japanese.

21

The Chinese party reflected the change. It appealed for a 'united front from below' against the Kuomintang leadership and the Japanese invasion. In April 1932 the Kiangsi Soviet declared war on Japan, a symbolic gesture but of great significance for nationalist opinion. By 1935 and the Seventh Congress of the International in Moscow, the Russian leadership was urgent in its demands for a new alliance. Mao resisted, and in particular was reluctant to accept the implication that the party give up slogans which might jeopardize the Kuomintang's social basis (notably, the attack on landlords). As late as July 1936, Chou En-lai could still promise Edgar Snow that any real war on Japan would destroy Chiang Kai-shek.[35] When in December two rebel Kuomintang generals interned Chiang in Sian, while the Russian press denounced them as traitors, Mao cabled his congratulations.[36]

However, the party's rebellion was brief. Mao despatched Chou En-lai to Sian to secure the release of Chiang. In February of the following year, the party agreed to end its programme of agrarian reform and once more to embrace Sun Yat-sen's Three People's Principles. In sum, Mao promised: 'We have already accepted a decision not to confiscate the land of rich peasants, and if they come to us to fight against Japan, not to refuse to unite with them. We are not confiscating the property and factories of the big and small merchants and capitalists. We protect their enterprises and help them to expand so that the material supply in the Soviet districts, so necessary for the anti-Japanese campaign, may be augmented.'

Furthermore, the events of 1927 were rewritten to highlight 'the glorious history of collaboration between the Communist party and the Kuomintang'.[37] Chiang himself, the former 'butcher of Shanghai', received a facelift: 'The Chinese Communist party has placed unquestioning confidence in Chiang Kai-shek's fixed policy of conducting a war of resistance. No one else can lead the war except Generalissimo Chiang.'[38]

What was initally a short-term tactic became part of the party's principles. By 1937 Chou En-lai was denouncing those party members who saw the united front as simply a tactic.[39] In 1939, Mao summed up the party's politics in the following form: 'Our eighteen years of experience show that the united front and armed struggle are the two basic weapons for defeating the enemy. The united front is a united front for carrying on armed struggle. And the party is the heroic warrior wielding the two weapons.'[40]

Thus, unlike 1927, the party now had *two* weapons, of which its independent military force was the decisive one. On that basis, Chou En-lai and other Communist representatives joined Chiang's Supreme

National Defence Council, subsequently renamed the People's Political Council. The Red Army became the 8th Route Army, and the Chinese Soviet governments were renamed as local authorities of the Kuomintang government.

The alliance in no way impeded the Japanese advance. On 7 July 1937 Japanese and Chinese forces clashed in the Marco Polo Bridge Incident, and the Japanese attack on China proper began. Chiang's forces rapidly evacuated the area. In August, Japanese troops invaded Shanghai, and in November, the Kuomintang abandoned its capital at Nanking while the Japanese were still 150 miles away. Undeterred by any serious opposition, the Japanese forces pillaged the city and inflicted one of the most barbarous massacres of modern times upon the citizens. The Kuomintang similarly abandoned its refuge in Wuhan and Chiang fled far west to Chungking.

Kuomintang China
The united front was justified by the Communists as a response to the threat of the Japanese. The threat was such, it was argued, that the class interests of workers and peasants must be subordinated to the national issue. Only in this way could there be a united national opposition to the invader.

However, under the impact of Japanese attack, the Kuomintang became increasingly tyrannical, its corruption a byword. Japanese forces purchased the Kuomintang evacuation of Shanghai without a fight. It is said that, in return for 80,000 dollars, the Kuomintang general thoughtfully provided petrol reserves for the use of Japanese trucks landing at the wharves. In Chungking, army officers and government officials moved into business – the State became the main employer – and used it to line their pockets. Finance Minister H. H. Kung is said do have made his fortune in this way. Mrs Chiang dealt in military aircraft contracts. United States military assistance, beginning in 1938, provided further opportunities for gain (comparable to the fortunes made by a few in Saigon twenty-five years later).

Kuomintang troops – five million in the field, and ten million in reserve – were cruelly mistreated. Officers and NCOs sold their equipment, clothes and even foodstuffs. In battle, units were abandoned, and the wounded left to the mercy of the enemy. Only terror could force them to face Japanese arms. Not even the Communist party could persuade them that Chiang's China was worth defending.

Yet the soldiers were better off than the mass of the population. After fleeing to the west, the Kuomintang lost its labour force in the east. It press-ganged villagers into the army and to forced-labour projects on

23

highways, railways and airfields. There was, occasionally, fierce opposition. As the war proceeded, so the burden of arbitrary taxes, appropriations and bribes grew. No political force championed the interests of the cultivators, nor showed how the defeat of the Japanese would alleviate their condition.

In the cities, it was scarcely any better. There was tight military control of the labour force to prevent revolt. Inflation and wage controls produced a disastrous decline in real wages. The Chungking retail price index (1937:100) reached 5,304 by March 1942, and 10,000 in 1944.[41] Real wages were halved in a year. Strikes were outlawed in 1937, and the death penalty decreed for those who disobeyed.

Yet the Communists continued officially to support the government and did not raise even elementary demands either at a popular level or directly with their 'allies'. As a supporter of the party notes: 'The Communists in 1937–45 opposed strikes as detrimental to the war effort, and undertook no independent organization of labour (or the peasants) in Kuomintang administered areas.'[42] The result was to increase the power of the Kuomintang and to weaken the resistance of the mass of the population to the Japanese, the supposed justification for the united front.

Chiang was no fool, and while independent Communist military forces existed, they were a perpetual threat to his power. There were armed clashes between Communist and Kuomintang forces through 1939, and a major battle in January 1941. An uneasy stalemate persisted through much of the war. Yet even this did not prompt the Communist leadership to end the alliance. To have done so would have been to betray the Russian government and its most prominent member, Joseph Stalin, now seated at the high table of allied power with Roosevelt and Churchill. Furthermore, in China itself, the Communist leadership endeavoured to win United States support away from Chiang. From 1942, the party persistently raised the question of US aid to their forces at Yenan (and succeeded in winning a visit from a US military delegation in June 1944).[44] The Communist political credibility turned upon the fact that it was a more determined advocate of national unity than the Kuomintang. Chiang, with splendid effrontery, threatened Washington that, if the US used its military aid to force the Kuomintang into coalition with the Communists, he would turn to the Soviet Union for aid.

Peasants, workers and the party
The years of the Second World War consolidated the party's policies.

Before the war, the party had gone some way to reconcile itself to landlordism. During the war, 'anti-Japanese' landowners became 'landlords who do not oppose fighting Japan'. Reforms must be introduced, the party argued, but not reforms which affected the basic material interests of the dominant classes. In sum, the party aimed at balance between existing classes rather than tilting the balance. As Mao put it: 'The workers have been advised not to put up demands which may be in excess of what can be granted by the enterprise in question. In the non-Soviet districts, it is our intention not to accentuate the anti-capitalist struggle.'[44]

The politics of balance were difficult to apply. Mao was obliged to overcome the confusion of the cadres. He stressed that reforms were needed to 'arouse enthusiasm' for the war effort, but arousing enthusiasm always tended to spill over into land confiscation. To avoid this, the reforms must be modest: 'this is not the time for a thorough agrarian revolution . . . On the one hand, our present policy should stipulate that the landlords shall reduce rent and interest, for this serves to arouse enthusiasm of the basic peasant masses for resistance to Japan, but the reductions should not be too great.'[45]

Or again, and more bluntly: 'Recognize that most of the landlords are anti-Japanese, that some of the enlightened gentry also favour democratic reforms. Accordingly, the policy of the party is only to help the peasants in reducing feudal exploitation but not liquidate feudal exploitation entirely, much less to attack the enlightened gentry who support democratic reforms . . . The policy of liquidating feudal exploitation should only be adopted against stubbornly unrepentant traitors.'[46]

The party reserved the right to administer the 'class struggle' as a punishment for moral failings. Only the most incorrigibly eccentric landlords could have favoured the Japanese in the Liberated Areas. (i.e. under Communist authority).

If the attack on feudalism – and so any attempt to improve the condition of the landless – was muffled, capitalism became positively desirable:[47] 'Recognize that the capitalist mode of production is the more progressive method in present-day China, and that the bourgeoisie, particularly the petty bourgeoisie, represents the comparatively more progressive social elements and political forces in China today.'[48] They should be encouraged, and State activity curbed, to stimulate private enterprise. In like fashion, foreign investment was to be welcomed in the new China.[49]

In the Liberated Areas, life was hard but ordered, austere but adequate, in striking contrast to the squalid corruption and barbarities of the Kuomintang areas. The land revolution might be postponed, but

25

nonetheless, party rule ended famine and oppression, and improved educational and health facilities. For those who escaped Kuomintang or Japanese rule, these were tangible benefits.

In Yenan, the party grew for the first time since 1927 into a significant political force. From its claimed membership of a few thousand, and forces numbering 20,000 at the end of Long March (the party claimed 300,000 troops at the beginning), it attained a membership of 40,000 in 1937, 800,000 in 1943, 1.2 million in 1945, and 3.3 million in 1950. The central cadre was quite small – Mao estimates that only 800 members survived from the early 1930s to 1945.[50] The seventy leading figures in the party were overwhelmingly drawn from the respectable classes, the *hsüeh-cheng* ('students from families of small farmers, merchants and even aristocratic official families').[51]

The party was a qualitatively different organization to that of 1927. In late 1944, it was estimated that ninety-three per cent of party members had joined since the outbreak of war, and ninety per cent of the recruits were of peasant origin. By 1945, the party had acquired a distinctive style, with a recurrent stress on education, rectification through cultural reforms and manual labour in the villages, continual campaigns against bureaucracy, authoritarianism, arrogance, and a growing cult of Mao Tse-tung thought.

Civil war and victory

The end of the world war found both contenders for China's national power poised to race eastwards to establish their claims. The first phase of hostilities ceased on American initiative in January 1946. By March of the following year, the pause – and the united front with the Kuomintang – was over, and civil war broke out in earnest.

Both the Soviet Union and the United States had endeavoured to create a coalition between the two forces, while offering main support to the Kuomintang. In August 1945, the Soviet Union signed a new treaty with the Kuomintang which restored Russian rights in Manchuria. Privately, Stalin advised the Chinese Communists to 'join the Chiang Kai-shek government and dissolve their army'.[52] The victories of the People's Liberation Army received no mention in the Russian press until the last year of hostilities. Indeed, in May 1949, when it was already clear that the People's Liberation Army was about to win the whole of China, the Russians renewed one of their treaties with the Kuomintang government. When Nanking fell on 2 February, the Russian ambassador, N. V. Roschin, was the only diplomatic representative to the Kuomintang government to flee with Chiang Kai-shek to Canton.

Land

Despite the end of the alliance, agrarian policy remained strikingly conservative between 1937 and 1945. Enthusiasm required rent reductions for the peasants, but the landlords must be permitted to make a living or they would join the Kuomintang. Furthermore, Mao said, without rent reductions, 'the masses in the newly liberated areas will not be able to tell which of the two parties, the Communist party or the Kuomintang, is good and which is bad'.[53]

In the north-east, the party confiscated and redistributed Japanese land. It encouraged landlords everywhere to move their assets out of land into urban industry, operating a tax policy and denationalizing some government assets to encourage them.[54] When peasants challenged this as a manoeuvre to escape retribution, Mao instructed the party to defend the urban properties of landlords.

Rent and interest reductions were invariably described as 'solving the land problem'. However, in May 1946, the party proposed a scheme to *purchase* the 'excess' land of landlords (landlords were permitted fifty per cent more acreage than middle peasants, and one hundred per cent if they had been active in the war against Japan), and sell it at half price to peasants with the funds to buy it.[55] At the end of the year, a draft law was issued for the compulsory purchase of 'excess' land in the Shensi–Kansu–Ninghsia Border Region (of which Yenan was the capital), indicating that in an area held by the Communists since 1935, the land had not already been redistributed.

In October 1947 a quite different land law was published. This decreed, for the first time, 'the confiscation of all properties of the landlords and all the surplus properties of the rich peasants, the assignment of supreme power in the disposition of confiscated properties to poor peasants and labourers, and the overthrow of the landlord class without mercy'.[56] However, the cadres were to retain the power of confiscation; the poor peasants and labourers were restricted to *distributing* the land. Nonetheless, the new law was a revolutionary step.

The moment was brief. There were too few cadres to curb the peasant masses in Hopei. The party was so slow in administering the act, the poor moved into direct action. Through the winter of 1947–8, peasant associations sprang up in the province, launching indiscriminate attacks on landlords, rich peasants and some of those officially classified as 'middle peasants'. Naïvely, they thought they knew who the landlords were without needing party instruction, and that their actions constituted 'the overthrow of the landlord class without mercy'. The party's conflicting and confused classification of the rural population was blown aside.[57] When the cadres loyally attempted to restrain the movement, they too were overturned. The peasants demanded complete equality in the countryside and the right to supervise the party itself. They seized all the land of those identified by the party as rich peasants, pursued and assaulted them, and marched to the towns to seize the urban, industrial and commercial properties of the rural rich.

The party leadership swung hard to the Right. Only three months after the introduction of the law, Party leader Jen Pi-shih demanded an end to redistribution until the peasants had been properly educated.[58] Six days later, Mao himself weighed in against 'Left excesses', urging that 'new rich peasants' in the old Liberated Areas should be treated as 'middle peasants', that former landlords and rich peasants could be reclassified, that no one should pursue landlords into the towns, that poor peasant associations should be compelled to admit rich peasants, landlords and the 'enlightened gentry': 'there has been an erroneous emphasis on "doing everything as the masses want it done", and an accommodation to wrong views existing among the masses, one-sidedly propagating a poor peasant–farm labourer line . . . that the democratic government should listen only to the workers, poor peasants and farm labourers, while no mention at all was made of the middle peasants, the independent craftsmen, the national bourgeoisie and the intellectuals'.[59]

In the spring of 1948, Mao himself arrived in Hopei to unite the war command again. He stressed that there was no urgency about introducing agrarian reforms; they could be left for 'one, two or three years'. There were three conditions: the enemy must have been wiped out, the masses must demand it, and the 'Party cadres must be adequate both in numbers and quality to grasp the work of land reform and must not leave it to the spontaneous activity of the masses'.[60]

Officially, policy returned to the promise of rent and interest reduction. The peasant war was not to contribute to the defeat of the Kuomintang or any popular revolution. It was postponed until after power had been won by military conquest. The party, perforce, must tolerate rich peasant and even landlord predominance in sections of the party.[61] We do not know whether some of the enormous numbers of 'bandits' destroyed by the People's Liberation Army were in fact the landless attempting to persist in the land revolution begun in 1947.[62]

The workers

The labour movement in the cities revived as the Japanese relinquished control. Strikes increased rapidly. Workers in Japanese factories seized the plants as the Kuomintang armies approached Shanghai. Once in power, the Kuomintang attempted to restore its former labour laws, but did not succeed in curbing the strike wave.

Post-war slump exaggerated the effects of the civil war. Hyper-inflation, large-scale lockouts, sackings and pay cuts afflicted workers, but few presented a political alternative. If they saw hope in the arrival of the People's Liberation Army, they did not (as in 1926–7 with the arrival of the Northern Expedition) seize the city to welcome the New Fourth Army.

To have seized the city, or even a factory, would have been to risk the displeasure of the Communist party leadership. Mao instructed workers to 'co-operate with the capitalists, so that maximum production can be attained'.[63] Many of the cadres who went into the cities, however, found this a difficult policy to argue, given the great excitement and hopes of city workers. They fell into what Mao called a 'relief standpoint': 'the one-sided and narrow-minded policy of "relief" which purports to uphold workers' welfare but in fact damages industry and commerce and impairs the cause of the people's revolution'.[64] The real task, he stressed, was to secure the co-operation of workers and capitalists in order 'to do everything possible to reduce costs, increase output and stimulate sales'.[65] Party leaders condemned the Labour Maintenance Law of October 1945 because it set wages too high, introduced 'excessive' labour welfare measures and reduced incentives to work.[66] They complained – in conditions of considerable unemployment – that too many people were employed, too many cadres promoted themselves without experience or competence in production, and wages were excessive.

The policies attacked had been encouraged when the People's Liberation Army held cities only temporarily. Then 'Left excesses' produced 'enthusiasm' which left a legacy of goodwill among workers that might encourage them to emigrate to the Liberated Areas or support the party in other ways. But by 1948, the party was no longer a temporary urban visitor. It was about to inherit the cities. It needed to take them seriously. As in the agrarian field, policy moved to the Right, and maintaining existing production took priority. The wage system then became, not a method of 'raising enthusiasm', but of making people work harder. Mao warned the cadres: 'Do not lightly advance slogans of raising wages and reducing hours. In wartime, it is good enough if production can continue and existing working hours and original wage levels can be maintained. Whether or not suitable reductions in working hours and increases in wages are to be made later will depend on economic conditions, that is, on whether enterprises thrive.'[67] Where possible, working hours should be increased, holidays reduced, staff pruned, politics not permitted to impede production, and the public sector used to assist the private.

The same standpoint covered all reforms in the cities. Mao adjured the cadres: 'Do not be in a hurry to organize the people of the city to struggle for democratic reforms and improvements in livelihood. These matters can be properly handled in the light of local conditions only when the municipal administration is in good working order, public feeling has become calm, surveys have been made.'[68]

And if the poor, not daring to hope for revolution, might yet think they would at least be fed: 'Do not raise the slogan, "Open the granaries to relieve the poor". Do not foster among them the psychology of depending on the government for relief.'[69]

The scale of the war was vast. Despite initially much smaller forces, the People's Liberation Army inexorably drove back the Kuomintang forces. The long years of isolation, of living off an impoverished land, constantly fighting against a more powerful enemy, now began to tell. By 1949, the outcome was clear. In January, Peking peacefully surrendered. On 1 October, Mao proclaimed the People's Republic of China. The 'protracted struggle', in terms of numbers and terrain the most gigantic struggle for national liberation in history, had reached victory. Now, at long last, the party was free to do as it chose, free of the tactical feints imposed upon it by the International.

NOTES

1. On China's early industrial history, see John Chang, *Industrial Development in Pre-Communist China*, Chicago, 1949; on the labour movement, see Jean C. Chesneaux, *The Chinese labour movement, 1919–27*, Stanford, 1968. The most outstanding political account of the period is Harold Isaacs, *The Tragedy of the Chinese Revolution*, London, 1938 edition

2. See his explanation of frictions with the Communists – they were jealous of Russian military aid – in *A Documentary History of Chinese Communism* edited by Conrad Brandt, Benjamin Schwartz and John K. Fairbank, New York, 1967, p. 63

3. 'Exploitation in [Chinese-owned] enterprises was generally greater than in foreign-owned industries; the technically backward and relatively under-capitalized Chinese firms were able to compete only by such methods', Israel Epstein, *Notes on Labour Problems in Nationalist China*, New York, 1949 mimeo

4. Sun Yat-sen, 1924 May Day speech: 'The difference between the Chinese workers and foreign workers lies in the fact that the latter are oppressed only by their own capitalists and not by those of other countries . . . The Chinese workers are as yet not oppressed by Chinese capitalists . . . They are oppressed by foreign capitalists'. Cited by Isaacs, *op. cit.*, p. 71

5. Cited by E. H. Carr, *Socialism in One Country, 1924–26*, London, 1964, III, p. 751

6. Zinoviev, then president of the Communist International, reported to the 14th Congress of the Soviet Communist party in December that 'The Chinese party received a directive proposing a certain putting on of brakes' – cited by Carr, *Socialism, op. cit.*, p. 761

7. General V. V. Blücher (Galin), Sep. 1925, *Prospects for 1926*, translated *CQ* 35, Jul.–Sept. 1968, p. 23

8. *Inprecor*, 7 Jan. 1926

9. See *Inprecor*, 53, 5 Apr. 1926, reprint from the Berlin *Rote Fahne*, 28 Mar. 1926. The Tass Peking correspondent specifically denied the allegations, 30 March despatch, cited Isaacs, *op. cit.*, p. 111

10. For example, see Leon Trotsky, *Problems of the Chinese Revolution* (documents); translated and published, New York, 1932

11. Circular letter of the Central Committee, CPC, 7 Aug. 1927 in *A Documentary History, op. cit.*, p. 102 *passim*

12. *New York Herald Tribune*, 21 Feb. 1927

13. Unpublished speech, cited by Vuyovitch as a challenge to Stalin at the 8th Plenum of the ECCI, May 1927. Stalin did not deny he made the speech, nor that it was in the terms quoted, but the official transcription was never published; cited by Isaacs, *op. cit.*, p. 185, from *Documents de l'Opposition Française*, pp. 36, 64, and included as second appendix to Trotsky, *op. cit.*, pp. 376–90. At the 8th Plenum, Stalin affirmed that events in China had 'proved the line laid down was correct' – 'Questions of the Chinese Revolution', *Inprecor*, 7/27, 28 Apr. 1927 (from *Pravda* 90, 21 April 1927)

14. Lenin, *CW* 31, p. 72

15. *Problems of Leninism*, Moscow, n.d. (written 1926), p. 264

16. From Lenin's Theses on the Colonial Question, 2nd Congress, Communist International, in Jane Degras (ed.), *The Communist International 1919–1943*, London, 1971, I

17. Isaacs, 1938, *op. cit.*, p. 51

18. See 'Five years of Kuomintang Reaction', *China's Forum*, Shanghai, 1932. See also Lowe Chuan-hua, *Facing Labour Issues in China*, Shanghai, 1933, p. 50. On the situation in the immediate aftermath of the 1927 coup, see Lo Chao-lung, 'The Chinese Trade Union Movement in 1928', *China Tomorrow*, Shanghai, 20 Feb. 1929

19. Nym Wales, *The Chinese Labor Movement*, New York, 1945, pp. 166–7

20. For example, the Moscow district party, with 5,320 members in May 1906, declined under police repression to 180 in 1908, and in 1910 ceased to exist – cited by Tony Cliff, *Lenin*, London, 1975, I, p. 240. As late as 1914, Krupskaya could complain: 'The illegal organization is cut to ribbons. There are no solid regional centres. The local organizations are cut off from one another, and in the majority of cases everywhere, there are only workers in the organizations, the professionals have vanished long since', cited from *Istoricheskii Archiv*, 1957, 1, p. 26, by R. H. McNeal, *Bride of the Revolution, Krupskaya and Lenin*, London, 1973, p. 145

21. Mao, Jan. 1930, in *Selected Works*, Vol. 1, p. 123 (*SW*; cf. Notes to Reader for explanation of edition employed)

22. Compare Manuilsky of the ECCI: 'Hitherto, we have regarded the partisans as the rearguard fight of a revolution in the course of a general retreat. Today, their character has changed. They form a constituent of the upsurge and one of the most important signs of the rising tide of revolution', *Inprecor*, 10

Mar. 1930, p. 267. By the autumn, the partisans had become evidence that the working class had a Red Army and a State even before the final victory of workers and peasants – *Inprecor*, 1930, p. 1065; cf. also Kuchynov, in *Communist International*, 8, 6, 1 Mar. 1930, p. 166, cited J. P. Harrison, *The Li Li-san Line and the CCP in 1939*, II, CQ, 15, Summer 1963, p. 154

23. See Mao's observation: 'When we started to fight battles, we depended on vagrants becaused they dared to die. There was a time when the army wanted to weed out the vagrant elements, but I opposed it', Forum on Central Committee Work, 20 Dec. 1964, in *Miscellany, op. cit.,* II, p. 421. For other sources, cf. Stuart Schram, *The Political Thought of Mao Tse-tung*, London, 1963, pp. 196, 200. The first efforts in the Chingkang Mountains obliged Mao to collaborate with two bandit chiefs, Wang Tso and Yuan Wen T'sai, cf. Snow, *Red Star over China*, London, 1937, p. 165

24. See comment by leading party member: 'When we say that we must distribute the land among the poor peasants and soldiers, this sounds good. But all of the available land is already being worked, and after it has been distributed, it will as before be worked by the same tenants. In such a case, where can one take the land for distribution among poor peasants and soldiers?', cited by Yun Taiying, in L. P. Deliusen, *Agrarno-krestianskii vopros v politike KPK, 1921–28*, Moscow, 1972, Chapter VII, pp. 326–75, translated in *Chinese Studies in History*, Summer 1974, VII/4, p. 41

25. In two districts of the Kiangsi Soviet, Mao claimed that between eighty and eighty-eight per cent of the males in the age group sixteen to forty-five years were serving in the Red Army – *Report* to the Second Chinese National Soviet Congress, Juichin, Kiangsi, 22 Jan. 1934, London, Sept. 1934

26. Mao: 'not only is such economic strain intolerable to the intermediate class, but some day it will prove too much even for the workers, peasants and Red Army men' – *SW* I, p. 89

27. In *Mao Unrehearsed, Talks and Letters, 1956–71*, edited by Stuart Schram, London, 1974, p. 97. See also 'On Policy', 25 Dec. 1940, *SW* II, p. 441, and 'The present Situation', Dec. 1947, *SW* IV, p. 169

28. The Hsinkuo hsien agrarian law is included in Liu Kung, *Reference materials for the study of the Agrarian Reform Law*, Shanghai, 28 Jun. 1950, and cited in Chao Kuo-chün, *Agrarian policy of the Chinese Communist party, 1921–59*, Bombay, 1960, pp. 67–9; the Kiangis Land Law is included in *A Documentary History, op. cit.,* pp. 224–6; see also Hsiao Tso-liang, *The Land Revolution in China, 1930–34* (Documents), London, 1969

29. Central Committee resolution, Aug. 1929, cited Isaacs, 1938, p. 416

30. In 1933, Mao alleged that the rich peasants dominated '80 per cent of the area of the central district, affecting a population of more than two million'. The re-examination of land distribution in the Soviet districts is the central task, *Red Flag*, 21 Aug. 1933, cited Isaacs, *ibid*, p. 420; see also *A Documentary History*, p. 219

31. See the Chinese version of Resolution on certain questions in the history of our party, Appendix to: Our study and the current situation, *SW* III, cited by John E. Rue, *Mao Tse-tung in Opposition, 1927–35*, Stanford, 1966, p. 13

32. See Nym Wales's comment: 'the Chinese Communists seem to consider their party itself equivalent to direct participation by the proletariat', in *Inside Red China*, New York, 1939, p. 221

33. Thirteenth Plenum, ECCI, Dec. 1933, in *Revolutionary China*, Peiping,

1933, p. 33

34. *Communist International*, 14/10, Oct. 1937; see also the call for an 'All-China United People's Government of National Defence' in *Revolutionary Movements in the Colonial Countries*, Seventh Congress, Communist International, New York, 1935, pp. 15, 20–21

35. *Random Notes on Red China*, Cambridge, Mass., 1968, pp. 56–7

36. And a proposal for a national conference in Nanking on 'the problem of how to dispose of Mr Chiang Kai-shek', text in Kuo, *Chinese Communist Party*, pp. 272–3, cited by Gregor Benton, The 'Second Wang Ming Line', *CQ* 61, March 1975, p. 61

37. Letter to Chang Nai-chi and others, in Mao Tse-tung *et al., China: the March Towards Unity*, New York, May 1937, p. 75

38. United Press interview with Po Ku, Chungking, 8 Nov. 1938; cf. the slogan, 'Let us support General Chiang to lead in the anti-Japanese war', cited in *China Today*, Shanghai, July 1937

39. 'Comrade Chang Hao's error at that time [during a course of lectures at Yenan University, Feb. 1937] was to consider the national anti-Japanese front to be a temporary tactical change whereas the Central Committee of the Party definitely views it as a revolutionary strategic change during a historical phase', *Chieh-fang pao*, 36, 29 Apr. 1938, pp. 11–12, cited L. P. Van Slyke, *Enemies and Friends, the United Front in Chinese Communist History*, Stanford, 1967, p. 60, from *Inprecor* 16, 10, p. 377

40. *SW* II, p. 295, also p. 445

41. Nym Wales, 1945, *op. cit.*, p. 120

42. Epstein, *op. cit.*

43. See *US Relations with China*, US Department of State, included in *Strengthening the Forces of Freedom*, Washington, 1950, pp. 2378–80; and *Yalta Papers*, Hurley to Roosevelt, 14 Jan. 1945, pp. 346–51; both cited by John Gittings, 'The Origins of Chinese Foreign Policy', in D. Horowitz (ed.), *Containment and Revolution*, London, 1967, p. 182 ff.

44. *China: the March, op. cit.*, p. 76

45. On Policy, 25 Dec. 1940, *SW* II, p. 446

46. *SW* II, p. 278

47. 'In the matter of raising wages and improving the living conditions of the workers in the rural areas, we must especially not make excessive demands on their behalf, or the peasants would protest, the workers would lose their jobs, and production would decline', *SW* II, p. 446

48. Decision of the Central Committee on Land Policy in the anti-Japanese base areas, 28 Jan. 1942, in *A Documentary History*, p. 278

49. Mao: 'We welcome foreign investments, if such are beneficial to China's economy and are made in observance of China's laws . . . we shall be able to absorb vast amounts of foreign investments', *A Documentary History*, p. 312; the passage is omitted from the version in *SW* III, p. 304

50. *Miscellany* II, *op. cit.*, p. 341

51. Nym Wales, *op. cit.*, p. 335

52. Reported by Vladimir Dedijer, *Tito*, New York, p. 322

53. Policy for work in the Liberated Areas for 1946, inner party document, 15 Dec. 1945, *SW* IV, p. 76

54. Report, Hsueh Yuah in *New International*, Dec. 1949, p. 329

55. This measure is omitted from *SW*, although referred to – *SW* IV, foot-

note 4, p. 118

56. Struggle for the purification of the organization of the party, cited by Chao Kuo-chün, *op. cit.*, p. 90

57. Mao repeatedly strove to restore the classification – see for example, 13 Jan. 1948, *SW* IV, p. 239; on the confused and contradictory nature of the classification, see Yaael Gluckstein, *Mao's China*, London, 1957, pp. 85–9

58. Some problems in land reform, 12 Jan. 1948, cited Chao Kuo-chün, *op. cit.*, p. 84

59. Correct the 'Left' errors in land reform propaganda, 11 Feb. 1948, *SW* IV, p. 197; on protecting landlord urban interests, see also *ibid*, p. 203

60. Tactical problems of rural work, 24 May 1948, *SW* IV, pp. 251, 255; see also The work of land reform, 25 May 1948, *ibid*

61. See 'Many landlords, rich peasants and riffraff have seized the opportunity to sneak into our Party . . .', *SW* IV, footnote, p. 166. Another party leader, Nieh Yung-jin, observed that: 'Those elements occupy most of the positions in our party . . . considered in the light of agrarian reform, our policy appears to reflect the views of the landlords and the rich peasants', 'Renewal of our Ranks', 1948, cited Hsueh Yueh, *op. cit.*, p. 328

62. For example: 'Everywhere we are making great progress in the work of exterminating bandits in central China. In Hunan province, during the past year [1948–9], about 38,700 bandits were killed, captured alive or forced to surrender. In Hupeh province, during the three months of May, June and July, the total number of bandits exterminated was more than 12,000' – New China News Agency (NCNA), Hunan report, 20 Aug. 1949

63. United Press correspondent, citing Peking Radio broadcast by Mao, 4 Jun. 1949; see also *SW* IV, pp. 397–8, 247

64. 27 Feb. 1948, *SW* IV, p. 203; also *ibid*, p. 219

65. *Ibid*, p. 203

66. See Ch'en Po-ta *et al.*, *On Industrial and Commercial Policy* (*Kuan-yu kung-shang-yeh te Cheng-tse*), NCNA, Hong Kong bureau, Oct. 1949, pp. 65–7, cited by Kenneth Lieberthal, 'Mao versus Liu? Policy towards Industry and Commerce', 1946–9, *CQ* 49, Jul.–Sep. 1971, p. 497

67. 8 Apr. 1948, *SW* IV, p. 248

68. *SW* IV, p. 248

69. *Ibid*, p. 248

PART II

THE PEOPLE'S REPUBLIC

3

THE FIRST PHASE

(i) The State

The new government of China faced many problems. For decades, the weakness of the central authority had led to the neglect of vital elements in China's economy; war, foreign occupation, and civil war had further exacerbated the situation. Industry was paralysed by hyper-inflation and the disorganization of trade and marketing. Agriculture had stagnated, and was now afflicted by drought, flood and typhoon. Most of the country outside the old Liberated Areas was still in the hands of landlords, petty gangsters and warlords. Finally, there was the threat of foreign intervention: the United States blocked the passage of the PLA to the last unconquered province, Taiwan, war threatened in Korea, and the French fought to recover Vietnam on China's southern border.

In 1920, the Soviet Union had faced comparable problems of devastation and disorganization, but with a much more advanced economy. The availability of foodgrains per head in China in 1952 (after post-war restoration of production) was only thirty-eight per cent of Tsarist Russia's in 1913 and forty-six per cent of the USSR of 1928. Soviet income per head in 1928 was between three and four times higher than that of China in 1952.

There was another important difference. China's small cultivated acreage (sixteen per cent of the land surface) was intensively farmed by millions of peasant households, cultivating tiny patches of soil as they had done for hundreds of years. The Soviet Union's land supply was much larger, including what only recently had been enormous estates which contributed the major part of Russia's marketable surplus of grain. Much of the land to the east had only recently been cultivated, and there was a vast acreage available for cultivation at low cost. Severe though the losses were as a result of collectivization in Russia, extensive agriculture made State direction infinitely more practicable than would have been the case with an agriculture dependent on a mass

37

of small cultivators. Any efforts to impose detailed control in China involved a vast network of supervisory cadres (themselves consuming a significant share of the surplus appropriated), and could only be brief since increased appropriations directly sapped peasant incentives, producing either a decline in output, or increased concealment. The new government of China accordingly made no sustained attempt to emulate Stalin's programme of collectivization. Yet neglect was not enough. For the more the State tolerated the leakage of the surplus into consumption, the more pressure on food supplies to the cities (themselves expanding rapidly as a result of industrialization), the stronger the stratum of relatively well-off farmers and accordingly the greater the danger of a political and social challenge from China's 'kulaks', expressed through demands for greater district and provincial autonomy. The State was thus obliged to intervene, even if briefly, to curb such processes on the countryside, only to draw back rapidly when output or appropriations seemed threatened. It was the problem of intensive agriculture which gave policy the appearance of zigzags and irresolution. The issue was never settled, nor could it be until an adequate flow of investment reached rural China and the supply of jobs outside agriculture expanded rapidly enough to employ a large part of the rural labour force. By contrast, Stalin was not obliged to draw back; once committed to collectivization, he was able to persist. What was a loss to the Chinese State was of considerable value to the Chinese peasants; Stalin's devastation of the Russian peasantry was not repeated.

Conditions in China were rendered more severe by the care with which the party had avoided or prevented the mobilization of those class forces which could have accelerated the achievement of power and the rehabilitation of China's economy. Without the spontaneous initiative of the masses – of poor peasants to settle the question of landlordism, of workers to seize factories and start production again under their own control – the régime was dependent on its own administrative capacities, on its followers and those that joined it. All changes were necessarily slow, and dependent on the restoration and expansion of production.

In Russia in 1917, Lenin continually stressed the need to destroy completely the old Tsarist State and those that then directed it, the provisional government. A new workers' State had to be constructed, a State appropriate to a new order of class power: 'The proletariat ... if it wants to uphold the gains of the present revolution and proceed further to win peace, bread and freedom, must "smash", to use Marx's expression, the "ready made" state machine and substitute a new one for it by *merging* the police force, the army and the bureaucracy with

38

the *entire armed people* . . . the proletariat must organize and arm *all* the poor, exploited sections of the population in order that they *themselves* should take the organs of State power directly into their own hands.'[1]

Lenin spoke of the the proletariat, not the Bolshevik party; of a class assuming social power, not a group taking over the old administrative apparatus. It was this which distinguished the socialist revolution – 'all previous revolutions perfected the State machine, whereas it must be broken, smashed'.[2]

However, the Chinese Communist party adhered to a united front, a class coalition. The New Democratic State was not to be the instrument of one, exploited, class over the rest. Far from 'smashing' the old Kuomintang State machine, the party aimed to absorb it. In 1952, three years after the assumption of power, the régime repeated that 'the People's government has adopted a policy of taking over all the personnel in the former Kuomintang government offices and educational institutions when the reactionary rule of the Kuomintang collapsed'.[3] It followed that there was no question of arming '*all* the poor, exploited sections of the population' lest they turn their weapons upon the other participants in the United Front.

One cause for optimism was the overwhelming military power at the party's command. Another was that the Kuomintang government had already appropriated such a large part of the industrial economy – for example, ninety per cent of the metallurgical industries, eighty-nine per cent of power generation and electrical equipment, seventy-three per cent of machine building, and seventy-five per cent of chemicals; indeed, Chiang Kai-shek had had the aim of the State taking over *all* private capital.[4] Furthermore, the State now acquired the massive share of Japanese industry (eighty-three per cent of all foreign capital in China). With this as the basic economic lever, it was felt industrialization would follow rapidly. A carefully administered land reform would both secure the régime in the loyalties of the rural majority and break the power of the landlords. Beyond that, only industrialization would permit the expropriation of land: 'Without the socialization of agriculture there will be no completion and consolidation of socialism. And to carry out socialization of agriculture, a powerful industry with State-owned enterprises as the main components must be developed. The State of People's Democracy must step by step solve this problem of the industrialization of the country.'[5]

All efforts must therefore be bent to building industry. The Soviet Union provided the model of how this was to be achieved. It included the use of the most exacting mechanisms for raising worker output. As early as 1942, Mao proposed what ought to be done: 'Next, there is the implementation of a ten-hour day and progressive piece-rate wage systems – using wages to increase production and raise labour consciousness . . . the egalitarian supply wage system obliterates the distinctions between skilled and unskilled labour and between industriousness and indolence – thereby lowering worker activism; we must replace the supply system with a progressive piece-rate system to stimulate worker activism and increase the quantity and quality of output.'[6]

The First Plan

During the period up to 1952, the régime consolidated its power in the countryside. It introduced an agrarian reform to eliminate the old landlord class, and established control of China's borders. In October 1950, the government despatched 'volunteers' to defend areas beyond its borders in Korea. The Korean war imposed an increased degree of centralization on the country and was an important factor in obliging the State to extend the public sector of industry; the State's share of national industrial output increased from thirty-seven to sixty-one per cent between 1949 and 1952. On the official figures, defence spending took between fifteen and eighteen per cent of the national income even after 1952, and twenty per cent of the national budget in 1956.[7] Defence deterred invaders, but did not prevent a noose of US bases round China's coastal waters – Korea, Japan, Okinawa, Taiwan, Guam, Philippines and Thailand. The effort took scarce resources out of civil investment, and skilled labour from the civil workforce.

Despite these heavy burdens, China, like many countries, experienced a remarkable expansion in output in the immediate post-war period. By 1952, output in many sectors had been restored to its pre-1949 peak, and the government began to undertake planned growth. The first five year plan (1953–8) embodied the promise of the revolution. Chou En-lai, citing Mao, put it in this form: 'The fundamental aim of this great people's revolution of ours is to set free the productive forces of our country from the oppression of imperialism, feudalism and bureaucratic capitalism and, eventually, from the shackles of capitalism and the limitations of small-scale production.'[8]

The core of the plan was the building of heavy industry in public hands to accelerate industrialization. Fifty-eight per cent of the planned investment went to industry, eighty-nine per cent of it in the State sector. Much of the rest went to communications, transport and defence, with seven to eight per cent for agriculture. Such a plan imposed some hardship on the people, as Chou En-lai admitted: 'It is of

40

course true that heavy industry needs more capital, takes longer to build and yield profit, and that most of its products are not for direct consumption by the people. Consequently, in the period when the State concentrates its efforts on developing heavy industry, the people have to bear some temporary hardships and inconveniences, notwithstanding the corresponding development of light industry and agriculture.' Such 'temporary hardships' would be alleviated by foreign aid. But this was the period of the Cold War, and assistance could be expected only from the Soviet Union and its allies. However, Russia was itself under pressure in its military competition with the United States and, for what assistance it gave, imposed fairly tough terms. Nonetheless, between 1949 and 1958, Russia and its East European allies made available 12,300 technical experts to work on a number of projects, the costs of which were advanced by Moscow and repaid out of China's agricultural exports to Russia (thus reducing China's already meagre domestic supply of foodstuffs). In addition, Russia took some 14,000 Chinese students and 38,000 apprentices for training. By early 1960, there were still some 7,500 Russian experts in China before the unilateral withdrawal of Soviet aid.

The government undertook the first plan without having fully centralized the economy under the State. In 1952, a third of modern industry, two-thirds of trade, and almost all of agriculture was still in private hands. The government tried to direct the economy through its control of the supply of raw materials for industry, government purchases and procurements of grain to feed the city population, tax policy and price controls. In the first Russian plan, control grew as a function of the need to plan, to secure adequate resources in the hands of the State. In China, although the régime had assured private business and trade that it would continue for many years and that collectivization of agriculture depended upon the prior existence of a powerful industrial sector, the logic of State accumulation now forced it to seek control of all activities. It did so hesitantly, pragmatically, preoccupied at every stage with the need not to disturb production. It was this – despite retreats and excessively rapid advances – of which the régime was later proud: 'The transformation of national capitalism in our country went through three stages [Mao said]. Each step was carried out by degrees. This kind of method made it possible to suffer no disruption and to develop during the course of improvement.'

Private business
The party had regularly stressed its promise to encourage the growth of

41

private capitalism and, initially, the government was as good as its word. A prominent Hong Kong business journal concluded early in 1950 that: 'The new régime has so far brought prosperous living conditions to all and sundry; the bankers and traders have no reason to complain, and, in fact, no substantial complaints are ever heard. Private trade is doing well and profits are high.'[9]

The number of businessmen in eight major cities had increased by twenty-seven per cent by the end of 1951, and the average rate of profit was a remarkable twenty-nine per cent in 1951 and thirty-one per cent in 1953.[10] There were said to be sixty-eight millionaires operating, and the owner of the Sing Sing Spinning and Weaving Company was reputed to be worth JMP 60 million (or nine million pounds sterling) in late 1956. Mao himself acknowledged that 'Mr Jung I-jen's capital is worth half of Peking'.[11]

The prosperity did not lack public approval. In 1952, Vice-premier Chen Yun assured the government-sponsored All-China Federation of Industry and Commerce that 'Private factories will be guaranteed a profit of around 10, 20, or even up to 30 per cent on their capital, under conditions of normal and rational operation'.[12] The *People's Daily* in like spirit forecast that: 'Our economic situation will continue to improve. Private industry and commerce will also have a more glorious future.'[13]

There were warning signs, however, which indicated where the power lay. From the end of 1951 to mid-1952, the 'Wu fan' campaign against five business errors (including bribery, tax evasion, theft of State property, fraud) led to the investigation of some 450,000 private businesses in nine major cities, producing some JMP 50,000 million in illegal profits. It also produced, however, a drop in private production, by possibly a third up to February 1952. The government relented by cutting the fines imposed, offering businessmen financial help and increasing the volume of State purchases.

The problem could not be left there as the first five year plan began to expand the economy. Private business tended to expand more rapidly, buying its way into a larger share of scarce raw materials (and so jeopardizing the supply to the State sector), whether this was done officially or through the black market. Skilled labour was scarce, and private firms with high profits were able to attract workers from the State sector. In boom conditions, the government controls collapsed, and public investment was threatened. Control was made particularly difficult by the mass of small private firms, outside State supervision. It needs no 'ideological' explanation to understand why the government needed to reverse its former policies and absorb the private sector. It was inhibited only by the wish to prevent a drop in production.

From 1953 onwards, business was rendered dependent through the provision of State finance (culminating in the creation of joint State–private enterprises) and State purchases. Both processes culminated in voluntary – or at least, painless – nationalization. The private share of industrial output declined from thirty-nine per cent in 1952 to sixteen per cent in 1955. By the end of 1955, eighty-two per cent of private output was purchased by the State. By 1956, all private industry had been absorbed into joint enterprises, and some fifteen per cent of shops.

The régime remained sympathetic to private businessmen. It paid compensation, guaranteed interest payments on the private capital appropriated, and it employed the former private businessmen at relatively high salaries as managers of the new joint or State enterprises. Initially, interest on capital was promised up to the end of the second plan (1963), but when many businessmen protested in the spring of 1957, the government relented and promised that interest payments would continue indefinitely. Mao was similarly sympathetic when he addressed China's leading businessmen in late 1956: 'We have reformed all capitalist industrialists and businessmen, eliminating them as a class and taking them all into our fold as individuals . . . we cannot say the bourgeoisie is useless to us; it is useful, very useful. The workers do not understand this because in the past, they have had conflicts with the capitalists in the factory. We should therefore explain the situation to the workers. Especially in view of the high tide of learning of the industrial and commercial circles and in view of your desire for learning, the workers would change their attitude towards you.'[14]

Their children were needed in new China. 'About 70 per cent of our college students are the sons and daughters of the bourgeoisie and the landlords. We need to rally them and educate them.' Big business was much more important than small, which had 'no decisive effect upon the nation's life'. But would not people say, 'the Chairman takes special care of the big capitalists but not the small capitalists. Is this Right opportunism?' Paying interest to big business on its capital would help to keep up output: 'The small enterprises and workers will object. The workers will say we are making it too advantageous for the capitalists. In their opinion, the interest payments should be cancelled immediately.' The workers would have to be convinced that 'we should not do anything detrimental to the interests of the large capitalists for they are beneficial to the State . . . Are we becoming a capitalist party? We have to explain to them that what we are doing is beneficial to the entire nation, to the workers, the peasants, the petty bourgeoisie, and the medium and small enterprises. They may not understand what "bene-

43

ficial" is at the moment.'[15]

The Cultural Revolution myth that Mao was prevented at this time by Liu Shao-ch'i from liquidating interest payments to private capital seems to have little basis in fact.

Mao's 'fear' was clearly absurd. No doubt his audience laughed politely at his humour. There was as little truth in the proposition that the Chinese State or party was controlled by private capitalists as there was in the idea that workers directed it. If it were the first, private capitalists would not have been slowly eliminated. If it was the second, as Mao admits, there would have been no interest payments, and no delay in expropriation in the immediate aftermath of 1949. Nor was the State 'balancing' between these rival claims simply in order to survive. It had another and separate interest, rapid expansion; it made or withdrew concessions entirely in the light of this central aim.

(ii) Agriculture and Employment

The party's approach to agriculture, to the movement from low-level traditional peasant assistance (Mutual Aid Teams) to State-guided co-operatives, was governed by similar considerations. In this case, it was the urgent need to secure control of industrial raw materials and foodstuffs for the urban population which forced the moves to co-operativization and State monopoly trading in agricultural commodities. By early 1956, a quarter of China's peasant households were in co-operatives, and by May of that year, ninety-one per cent. The government began to assume control of the grain trade in 1953, and then moved on to establish a monopoly of trade in cotton and cotton cloth, oil-bearing crops and the urban rationing of grain. In August 1953, the first steps in rural grain rationing began.

The first year of real peace was 1954 and, in 1955, industrial output was accelerated, a speed-up that continued through to 1956. By the standards of a poor country, the effort involved was very great. Up to 1957, the level of investment approximated to that of Japan in the last quarter of the nineteenth century (but below that of the Soviet Union in the first five year plan period). The acceleration of 1958–9 carried it up to the Soviet level of eighteen to nineteen per cent of national income, roughly comparable to that of Japan after the Second World War (when Japan was a much richer country). Over the period 1949–57, industrial output grew by roughly a fifth to a quarter on average each year, and industrial employment by 12.6 per cent.

The expansion was curbed by the inadequacy of basic inputs – power, raw materials, transport, foodstuffs – and the increasing disparity in the growth of different sectors. The growth in industrial employment and the flight of peasants from agriculture as a result of co-operativization led to a massive increase in the city population, all needing to be fed from the public granaries. The 1949 city population of 49 million nearly doubled by 1956 and reached 130 million in 1961.[16] The supervisory bureaucracy swelled rapidly. The expansion of higher education produced a stream of educated labour beyond the supply of jobs. Unemployment became severe.

The State's compulsory procurement of agricultural goods weighed heavily on the peasantry without providing sufficient food for the cities. In the winter of 1955–6 the peasants in certain areas rebelled; as Mao put it: 'Old women blocked the way and wouldn't let the food be taken.'[17] Grain was burned and livestock slaughtered to prevent the government taking it. This added a meat shortage to the grain shortage in the cities. Neither the black market nor early morning queuing resolved the problem, and workers and students took protest action. At the time, Mao warned the cadres to be careful: 'Trouble-making by the people is worth looking into. This is a new problem . . . In the past, we stood side by side with the people to struggle against the enemy . . . The people are staring at us with hostile eyes. We should prepare for constant trouble-making by a small group of people.'[18]

The leadership recognized the problem but kept up the pace. Minister of Finance Li Hsien-nien boasted that 'the profit derived from State industries in 1955 was over ten per cent in excess of the target set'; and that labour productivity should increase by seventeen per cent in 1956.[19] But the chairman of the State Planning Council acknowledged that there had been too much pressure on the peasants, and 'In 1955, in particular, the adjustment of wages and the construction of living quarters were ignored to some extent, thereby preventing the workers and staff showing enthusiasm for work'. The party congress briefly relaxed controls on small private traders and free markets in 1956, but the basic drive remained the same. Mao urged the cadres: 'We should pay attention to foodgrain production. It will be disastrous if we don't. When we have food, we have everything . . . food to eat, raw materials for industry, a rural market for industrial goods, and agricultural exports to purchase imports for the development of heavy industry.'[20]

In November 1957, Mao flew to Moscow, officially for the world conference of Communist parties, but perhaps also to plead for Russian aid to sustain China's industrialization. Otherwise, there seemed no alternative but retreat. In 1957, the pace was slackened, heavy industry curbed and the output of consumer goods increased. A succession of revolts in Eastern Europe, Poland, East Germany and Hungary in 1956, were danger signals. Mao introduced the 'One Hundred Flowers' campaign to allow public expression of grievances. As he put it: 'There is advantage in having "a hundred schools contending", for then all the evil elements will be exposed.'[21] Later he claimed 'over four hundred thousand rightists had to be purged'.

Between 1955 and 1958, the government developed a set of policies to deal with immediate obstacles to building heavy industry, policies which came to be seen as a distinctive 'Chinese model of development'. There were three immediate problems – the growth in consumption by city-dwellers, the growth in their numbers, and rural unemployment. All three were related – rural unemployment produced peasant migration to the cities which strained food supplies. Unemployment – the incapacity of the productive base to provide work for all the available manpower – was particularly pressing. In January 1956 Chou En-lai estimated that agricultural production required 30,000 millions eight-hour labour days, but 45,000 millions were available in the rural areas.[22] The government planned to increase the number of labour days by 15,000 millions, so that all adult males would work 250 days per year, females 120, still a high level of underemployment.

To limit the growth in the city population, the régime introduced: the use of ration cards, residence permits and movement passes to prevent newcomers entering the cities illegally; controls over managers to prevent them hiring labour, with occasional bans on hiring rural workers for city work. The government also fixed the volume of output of firms, the number of workers, and the total wage bill, while banks were instructed to exercise tighter controls over firms' finances; and a new form of 'sending down' labour from the cities to the rural areas, *hsia fang*, helped to thin 'non-productive' labour, and strengthened the cadres on the rural 'production front'.

These measures limited urban consumption. But in addition, the government tried to achieve overall control of wages through its major wage reform of 1956. With this reform – impossible without State control of all industry – the régime also adopted a policy of keeping the lowest rate of city wages close to rural earnings. However, controls on entry to the cities created an artificial labour scarcity which sooner or later would have produced wage pressure. The government escaped this by diluting the relatively high-cost permanent city workers with much lower cost temporary and contract workers who numbered some 12 millions by 1958.[23]

To tackle urban educated unemployment, the government reformed the educational system to reduce the numbers and relate education more directly to production needs. Mao issued instructions that middle and primary schools should contract with rural co-operatives to supply them with labour; universities and urban middle schools should start their own factories, workshops and farms.

To tackle rural unemployment, efforts were made to create jobs without calling on central funds, through the 'decentralization' of 1957, which increased local decision-making powers at the provincial level, but retained central control of heavy industry and accumulation; as Mao put it in 1958: 'Concentrate important powers in one hand/diffuse less important ones'; through the dispersal to rural areas of some light industrial, warehousing and storage activities; and through campaigns to reduce rural hoarding so that funds would be available for local investment.

Many of the items will be discussed later. It should be stressed that the measures were not part of any general 'model' or plan; they were pragmatic responses to particular obstacles in China's industrialization programme. Only in retrospect do they form a whole: the maintenance of the drive to build industry in conditions of great backwardness.

4

THE GREAT LEAP FORWARD
AND AFTER

China's economy is backward and China is materially weak. This is
why we have been unable to take much initiative; we are spiritually
restricted. We are not yet liberated in this sense. We must make a
spurt [forward in production]. We may have more initiative in five
years and more still in ten. After fifteen years, when our foodstuffs
and iron and steel become plentiful, we shall take a much greater
initiative.[24]

(i) The Great Leap Forward

The Great Leap Forward of 1958 was a spectacular attempt to break
through the limitations of backwardness, to ward off the pressing demands of the mass of the population for some improvement in their
living standards, and to accelerate vastly the growth of all sectors of industry. It was 1929–31 in the Soviet Union all over again; except in a
much more backward country that could not tolerate the extremities of
forced growth. Intensive agriculture and the albeit modest incentives of
millions of peasant households provided no long-term basis for a 'War
Communist' supply system, with all subordinated to serving the State.
As a result, whereas the Russian régime was able to persist in the acceleration, China was forced very rapidly to retreat.

Up to mid-1957, the régime was officially committed to a temporary
relaxation in the final phase of the first five year plan, and to the com-
mencement of the second, which would carry the country through to
1963. By September, however, there was a certain reorientation. The demands, that the supply of consumer goods be increased and living standards improved, continued. The 8th party Congress (1958) noted the
'need to increase consumption, otherwise there would be a serious contradiction between the Party and the masses which would lead to unfor-
givable errors'.[25] But at the same time, Mao was preparing a complete

reversal of any such trend. He dismissed the complaints of the rural party cadres with: 'What kind of people were these cadres? They are well-to-do peasants, or formerly poor and lower middle peasants who had become well-to-do.'[26]

He attacked the politburo of the party itself for conservatism and lack of boldness, complaining that his orders were diluted and the committee just a voting machine; as a result, he was on strike: 'For two years, I have not read your documents and I do not expect to read them this year either.'[27]

What alternative was Mao proposing? It is not clear that he had any coherent plan, only the belief that the campaigning spirit could break through bottlenecks and beat back the demands for increased consumption. Nor is it clear how he managed to sweep away the anxieties of the party leadership. Certainly, they must have agreed when he formulated the slogan, 'Catch up and surpass Britain in the output of major industrial goods within fifteen years'. Shortly afterwards, he reckoned this slogan had itself become conservative – 'It looks as if in three more years we can overtake and surpass Great Britain'. As the cadres strained their muscles – or rather, strained the population's muscles – the ambitions soared:'With eleven million tons of steel next year, and seventeen million the year after, the world will be shaken. If we can reach forty million tons in five years, we may possibly catch up with Great Britain in seven years.'[28]

That was in May, but by December he was speaking of fifty to sixty million tons of steel by 1962. He later confessed that he had hoped for 100 to 120 million tons.[29] By the mid-1970s, China's steel output had reached the very creditable level of some 25 million tons.

The party Congress in February 1958 was persuaded to demand a 'Great Leap Forward'. The targets were all to be raised – steel by nineteen per cent, to 6.2 million tons; and in August, to 10.7 million tons (or double the 1957 level); electricity generation by eighteen per cent. The cadres were instructed to ensure that workers surpassed all previous records. The provincial party secretaries competed to outdo each other. Some promised to meet 1967's targets in 1958. The 14.6 per cent target for overall industrial output ratified at the February Congress was in March raised to thirty-three per cent. By the end of 1958, some half million small 'factories and workshops' had been set up in Hopei province. By October, 600,000 small blast furnaces, many in rural areas, were at work.

To achieve the expansion, all rules had to be scrapped. Management in urban industry was pushed into the background in order that cadres could press workers to 'exceed all records'. The safety, rest and recreation of workers were inevitable casualties. Quality collapsed as output rose – the mines met their impossible targets by loading rubble.

The rural areas were mobilized in even more radical fashion. The logic of industrial expansion in backward rural areas (without central financial help), and the need for vast labour-intensive schemes (major irrigation, land reclamation and flood control works) already made the new co-operatives obsolete. The Honan provincial party drew the lesson in April, merging the co-operatives. Liaoning province announced in June that 9,200 co-operatives were being merged into 1,500 (each containing an average of 2,000 households). In July, Mao confessed that no one in the central leadership had foreseen this beginning of the commune movement.[30] By August, Honan claimed to be setting up 'People's Public Associations' or Communes, and by November 26,000 had been created, covering ninety-eight per cent of the farm population (each including thirty co-operatives, between forty and one hundred villages, and an average of 25,000 people).

The communes enabled the cadres to be effective over much larger areas than before. The party leadership understood this: 'Why do we say that with the setting up of People's Communes, the Party leadership will be strengthened? . . . a large-scale, highly-centralized organization is naturally easier to lead than a small-scale, scattered organization.'[31]

It was possible to hunt out the hoarder, to end rural markets, to expropriate a bigger share of the equipment and animals still privately owned and to impose a much stricter rationing system. Monthly pay was reduced and controlled, and free services substituted in the form of foodstuffs, through communal canteens. Enormous labour-intensive schemes on the land were organized by the commune authorities. To run the new rural industries, men were taken off the fields – sixty millions to iron smelting and steel refining alone producing a labour shortage during the excellent harvest of 1958.

It was not enough that this vast effort to break out of backwardness should be made. An heroic ideology was required. Its flavour was captured by the party's resolution at the end of 1958: 'In 1958, a new social organization appeared, fresh as the morning sun above the broad horizon of East Asia. This was the large-scale people's commune in the rural areas of our country which combines industry, agriculture, trade, education and military affairs . . . the gradual transition from collective ownership to ownership by the whole people in agriculture, the way to the gradual transition from the socialist principle of "to each according to his work" to the Communist principle of "to each according to his needs", the way to the gradual diminution and final elimination of the differences between rural and urban areas, between worker and peasant

50

and between mental and manual labour, and the way to the gradual diminution and final elimination of the domestic functions of the State.'[32]

According to the *People's Daily*, China could make the transition to 'property of the whole people' in three to six years, and the transition to communism a few years later.[33] Backwardness was just a bad dream. Free supply of rations instead of cash was not the introduction of a form of national military service in which the troops were fed directly, but the very goal itself, communism.

(ii) The retreat

The moment of heroism was brief. Backwardness proved a more obdurate master, no 'paper tiger'. The party leadership were lulled by the harvest of 1958; Mao's gamble had been favoured by wind and water. But by the end of the year it was clear something was wrong – a spectacular harvest coexisted with food shortages and queues in the cities. Who was to blame? The national leadership for setting such absurd targets and harrying the cadres to achieve them? No, the cadres must be blamed. The press began to criticize their arbitrary and ruthless behaviour – 'commandism'. Even in the spring, Mao attacked the 'very bad work style' of some cadres who used force rather than persuasion to achieve their targets, and proposed a 'Big Character' poster campaign as a method of checking them. The party launched a rectification campaign, instructed the cadres not to overwork commune members, to allow them time to sleep and rest. Some restrictions were relaxed, and the right to private property reaffirmed (indicating that the cadres had been trying to meet targets by expropriations). Mao insisted: 'If we "blow a communist wind", and seize the property of the production brigades and work teams, helping ourselves to their fat pigs and big white cabbages, this is quite wrong.'[34] How else were the cadres to meet Mao's targets? There was no magic method of conjuring plenty from poverty.

The targets began to be dropped. The local claims which had made up the national output total were now seen to have been designed to win praise rather than reflect performance. The figure for the 1958 harvest, originally put at 375 million tons of grain, was cut to 250 millions, and the 1959 target cut from 525 to 275 millions.[35] Severe shortages persisted however, and, in the south, there was a campaign to eke out the flour supply by mixing it with vegetable stalks and roots, and to collect wild plants for consumption.

The peasants themselves were going on strike. Mao tried to reassure them by proposing a rate of rural accumulation which would guard against the arbitrary depredations of the cadres (but which made no allowance for the enormous differences between rural communes). By May 1959, he had decided the government could not persist in the expansion of heavy industry without some improvement in consumption, the conclusion of 1957. The retreat had begun: 'We have to restore the primary market in rural areas'.[36]

The supposed 'communist achievements' of the Great Leap Forward now came under attack. The party inspection teams despatched in 1959 to implement the rectification campaign were instructed to combat egalitarianism; as Mao put it: 'it would be unreasonable to use equalization on the poor and rich brigades and the poor and rich villages; it would be banditry, piracy'.[37] Authority must be centralized once more, removed from the commune leadership, for: 'there is now semi-anarchism. We have granted too much of the "four powers" and too soon, causing the present confusion. We should now emphasize unified leadership and centralization of powers. Powers granted should be properly retracted. There should be proper control over the lower level.'[38]

The communes in their original form were scrapped. The name continued to disguise the defeat but now referred to little more than the lowest level of the administrative structure, covering a much reduced area and with drastically curtailed powers. Mao indicated the failure was not unexpected: 'We were prepared for the collapse of half of them, and if seventy per cent collapse, there would still be thirty per cent left. If they must collapse, let them.'[39] Henceforth, the production brigades – and in some cases, the production teams – corresponding to the old co-operatives, became the basic accounting unit, the locus of rural power and economy; as Mao summarized the change, the commune became no more than a federation of brigades, far from the old 'sprouts of communism'.[40]

There was a similar retreat in industry. Vast increases in production were claimed – at the end of 1958, a sixty-five per cent increase in total industrial output over 1957. But severe disproportions between sectors had arisen – the stream of capital goods could not be used because of the lack of complementary inputs. The growth of local metal refining led to a lack of transport throughout the economy, curbing the modern industries. Mao put it vividly: 'Coal and iron cannot walk by themselves; they need vehicles to transport them. This I did not foresee. I and XX and the Premier did not concern ourselves with this point . . . I am a complete outsider when it comes to economic construction.'[41]

Quality had suffered severely. In August 1959, it was officially admitted that the three million tons of iron output from 'backyard furnaces' – a quarter of national production – was too poor in quality to be refined further.[42] The lack of investment in the small plants, of proper engineering design and skilled metallurgical workers could not be made up simply by cadre enthusiasm. The 1959 steel target was successively dropped from thirty to thirteen million tons. By the end of the year, the government was rationalizing all 'backyard furnaces' – from 600,000 claimed at the height of the Great Leap Forward to 1,300 by April 1960.

Central control, managerial authority (as opposed to the cadres), the restoration of 1957 incentive payment systems, and the restoration of factory rules, were now at a premium. Instead of stressing the potential of enthusiasm, the party leadership now complained: 'It is intolerable to find in production and basic construction that no one takes up any responsibility, and that all necessary rules and regulations are being violated.'[43] Up to 1961, these changes slowly restored financial control to managers and the restriction of party factory committees to education and welfare matters. The stress now was not on a production offensive, but on protecting what there was, on economies, profits, costs, labour productivity.

The disagreements in the party leadership over these two sharp turns must have been severe. Did the disagreements lead to the removal of Mao as head of State in 1959? It does not seem so, since Mao himself raised the question *before* the Great Leap Forward developed. He wanted, he said, to 'step down' to 'save a great deal of time in order to meet the demands of the Party'. In December, he said he was already working only half-time, without responsibility for daily work, and he would soon resign. It seems that, although there were inevitably disagreements, they were not with Mao personally nor sufficient to enforce his removal. Indeed, it would be difficult to see how the Great Leap Forward could have been implemented in the face of the opposition of the central leadership who were responsible for the day-to-day work and the actual implementation of policy. Those who did disagree with it – Defence Minister P'eng Te-huai and Chief of Staff General Huang K'o-ch'ing – were not promoted as a result of its failure; they were dropped from the leadership.[44]

Mao volunteered – or was induced to volunteer – to be the scapegoat for the disasters, perhaps because he was already resigning or his prestige was so great, it could engulf any opposition. At the Lushan Plenum in July 1959 he made his confession of errors: 'I understand nothing about industrial planning . . . But comrades, in 1958 and 1959, the main responsibility was mine, and you should take me to task . . . Who was responsible for the idea of the mass smelting of steel? I say it was me . . . With this, we rushed into a great catastrophe, and ninety million people went into battle . . . The chaos caused was on a grand scale, and I take

53

responsibility. Comrades, you must all analyse your own responsibility. If you have to shit, shit! If you have to fart, fart! You will all feel much better for it.'[45]

The excellent harvest of 1958 had blinded the leadership to the dangers. But the harvest in 1959 was poor, and in the two following years, disastrous. In 1960, the government still persisted in trying to keep up the growth of industrial output despite the evidence of famine in some parts of the country. But industry's efforts disintegrated before the shortage of raw materials and foodstuffs. The value of 1960's agricultural output was considerably less than 1957's.[46] In the middle of the year, the sudden withdrawal of Soviet assistance – including the technicians manning Soviet-sponsored projects – exacerbated the downturn in the heavy industrial sector. Retreat became a rout, recession a slump. At long last, four years too late, the government curbed the expansion of heavy industry, and increased its assistance to light industry, handicrafts, family sidelines and suburban agriculture in a general policy of 'readjustment, reinforcement and improvement'. Without special permission, all basic construction work was suspended, loss-making industrial units closed and managers forbidden to hire rural labour for three years. In March, 1962, Chou En-lai urged a further contraction in basic construction work and a cut of 20 millions in the size of the urban population.[47] Private handicrafts would, it was now said, continue for a long time to come; private markets and private cultivation were fully restored. The party duly produced an obscure phrase to suggest that the changes were all part of the plan, 'agriculture as the foundation of the national economy, with industry as the leading factor', and 'walking on two legs', as if walking on one leg had ever had much sense! Stalin was never obliged to formulate such obscure phrases; once collectivization was launched, although the pace might be varied, there was no reversal. The Russian peasantry never had such power to oblige the general secretary to retrace his steps, to use 'both legs'.

Reality had caught up. Now, instead of breaking the grain bottleneck, China was compelled to import grain in massive quantities from Canada and Australia – sixteen million tons between 1960 and 1963. The time horizons lengthened dramatically. In 1955, Mao had proposed that ten years would be required to 'build socialism', and fifty to seventy years 'to catch up with, or overtake the United States'.[48] But by 1962, the prospects were less sanguine: 'As for the construction of a strong socialist economy in China, fifty years won't be enough; it may take one hundred years or even longer . . . China has a large population, resources are meagre, and our economy backward, so that in my opinion it will be impossible to develop our productive powers so rapidly as to

54

catch up with and overtake the most advanced capitalist countries in less than one hundred years.'[49] No more was said of making the 'transition to communism' only 'a few years' after the communes had established 'property of the whole people'. Even by the spring of 1959, Mao was advising the cadres: 'At the moment, too much activity should be avoided.'

The 'three hard years' tested the party severely. There was rebellion on the western border province.[50] Peasant grievances in 1960–61 spread into armed rebellion in at least two provinces, Honan and Shantung (and possibly a third, Kansu), involving mutinous members of the rural militia.[51] In 1962, there was a massive flight of refugees from China to Hong Kong, encouraged or tolerated by the desperate local authorities of neighbouring Kwantung province.

The drop in farm production paralysed the whole economy. A foreign estimate put the cost high; the Great Leap Forward 'may have cost a decade of economic growth, for the gross national product in 1965 does not seem to have been above the 1958 level'.[52] Yet party control survived intact and the strategy remained the same, even if pursuing it now demanded a diversion. Mao described what the strategy was: 'Our method is, *on condition that priority is given to the development of heavy industry*, to enforce the simultaneous development of industry and agriculture . . . If agriculture does not turn up, many problems cannot be solved . . . *If we want heavy industry to develop rapidly*, we must make everybody happy and enthusiastic in his work. And if we want this to happen, we must promote industry and agriculture, and light and heavy industry simultaneously.'[53]

(iii) The Socialist Education Campaign

Material backwardness and intensive patterns of cultivation in national isolation are constantly tending to recreate the social formations of a small producer economy. In China, the process was variously described in the 1950s as the revival of a 'rich peasant economy' on the one hand, and the corruption and decay of the rural party on the other (it was often the same process since the cadres behaved as, or in close collaboration with, rich peasants). Campaigns and the high rate of expansion in the first plan did something to curb both trends, and the Great Leap Forward was a sustained assault on the imperatives of peasant agriculture. But the forced retreat of 1959–62 either permitted the open expression of what had existed covertly before or created a situation in which the power of the party in the rural areas appeared threatened.

The power of the party leadership to curb, let alone eliminate, the trends was limited, which is why it so frequently relied on moral exhortation. Too severe a threat to the rural cadres could destroy or demoralize party authority in the rural areas altogether, thus endangering the supply of foodstuffs and raw materials to the cities, and raising the possibility of peasant rebellion. Alternatively, the cadres might unite with the rich peasantry to defend local autonomy, a situation which, when matched by the resistance of provincial leaders to central control, raised the hydra of what were attacked during the Cultural Revolution as 'independent kingdoms', warlordism in the party itself. On the other hand, toleration of rural decay would sooner or later threaten the national power of the party and the strategic aim of State accumulation.

A set of party documents from a county in Fukien province[54] gives some idea of the problem. The commune was densely populated (in two brigades there was only one *mou* – about a sixth of an acre – of land per head), and employment in the public sector yielded an inadequate income. As a result, there was much absenteeism among the peasants, many turning to private work during the day and making up on public work at night. The range of private jobs was wide – sewing, knitting, bee-keeping, peddling, odd labouring jobs, stone mason work, money-lending. Legally, peasants were entitled to cultivate privately between five and seven per cent of the total cultivated acreage, but the average was nearer 9.5 per cent. Reclaimed land and the area for fodder growing were excluded from these calculations and were wholly in private hands. In all, some thirty per cent of the total crop area was privately cultivated, and for some teams, over fifty per cent. Other sources make even larger claims – for example, that in 1962 Yunnan's private grain harvest was larger than the collectives', and privately cultivated land in the province was half the total; that as late as 1964, in Kweichow and Szechuan provinces there was more private than collective cultivated acreage.[55]

The income received from these activities was put at RMB 88 (just over £18 sterling) per year per head for the peasants, and RMB 130–53 for party cadres. However, cadre real income was increased by a number of malpractices: the usurpation of public property (cutting down State woodlands – 500 cedar trees are mentioned – for private building work or sale), use of public funds and foodstuffs for private celebrations (e.g. weddings, births), participation in, or favouring, private enterprise, speculation, peddling, gambling, illicit brewing, and slaughter of livestock. In sum, traditional practices of Chinese rural clan rule were threatening to re-establish themselves, complete with appropriate ideological forms among the cadres – religious festivals, paying bride prices, spiritualism and witchcraft.

The socialist education movement, launched in September 1962, included a number of elements – a propaganda campaign, a rectification movement among rural cadres, and a purge. The propaganda repeated familiar themes, attacking cadres who 'indulge in idleness and hate work, eat too much and own too much, strive for status, act like officials, put on bureaucratic airs, pay no heed to the plight of the people, care nothing about the interests of the State'.[56]

From the beginning, Mao assessed the threat as affecting the balance of power. Contrary to the decision Mao formulated in 1957 – that the contradiction between the proletariat and the bourgeoisie had been fundamentally resolved – there was now a danger that the dictatorship of the proletariat could be turned into 'a bourgeois dictatorship, into a reactionary fascist type of dictatorship'.[57] 'In our state at present, approximately one-third of the power is in the hands of the enemy, or the enemy's sympathizers. We have been going fifteen years, and we now control two-thirds of its realm. At present, you can buy a Party secretary for a few packs of cigarettes, not to mention marrying a daughter to him.'[58] And again: 'Middle and low-ranking Kuomintang officers, secretaries of *hsien* [county] party offices etc., have all crept in. No matter what guise they have been transformed into, we must now clean them all out. Everywhere there is class struggle, everywhere there are counter-revolutionary elements.'[59]

It will be recalled that it was party policy in 1949 to 'absorb' the former Kuomintang officials. The statistics were wrong, for now it could not be taken for granted that the social classification of the rural population had been reliable: 'In the past, there have been instances in which some upper-middle peasants, petty merchants, and even landlords and rich peasants were mistakenly classified as poor or lower middle peasants.'[60]

Given this assessment, the reaction of the party leadership was strangely mild. Liu Shao-ch'i favoured a thorough purge of the rural party. But Mao was for moderation – as he explained: 'I am somewhat on the right. There are so many . . . that they might constitute twenty per cent of the people.'[61] The cadres should be treated leniently, even in cases of large-scale corruption ('several thousand yuan', or thirty to forty times the average annual income of the peasants in Lieng-chiang county). The money should in part or whole be repaid, but 'We need not talk about "thoroughness"'.[62] There were large sums at stake – a Central Work Conference in 1964 recorded that in one area in two months, RMB 20,000 of illicit cash and 100,000 catties of grain were recovered.

In 1962 Mao was firm that violence was ruled out: 'It isn't good to kill people. We should arrest and execute as few people as possible. If we arrest and execute people at the drop of a hat, the end result would be that everybody would fear for themselves and nobody dare to speak.'[63] But by 1964 he is less sure: 'It is impossible for us not to kill, but we must not kill too many. Kill a few to shock them . . . the one killed by mistake won't resurrect.'[64]

The work teams sent to investigate were apparently not effective. The poor and middle peasant associations that had been set up to supervise the cadres were selected by the cadres themselves.

Liu Shao-ch'i and his wife, Wang Kuang-mei, stepped up the disciplinary element in the campaign. In mid-1964, Wang addressed 3,000 cadres in Shanghai on her 'Taiyuan experience' after staying six months in a Hopei production brigade.[65] She concluded that forty of the forty-seven brigade and team leaders were corrupt and needed to be replaced by handpicked cadres through a process of mass struggle rallies, public accusation meetings and forced confessions. In July, Liu and Wang travelled in the south-central region, and concluded that possibly a third of the cadres were corrupt, and a much longer period of reform was required (five to six, rather than two to three, years). Unless the central work team returned to an area to check its earlier recommendations had been implemented, the peasants would remain intimidated; higher level cadres would ignore them in order to protect the lower cadres upon whom the administration depended. The purge began in September, and one estimate suggests seventy to eighty per cent of sub-village level cadres were removed – a powerful source of hatred towards Liu and Wang.

The revelations of corruption, bribery and extortion mounted.[66] There were cases of physical assault by the peasants on the cadres, and of cadre suicide. Wang's work teams had disturbed a hornet's nest. They discovered, for example, that Ch'en Hua, party secretary in Shengshi, Kwantung, a 'five good' cadre and national labour hero who had been received by Mao, was a brutal petty dictator; he was caught attempting to escape to Hong Kong in his launch (a remarkable symbol of wealth) and killed. In October, the work teams collided with another 'national model Party secretary', Ch'en Yung-kuei of the famous Tachai production brigade. But Ch'en was shrewd and had powerful friends. He gained an audience with Mao, and was nominated, perhaps as a result, to the praesidium of the third National People's Congress. Tachai was praised publicly in Chou's report to the Congress; Ch'en was permitted to make a speech, and a photograph of him with Mao appeared on the front page of the *People's Daily*.[67]

In late 1964, Mao endeavoured to restrain the movement, but without criticizing Liu and Wang. Now the cadres needed to be *educated*, and more importantly, at the level of the province rather than the village; it was here that there were 'powerholders within the Party who take the capitalist road'. By contrast with his earlier assessment, the 'normal good and relatively good' cadres constituted 'the absolute majority', and the work teams should rely on them rather than attack them. The mood was mild and conciliatory; as usual, Liu was praised as Mao's 'closest comrade in arms'.

5

THE CULTURAL REVOLUTION

It seemed Chinese society had not been fundamentally changed. A new political order had been grafted on to the basic rural society. China was still not equipped to undertake sustained capital accumulation. The 'three bad years' revealed a social structure hidden in the pre-1959 years of growth. Yet to tackle the problem head-on with a purge of the party was to risk the collapse of party rule itself, to destroy the basis of the power of Mao and the central leadership. Mao instinctively opted for a classical reformist strategy – the transformation of *education*, not the distribution of power. By this means, the 'superstructure' would be brought into conformity with the needs of the 'material base'.

What were the symptoms that the educational system needed reform? Young people were unaware of the barbarities of Kuomintang rule; they had grown up in the People's Republic and were not grateful for its achievements. They were urged to listen to the old people tell of the past. The educational and cultural institutions would have to be reformed to accord with the need for accumulation. The present educational system imposed too many years of study, the content of which was irrelevant to the drive for output; it was also too expensive – 120 yuan per ordinary middle school student, in comparison to 6.80 yuan per agricultural middle school student.[68]

The educational curriculum must be changed, shortened and lightened not in order to eliminate expert technical knowledge but to oppose the *cult* of the expert, the demand for special privileges and consumption on the basis of formal qualifications. But, on the other hand: 'Those who have no practical knowledge are pseudo-red, empty headed politicos.'[69]

Culture must be purged of diversity. The reality of life in China – such of it as was still reflected in literature, opera, film and radio – must be eliminated to create simple sagas of moral heroes totally devoted to the interests of the State. The changes in Chinese opera were only one form of this 'aligning of the superstructure'. Pre-1949 writers, including

60

some, like Confucius,[70] much-praised by Mao himself, were banned. Yang Heng-sheng, former vice-chairman of the Federation of Literary and Art Circles, was condemned for praising Shakespeare, Molière and Ibsen, and Chao Feng for playing Beethoven's Ninth Symphony, a work much appreciated by Lenin. The highest achievements of bourgeois culture were not to be absorbed into socialism, but eliminated lest they impede the effort to extort sacrifices.

We can only surmise at the motives which led Mao to take his case outside the party. All his life, he had endeavoured to protect and build the party. The disputes inside the party were not broadcast to the world at large until after they had been settled, when ignominy would be publicly heaped upon the defeated. But in the winter of 1965–6, Mao went far beyond this procedure to appeal to an audience outside the party to settle the dispute within it. Even the arguments within the party are not clear – we have only Mao's side of the case. His closest followers for many years remained loyal to his own record; they attempted to defend the party against radical change lest it destroy the party and so the very basis for Mao's own influence. Did Mao hope to create a new party from the youth, a body of cadres completely devoted to the cause of accumulation, or did he hope to do no more than scourge the provincial and national leadership as the basis for establishing a stronger loyalty to them and so the stability of the régime after his death (as he himself once suggested)? How far was the Cultural Revolution not *planned* at all, but merely the result of a sequence of events in which Mao felt himself increasingly hampered in the effort to reshape the party? Without access to the inner party discussions, the answers cannot be verified.

The recorded pretext was slight.

Mao's wife, Chiang Ch'ing, claimed that in the autumn of 1965, a number of articles in literary criticism by Mao were refused publication in Peking. Mao was obliged to have them published in Shanghai.[71] Possibly on the basis of this experience, he concluded: 'The central Ministry of Propaganda is the palace of the Prince of Hell.'

A 'cultural revolution' was required: that is, a purge and rectification in the fields of propaganda, education and cultural work. The resistance of the Peking party was another problem, affecting directly the senior party leader concerned, P'eng Chen, deputy general secretary. The national centre, the Politburo, agreed to establish a Cultural Revolution Group, backed by the PLA, to supervise work teams to implement the programme.

However, as in the socialist education movement, the work teams compromised with leading officials. From April 1966 Mao publicly attacked particular individuals – P'eng Chen, Lu Ting-yi (Minister of

Culture and chief of the Propaganda Department), and now Lo Jui-ch'ing, PLA Chief of Staff. In May, Mao secured from the Politburo dissolution of the Cultural Revolution Group, a revocation of its report, and the closure of all institutions of higher education for six months in order to reform the curricula. The students must be involved in the reform; and as an inducement, it was promised that students of worker or peasant origin would receive preference in higher education (although their share in higher education had already risen from thirty-six to sixty-seven per cent between 1957 and 1962).

(i) The revolution

There was another audience for these disputes within the party – the students themselves. Elements of what Mao had to say appealed directly to them, although for quite different reasons. The students were for 'revolution', but for the emancipation of people rather than productive forces. Indeed, many of them supported Mao in order to *fight* the social obsession with accumulation, the tyrannical work disciplines made necessary by that obsession. Some of them pursued aims the precise opposite to those of Mao – the desire for privilege without having to acquire technical competence. Now at last they were given an opportunity to torment their tormentors, the local instruments of the national plan, teachers, headmasters, professors. They were the tangible 'persons in authority taking the capitalist road', and any form of discipline must represent capitalism. From May, groups of students began seizing the schools and the dossiers upon which their future careers depended.[72] The work teams of the party attempted to defend a stable administration, and, as a result, were attacked both directly and through the Big Character posters that blossomed on the walls of the cities. The work teams likewise must be 'those taking the capitalist road' inside the party. The work teams appealed to the party centre, which in turn attempted to defend the administration, without which the central production control system would break down. The 'anti-party group' now came to include all or part of the central leadership of the party.

A Peking student – Nieh Yüan-tzu – in collaboration with Mao, provided the signal for an explosion of student militancy. Mao's excitement was extreme. He had apparently found a brand new cadre force outside the old party: 'Nieh Yüan-tzu's big character poster of 25 May is the declaration of the Paris Commune of the Sixties of the Twentieth century; its significance far surpasses that of the Paris Commune.'[73] Suddenly, the rectification campaign began to recede in importance before the prospect of the transition to communism itself – just as the merging of the rural population in the Commune movement had in 1958 promoted the same utopian idea: 'The present Cultural Revolution is a heaven-and-earth shaking event. Can we, dare we, cross the pass into socialism? This pass leads to the final destruction of classes and the reduction of the three great differences.'[74]

Mao and the students might raise the slogan, but workers and peasants still had to report for work each day. The maintenance of China's output also required that the party continue its supervision, and if the party faltered under attack, the People's Liberation Army was required to maintain elementary administration. The PLA, under Defence Minister Lin Piao, Mao's strongest supporter at the centre, was not attacked. Indeed, military discipline – without talk of pay or reward – had become increasingly the ideal put forward by the party. Lin Piao and the PLA did not isolate Mao and, in return, Mao identified himself with the army. The main Cultural Revolution statements now appeared first in the leading army newspaper, *Liberation Army Daily*. Mao regularly appeared in army uniform (aped by the Red Guards), as did the other leading members of the reorganized Cultural Revolution group. The army was only three million strong, quite inadequate to change the cultural orientation of China. For that, a more widespread force was required, and one not tethered to the material interests of the majority, workers and peasants. If the majority were involved, they were liable to confuse cultural change with urgent material demands. If these were conceded, it would reduce accumulation. Indeed, workers, peasants and soldiers reacted initially by opposing the student Red Guards, accusing them of being pampered children of the bourgeoisie. In the 'dictatorship of the proletariat', Mao instructed: 'The workers, peasants and soldiers should not interfere with the students' great Cultural Revolution' (23 Aug. and 7 Sept. 1966).[75]

Throughout the first phase, there were hints by Mao of a party conspiracy to stifle the Cultural Revolution, based upon the link between the work teams and the party centre. The evidence for a conspiracy is little more than that the centre, like Mao, wished to protect production from being disturbed by student activities. But Mao was now responding to an audience whose expectations pushed and pulled him in other directions. The hints – such as dropping Liu Shao-ch'i's name from its customary second rank to seventh at the first Red Guard rally – were still opaque, but became clearer in Mao's first wallposter: 'in the last fifty days or so, some leading comrades have enforced a bourgeois dictatorship and struck down the surging movement of the great People's Cultural Revolution' and in the startling slogan, 'Bombard the

63

headquarters'.[76] There is a gap between the 'comrades' criticized and the rhetoric of enforcing a 'bourgeois dictatorship', a gap of vagueness which permitted Mao complete freedom to manoeuvre, to speak the language of revolution while persisting in a programme of limited reforms.

The Eleventh Plenum of the party – when the central committee permitted admission to unelected Red Guards – sanctioned a sixteen point programme to guide the movement. The programme limited the Socialist Education Movement to basic production units, and the Cultural Revolution to cultural and educational bodies and leading party and government organizations in the cities. The Cultural Revolution should *not* be launched in basic production units, a point firmly repeated by Chou En-lai when he forbade Red Guards to enter factories and villages.[77]

Mao must have been already sensing the possible divergence of interests in the Red Guard movement and the potential for open warfare both between Red Guards and party and between different Red Guard factions. On the draft sixteen points he scribbled, 'Do not beat people up'.[78]

(ii) Sound the retreat

By the autumn of 1966, with some eleven million students visiting Peking and others in other cities, with fighting between different Red Guard factions, with transport and food supplies strained to serve the students, Mao began to draw back, as quickly as he had done in 1947–8 when faced with the beginning of a peasant revolution: 'I had no idea that one big character poster, the Red Guards and the big exchange of revolutionary experience would have stirred up such a big affair. Some of the students did not have a terribly good family background, but were our own family backgrounds all that good?'[79] As at the Lushan Plenum, to the senior leaders of the party he again confessed: 'Since it was I who caused the havoc, it is understandable if you have some bitter words for me . . . Perhaps the movement may last another five months, or even longer.'[80]

In fact, it was to last another two and a half years.

The Red Guards achieved another unexpected result. They forced a defensive reaction by the party leadership. Mao disingenuously complained: 'I wanted to establish their prestige before I died. I never imagined that things might move in the opposite direction.'[81] Thus, on his own estimate, there had been no longer-term 'capitalist road' conspiracy in the party, no permanent struggle between two lines; that was to be invented in later years, weaving past and current disagreements into a consistent historical record. Mao resented the defensive reaction of the provincial leaders, setting up 'independent kingdoms', like their warlord predecessors, and their failure to consult him: 'It's not so bad that I am not allowed to complete my work, but I don't like being treated as a dead ancestor.'[82]

Nonetheless the irritations – despite the grandiose language which caught the imagination of the students – still did not mean that the 'top persons' should be cast out: 'Cliques and factions of whatever description should be strictly excluded. The essential thing is that they [the criticized leaders] should reform, that their ideas should conform, and that they should unite with us. Then things will be all right. We should allow Liu and Teng to make a revolution and to reform themselves.'[83] Or again: 'We shouldn't condemn Liu Shao-ch'i out of hand. If they have made mistakes they can change, can't they? When they have changed, it will be all right. Let them pull themselves together, and throw themselves courageously into their work.'[84] The language of 'bourgeois usurpation of the proletarian State' suddenly faded into 'mistakes'; apparently, the potential capitalists could cease to perform their social role just by trying.

There were now many other forces and motives at work. Lin Piao and his supporters (the 'Left', led by the Cultural Revolution group) saw the chance to remove their main rivals within the party, Mao's heir Liu Shao-ch'i and general secretary Teng Hsiao-p'ing. Lin Piao would then stand close to inheriting the supreme leadership on the retirement of Mao. Secondly, the party cadres disgraced by Liu and his wife during the socialist education movement now had a chance to destroy Liu, and secure their rehabilitation. Finally, the Red Guards, young and innocent, were prey to any ambitious leader prepared to speak in extreme terms. By October, the numerous Red Guard factions were involved in almost continuous warfare among themselves, manipulated by different party leaders. The one thing that could unite them was a common enemy, a scapegoat.

Thus, there were already powerful forces striving for Liu's destruction. In October Mao decided that the sacrifice of Liu, Teng and the rest was required as the price of the survival of his own authority. Liu and Teng were obliged to make a public confession, accepting a version of the past that was clearly false – for example, that they alone were responsible for the changes introduced after the Great Leap Forward. The confession did them no good. Mao could no longer protect them. From December, Liu ceased to appear in public and retired to his State villa in Chung Nan Hai. Thus the head of State, central committee

65

member, and heir to Mao, suddenly became a 'capitalist roader', the source of all ills for hundreds of millions of Chinese.

(iii) Workers intervene

From November 1966, the party centre made strenuous efforts to end the Red Guard movement. The students were directed to leave Peking, to 'go on a Long March' to wherever they came from. To no avail. Having escaped from the dreary routine of school, the youth would not lightly return. Furthermore, their agitation was drawing in young workers, resentful that the new freedom to travel, discuss and avoid the tedium of work was restricted to those in full-time education. Once workers were involved, a mass of new demands appeared, no longer confined to the area of education. In somewhat desperate tones, the Cultural Revolution group repeated the instruction to 'promote production' while 'grasping revolution . . . The production command system of the factories must not be interrupted.'

It was too late. Workers did leave production. Delegations flocked to Peking to present their demands, to show how they had been oppressed by Liu Shao-ch'i with poor wages and conditions. Many took strike action – in the Shanghai docks, on the railways, in transport, power stations, and elsewhere.[85] Free rail travel permitted thousands of those exiled to the rural areas to return to their cities legitimately, and to fuel the growing militancy on the streets.

The party centre denounced the agitation, blaming the strikes not on the objective conditions facing workers – the result of the State's accumulation drive since 1949 – but on the 'handful of party persons in authority taking the capitalist road'. 'These capitalist roaders have been even fomenting strikes, instigating the *masses who do not understand the actual situation* to flock to the banks and withdraw their deposits by force'.[86] In the State where supposedly the self-conscious masses governed, it seemed absurdly easy to 'mislead' them.

(iv) The army must save the country

The PLA endeavoured to hold the line. It was the only secure base of power for the leadership. But it was small, spread thinly, aware of the dangers lurking beyond China's borders – Russian troops in the north and east, and a major US military operation in the south in Vietnam. Furthermore, some of the rebels attacked the soldiers, and possibly some of the soldiers were infected with the radical demands: they had their own persons in authority taking the capitalist road. The central authorities might urge that 'no person or organization may attack the organs of the PLA'; that radio stations, prisons, warehouses, roads, bridges, banks and other important installations were out of bounds; they might forbid soldiers to participate in the Cultural Revolution.[87] But a real class struggle had broken out and it was not to be tamed by edict.

The PLA was instructed in January 1967 to intervene, not just to separate belligerents or protect installations, but to *lead* all legitimate organizations: 'In all institutions where seizure of power has become necessary, from above to below, the participation of the PLA and militia delegates in the temporary organs of power of the revolutionary triple alliance is indispensable. Factories, villages, institutions of finance and commerce, of learning (including colleges, secondary and primary schools), party organs, administrative and mass organizations, must be led with the participation of the PLA . . . Where there are not enough PLA representatives, these positions should better be left vacant temporarily.'[88] The task was to implement Mao's latest thought: 'Economize on consumption and carry on revolution. Protect the property of the country.'[89]

In the din, very little could be heard of what Mao actually proposed. So great was the 'upsurge of bitterness' at the years of the party's rule, it drowned all lesser questions. The press continued to divert all grievances towards one target – as one Shanghai newspaper urged its readers: 'Concentrate the Greatest Animosity on "A Handful" of Those at the Top'.[90] The effect on the youth was poignant. For example, one confessed: 'Today I heard a class brother accuse counter-revolutionary revisionist Lo Jui-ch'ing of his crimes . . . tears ran down my face and I was very angry. At that time, I looked at the "Quotations of Chairman Mao" in my hand, and thought that, but for Chairman Mao and the Great Proletarian Cultural Revolution led by him, how could we be able to accuse Lo Jui-ch'ing here? This deepened my reverence and adoration for Chairman Mao.'[91] Mao meanwhile was endeavouring to restore the position of the battered party cadre: 'The old cadres before the power struggle and the new cadres after it should co-operate in working together and preserve the secret of the State.'[92] The method of winding down the 'peasant war' of 1947–8 had been to admit middle and rich peasants and landlords into the poor peasant leagues. Now Mao attempted a similar tactic – to build a new organization with the old party and the new rebels, held together by the PLA: a 'triple alliance' which subsequently became the revolutionary committees. The party held power and commanded the structures, so that it would inevitably master the incoherent and fluid rebelliousness of the 'mass organizations'.

To help matters along, the press declared in March that many good cadres had been wrongly dismissed by Liu Shao-ch'i, but that now the revolution had triumphed, they could return. Furthermore, the press deplored 'indiscriminate attacks on all persons in authority' since this 'robs the nation of the mature political and organizational skills of experienced men'.[93] Petty corruption and even a bad work style were now small details in comparison to the threat to the State. Mao added his quotation to clinch the point: 'We must believe that more than ninety per cent of our cadres are good or comparatively good.'[94] He drew the limits more sharply: 'The method of simply rejecting everything and negating everything, of directing the struggle against cadres who shoulder most of the responsibilities and do most of the work or against the "heads" [of departments] must be abandoned.'[95] In mid-1966 Mao had compared the movement to the Paris Commune. Now he rejected any idea of a Shanghai Commune.

(v) Sheng-wu-lien

In the upsurge of late 1966, the workers lacked any organization which could present their demands, whether trade union or independent political party. It was the strength of the State, with its monopoly of armed power and serried ranks of disciplined bureaucrats, which meant it would inevitably win unless alternative organizations were created.

The longer instability continued, the more likely some such organization would be created. Then the fears of the leadership would become a reality – there would exist, in their terms, a 'counter-revolutionary' alternative. A number of organizations arose spontaneously which aspired to champion the revolt. One of the most interesting was Sheng-wu-lien, the Hunan Provincial Proletarian Revolutionary Great Alliance Committee.

This Hunan federation of organizations was attacked by most of the central leadership. Minister of Public Security K'ang Sheng expressed their indignation: 'They describe the State and the party led by Chairman Mao as a privileged class, similar to Khrushchev's party . . . They say the Great Cultural Revolution has just begun, that the Great Cultural Revolution in the past was merely reformism, and that it has really begun only since the emergence of "Sheng-wu-lien" . . . They say that the provincial revolutionary committees and preparatory groups for these committees set up in the Great Cultural Revolution are all reformists . . . In this way, isn't Chairman Mao's thought reformism too? In this way, they slander our great leader, Chairman Mao.'[96]

Sheng-wu-lien's case was as follows. China was governed by a 'bureaucratic bourgeoisie', a decaying class of 'Red' capitalists who were hindering the progress of history. A revolution, according to Lenin, was a change in the classes governing a country, yet in China the attack had been solely on particular individuals, not on the State itself: 'As a result, the fruit of the revolution was in the final analysis taken by the capitalist class . . . The revolution by dismissal of officials is only bourgeois reformism which changes in a zigzagging way the new bureaucratic rule before the Cultural Revolution into another kind of bourgeois rule of bourgeois bureaucrats.'

The triple alliance, the revolutionary committees, amounted 'to a reinstatement of the bureaucrats already toppled in the January revolution. Inevitably, it will be the form of political power to be usurped by the bourgeoisie, in which the local and national bureaucrats are to play a leading role.' Of course, great claims were made by the party, but 'The bourgeoisie always represent the form of political power of their rule as the most perfect flawless thing in the world that serves the whole people. The new bureaucratic bourgeoisie and the brutes of the Right-wing of the petty bourgeoisie who depend on them are doing exactly that.'

As a result of this analysis, 'the real revolution, the revolution to negate the past seventeen years, has basically not yet begun'. Its task was not reform or the removal of selected individuals, but: 'The rule of the new bureaucratic bourgeoisie must be overthrown by force in order to solve the problem of political power. Empty shouting about realizing the May 7th directive [Mao's instruction on the rectification of the army] without any reference to the seizure of real power and the utter smashing of the old State machinery will of course be a "utopian" dream.' The question therefore became one of armed struggle against the party. 'Before the Cultural Revolution, the bureaucrats dared not really hand over arms to the people. The militia is only a façade behind which the bureaucrats control the armed strength of the people. It is certainly not an armed force of the working class, but a docile tool in the hands of the bureaucrats.' The aim was to destroy the bourgeois class, to create a 'new society free from bureaucrats', one People's Commune of China.⁹⁷

It is understandable that the party leadership were alarmed at this startling reappearance of Leninism after all the years of cultural control and social discipline. All efforts were now bent to root out this 'counter-revolutionary Hotch Potch' as a leading Hunan newspaper described it.

(vi) The Long March back

The rebels became more violent and embittered. They had been promised a revolution, but were now faced with most of the old faces at the local level. The PLA could provide no guide as to what 'Mao Tse-tung thought' meant. General Chen Tsai-tao, the Wuhan commander, backed the wrong group, the One Million Heroes Rebel Group for the 'triple alliance', and was said to have imprisoned Peking's emissaries (Minister of Public Security Hsieh Fu-chih, and Propaganda Chief Wang Li) who were sent to remonstrate with him. The Red Guards stayed in Peking, fighting, attacking foreigners, and in August sacked the office of the British chargé d'affaires, to the government's embarrassment.

In the summer of 1967 Mao made a tour through China. He concluded: 'it is said that there is no civil war in China, but I think there is . . . This is an armed struggle.'[98]

Lin Piao reported that a thousand houses in Kwangsi had been razed to the ground because no one would let the fire-fighting equipment be used. Chiang Ch'ing said the siege of Kwangsi had lasted two months, and Mao reported that 'in Szechuan, the fighting is real war. Each side has tens of thousands of men. They have rifles and cannon'. He deplored the way cadres were forced to kneel and wear dunce's hats, for they were not the same as landlords; yet it was Mao who had identified bad cadres as an exploiting class, the bourgeoisie. There were even people, he said, who 'instigated the soldiers to oppose their superiors, and saying that while you are making only six yuan [RMB] a month, the officers are making much more and enjoying the luxury of riding in automobiles'.[99]

A year later, he was again attempting to force the Red Guards back to their localities of origin. He summoned the four leading members to tell them firmly: 'I am the black hand that suppressed the Red Guards'.[100] Lest they lied when they reported back to their followers, he had the reproof tape-recorded: 'Otherwise you might just quote what you pleased on your return. If you do, I'll just release the recording.'[101]

Progress was, for the leadership, agonizingly slow. Twenty-two revolutionary committees were to have been created by January 1968 but, in fact, only seven existed by then. The old cadres were not easily accepted by the mass organizations, and there were now many new rivals for power – both old cadres and new 'rebels'. The civil war seemed to break out in new areas as soon as it had been mastered in one place. In June 1968, the forty-one corpses washed up in Hong Kong bore witness to continuing conflict. There was a conspiracy to seize the railways. In July, railwaymen were said to have attacked a station in

Canton, stealing arms and calling the PLA a 'royalist army'.[102]

If any faction in the leadership had considered persisting in attempts to unseat the national centre, the Russian invasion of Czechoslovakia in 1968 gave reason to hesitate. The Russian forces concentrated on China's northern borders could be used for a similar exercise against China, and in 1969 armed clashes between Russian and Chinese troops on the Ussuri and Amur rivers made it urgent to restore order.

In April 1969, the Ninth Party Congress met to clear up the debris, to attempt to restore some of the decimated national leadership in the face of the Russian threat. The destruction had been, whether Mao intended it or not, severe. A Western account estimates that, of the ninety-three full members of the central committee elected at the Eighth Congress, fifty-four had been purged after 1966, including four of the six first secretaries of the regional bureaux of the central committee, and twenty-three of the twenty-nine provincial party secretaries. At least some of the Central Committee members must have recalled Khrushchev's speech on Stalin's rule to the 20th Congress of the Soviet Communist party. But people had not been killed, and in the years following, many of those disgraced were allowed to return quietly to positions of authority.

The purge of the armed forces had been relatively light. At the Ninth Congress, the PLA was rewarded for having held the line. Of the 170 full members of the new central committee, exactly half came from the PLA, and only eighteen per cent from the 'rebel mass organizations'. On the Politburo, there was again exactly half the members from the PLA (twelve), with nine from the party, and three from 'mass organizations'.

The Cultural Revolution was important in revealing the reality of China. The twin bases of power, the PLA and the party, survived intact. It would have been impossible to sustain production if either had been seriously damaged. The economy did not go through the wild fluctuation that occurred during the Great Leap Forward – in the worst year for external trade, 1967, exports fell by twelve per cent. Other key institutions escaped disruption. Scientific research did not suffer; China made its sixth hydrogen bomb test in June 1967, and there were rumours of a seventh in December. A year later, a test was officially announced: 'hundreds of millions of revolutionary people throughout the country are greatly inspired by the happy news that China has successfully conducted a new hydrogen bomb test'.[103]

We are left with a paradox – a reform movement described in revolutionary terms, moving into a popular revolution outside the control of the party, but eventually frustrated. The paradox promotes self-contradiction as, for example, in the account of a French supporter of

71

Mao (whose final chapter is headed, 'The Victory of Moderation'): 'It is no longer possible to dispute that the Cultural Revolution really was a revolution . . . The movement called into being was so strong that it almost became another revolution, sweeping away the Communist Party'.[104]

The task, as he saw it, was to awaken 'political consciousness' while 'saving the revolutionaries from their besetting temptation to exploit the revolution for their own pleasure'; or 'to give the Chinese the taste for peaches, and to keep all the fruit on the tree'.

6

AFTER THE CULTURAL REVOLUTION

The history of the Chinese State after the Cultural Revolution falls into three phases, each punctuated by yet another upheaval in the central leadership. During the Cultural Revolution, Mao did not transform the basic institutional apparatus of State, party and PLA, but he did graft on a group of newcomers. The first phase consisted of an assault on the newcomers, leading to the downfall of their leader, Minister of Defence Lin Piao; the second ended in a minor victory for the newcomers by the removal of Teng Hsaio-p'ing; and the third, following the death of Mao, saw the removal of those newcomers remaining in the leadership. Each of the changes took place without any 'popular participation'. The fall of Lin Piao was not publicly admitted until eighteen months afterwards; Teng's removal was made by the party centre; and finally, the removal of the remainder of the newcomers, the 'gang of four', took place in cabal, and only after the event were the crowds mobilized to offer praise.

The changes in leadership did not reflect major differences in policy. Both sides agreed on the basic orientation, although they disagreed over certain symbolic, and sometimes obscure, issues – over works of literature like the novel *The Water Margin* and the writings of Confucius, or over the role of private plots in agriculture and overtime pay in factories. But the emphases the national government placed on each element did not vary with the leadership changes – broadly, policy was to the 'Right' between 1969 and 1973, then moved to the 'Left' between 1973 and 1975 (during Teng Hsaio-p'ing's rise to office). The newcomers, the supposed 'Left', were more strongly in power during the 'Right' phases, and the 'Right' in the ascendant during the 'Left' phases of policy.

The paradox only arises because the labels are misleading. The symbols of debate were of marginal significance for policy in comparison to the basic strategic agreement; and when in power, objective necessities guided policy in much the same direction, regardless of the personnel.

73

Whether or not people read *The Water Margin* or farmed private plots was not a decisive question for the difference between 'socialism' and 'capitalism', except in a demonological universe.

The newcomers and the apparat differed more in terms of an aspirant and an established leadership. The outsiders tried to secure a stronghold, utilizing originally forces outside the party, the youth of the Cultural Revolution; they won the mass media (press, radio, opera etc.) as opposed to the established mechanisms of power in party, government and armed forces. The apparat never lost control of China, and it was vital for Mao's position that they did not do so; the newcomers never penetrated the real centres of authority except in Shanghai, and depended entirely for their influence on Mao's continuing goodwill. The only alternative for the newcomers was to step outside the bureaucracy, and to appeal to the mass. But that demanded both a popular programme and a popular revolution, against just that power order the newcomers aspired to command.

The inheritance of the Cultural Revolution is as ambiguous as its meaning. Take for example, the 'May 7th Schools'. They were created to provide party cadres working in government with the opportunity to 'participate' in manual labour, but on an exclusive basis (that is, the schools were a retreat from the idea of participation in manual labour *with* the peasants). However, quite quickly the schools became simply cadre schools for political training, with an option for participants to do a little weekend gardening if they so chose.[105]

The period of education was for a time reduced from ten to seven years. Schools and universities continued, as urged by Mao in 1957–8, to run their own factories and farms, to supply students as contract labour to enterprises. The supervision of these activities by factory work teams continued, although the 'working class' – as opposed to the party – no longer seemed to supervise educational institutions. Students were required to do three years' manual labour before receiving higher education, a procedure which had the incidental advantage of reducing the numbers applying. The experience in manual labour earned potential students the title of 'worker' or 'peasant', rather than that of their original family background. An English student who spent two years between 1973 and 1975 at two institutions of higher education in China reported that about a third of the student's time was spent on labour projects outside the university. This work also involved participation in political education or 'criticism' sessions: 'The word criticism in China covers anything from the bitter struggles of the Cultural Revolution to the reading of a stereotyped article on Confucius; and I carry an indelible memory of one factory meeting I attended which resembled nothing so much as a non-conformist weekly religious meeting, not in content, but in the fact that it began and ended with a song in which all present more or less participated and the middle consisted of the reading of prepared texts on the theme, through which the majority of those present gently dozed. At the end, the Chairman said: "We have criticized very well – let's wind up today's criticism here".[106]

The work pace in Chinese factories is intense enough to explain the tendency to sleep. It was the same at harvest time on a commune – 'many fell asleep, others chatted among themselves and others played with the ever-present babies. Chinese audiences in any case frequently give disconcerting evidence of inattention.' It seems that 'politics' for much of the time is what the cadres choose to do, and patriotic citizens – or, at least, those without strong objections – tolerate their rituals. Another visitor makes a more general point: 'People whose sole contact with China has been through articles in the press beginning "the Chinese people are advancing inexorably towards the conquest of Nature", are surprised, when they get there, by the stability and tranquillity of the social climate.'

There was a sharp increase in *hsia-fang* (the sending down of urban dwellers to the countryside) in the years immediately after the Cultural Revolution, perhaps in order to break up what was left of the Red Guards, and expel those who had returned during the upheavals, and to reduce the urban population proper. Between 1968 and 1973, eight million school-leavers were sent out of the cities, and a further two million in the following two years. Shanghai sent fully one million (1968–73), and Wuhan 300,000 (1970–73). There was another sort of 'sending down' in 1972, the highest year since 1962 for legal and illegal immigration to Hong Kong (an estimated 80,000 arrived, 20,000 by the dangerous method of swimming). Half of the immigrants were former Red Guards who had been 'sent down' to rural Kwantung province.

As in earlier waves of *hsia-fang*, the press urged the young to embrace the task eagerly, to reject 'Confucian' expectations of a white-collar job in the city. The press also urged peasants not to resent the arrival of these extra mouths with untrained hands: 'People should not seize opportunities to laugh at them or mock them or to take an uncouth attitude to them.'[107] The government offered a public subsidy of RMB 200–240 (£46–55) per head per year to soften the impact.

(i) The Lin Piao affair
The Ninth Party Congress in April 1969 offered only modest rewards for most of the newcomers. Nonetheless, their main leader, a man

originally of the old order, Defence Minister Lin Piao, formally secured the position of Mao's heir. But for the rest, it was part of the old apparat, the PLA, which inherited the post-revolutionary order.

It took only a few months for a leading Cultural Revolutionary, Chen Po-ta, who had been Mao's private secretary for thirty years and was nominated as fourth in the party hierarchy at the Ninth Congress, to become a 'sham Marxist and political swindler'. And two and a half years after the Ninth Congress, Mao's 'close comrade in arms', Lin Piao, a leading military figure in the party for forty years, became 'that bourgeois careerist, conspirator, counter-revolutionary double dealer, renegade and traitor; and his resolute defence of Mao's proletarian line now became 'trash [representing] the wishes not only of the toppled landlord and bourgeois classes for restoration but also of the new bourgeois elements in socialist society'.[108] Either this was libel, or Mao was guilty of criminal negligence in tolerating such a scoundrel for forty years and permitting him to be promoted to such a high position.

The party documents to some extent recognized the anomaly. Party history was rewritten – the triumph of Lin Piao's civil war career, the victory against the Kuomintang on the Liaohsi–Shenyang front, was now abruptly attributed to Mao. It was also now claimed that Mao had secret suspicions of Lin, and a most opaque letter to Mao's wife used in evidence.[109] Clearly politics was not of the kind for mass involvement, but the secret opinions of a cabal; had it been otherwise, Mao could scarcely have refrained from publicizing his doubts, rather than supporting Lin for promotion to the position of his heir. The credibility gap was not closed by the official account of the conspiracy to murder Mao,[110] except to reveal something of the internal relationships of the leadership, and the fact that, despite all the claims for the Cultural Revolution, Lin Piao's twenty-four-year-old son, Lin Li-kuo, was deputy director of the Chinese Air Force logistics department, a surprising piece of nepotism under the 'dictatorship of the proletariat'. The affair took place on the 11–12 September, and on the 30th, Moscow announced recovery of a bullet-riddled Trident aircraft from a site in Outer Mongolia. The corpses, it was suggested, were those of Lin Piao, his wife and Politburo member, Yeh Chün, and seven others, including those apparently involved in the plot, Air Force Chief of Staff Huang Yung-shang, PLA general (Chief of Logistics) Ch'iu Hui-tso, Chief Naval Political Commissar Li Tsu-p'eng, Air Force Chief General Wu Fa-hsien. Subsequently however, the Russians denied Lin was on the Trident.

Was this the first attempt by the old apparat to dislodge the newcomers? If so, it was only partly successful, because the main section of the newcomers, led by the 'group of four' were able, with Mao's protection, to dissociate themselves from their leadership. Mao apparently made no effort to defend Lin. He permitted – or at least made no public protest against – the dropping of a third of the politburo so recently elected at the Ninth Congress. Subsequently, efforts were made to reduce the PLA role in the party – in late 1973, eight of the eleven area military chiefs were posted and, in the process, disentangled from their party responsibilities; at the Tenth Party Congress in August 1973, the PLA share of party posts was radically reduced. The cadres of the party were not informed about the events of mid-September until November, and the Chinese masses not for eighteen months.

(ii) Domestic policy

The armed clash with Russia in 1969 had exposed the risks of domestic disunity. Perhaps that is the reason for the conciliatory policies pursued between 1969 and the Tenth Party Congress in August 1973. A minor wage increase for low-paid workers was allowed in 1971, and prices were cut for some consumer goods – television sets, transistor radios, silk, watches and bicycles. State purchasing prices for some agricultural commodities were increased – by fifteen per cent for sugar and seventeen per cent for oil seeds. In both cases, the main effects were on the better-off: workers able to buy consumer durables, and production teams with high marketable surpluses.

For the peasants, private plots became respectable again; in 1971 they were praised and cadres assured that their existence was nothing to do with any 'capitalist road'; on the contrary, they damped down the black market that State procurements with scarcities inevitably tended to create.[111] The *People's Daily* went so far as to deplore 'time-wasting' meetings in rural areas.[112]

In 1969 the government radically cut central expenditure, making communes responsible for spending on social services, administration and education (expenditure on these items amounted to a quarter of government spending in the 1950s). This change obliged communes to finance their own expenditure and allowed the government to make a sharp increase in defence spending. It would also have increased the differences between rich and poor areas. In July 1971 the government resumed more central control, perhaps to offset this effect.

In the factories, much of the capacity constructed in the 1960s was now brought into production, and industrial output expanded rapidly, assisted by an unprecedented expansion in China's imports of technically advanced goods.

77

Despite the hold of the newcomers on the mass media, there was a cultural relaxation which persisted until 1974 – the London Philharmonic, the Vienna Philharmonic and Philadelphia orchestras made visits to Peking to play the works of 'capitalist composers'.

Simultaneously, the party was being restored. By March 1971, twelve of the twenty-nine provincial party committees had been re-established. The party slogan had shifted from 'Bombard the headquarters' to 'It is the party that exercises leadership in everything'.[113] Thousands of cadres now secured rehabilitation, including the most prominent 'capitalist roaders' (Liu Shao-ch'i had already died). Teng Hsiao-p'ing, second in command of the 'bourgeois dictatorship', appeared at a reception for Cambodia's Sihanouk on 12 April 1973; in May he appeared in the position of honour with Mao at a reception for Bhutto of Pakistan. Lo Jui-ching appeared on the saluting stand at the Army Day celebrations in 1975. Chao Tzu-yang was appointed First Secretary of the Canton party. General Hsiao Hua reappeared in October 1974, and many more.

The former Cultural Revolutionaries suffered accordingly. Some of those accused of being 'ultra-Left' were put on trial in a number of provinces in the spring of 1970 (Kwantung, Peking, Honan, Chekiang, Fukien), and there was a press campaign against those who 'negate everything . . . see only trivial facts of behaviour and not a person's integrity, and see only the past and not the present'.[114] The 'May 16th Group' came in for particularly harsh criticism, being accused of sacking the office of the British chargé d'affaires in 1967 (in June 1970, a foreign ministry official was gaoled for the same offence). No doubt, restored cadres settled other scores with their former tormentors with less publicity – consigning them to rural areas or factory labour instead of party office.

(iii) The Tenth Congress (August 1973)

Having effectively separated the newcomers who achieved prominence in the Cultural Revolution from their base (the Red Guards and Red Rebels), the Tenth Party Congress both recognized the rehabilitation of the old disgraced cadres – Teng became deputy Prime Minister and effectively Chou En-lai's heir – and made room for a larger number of the newcomers. The military component in the central committee was reduced to thirty-two per cent of the total; the newcomers' share rose to ten per cent, and forty per cent on the Politburo (where eight new members were added). Shanghai worker Wang Hung-wen, the most authentic of the 'newcomers', became officially third in the party hierarchy. The Congress also ended the 'conciliatory' phase – there needed to be, once more, a 'revolution in the superstructure . . . Some unhealthy tendencies in State organs and defects in some links of the State system stand in contradiction to the economic base of socialism'; and some cadres still failed to perceive 'the hindering effect of bourgeois ideology, idealism and metaphysics on the socialist revolution and construction'.[115] Whereas Lin Piao had hitherto been accused of being 'ultra-Left', he was now transformed into opposition from the Right.

The 'four clean-ups' campaign – against embezzlement, speculation, profiteering and luxury consumption by the cadres – had been resumed early in 1970. Class enemies who sought 'to corrupt and win over cadres . . . now frequently employ such tactics as giving banquets, handing over gifts, enticing with money or women, or engineering nuptial relations or sworn friendships'.[116] Despite the Cultural Revolution, such people, 'although they have lost their political power, still have money and vast social connections, and these have become the material foundation supplying them with commodities and money for corroding the proletariat'.[117] Particularly at risk were cadres and leading members of the party, some of whom 'do everything to oppose the socialist revolution and protect their own interests. They have good houses, they have cars, their salaries are high and they have servants – they are worse than capitalists.'[118]

What sort of cases did the press present? Cadre Hsieh Ho-hsun was murdered in December 1974 for trying to stop the use of quarry vehicles to steal rocks for private house building.[119] A Peking hotel reported how its staff regularly refused invitations to dinner, the offer of tickets to the theatre or sporting events, special privileges in buying bicycles and other goods; at one point, some 300 catties of Tientsin pears arrived from a procurement clerk 'for the obvious purpose of securing privileges should he stay at the hotel another time'.[120] A school in Anwhei province found 'a small number of students who were influenced by bourgeois ideology, indulged in reading bad novels, telling bad stories and singing bad songs'. In Hopei, 'there sprang up in society a gust of wind which claimed that when cadres give up their posts or retired, they could be succeeded by their own children'.[121] Finally, there were numerous cases of cadres openly expressing their superior power – 'Instead of regarding themselves as part of the masses of the people, they put on pompous airs, follow a bureaucratic routine, reprimand the rank and file whenever they feel like it and are reluctant to treat people on equal terms . . . Instances like these are too numerous to be cited.'[122]

Big character posters spluttered into life through 1974 and 1975, but were usually under close supervision by the authorities. However, some posters attacked unofficial targets – Generals Yang Cheng-wu, Yu Li-chih, Chen Hsi-lian (Shenyang), Hsi Chen-hua (Taiyuan First Secretary), and even General Li Teh-sheng (Politburo Standing Committee member and Vice-chairman of the party) and Hua Kuo-feng. Posters attacking leading party members were promptly torn down. Other posters criticized managers in Kunming (Yunnan); party cadres for black market trading in eggs and oil, for kidnapping, fraud in timber dealing; the police in Nanch'ang (Kiangsi) for arbitrary arrests and brutality; one even claimed that 2,000 had been killed in gang warfare in Juichin. In Peking, the 'Golden Monkey' with his or her complaints that the city had been for eighteen years under revisionist control achieved international fame.[123]

There were posters which went well beyond these individual complaints. Li Yi-che – the pseudonym of three authors, Li Cheng-t'ien, Ch'en Yi-yang and Huang Hsi-che – indicted the régime in 'On socialist democracy and legality under socialism', a set of seventy-seven sheets posted on the Peking road, Canton, in early 1974.

The authors argued that the removal of Lin Piao had not changed the system which had created and sustained Lin Piao – a 'social-fascist dictatorship of a feudal type'. As in the Soviet Union, a new bourgeoisie controlled the State, robbing the community and sustaining a quasi-hereditary rule of privilege based upon the arbitrary and brutal use of power. The brief first phase of the Cultural Revolution was the only time when the masses had secured certain minimum rights and liberties – of press, opinion, association and movement. Lin Piao's usurpation of power in 1968 had ended this and restored the old clique to power. The writers appealed to the forthcoming National People's Congress to establish popular control of the State, the right of popular recall of all party and government officers, and elementary civil liberties (to prevent arbitrary arrest, rigged trials, use of torture on prisoners, political arrests).

It was an echo of the old 'ultra-Left' of 1968. Indeed, it is said that Li Cheng-t'ien spent a year in prison in that year for his beliefs. In 1976 and '77, Hong Kong sources claimed the group behind the posters had been publicly attacked as proponents of 'social feudalistic fascism'. Li Cheng-t'ien was said to have been sentenced to 'indefinite imprisonment', the others to long periods in labour reform camps.

(iv) Fourth National People's Congress
In January 1975 some 2,864 representatives met at the Fourth

National People's Congress to ratify a new constitution for the State and endorse the government. Under the constitution, private farming plots were guaranteed, and the practice followed since the mid-1950s of permitting strikes was recognized. Chou En-lai, reviving a perspective outlined by Mao in 1965, proposed the building of 'an independent and relatively comprehensive industrial and economic system before 1980', the doubling of national income between 1970 and 1980, and the mechanization of agriculture. Teng's position was recognized as next in line of succession after Chou – he was now deputy premier, Vice-chairman of the party, member of the Standing Committee of the Politburo, and Chief of Staff of the PLA. One of the newcomers, Chang Chun-chiao, advanced parallel with Teng – a deputy premier and head of the PLA Political Department.

However, when Chou En-lai died a year later, the press began a campaign against 'China's Second Khrushchev'. One month after Chou's death, Hua Kuo-feng, himself a relative newcomer (from district party secretary in Hunan he had risen on the occasion of the Lin Piao affair to become Public Security Minister), became Acting Prime Minister. It seemed that, in the inner party centre, the newcomers (supported possibly by Mao) had had sufficient power to block Teng's automatic inheritance, but insufficient to promote any of the 'group of four'. The press dutifully harried Teng, but insisted that there be no movement of activists between cities, no special groups formed, and the cadres remain fully in control, lest the 'Rightists . . . use the sabotage of production to sabotage the revolution'. As in the past, the accused was given no opportunity to present his views, so the mass of the population could not judge the rights and wrongs of the case.

Teng had been blocked but not politically destroyed; he remained a candidate of the apparat. In the spring of 1976, his political destruction was achieved in the last coup of the newcomers. At the Ching Ming festival on 4 April, some 100,000 people gathered in Tienamin Square to mourn the death of Chou En-lai, far too many to represent a spontaneous demonstration (wreaths were said to have been sent by the headquarters of the second artillery section of the PLA and cadres in sections of the State Council), but there was no evidence of overt support for Teng. Nonetheless, some force removed the wreaths and posters overnight, as a result of which the largest riots seen in Peking since 1949 broke out. Vehicles were burned and a public security office sacked. On the 6th troops occupied the area, facing sullen crowds, when it was announced that Teng had been officially dismissed from all posts (but not expelled from the party).[124]

It was a Pyrrhic victory. We can presume that the entire apparat was

81

outraged at the public display of arbitrariness, yet obliged to accept it while Mao insisted on protecting the newcomers. But in September, the Chairman died. Within one month, the central leadership had eliminated its tormentors, the 'gang of four' (Mao's wife, Chiang Ch'ing, and Chang Chun-chiao, Yao Wen-yuan, Wang Hung-wen). The Cultural Revolution had finally come to an end.

The purge of the opponents of the old leadership (whether they were supporters of the 'gang of four' or not) continued through the following year. A larger number of people than normal seems to have been executed in this campaign; no doubt old scores were settled. Now all the standard accusations levelled at Liu, Teng and Lin were directed at the four, including charges of attempted murder, organizing civil war and high treason. Chairman Hua, like many before him, enthused: 'genuine Marxism has triumphed over sham Marxism'.

Ten months later, the party sanctioned these changes at its Eleventh Congress. Teng became once more Vice-chairman of the party, as well as Vice-premier, chief of staff of the PLA and Vice-chairman of the Military Affairs Commission. Most of the newcomers who had achieved prominence at the 1973 Congress were removed from the new Politburo and Central Committee, and replaced by representatives of the 'old guard', particularly those from the military high command. Shortly afterwards, the Fifth National People's Congress was announced for 1978 to sanction the new hierarchy of the State.

Politically, the fitful swing to the 'Right' of 1970–74 was resumed, but now with much greater determination. In industry, for example, the leadership made it explicit that profits were to be the key measure of performance, output should determine pay, and that foreign imports were a vital means of modernizing the economy. In higher education, examinations were restored as the primary method of entry, and entry from school, not from manual occupations in farm or factory. For the PLA, the improvement of weaponry became an important element in future planning. None of this was new in the history of China, and there were numerous speeches by Mao to support such policies from the years before the Great Leap Forward (now edited by Hua and published as the long-delayed fifth volume of Mao's *Selected Works*) as well as from the period 1961–5. But mere restoration showed how shallow the commotion of the Cultural Revolution had been, how utopian the hopes of the youthful rebels of 1966.

The events following the death of Mao illustrated yet again the consistency of the history of the Chinese State since 1949. There were many detours, but the central authority never diverged for long from its purpose of building a powerful national State, weaving between the obstacles set by a hostile world order and the obdurate backwardness of China's rural majority. The performance was remarkable, given the scale of obstacles and pitfalls on the way, and the fact that the party itself was not an unchanging entity.

The party claimed that the tasks it set itself were laid down and directed by the workers and peasants of China. It was said that, for this reason, although there were many diversions, the basic direction remained true to the original aim. What was the role of these two classes in the new society of the People's Republic? We need now to examine in more detail the position of workers and peasants in order to appraise the legitimacy of the party's claim.

NOTES

1. *CW* 23, pp. 325–6, stress in the original
2. State and Revolution, *CW* 25, p. 406
3. Decisions on Employment, GAC of the Central People's Government, 25 Jul. 1952, in *Labour Laws and Regulations of the People's Republic of China*, Peking, 1956, p. 65
4. *China's Destiny*, London, 1947, p. 173
5. On the People's Democratic Dictatorship, 1 Jul. 1949, *SW* IV, p. 419
6. Economic and financial problems, 'Ching chi wen t'i yü ts'ai cheng wen t'i', Hong Kong, 1949, cited Christopher Howe, *Wage patterns and policy in Modern China, 1919–1972*, Cambridge, 1973, p. 59
7. Report of Li Hsien-nien, Minister of Finance, 3rd session, 1st National People's Congress, 1956, in *New China Advances to Socialism*, Peking, 1956, p. 65
8. Report on the work of the government, 1st session, National People's Congress, 23 Sep. 1954, Peking, 1954, p. 1
9. *Far Eastern Economic Review*, 26 Jan. 1950
10. *Development of State capitalism in China's industry*, Statistical Work Bulletin, Peking, 29 Oct. 1956, cited Gluckstein, *op.cit.*, p. 198
11. Address to the All-China Federation of Industry and Commerce, 8 Dec. 1956, *Miscellany* I, pp. 43–4
12. NCNA; Peking, 24 Jun. 1952
13. *JMJP*, 1 Jul. 1952, in *CB*, 1952, p. 199
14. Address, *op.cit.*, *Miscellany* I, p. 38
15. *Ibid*, p. 43
16. For 1949 and 1956, see Data on China's population from 1949 to 1956, *Statistical Bulletin*, No. 11, 14 Jun. 1957, *ECMM* 1957, pp. 22–5, and Table I, John S. Aird, 'Population growth and distribution in Mainland China', in *An Economic Profile of Mainland China*, Washington, Feb. 1967, 2, p. 353; 1961 from Po I-po, Chairman State Planning Council, in Anne Louise Strong, *Letter from China*, Peking, 1964

17. Symposium, 21 Feb. 1959, in *Miscellany* I, p. 160
18. Jan. 1957, in *Miscellany* I, p. 47
19. *New China Advances, op.cit.*, p. 40
20. Jan. 1957, *Miscellany* I, pp. 51, 61
21. Jan. 1957, *Miscellany* I, p. 57
22. Edgar Snow, *Red China Today: the other side of the river*, London, 1963, p. 426
23. Note 31 (with official sources), in John Wilson Lewis, (ed.), *The City in Communist China*, Stanford, 1971, p. 404
24. Sixty Points on Working Methods, 19 Feb. 1958, No. 21, in *Mao Papers*, p. 63
25. Cited Jan Deleyne, *The Chinese Economy*, London, 1973, pp. 185–6
26. Speech, 8th Party Congress, 2nd session, 17 May 1958, in *Miscellany* I, p. 102
27. Talks, Nanning Conference, 11–12 Jan. 1958, in *Miscellany* I, p. 80
28. Speech, 8th Party Congress, 2nd session, 18 May 1958, *Miscellany* I, p. 122
29. Sixth Plenum, 8th Central Committee, 19 Dec. 1958, *Miscellany* I, p. 144
30. *Ibid*, pp. 138–9
31. Che Hsueh Yen Chiu, *Philosophical Studies*, No. 5, 10 Sep. 1958, *ECMM*, 149
32. Central Committee resolution, 10 Dec. 1958, NCNA Peking, 18 Dec. 1958, in *CB* 542, pp. 7–22, and *SCMM* 138, p. 16
33. *People's Communes in China*, Peking, 1958, p. 8, and *JMJP*, 3 Oct. 1958
34. 23 Jul. 1959, Lushan Plenum, in *Mao Unrehearsed*, p. 135; see also 21 Feb. 1959, *Miscellany* I, p. 162
35. *JMJP*, 27 Aug. 1959
36. May 1959, *Miscellany* I, p. 183
37. 21 Feb. 1959, *Miscellany* I, p. 159
38. Mao, *Miscellany* I, p. 184
39. Lushan Plenum, 23 Jul. 1959, in *Mao Unrehearsed*, p. 142
40. 21 Feb. 1959, in *Miscellany* I, p. 160
41. Lushan Plenum, 23 Jul. 1959, in *Mao Unrehearsed*, pp. 42–3. XX is not identified in the text available
42. *JMJP*, 27 Aug. 1959
43. *JMJP*, 19 Apr. 1959; see also: Tsai T'i-chiu, 'Mass movement and centralized leadership in industry', *JMJP*, 24 Oct. 1959; see also Hsu Hsin-hsueh, in *Hung-ch'i*, 16 Oct. 1961
44. 19 Sep. 1959; cf. Mao's warm reply to P'eng's acknowledgement of error: 'We should take this two-sided attitude to help an old comrade who has been with us for thirty-one years', *Miscellany* I, p. 187
45. Lushan, in *Mao Unrehearsed*, pp. 142–3, 146
46. Snow, *Red China Today, op.cit.*, p. 188
47. Po I-po, to Anna Louise Strong, *Letter from China, op. cit.*
48. Sixth Plenum, Seventh Central Committee, Sep. 1955, in *Miscellany* I, p. 25
49. Mao, Enlarged Work Conference, 30 Jan. 1962, in *Mao Unrehearsed*, pp. 174–5
50. 'In 1962, under the instigation and direction of external forces, a group of the most reactionary protagonists of local nationalism staged a traitorious

counter-revolutionary armed rebellion in Ining, Sinkiang, and incited and organized the flight to foreign territory of a large number of people near the frontier' – Chou En-lai, Third NPC, 21–2 Dec. 1964, cited by William Malden, 'A new class structure emerging in China?', *CQ* 22, Apr.–Jun. 1960, pp. 84–5; an edited version of his report is translated and published, *ibid*, pp. 70–74

51. *Bulletin of Activities (Kung-tso T'ung-hsun)*, PLA confidential documents, No. 1, 1 Jan. 1961, pp. 29–32, and No. 5, 17 Jan. 1961, pp. 5–15, cited by John Wilson Lewis in discussion of these papers, *CQ* 18, Apr.–Jun. 1964, p. 76; Mao refers to 'serious problems' in three provinces due to food shortages and errors of leadership, in speech, Ninth Plenum, Eighth Central Committee, 18 Jan. 1961, in *Miscellany* II, p. 240

52. Alexander Eckstein, in Alexander Eckstein, Walter Galenson and Ta-chung Liu (eds.), *Economic Trends in Communist China*, Chicago, 1968, p. 7

53. Notes on Soviet Union's 'Political Economy', 1961–2, in *Miscellany* II, p. 277: stress added

54. *Rural communes in Lien-chiang, documents concerning communes in Lien-chiang county, Fukien province, 1962–3*, translated and edited by C. S. Chen, Stanford, 1969

55. E. L. Wheelwright and Bruce McFarlane, *The Chinese Road to Socialism*, London, 1973, p. 70, citing R. Wilson, 'The China after next', *Far Eastern Economic Review*, 1 Feb. 1968, p. 193

56. *Hung-ch'i*, Nos. 13–14, 1963, p. 11

57. Enlarged Work Conference, 30 Jan. 1962, in *Mao Unrehearsed*, p. 167

58. 18 Aug. 1964, in *Mao Unrehearsed*, p. 217

59. 5 Jul. 1964, in *Mao Unrehearsed*, p. 244

60. Revised Second Ten Points, Article IV, translated by Richard Baum and F. C. Tiewes, *Ssü-Ch'ing: The Socialist Education Movement of 1962–66*, Center for Chinese Studies Research Monograph, Berkeley, 1968, Appx. E

61. Talks on the four clean-ups movement, 3 Jan. 1965, *Miscellany* II, p. 414

62. Dec. 1964, *Miscellany* II, p. 416

63. Enlarged Work Conference, 30 Jan. 1962, *Mao Unrehearsed*, p. 185

64. 20 Dec. 1964, in *Misellany* II, p. 426

65. This account is derived from Richard Baum, *Prelude to revolution: Mao, the Party and the Peasant Question, 1962–66*, New York, 1975, for which see Chinese sources, p. 84 *passim*

66. For example, *Nan-fang JP*, Canton, 11 Oct. 1964

67. cf. *SCMM*, 578, p. 28 and *CB* 824, and Baum, *op.cit.*

68. 13 Feb. 1964, in *Mao Unrehearsed*, p. 206–7

69. *Ibid.* p. 203: cf. also 5 Jul. 1964, *ibid*, p. 248

70. 13 Feb. 1964 – Mao praises Confucius as a model of educational simplicity; in *Mao Papers*, p. 93

71. The articles criticized the work of historian Wu Han, deputy mayor of Peking; Kuo Mo-jo, President of the Academy of Sciences; and later Teng T'o, former editor of *JMJP*; cf. *Miscellany* II, pp. 456–7

72. cf. Interview with former Canton Red Guard by Tariq Ali, in *International*, 3, London, Summer 1974, pp. 35–9

73. July 1966, in *Mao Papers*, p. 24

74. July 1966, in *Mao Unrehearsed*, p. 254

75. 23 Aug. 1966, in *Mao Papers*, p. 36; repeated, 7 Sep. Directive of the central committee, *ibid*, p. 130; repeated 11 Sep.

76. In *SCMP*, 3997
77. 15 Sep. 1966, *SCMP* 3785, pp. 3–5
78. 31 Jul. 1966, in *Mao Papers*, p. 129
79. Oct. 1966, in *Mao Unrehearsed*, p. 268. See also *ibid*, p. 271, and *Mao Papers*, p. 43
80. *Ibid*, p. 271
81. *Ibid*, p. 270
82. *Ibid*, pp. 266–7
83. *Ibid*, p. 267
84. *Ibid*, p. 268; cf. also 'Nor can we put all the blame on Comrade Shao-ch'i and Comrade Hsiao-p'ing', *ibid*, p. 274, and slightly different translation, *Mao Papers*, p. 45
85. For details of some of the strikes, cf. on fortnight's dock strikes, *Hung-ch'i*, 1 Feb. 1967, *SCMM* 564; railway strikes, Shanghai to Hangchow and Nanking, 30 Dec–10 Jan. 1967, NCNA, 9 Feb. 1967; Yangshupu power station strike, NCNA, 16 Jan. 1967; Nanking transport strike, NCNA, 14 Jan. 1967; Taching oil field strike, NCNA, 15 Jan. 1967; Shanghai No. 17 textile mill strike, NCNA, 9 Jan. and 28 Jan. 1967; Shanghai glassmaking machinery factory strike, NCNA, 15 Jan. 1967; Shanghai No. 2 camera plant – because of strike, 'only 9.2 per cent of the target was completed', NCNA, 17 Feb. 1967; Peking No. 2 machine tool plant, *JMJP*, 2 Feb. 1967, *SCMP* 3881
86. cf. *Wen Hui Pao*, 18 Jan. 1967, *SCMP* Suppl. 164, 28 Feb. 1967, p. 24, stress added
87. Central Committee, Circular concerning prohibiting directing the spearhead struggle against the armed forces, 14 Jan. 1967
88. Order of the Central Military Commission, 28 Jan. 1967, and also Regulations of the Central Military Commission on the seizure of power in the armed forces, 16 Feb. 1967; and also Document of the Central Committee, State Council and Central Military Commission, 19 Jan. 1967 and 26 Jan. 1967
89. *JMJP*, editorial, 26 Jan. 1967, in *Mao Papers*, p. 134
90. *Chieh-fang JP*, 8 May 1967, *SCMP* 191, 14 Jul. 1967, p. 28
91. *Chan Pao (Battle News)*, 18 Jan. 1967, *SCMP* 165, 10 Mar. 1967, p. 25
92. 27 Jan. 1967, in *Mao Papers*, p. 48
93. *Hung-ch'i*, 22 Feb. 1967
94. 13 May 1967, in *Mao Papers*, p. 154
95. 12 Jun. 1967, *ibid*, p. 141
96. 24 Jan. 1968, in *SCMP* 4136
97. All citations in this section from *Whither China?*, document of Sheng-wu-lien, *SCMP* 4190; extract republished in *International Socialism* 37, Jun.–Jul. 1969, pp. 23–7
98. Dialogues during an inspection tour, Jul.–Sep. 1967, in *Miscellany* II, p. 464: cf. also 'A wind of armed struggle is developing in several regions', *JMJP*, 19 Aug. 1967
99. *Ibid*, p. 465
100. Capital Red Guard Congress, 28 Jul. 1968, *Miscellany* II, p. 480
101. Cited from *Long Live Mao Tse-tung thought*, by Roderick McFarquhar, *The Times*, 5 Sep. 1973
102. *San-chün Lun-wei Chan-pao*, 9, 7 Sep. 1968, in *SCMP* 4338, 15 Jan. 1969
103. NCNA, 29 Dec. 1968, *SCMP* 4331, 6 Jan. 1969

104. Jean Esmein, *The Chinese Cultural Revolution* (translated from French), New York, 1973, p. 330

105. Visitor's observation – Gilbert Padoul, 'China 1974: Problems not Models', *New Left Review* 89, Jan.–Feb. 1975, p. 73

106. Isabel Hilton, *Sunday Times*, London, 25 Jan. 1976

107. *Hung-ch'i*, Nov. 1973

108. *JMJP*, 22 Apr. 1975, *SCMP* 5846, 6 May 1975

109. Published outside China, from spy sources in Taiwan; French translation in *Le Monde*, 2 Dec. 1972; validity confirmed in Peking by Wilfred Burchett, cf. *The Daily Yomiuri*, Tokyo, 17 Aug. 1973, and *Far Eastern Economic Review*, 81/33, 20 Aug. 1973, pp. 22–4

110. Burchett, *ibid*, claims his account was written in consultation with authoritative sources in Peking and in the light of the dossier prepared by the Central Committee for the Tenth Party Congress

111. *JMJP*, 22 Oct. 1971

112. *JMJP*, 23 Oct. 1971

113. *JMJP*, 1 Jul. 1974

114. *Hung-ch'i*, 12 Jul. 1970

115. *Hung-ch'i*, Aug. 1973; cf. also Su Hsi, *JMJP*, 11 Jan. 1974, *SCMP* 5547, 6 Feb. 1974

116. Harbin radio, in *SWB* FE/4856, 3, BII/5, 18 Mar. 1975; cf. also Peking radio, 12 Mar. *ibid*, BII/II

117. *Kuang-ming JP*, 17 Apr. 1975, *SCMP* 5834

118. *Kuang-ming JP*, 28 Jun. 1975; see also *JMJP*, 21 Mar. 1975, in *SWB* 4862/i 24 Mar. 1975; *Hung-ch'i*, Aug. 1975, and Peking radio, 7 Aug. 1975, *ibid*

119. Hupeh provincial service, Wuhan radio, 30 Jun. 1975, *SWB* 4947/BII/12

120. Advance in the struggle against corruption, Chingwenmen No. 2 Hotel, *Hung-ch'i* 4, 1 Apr. 1975, in *SCMM (SPRCM)* 819–20, 28 Apr.–5 May 1975

121. *JMJP*, cited *Far Eastern Economic Review*, 1 Aug. 1975

122. *Study and Criticism*, Shanghai, *ibid*

123. Peking correspondent, *The Times*, London, 26 Jun. and 6 Jul. 1974

124. NCNA Peking, 6 Apr. 1976; cf. also *Far Eastern Economic Review*, report from Peking, 16 Apr. 1976, and Hua Lin, *Minus 8*, Hong Kong, Jun.–Jul. 1976

PART III

WORKERS AND PEASANTS IN THE PEOPLE'S REPUBLIC

7

WORKERS IN THE 1950s

(i) Restoring production

Between 1949 and 1953 the economy was restored. The government then began a programme of planned expansion, at the core of which – so far as workers were concerned – were sustained efforts to increase labour productivity. Accordingly a new set of regulations was introduced, the draconian Model Outline of Intra-Enterprise Discipline Rules.[1] The All-China Federation of Trade Unions (ACFTU) was required to publicize and assist in the enforcement of the new regulations. Article 17 of the rules reads 'Late arrival or early departure without good reason, or playing around or sitting idle during working hours shall be subject to proper punishment or dismissal as the case may require'. Article 21 stipulates that: 'If due to non-observance of working procedures or irresponsibility, rejects are turned out or the equipment is damaged, the worker or staff member shall be held responsible for part or whole payment of compensation for the material loss as conditions may require, whether he is punished or not. The amount of compensation shall be decided by the management and deducted from his wages until it is completely paid up, but the maximum amount to be deducted each time must not exceed 30 per cent of his actual monthly wages.'

As if this 'foreman's charter' (prosecution, judgement and jury were all in the same hands) were not enough, penalties were stipulated for managers who failed to punish the workers concerned.[2]

To ensure that workers with poor records could not escape particular managers by changing jobs, the Ministry of Labour introduced a labour book containing the worker's record; the worker could not obtain legal employment without presenting the book to his employer for inspection. Special tribunals were created in 1953 to enforce the disciplinary code, with the court of final appeal being the Supreme People's Court. Under supervision by local courts, factory managements were required to set up internal courts with the power to make public criticism of the

91

performance of particular workers, to warn them and to penalize them by cutting pay, demoting, suspending or dismissing them. For more serious charges, labour correctional camps were created; the ordinary courts took over after that, with the power to imprison or in extreme cases to impose the death penalty.[3]

The combined effects of poor machinery, poor health and the general speed-up in production created both high accident and sickness rates as well as forms of worker resistance. In response, the ACFTU undertook regular campaigns, not to protect workers by securing a slackening of the pace, but by intensifying discipline and setting up union commissions to try offenders. The press complained regularly of labour 'indiscipline'. One newspaper maintained that: 'Workers in general are late for work and early to go home, and always absent without leave; they break working regulations, disobey transfer orders and technical instructions and resist the authorities negatively, causing a fall in the quality of their work; sometimes they purposely go slow in their work or even stage a strike.'[4] The trade union newspaper explained: 'Since a large number of the new workers who have been recruited by various enterprises come from the petty bourgeoisie or even from the exploiting classes, they brought many backward ideas such as selfishness, irresponsibility, and laziness.'[5] As so often, resisting the régime's purposes was attributed to hostile classes. In fact, by 1953 the rapid expansion in employment had not gone beyond taking up the existing unemployed.

The press also attacked go-slows and strikes. The *People's Daily* summarized the irritation of the new government: 'The phenomenon of idle strikes, insubordination and violation of labour discipline, are still prevalent among staff and workers in various enterprises, causing tremendous damage to our national economy.'[6]

The cadres were also guilty of not applying the proper sanctions: 'The leadership cadres in some of our departments and enterprises have cherished an erroneous conception of the problem of labour discipline, considering that strict implementation of discipline is a "capitalist way of management", a "warlord style of work", or "commandism". Therefore they consciously or unconsciously adopt a compromising attitude towards acts of breach of discipline, nor do they take any drastic action against them.'[7]

The work performances criticized might have been tolerable had they not been measured against the spectacular output achieved by 'model workers', the 'Stakhanovites'. 'Stakhanovism' was a feature in the organization of labour in Stalin's Russia. A miner, Alexander Stakhanov, claimed to have produced 102 tons of coal in five hours, fourteen times the normal output. This 'model' was then employed to force all miners to compete to achieve the new – and clearly ludicrous – target, raising the norm progressively so that the average miner could never reach it but productivity went up by leaps and bounds. In China, the 'model worker' concept was used from the beginning with the same aim. By the end of 1950, there were some 200 publicized national and several thousand provincial models as well as model enterprises; by 1958, there were five and a half million model workers. The Wang-chia-yuan colliery in Kiangsi province, for example, claimed to have broken the national record six times running (though the claims were subsequently said to be forged).[8]

In Western countries, 'rate-busting' by individual workers is a notorious method of raising output, setting workers against each other, and ruining their health through exhaustion and accidents (it penalizes all except the most robust, especially women and older workers). But in China, Stalin's formula was described as 'socialist emulation': 'it transforms labour from a degrading and painful burden, into a matter of honour, glory, valour and heroism'.[9]

Pay was geared to reward the rate-buster. There were numerous other privileges for model workers – titles, opportunities for promotion, attending conferences, being introduced to national leaders, opportunities to join the party or be elected to political or governmental bodies, special holidays in trade union rest homes, travel privileges, gifts in kind, and – perhaps the most important of all – special treatment in the provision of housing. Sometimes the rewards were not to individuals but to a gang or team. In the early 1960s, there was even a 'family emulation drive' in which members of a family working in the same factory were supposed to check each other's shortcomings in order to keep up the family output.[10] There were also interplant contests, and the mass meeting was used to expose the laggards.

The model workers' system proved a mixed blessing for the régime. Apart from the problem of forged credentials – workers and management colluding to win prestige – stable production was often wrecked by individual *blitzkrieg* tactics. Wang Jung-lun of the Anshan iron and steel complex was so far ahead in his work, he would have been halfway through the Fourth Plan while the rest of the work force was only completing the First, something of a problem if production is collaborative.[11] For different reasons, managers and workers had cause to be hostile to the scheme. Furthermore, model workers had an exceptionally high casualty rate, not a good advertisement for other workers; of 192 model workers discussed in one source, seventy-six later collapsed from overwork, and ninety others subsequently failed to make the political or moral grade.[12]

Efforts were made to lengthen the working day. However, the cost to men and machines was high. As a result, the original eight to ten hour day was revived, with, where possible, three-shift working. However, plant targets remained, often forcing managers to extend working hours well beyond the official period. In 1952 the government reproved the practice: 'Under the slogan of "accomplishing the production mission" and "implementing the economic accounting system", the leadership personnel in certain factories demand an unlimited stretch of labour of the workers, extend their working hours, and encourage them to "throw themselves into the boiling water and burning flame". For instance, the brick factory of Ma Chia Kou, Kailan, failing to keep up its production previously, mobilized workers to pull bricks out of the hot kiln heated to 130 degrees centigrade in order to fulfil its contract in time to avoid a fine . . . The result was that forty-one of the forty-three workers sustained injury through burns, some proving fatal.'[13]

Despite the reproof, the pressure of targets – and the sanction of fines or worse – continued to force the pace. The press carried accounts of people working twenty-four hours or more at a stretch; one railway 'hero' worked for thirty-nine hours continuously. At the Anshan steel works in 1955, it was reported that: 'During a week in April, some workers in this enterprise worked as long as thirty-five hours at a stretch; others, seventeen hours.'[14] Even the head of the ACFTU, Lai Jo-yü, was prevailed upon to complain: 'There has been no limit to the prolongation of working hours; individual workers have worked continuously for seventy-two hours through additional shifts and working hours. In order to fulfil their tasks, individual factories have required their workers to work Sundays for a period of ten months . . . As a result of exhaustion, sickness and casualties have been serious . . . In individual factories, increased shifts and working hours reached 260,000 hours, but the number of hours lost due to sick-leave amounted to 220,000.'[15]

The government also made continuing efforts to economize on manpower. In his 1958 Sixty Points on Working Methods Mao praised the amalgamation of Kwangsi commercial enterprises which cut their workforce 'from 2,400 to 350'. In the 1950s, jobs expanded rapidly enough to conceal the simultaneous decline in the volume of labour per unit of output. In the 1960s, output increased less rapidly, but there was no relaxation in the efforts to reduce the labour force. For example, at the Hsiao Ch'i-pa Iron and Steel Works (Chieng-yu county, Szechuan), the 1960 production plan was fulfilled one month ahead of schedule while the workforce was cut by a fifth; the management aimed to cut the workforce by another fifth in 1961, but then decided to raise the targets and drop a third of the workers.[16]

With tight curbs on labour costs, the appropriation by the State from current production was enormous. The Chairman of the ACFTU in 1954 reported that: 'In 1952, the workers of State-operated enterprises produced a yearly average value of JMP 100 million per capita. Of this, except for JMP 500,000 as the average monthly wage for workers, ninety-four per cent represented capital created for the State.'[17]

The Great Leap Forward accelerated the drive to increase output and lower labour costs. The rules governing hours and conditions were swept away in the frenetic drive for expansion. Now even increased pay for increased output was denounced as capitalist 'material incentives'. Military and guerilla imagery came to dominate production – model teams and Red Banner Bearers led 'surprise attacks' in competition with other teams and factories; 'combat corps' were mobilized for assaults under the slogan, 'no respite without victory'. Tales of triumphs poured in – the cadres of Ku-hsien steel works, Shansi, claimed to have increased daily steel output from 714 to over 2,000 tons.

(ii) Wages

According to theory, under capitalism, wages induce people to work; they must work to secure the means of their survival. Differences in wages induce workers with different skills to take different jobs; the labour force is distributed between jobs. Differences in the profit margins between competing firms permit, in theory, different levels of wages, which induce workers to move from less to more profitable firms. The role of wages in distributing workers would be unnecessary if skills and abilities were universal or the nature of production required no skills. In a State-owned economy, subject to a central plan rather than different profit rates, if differences in wages are not used to distribute workers between jobs, it can only be done by decree, by instructing workers to do particular jobs, a task which requires a large directing bureaucracy. The discussion of wages in China must, therefore, include an account of how the Chinese government secures such a distribution of workers.

Both the Soviet Union and the United States had, during the main stages of capital accumulation, a *relative* shortage of labour, especially skilled workers, and in both countries there was a sustained drive to the most intensive exploitation of labour with sharp differences in wages between workers. In China, like Japan and India, the supply of labour appears in the early stages of accumulation to be unlimited, although there is a grave scarcity of skilled labour. In Japan, this situation produced not the high and finely graded wage differences of the United

States, but a small core of permanent workers alongside a very large workforce of temporary and contract workers; it was not so much the wage differences that were the mechanism for distributing workers, but differences in the security of employment. On coming to power the new Chinese régime made some efforts to copy a Russian style of wage payments (although it was never so extreme), but already by the mid-1950s was moving towards what we could call the 'Japanese' model.

The subject of wages is much confused by the distinction between 'material' and 'non-material' incentives. It is said, in China, that working for money is 'selfish', and people should work for patriotism or a similar purpose. Employers in the West have not been at all averse to urging workers to 'work for Britain', and capitalism has always employed 'non-material' incentives – usually negative (a fear of unemployment) but sometimes positive (patriotism, loyalty to a particular employer); there are other 'non-material' incentives, of course, like the use of the law, police and troops to intimidate workers into working. There must therefore be some care about praising 'non-material' incentives as if they were somehow superior, and confusing a situation where material scarcity has been abolished so that the basic drive – to secure material survival – is no longer paramount with one of great scarcity, where workers are not even paid in relationship to their work. In the second case, we are closer to forms of serfdom or military service (the second existing under capitalism) than communism.

We will look at incomes in China as a whole in the next section, but what was the picture of the wage system before the Cultural Revolution? Initially, the régime organized an eight grade wage point system, with fixed wage points related to skill, industry, area and job (the wage points were related to five staple items of consumption: grain, oil, salt, cloth and coal). The national range was not wide (3:1), but between industries and areas much wider. With the beginning of the First Plan, new priorities – of area and industry – were added; for example, a special bonus was given for metal working in Shanghai and Taiyuan (nine to ten per cent) and for Kansu petroleum workers (ten to thirty per cent). The government made consistent efforts to increase the proportion of pay made under piece-rate systems (at their maximum extension, piece rates were officially said to cover forty-two per cent of workers) and to widen differences in pay. Inequality of income was a deliberate act of policy – as Chou En-lai, quoting Mao (and Stalin), explained: 'some confusion still exists, and, in many places, egalitarianism has not been overcome. Egalitarianism is a type of petty-bourgeois outlook which encourages backwardness and hinders progress. It has nothing in common with Marxism and a socialist

96

system. It damps down enthusiasm of workers and employees in acquiring technical skill and raising productivity; it harms the growth of our economic construction. We must therefore oppose egalitarianism.'[18] The justification for inequality is not, here, seen as a temporary matter; equality is incompatible with a socialist system!

If the government strove to increase differentials, it was also concerned to minimize labour costs, particularly by eliminating payments which were not related to work performance. For example, from 1951, efforts were made to reduce the bonus customarily paid at the New Year. Drastic limits were laid down on the size of the bonus, and employees of the government and banks were forbidden to receive it.[19]

Despite inflation the expansion in jobs and increase in stability of employment after 1949 must have seemed to most workers a dramatic improvement. Wages did not rise much – one estimate suggests that the average wage in the early 1950s, about JMP 40–50, was not in real terms very different from the average in the early 1930s.[20] But there was now greater stability and, because more family members could expect to secure work, a higher level of *household* income, despite the increased level of deductions – for example, for State Bonds, Aid Korea Bonds, savings and fines. The beginning of the Plan imposed rigorous targets on managers and made the scarcity of skilled labour severe. Managers began to compete to secure skilled workers, bidding up top wage rates. In 1953, as a result the government seems to have lost control of the wage system, and only re-established some measure of guidance through a general tightening up of financial controls over managers.

In 1956 the government introduced the only major reform of the wage system under the People's Republic. The aim was to restore incentives and differentials. 'This revision', an authoritative commentator argued, 'will effectively eradicate egalitarianism and the state of unreasonableness and confusion obtaining in the current wage system [and] serve as a powerful material factor setting in motion the extensive masses of workers and office employees to strive for fulfilment of the First Five Year Plan ahead of schedule.'[21]

However, a straight rationalization would have had to include substantial wage cuts for many workers. Given the rash of industrial disputes mentioned earlier, and the resistance of party cadres in the factories to pay cuts, the government permitted wages to rise to secure the rationalization – by some twenty per cent on the former total wage bill. On the basis of the minimum wage needed to maintain two adults in an urban area – an innocent implementation of Marx's 'socially necessary wage' – eight new grades of pay were established, varying between different industries and eleven geographical areas (the variation was

97

about thirty per cent). Piece rates and incentive bonuses were expanded at the same time. The lowest manual workers' rates were kept down (and reduced even further in November 1957) to narrow the gap between rural and urban pay and so discourage peasant migration to the cities.

The State retained strict control over the total wage bill of the enterprise and the size of its workforce (controls weakened during the Great Leap Forward, were restored from 1961, and tightened during the Cultural Revolution). The eight grade system has governed the structure of wages up to the present, although there were minor adjustments in 1963 and 1971.

In the heyday of the system piece rates covered some forty-two per cent of the workforce, compared to a maximum of seventy-two per cent in Russia. During the Great Leap, the party attempted to lower labour costs at the same time as accelerating production; instead of raising the piece-rate norms, it began to move away from piece rates altogether. As one newspaper described it: 'during the Great Leap Forward movement, workers voluntarily abolished the piecework system and extra pay for extra work system. People now work not eight hours, but ten hours, or even twelve hours. If work requires, they work throughout the night.'[22]

Nonetheless, in 1959 piece-rate payment systems still covered thirty-five per cent of the workforce. In 1960 the effort to substitute party discipline for cash payments was then reversed and efforts were made to restore cash incentives (although not necessarily through piece rates). A commentator described the problem in the mines: 'some workers began to think that how much they worked made no real difference and relaxed their effort gradually'. It was found that the restoration of incentives radically reduced absenteeism and increased 'work enthusiasm'.[23] However, there was no relaxation of the tight controls over the hiring and direction of labour as employment contracted in the disaster years of the early 1960s.

(iii) **Welfare**
What about the living standards of urban workers and their families? Wages are not the only factor in assessing this. The price of goods determines the real value of wages. Since 1949, official food prices have been held stable, and in some cases slightly reduced. Of course, official prices do not indicate whether foodstuffs are available at that price. Speculation in commodities and the smuggling of foodstuffs in the cities have been a periodic preoccupation of the newspapers, indicating that

the black market has been important in the supply of goods not available through legal channels. Except in years of exceptionally poor harvest this applies less to the most tightly controlled agricultural product, grain, and more to horticultural foodstuffs (tomatoes, fruit) and meat, much of which is raised on private plots by the peasants and traded through rural free markets.

The official grain ration – varying with the type of work and age of the consumer – was in the 1950s relatively small, varying between twenty-five and fifty-five catties per month (12.5 to 27.5 kilograms). In 1953 it was estimated that the average adult required seventy-one catties per month, with an actual average consumption in 1954 of forty-nine catties.[24] Since the mid-1950s, the State procurement of grain has increased substantially, but at a rate not much faster than the increase in population, so that it is unlikely the grain ration has significantly increased. However, the supply of other foodstuffs – meat, eggs, milk, sugar and even edible oils – has improved, as has the stability of supply, so that the long queues from four or five in the morning seen in the big cities in the 1950s are less common today.

Housing has remained a problem. The housing stock was disastrously depreciated in the twelve years before 1949, and the new régime directed most of its investment into industrial production. In the 1950s, efforts were made to clear the slums in the largest cities and rebuild at standards which, however, were not met in subsequent years. Since the government has no national housing programme there is little information but it seems the addition to the housing stock was very small outside a few favoured areas. Standards were generally low – four or five persons per room – and some brand-new residential areas, lower.[25] In Taiyuan, for example: 'Housing conditions of workers are deplorable. It is rather a common phenomenon that over twenty workers are crowded into one small room. One room, formerly a toilet, is now accommodating six workers. In a coal mine outside Taiyuan, 250 worker families are housed in 123 rooms. In one room (ten by ten feet) are housed three worker families. Most of the houses are leaking.'[26]

In the 1960s, with strict controls on the increase in the city population and on marriage (so controlling the rate of creation of new households and the demand for separate living quarters), housing policy was concentrated on building factory dormitories for single workers, six to eight persons to a room. In the new industrial areas, little provision was made for housing at all. Workers in the Taching oilfield started work living in tents or holes dug in the ground to escape exposure to frost; in the early 1960s mud huts were built by the workers in their spare time; now, with half a million people living there, 'Even new houses have no running water, only outside toilets shared by a dozen or more families and communal bath-houses'.[27] This is 'self-reliance' with a vengeance! No wonder the State is so proud of the surpluses which Taching has provided.

In the 1950s more was done to improve basic services in the big cities, – electrification, water and sewage facilities, the provision of public latrines, bath houses, clinics and schools. Prices were kept low for those with the right to utilize them, primarily permanent employees in large-scale industry. Rents were held at four to five per cent of the worker's income. It is not clear what the situation was for those outside this group – temporary workers not housed in dormitories, small plant workers, casual labour, or even those without jobs (widows, pensioners, etc.). In the 1950s, there is evidence of at least some rents varying, not with the wage packet, but with the quality of accommodation. In 1955, the Minister of Finance, Li Hsien-nien, complained about one housing project in the following terms: 'The dormitories newly built for workers of the Tsitsihar Locomotive and Wagon Factory were beyond the means of workers because the rental on each flat ranged from JMP 18 to 41 per month, or two to six times higher than the old dormitories.'[28]

State and municipal expenditure on housing is so slight in relationship to need that enterprises and offices have generally built housing for their own staff. This system of 'tied cottages' gives great power to management and party cadres, and the allocation of housing can become one of the rewards for good behaviour. It also means that loss of job can entail, if not exile to a rural area, loss of the worker's home. However, the system affects only the minority employed in enterprises employing 100 or more workers (possibly a quarter of the sixty million or so employed outside agriculture). For the rural majority, there is no central housing provision; traditional 'self-reliance' must make up the gap.

The same minority is the recipient of the welfare services provided by the trade unions – canteens, clubs, housing, medical facilities, sanatoria, nurseries, and pensions. Half the cost of medical care for dependents of permanent workers is also met. Some factories provide schools for workers' children, as well as 'spare-time universities' for their parents. Social insurance benefits are graded according to wages, with special rights for model workers, combat heroes and others. Sickness benefit varies between sixty and 100 per cent of the wages received, provided the sickness or accident can be attributed to the worker's employment. Retirement pensions are some fifty to seventy per cent of the average wage received at retirement (seventy per cent for those who have worked at the same place for more than fifteen years). By 1960 some nine million workers were covered by the scheme. Trade union activities are financed by management deducting three per cent from the total wage bill; cases are mentioned in the press of a much higher proportion being deducted by the cadres and distributed as and to whom they think fit.[29]

For permanent workers in larger enterprises conditions are adequate without being lavish. The standard of living depends very much on the seniority of the head of the household and the number of household members who are working. For example, in 1972 the Chinese press quoted with approval the case of the family of an elderly chemical worker (working, incidentally, three years after the official retirement age): Chang Tien-cheng, aged sixty-three, of Hsiku district, Lanchow. Formerly, he had been an odd-job man, 'and no matter how hard he toiled at that time, he could not feed his family of five'. Presumably, the children were not of working age. 'They had to eat wild plants from time to time . . . Now, having five workers, the family income has risen while the cost of food grain, fuel and utilities and rent is stable or lowered. The family now has a flat in an apartment building. Rent and utilities cost less than one-eighteenth of the father's wage. They had a gas stove installed that costs one yuan per month . . . everyone who is working in a factory has a watch. The family possessions include two radio sets, three bicycles, a sewing machine, wool blankets, fur-lined coats and furniture.'[30]

After an extensive visit to China, Richman calculated the number of labour days required at present Chinese wages to purchase some of the items Chang Tien-cheng's family owns. We can compare them with how long it takes a British worker to earn enough to make the same purchases (the figures in brackets): five to six days for a watch (half to one day); between twenty-five and fifty days for a wireless (one day); between thirty and fifty days for a two-piece woollen suit (two to three days); between sixty and ninety days for a bicycle (three and a half days); 165 to 425 days for a television set (seven days); 12,000 days for a car, if permitted (155 days).[31]

The condition of the permanent workers has improved considerably since the period of Kuomintang rule (and more dramatically by comparison with the years of civil war). But the improvement is mainly from stability of employment and the increased number of jobs available, rather than changes in pay or prices or government investment in public services. For the majority of workers conditions remain austere.

(iv) Unemployment
The rapid economic expansion of the first half of the 1950s brought into

employment much of the reserve army of urban labour. But the increased labour productivity of these years meant also that, as output soared, the number of new jobs tended to decline. In the first eight years of the People's Republic, the number of industrial workers increased by fifty-one per cent; but in the period of the First Five Year Plan (1953–7), the number increased by only five per cent. Simultaneously, bureaucratic jobs grew more rapidly than those in industry, the result of extending State control. In China, the movement of peasants to the city also remained a problem, and put increasing pressure on State procurements of grain from the countryside.

By 1955, initial optimism that industrial growth would quickly eliminate unemployment was waning. The Chairman of the State Planning Council postponed a remedy for several years: 'The phenomenon of unemployment left over from the old China cannot be completely eliminated yet, and the surplus labour force still cannot be fully utilized. These problems will have to be solved by our continued efforts in the Second or even the Third Five Year Plan.'[32]

The policies designed to remedy this situation – from banning rural inmigration, rationing and passed, to increasing rural work – have already been discussed. However, rural disaster still produced a flight to the cities – for example, the Minister of the Interior complained that over half a million peasants had fled from famine areas to the cities in six months in 1957.[33] Every slackening in the industrial economy, as in 1961–6, threatened to re-create the old pool of urban unemployment unless *hsia fang* (sending down) worked with great speed and efficiency.

Despite the physical removal of the unemployed, the panoply of controls and propaganda, the attraction of the cities remained strong. The Minister of Agriculture remarked to a cadre audience in 1966 that: 'Everyone wants to go to the towns. There a man can earn thirty to forty yuan a month just by sweeping the streets, whereas in the country he can earn no more than twenty yuan a month. Among those present here, who would voluntarily become peasants?'[34] The pressure was not simply from the peasants. Those 'sent down' were frequently eager to return, whether with a job or not, and the weakening of police controls in 1966 led to a large influx of people to the cities.

Officially, the problem of unemployment in China is at an end, and in the cities, depending on the efficiency of the police and administrative controls, this is broadly true. It does not, of course, mean that the permanent city worker is relieved of the worry of redundancy; redundancy now can mean exile from the city to the countryside, with a sharp drop in the standard of living. However, isolating the urban economy in this way creates, when industry expands, a different problem: an artificial scarcity of labour. Managers, under the pressure of sanctions if they fail to meet the plan targets, are obliged to defy the regulations and pay their skilled workers above the going rate to prevent them moving to other enterprises for higher pay (a movement which is illegal, but which would require a vast police and administrative structure to prevent); and by hiring workers illegally either from the casual labour force in the city or from adjacent rural areas. In such circumstances, the government has been once again in danger of losing control. It has needed a method of making temporary cheap labour available if it is to safeguard its authority and sustain State accumulation. This has been achieved, as we shall see in the next chapter, by the system of temporary and contract labour.

In the rural areas, constant efforts are needed to keep up the level of employment, particularly when the State concentrates its attention on modern industry and urges the rural areas to be 'self-reliant'. The problem is severe. The working-age population of China has increased by about twenty to twenty-five million people per year on average since the early 1960s. Not all of them are looking for jobs – some continue in education, some marry and leave the labour force to raise children, some go into the armed forces; and so on. If we assume, fairly generously, that ten to fifteen million new jobs are needed every year to keep up the present level of employment, we get some idea of the problem. If the industrial economy is expanding, there may be half a million new urban jobs created each year. For the rest, the rural areas have to feed them and find things for them to do without permitting them to strengthen the forces of petty capitalism. There is little room to manoeuvre.

(v) Trade unions

What should be the role of trade unions – organizations supposedly designed to defend the interests of workers – in a State embodying the interests of the working class, 'led by the proletariat'? In Russia, there was no definitive answer in the early years. The exigencies of the period of War Communism led to the subordination of the unions to military imperatives. But in the retreat of the New Economic Policy, there was considerable debate over the question. One group, whose most prominent spokesman was Leon Trotsky, continued to defend the position of the party during the phase of War Communism; workers needed no defence against their own State, and therefore the trade unions should be instruments to achieve the production targets of the proletarian State. At the other extreme, the 'Workers' Opposition' argued that, since the trade unions embodied directly the essential interests of workers, the unions should take over the control of production and, indeed, the State itself.[35]

The two arguments ignored the complexities of the new régime – in a backward country with a minority working class, they were, in Lenin's term, 'abstract'. The Soviet Government, in fact, directed not a 'Workers' State', but a 'Workers' State with bureaucratic distortions'.[36] The 'distortions' entailed that the unions had a definite role, independent of the aims of the State: 'Our present State is such that the entirely organized proletariat must protect itself, and we must utilize these workers' organizations for the purpose of protecting the workers from their own State and in order that the workers' organizations may protect our State.' Lenin's formulation implied the right of the unions to use what strength they had against the State, to strike, in order to defend their members. Up to 1928, this was indeed the case, although bureaucratization led in practice to the suppression of many strikes.[37]

In the first years of the People's Republic, there was no debate on the role of the trade unions. Their role had been defined in the preceding period in the Liberated Areas; they were instructed to assist in meeting the production targets of the State; Mao, like Stalin, apparently adhered unquestioningly to the position advanced by Trotsky in 1920. The ACFTU whose claimed membership rose from 800,000 in 1945 to thirteen million in 1955 and sixteen million in 1958, had the role of its affiliated unions specified by law: 'To educate and organize the masses of workers and staff members to support the law and regulations of the People's Government . . . to adopt a new attitude to labour, to observe labour discipline, to organize labour emulation campaigns and other production movements in order to ensure the fulfilment of the production plans . . . to protect public property . . . to promote in privately owned enterprises the policy of developing production and of benefiting both capital and labour.'[38]

There was nothing about defending the interests of workers, nor about any rights the unions might have in this pursuit. Li Li-san, concurrently vice-president of the ACFTU and Minister of Labour, left no ambiguity: 'the central task of the trade union organizations is to increase production. Only in this way will the trade unions be able to take fully into consideration the interests of the working class.'[39] Contrary to Lenin's view, there was no difference between the interests of workers and the production targets of the State (a view usually espoused by employers in capitalist countries); only later was the halfway house of a 'non-antagonistic contradiction' constructed to shelter strikes. Those entrusted with the achievement of production targets were the managers, and it followed that there was no difference between the interests

104

of workers and managers. Indeed, since managers worked, they too ought to be members of trade unions; managers were frequently prominent in the unions as delegates at the annual conferences. It was the party which encompassed all, workers, managers and unions. In like fashion, the party appointed the trade union leadership from its own ranks, not from those with experience of workers or trade unions (let alone permitting the election of trade union leaders by union members).

In such circumstances, it was difficult for workers to distinguish trade union officials from management. From time to time senior party leaders complained of the resulting isolation of union officials; in 1950, for example, one military authority observed that: 'Many of the factory trade unions have recently adopted the position of the capitalists, issuing the same slogans, speaking the same language, acting like them. The unions defend management . . . In certain factories the capitalists could have accepted the demands of the workers, but the union proceeded to convince them to withdraw these demands . . . in the coal mines of Ta Hae, the workers, when they learned of the dismissal of the union chairman, were as joyful as if they had learned of the liberation of Taiwan or a rise in wages.'[40] The reproach was unkind, since the luckless cadres were doing no more than carrying out the instructions of the party leadership.

Party cadres working in the unions had the unenviable task of trying to retain the confidence of workers (important for their political duties), while ensuring that production targets were met. If too much was conceded, the cadres were liable to be dismissed for 'economism', giving in to the 'sectional and one-sided interests' of the working class. Li Li-san and his associates (a third of the ACFTU's executive) were criticized and removed from union leadership for holding the view that 'management should represent the long-term interests of the whole, while the trade union side should represent individual and immediate interests; management should represent production, while the trade union side should represent distribution'.[41]

Li Li-san had had no recent experience of trade union work (he spent the years of war and civil war in Moscow), and his replacement, Lai Jo-yü was even less experienced (he was a provincial party leader). A comparable sequence of events overtook Lai in 1957, although he was preserved from disgrace by his death the following year. In the unsettled conditions of 1956–7, Lai advanced the idea that local trade union branches should be responsible to the national trade union leadership rather than to factory or district party leaderships.[42]

The ACFTU despatched study teams to examine relations between union branches and local party committees; in the final report, it was

105

concluded that nowhere were the two separate. The report of the deputy director of the ACFTU General Office went further, saying the workers had 'cast aside' the unions because their sole function was to co-operate with management; the trade union officials were known to the workers as 'the tongues of the bureaucracy, and the tails of the administration and the Workers' Control Department'.[43] The local official, it was said, did nothing about bad working conditions or excessive hours; he was afraid to raise the complaints of workers lest the administration attack him as a trouble-maker. One cadre complained: 'I am told that I should study the problems with the leadership and not with the masses, and that to talk with the masses means "becoming the tail of the masses" . . . I am regarded as a trouble-making Party member.'[44] The trade union party cadre was the lowest in the party hierarchy, and few above him would listen to complaints. If he mobilized workers against the management, he would be sacked and expelled from the party. The party members among the workers – between ten and twenty per cent of workers and staff in 1956 – were hostile to the trade union cadre and sometimes were not even members of the union; those that were, did not attend union meetings, report or pay dues.[45]

The party centre again intervened to settle the question: the local union branch was to be directed by the local party committee, a position which left no role for the national union leadership except as a propaganda arm of the party centre.[46] When Lai Jo-yü fell ill in 1958, Liu Ning-yi who worked in the foreign affairs department of the party Central Committee was appointed to replace him and undertook a purge of Lai's associates lest they harbour secret ambitions to create autonomous unions.

No one questioned the idea that the role of the unions was to maintain production and implement the directives of the State. The unions played no role at all in the labour agitation in the mid-1950s. In general Mao displayed no interest in the unions, but when he did, it was to repeat that 'the principal task of a trade union is to develop production'.[47] His constitution for the Anshan Iron and Steel Company makes no mention of unions.

The unions – like management, of which the local union leadership was part – retreated into the background during the Great Leap. The party committee assumed the leading position. In the retreat, the unions were resuscitated as part of the effort to save production and stabilize activities. There was no question of this role involving an independent defence of workers. The trade union newspaper repeated the official line: the local union must strengthen its unity with management for its 'basic task is the same – to run socialist enterprises successfully

106

by relying on the masses for fulfilling the tasks assigned by the Party and the State'.

However, in the first year of the Cultural Revolution, the trade unions were unilaterally abolished, along with the trade union newspaper and the Ministry of Labour. None of the claimed millions of union members protested (the main functions of the local unions in welfare and education continued to be fulfilled). The party explained that the unions were dominated by 'revisionists' who concentrated solely on production and the 'economist' demands of workers, instead of 'production, livelihood and education in one with production as the centre', a formula notable for its obscurity.[48] The old unions were not resuscitated.

Yet the labour force required organizing for particular purposes. From 1967 the revolutionary committees began to sponsor local worker congresses for political education and 'combatting self-interest'. By 1973, these had moved into district or provincial congresses in major centres, the preparation for a reconstructed ACFTU.

In the early days of the régime, unions had been involved in wage negotiations with private employers, and on occasions were even able to claim that they had 'corrected the mistaken activities of management'. But the elimination of the private sector ended this. From 1957 the government tightened its control of jobs and the wage bill, removing as much discretion as possible from local management, let alone union officials. Today, the national government determines the wage bill, and the unions have no role even in distributing wages within the plant. The trade union function is restricted to educational and welfare activities, and only where unions exist – in the large plants of advanced industry. Thus, Chinese unions are not 'trade unions' at all in the ordinary sense, but rather the welfare departments of management (the role of factory committees will be discussed later).

8

TEMPORARY AND CONTRACT LABOUR: THE WORKER–PEASANT SYSTEM

In China, as in Japan and other countries, employers safeguarded their profits against fluctuations in business activity by employing a large part of their workforce on a temporary basis. In a boom, they took on temporary workers, and in a slump, laid them off. The 'permanent' workers were those who, by reason of skill, experience or personal favour of the management were kept on in a slump. Apart from relative security of employment, the permanent workers usually received higher pay, better conditions and other benefits. Often permanent workers were city born and bred (and had received more education and possibly an apprenticeship training), while the 'temporaries' were former peasants who had moved to the city in search of work, returning to the village when they were dismissed. Some groups of rural workers moved seasonally to the cities. In both China and Japan, some of these temporary workers were contracted for fixed periods of time; for example, parents would sell their daughters to textile mill owners for three to five years. Labour brokers would recruit gangs of rural workers for set tasks in plantations or on the roads. In some cases, the 'recruitment' was little more than conscription by the State for its construction or maintenance work on roads, dams, irrigation channels and so on. We have seen how in the late 1930s the Kuomintang conscripted labour for major road, rail and airfield construction. In pre-revolutionary France, the '*corvée*' the feudal obligation to work for a set period on the King's highway, was one of the most hated duties imposed on the peasants.

In China, temporary and contract work of this kind was regarded as one of the most vicious forms of oppression. The Communist party at its Second Congress in 1922 condemned the practice and promised to abolish it. The party recognized the political dangers of a division between permanent and temporary workers, with the unscrupulous only too willing to divert the attention of rural workers from employers to their permanent co-workers, and to appeal to permanent workers to fasten their hostility not upon the capitalists but upon the poor down-trodden rural inmigrant. The rural workers who came to the city could be used in exactly the same way as immigrants are used in the indus-trialized countries today – a pool of cheap labour in a boom, and the scapegoat for the failure of the ruling order in conditions of slump, a tactic excellently designed to divide the opposition and set them at each other's throats.

The change of régime in China did not dissolve the objective con-ditions which had created the temporary labour system. Indeed, the policy of restricting the city population, producing in a boom con-ditions of labour scarcity, made the need for some sort of comparable system even more urgent. From the foundation of the People's Repub-lic, it seems, temporary workers were tolerated (although it is not clear whether they were permitted in the cities in the 1950s). During the Cul-tural Revolution, it was alleged that temporary labour had been used for seventeen years,[49] that there were 2·4 million such workers in 1957, and that, under the impact of the Great Leap Forward, this figure rose to twelve million (that is over a quarter of all workers and staff employed outside agriculture at that time). Such workers were not in-cluded in the plan estimates for labour, and were used as a buffer by managers and cadres in sudden spurts to meet changes in target dead-lines. They were paid much less than permanent workers and received none of the fringe benefits (housing, medical and educational facilities, holidays, pensions, bonuses or allowances).[50] Sometimes their wages were paid from 'miscellaneous expenditure' funds to keep their employ-ment concealed from the State. As in capitalist countries, the con-struction industry with its unstable seasonal pattern of work had a high demand for such workers; illegal inmigrants could get work without questions being asked, and so secure a niche in the city. In the 1950s private labour brokers recruited in the villages for city enterprises, and also found jobs for those who were unemployed in the city, criminals, ex-prisoners and so on.

In the early 1960s, the use of temporary labour became more wide-spread, and was formalized in various State-guided contracts by which the government could regulate the scale of employment and tighten up the financial administration of enterprises. An extension of municipal boundaries in 1962 to include large tracts of the countryside brought a large pool of rural labour under city administration. By 1964, tempor-ary workers were being used not only in seasonal agriculture and con-struction, but in mining, agricultural processing industries, cotton gins, textiles, timber, power generation, road construction and maintenance, post and telecommunications and commerce.[51] It was also becoming clear that, unlike the general situation under the Kuomintang, temporary labour in the People's Republic was being used systematically to *displace* permanent workers, to dilute the labour force.

The 'system' was publicized as a fundamental break with capitalist labour practices, and a gigantic step forward in the abolition of what Mao saw as one of the Three Great Differences of capitalism surviving in China – the contradiction between town and country. Under the 'worker-peasant system', permanent city workers would be 'sent down' to the countryside (where they would receive none of the benefits of being city workers, at considerable savings in labour costs to enterprise and municipality) and young peasants would come into the city to work on temporary contracts (without receiving any of the material benefits of being permanent city workers, again with considerable savings on costs to enterprise and municipality). In the Chinese press, the 'worker-peasant system' was lauded as an exemplary instance of 'putting politics in command' and 'following Mao Tse-tung thought'.

The savings in labour costs were considerable. On a Hunan road maintenance scheme, Ch'ao-shui commune was paid RMB 150 per kilometre per year for a stretch of seventeen and a half kilometres of local highway – RMB 187·5 per worker employed on the task for the commune, RMB 126 for the worker's production team, and RMB 36 for the worker himself. The work was not full time, but even then, RMB 36 for a year's work compared very favourably for the régime with a month's full-time work from a permanent city worker at RMB 50–60.[52]

The press was lyrical in praise of the virtues of these arrangements – it improved the roads; contributed to commune income: 'the rural labour force is put to rational use' [i.e., underemployment was reduced] . . . State expenditures are reduced, and the supply of commodity grain is decreased [i.e., where the team fed the workers, the State did not have to supply grain].'[53] Some 4,500 people had worked on such schemes in the region, and in comparison to the time when only permanent road workers were employed, 'this represents a saving of 100,000 yuan in wages, and 400–500 catties of commodity grain'. However, the writer warned authorities who might like to copy the scheme, that the workers must be carefully selected, politically sound, physically healthy, and 'between eighteen and forty years old'.

Finance and trade departments were also urged to adopt the system. In this case, 'in order to cut down the State supply of commodity grain, the worker-peasant labourers who work in the basic level units of finance and trade departments must provide their own food rations, and the State will supply a part as subsidy only when it is necessary to do so'.[54] Cadres were instructed to ensure that 'the quality of commodities and services is improved and the cost of production and the cost of circulation are cut down without increasing the total amount of wages'. The aim, the writer argued, was to create useful work in slack seasons and at slack times of the day, involving all rural inhabitants: 'The subsidiary labour power of the aged and children and the idle labour power in the rural areas may also be utilized.' He outlined the schemes to be employed, including the fact that in some cases, 'the finance and trade departments pay for labour in kind (fertilizers, animal power, animal fodders)'. Such schemes were necessary because 'objective economic development demands that the differences between workers and peasants and town and country be gradually diminished through the introduction of the worker-peasant system'.

The *People's Daily* gave considerable prominence to this new 'higher type of social organization of labour'. In the Anyuan coal mines in Kiangsi (total labour force, 2,000 in 1965) 207 permanent – and older – miners had been 'sent down' to a rural area, and 207 rural recruits, aged on average twenty-four years, had replaced them in 1965. The cadres hoped that, in five years, they would have achieved the complete turnover of the entire labour force (that is, the complete end of any permanent employment). During the winter season of 1965–6, sugar refineries were able to lay off 7,800 permanent workers so that 'the State has saved wages amounting to 2·5 million yuan'. The savings were further increased because the temporary workers did not bring – or, at the wage received, could not bring – their families with them, so food and housing costs were very low (the same discovery was made by European employers – if immigrants could be separated from their dependants, the returns were vastly increased). The Chengtu Storage and Transport Corporation in December 1965 employed 172 permanent workers, and contracted with fifteen communes for 800 temporary workers for warehouse loading work, 'Because the commune members come when there is work, leave after having done their work, and ask for no food and living quarters from the corporation, it was possible to save for the State a sum of more than 270,000 yuan'. The *People's Daily* argued that 'various production teams near the warehouses can earn more income for the collective and solve the problem of the blind outflow of manpower owing to insufficient farmland'. In yet other cases, the savings were made simply by reclassifying the permanent workers as temporary; in four mechanized sugar refineries, the State saved RMB 108,000 in wages and 132,000 catties of commodity grain by reclassifying 629 permanent workers in 1965.[55]

It is inconceivable that such a far-reaching change, widely publicized and much praised in the press, could have been introduced without the support of the party leadership. None of them – including Mao – criticized the system. Indeed, the particular way in which it was justified – as abolishing one of the Three Great Differences – suggests that the 'worker-peasant' system might have been inspired by Mao himself. Until the end of 1966, through the upsurge of the Red Guards and their assault on all manner of malpractices, in the successive defining rules and documents of the Cultural Revolution, there was no mention of the condition and problems of temporary workers. Indeed, at one stage, it seemed as if an *extension* of the system might be one of the aims of the Cultural Revolution. When Canton radio, on 13 August 1966, broadcast instructions for implementing Mao's directives for the Cultural Revolution, the worker-peasant system was cited as a prime example of 'politics in command'; all suitable enterprises in the province should introduce it, gradually turning 'a number of permanent workers into worker-peasants', moving selected industries (particularly agricultural processing) to rural areas to utilize rural manpower, sending industrial workers to assist in farming and so on.[56]

A setback to the enthusiasm – or, at least, complacency – of the leadership was provided by the outbreak of worker militancy in late 1966. It is possible that efforts by the cadres to extend the 'worker-peasant' system was one factor in instigating worker agitation. A number of different demands coincided – of permanent workers for the restoration of bonuses and allowances abolished earlier; of temporary workers for the payment of back wages (presumably held to keep the workers obedient for the period of the contract) and an equalization of conditions with permanent workers; of apprentices for a general improvement; and of workers and students 'sent down' for a legal return to city employment.

Red Guards had begun to raise the issue of the conditions of temporary workers in September 1966.[57] Both temporary and permanent workers were laid off in November in a number of plants (for reasons that are not clear), and they sent delegations to Peking to complain to the government. In the charged atmosphere of the time, the centre had little alternative but to authorize their reinstatement and the payment of back wages to temporary workers. This seems to have provided the basis for general demands for the payment of wages with-held, bonuses removed, and for the return of jobs. Late in the month, the centre announced an extension of the Cultural Revolution to farms and factories (but in carefully circumscribed terms) and warned managers not to retaliate to criticism by sacking workers or with-holding pay.

Simultaneously, posters in Canton alleged that a delegation of temporary and contract workers had been received by Chiang Ch'ing and the Cultural Revolution Group of the Central Committee of the party.[58]

Chiang Ch'ing, Mao's wife, is said to have denied that Mao had any knowledge of the conditions of temporary and contract workers, and placed responsibility for the system on Liu Shao-ch'i, the Ministry of Labour and the ACFTU. Shanghai posters reported that Chou En-lai showed greater courage on the question, arguing that 'because of the circumstances in China', it was necessary to retain the system.

Chiang Ch'ing's accusation – that it was all the fault of Lui Shao-ch'i – sanctioned the agitation of Red Guards, Red Rebels and the temporary and contract workers themselves. In Shanghai, the rebels declared: 'Lui Shao-ch'i is the chief culprit', and 'the system of temporary workers and contract workers means capitalist relations of production between employer and employee . . . [and is] absolutely incompatible with our country's socialist system.'[59] The case of a Shanghai Fodder Work Section was cited. Workers were so intimidated they 'dared not express their anger in words. They patiently bore it! Why? The reason was that the moment you raised objection, you would immediately be fired.' Furthermore, temporary workers were excluded from membership of the party, the Young Communists, the militia, and were not eligible for election or nomination as deputies, members of Cultural Revolution committees, labour model heroes and so forth.

Early in January a leading Shanghai newspaper reported, under the headline 'Thoroughly abolish the system of temporary labour and outside contract labour', a demonstration in People's Square by 100,000 people protesting against the temporary labour system and calling for 'a brand-new labour system in conformity with Mao Tse-tung thought'.[60] Speakers denounced the fact that temporary workers 'could not join the political study classes of their factories or take part in other political activities. Nor could they get the labour protection they deserved.' When they protested, 'the power-holders even kept back part of their wages and suspended their work'.

The revolt was brief. Back wages were paid, and possibly other wage demands met. There was a run on the banks and a spending spree. On 9 January Shanghai 'rebel organizations' ordered all bank funds to be frozen except authorized expenditure; the 'readjustment of wages, payment of back wages and material benefits shall in principle be dealt with at a later stage'. Nonetheless, some of the Red Guards persisted in the face of what was now the disapproval of the party leadership. On 10 January, for example, the Capital Red Guards' newspaper attacked the temporary and contract worker systems, saying they were attempts to 'raise the greatest amount of cheap labour and to extract the maximum profits'.

On 16 January, the *People's Daily* outlined the leadership's case: 'The handful suddenly show concern for labour insurance and the well-being of the masses of workers and talk about their promotion, subsidized housing, etc. They vigorously use material incentives to corrupt the fighting spirit of the revolutionary masses. They incite some people to make trouble by demanding economic welfare.'[61] The source of the trouble afflicting the masses was not the conditions of sweated labour, the dedication of the State to the accumulation of capital, it was a strange psychological weakness, 'Economism', incited by 'the handful'. The error must be eradicated: 'We should educate the comrades of trade unions and the working masses, so that they understand that they should never see the immediate, one-sided welfare benefits exclusively and forget the far-reaching interests of the working masses.'

The line had swung into reverse, but the party had to campaign hard to hold wages stable and to eject workers and students who had returned from the countryside – a return, of course, engineered by nothing more complex than the reactionaries launching the slogan 'reverse the injustice of moving to the interior'. They were assured that 'the question of finding work for workers who have gone to the countryside . . . can be solved gradually', provided they returned to the countryside. If there were genuine grievances after people had returned, 'they can expose and criticize the power-holders by writing letters or by sending big character posters.[62] Whatever else, they must relinquish their only hold on power – access to the urban mass.

On 17 February, the Central Committee and the State Council declared that the doctrines of the National Rebel General Corps of Red Labourers and other temporary worker organizations were illegal. The party admitted that 'the systems governing the employment of temporary workers, contract workers, rotation workers and piece workers are rational in some cases, but are very irrational and erroneous in others'. However, 'before the Party Central Committee arrives at a new decision, the established methods are to be followed as usual'.[63] In the meantime, temporary and other workers should have the same *political* rights as permanent workers; the circular made no mention of the real and vital issue, equal economic rights.

On 27 February, the party – new and old cadres – had mastered the Shanghai situation sufficiently to purge the opposition. Shanghai radio reported that the Liaison Headquarters for Opposing Economism of the Shanghai Municipal Revolutionary Committee 'today took over the property and funds of organizations of contract and temporary workers and liaison centres of young intellectuals working in rural areas, of youth working in support of frontiers, and of State farm workers'.[64] All other bodies were forbidden to help or support the proscribed organizations. Obediently, 'seventeen revolutionary organizations in Shanghai [offered their] warm support for the Central Committee's wise and correct notice on temporary workers'.

The festival of the oppressed was over, but the battles were not. Nor were the grievances of temporary workers. Their resentment at the injustice of being promised a revolution, only to have it snatched away at the first sign of serious change, was no doubt one of the threads in subsequent events. For example, in May Canton radio reported a demonstration of 'several thousands' demanding an end to rotation work in agriculture. But officially, the establishment had closed ranks. The cause of the temporary workers was thrust into the background. The brief episode has illustrated some of the reality of discrimination against temporary workers and those subject to *hsia-fang*. One poster on a Shanghai wall gave a poignant twist to the latter: 'We are old workers (between fifty and eighty years), illegally sent to the countryside . . . If we have to leave Shanghai, where we have lived for twenty or thirty years, and go back to the villages where we have been for only four or five years, this is like gathering the sesame seeds but losing the melon.'[65] Their despair was of less concern to the authorities than saving the price of a pension.

The campaign on behalf of the temporary workers was a microcosm of the Cultural Revolution. A section of the leadership flirted with class issues in order to destroy its rivals within the party, but drew back in alarm when the issues became a real class war. The rebels were only 'revolutionaries' in so far as they implemented the aims of this section of the party, which, like its rivals, had no interest in disturbing the basis of its power, the existing production system. That required the 'rebels' to oppose any independent initiative by workers, any raising of their real interests (as opposed to the pieties of 'political rights'). Some rebels went so far that they had to be reminded not to 'regard all workers as conservatives and fight civil wars against them. We must be aware that, except for a few diehards, most of the workers misled by conservative groups are our class brothers'.[66] Some of the rebels were clearly in danger of forgetting who the 'leadership' was.

One solid achievement of the Cultural Revolution was the silencing of any public discussion of the 'worker-peasant' labour system. Had it been abolished, reduced or radically changed, the government would not have failed to inform the mass of the population through press and radio and thereby win credit for ending such an oppressive feature of employment. The silence indicates that the promises made in January 1967 were not honoured. Indeed, the following September, Wuhan radio once more reported without apology or even a nod at the

Shanghai rebels, that 1,600 worker-peasants had been hired in Hupeh cotton-processing centres, and 10,240 in sorting and cotton ginning plants.[67] The temporary and contract worker continues, victim and scapegoat.

THE WORKING CLASS AFTER
THE CULTURAL REVOLUTION

After the Cultural Revolution, the government set about restoring labour discipline and made renewed efforts to establish what, in sum, might be called a 'high productivity–low wage' economy. The watchword again became 'race against time to speed up socialist construction'.[68] Those who found work onerous were automatically 'bourgeois', for 'to love manual labour is the intrinsic virtue of the proletariat and other working people'.[69]

In the Number 1 Blooming Mill at Anshan (the largest in this, the largest steel complex in China), the cadres urged the workers to 'seize every minute, every second, to produce more steel'.[70] To this end, an example was given of a veteran worker who braved the searing heat of the rolls to replace a loose bolt rather than shut down the whole operation to allow it to cool before making the adjustment. Safety of workers was clearly not the first consideration. Nor, in the coal industry, were the hours worked. The mines exceeded their targets 'under the inspiration of the Second Plenary Session of the Communist Party's Tenth Central Committee and the Fourth National People's Congress . . . Most of the coal mines continued production during the Spring Festival . . . Many young workers deferred their wedding ceremony or gave up their holidays after marriage so as to cut more coal.'[71]

A Tientsin building company reported that, between 1966 and 1973, labour productivity had been increased by seventy-four per cent, and work completed by fifty-eight per cent.[72] The work was mainly small construction projects. Morale was high. 'Trusting the enthusiasm of the masses' had led them to use only the workers' spare time for work preparation, maintenance of equipment and moving between sites; an example that inspired the medical and nursing staff to follow suit, 'so that most of the workers and staff members who were slightly indisposed or had chronic diseases could come to receive medical treatment without encroaching upon the time set aside for labour'. Three examples were offered to illustrate the spirit: firstly, on the Liut'an site, the land was not levelled, half covered by an old concrete road, twenty centimetres in depth and the 'earth was frozen and its surface was very hard'. There was no power or water available. Nonetheless, the team refused to wait for power drills, and set to with ordinary iron spades to dig through the soil under the road, breaking it, fragment by fragment, by dropping heavy weights on the surface. Secondly, on another site, the team were required to sink a drainage well, but there was no power to operate the pumps. However, the workers 'rushed to carry out their work in the well. In the waist-deep water, they scooped out the mud, spadeful by spadeful'. And thirdly, another gang were building a dormitory. Parts weighing seven to eight hundred catties (roughly seven to eight hundredweight, or 350 to 400 kilograms) arrived at the site, but without hoists to lift them. Nevertheless, 'four young workers of the framework group . . . insistently carried on their shoulders all these structural parts in the five blocks of the four storey dormitories'. The article received prominent display in the *People's Daily*, and the honour of a special recommendation by the editor, stressing its great importance for all cadres.

It was not all plain sailing. There were obstacles to labour discipline. But happily, they were attributable not to bad working conditions but alien class forces. A number of 'educated youths' were hostile to the dirty and tiring work. One of them 'often associated with some ideologically backward people and often feigned to be suffering from lumbago in the course of work'. However, the 'malingering' was short lived. Veteran workers and others called on his home 'more than ten times', and enlisted the help of the man's parents. In due course, the son gave in.

The ideological climate encourages the most touching complaints. Consider, for example, the case of Chang Chen-an, worker in a Lanchow fertilizer plant, whose contribution to the *People's Daily* in 1974 was entitled by the editor, 'A warm and sincere letter'.[73] Chang explained that his plant had fulfilled their production target twenty days ahead of schedule, so the management planned 'a general meeting in celebration of victory by sounding drums and gongs and letting off firecrackers. Furthermore, the factory also plans to give everyone a large tea cup and a free meal ticket.' Chang opposed the proposals because they were extravagant and wasteful, leaving the door open to bourgeois influences. The leading cadres in the factory, he concluded, lacked revolutionary spirit. We are not told whether Chang won his promotion. The miserly millowners of eighteenth-century Lancashire would certainly have made him a foreman.

To ensure that the expansion in output was not offset by increased wage bills, the number of workers in any given plant had to be kept constant or even reduced. Chiangnan Locomotive section claimed to 'make very economical use of labour resources'; the Wuhan railway sub-bureau boasted that, between 1969 and 1971, the volume of goods carried increased 53.6 per cent, staff by five per cent, and labour productivity by 46.2 per cent.[74] T'angshan Locomotive and Rolling Stock Plant raised the question in terms of 'two lines of ideology'. One 'line' was 'to improve labour productivity and strive for increases in production with no additional workers or just a slight increase in personnel but through tapping the potentialities within the enterprise is a principal way for socialist enterprise to increase production'. The other stated that 'to try to increase production with little or no increase in workforce is tantamount to "requiring a horse to gallop without feeding it" – something that can't be done'. The horse, in this case, was the Chinese working class. However, the writers from T'angshan claimed vindication – the work load had been nearly doubled between 1969 and 1970, the targets being fulfilled forty days ahead of schedule, 'while cutting the original workforce by ten per cent'.[75] In this way, Mao's instruction to make the 'maximum economical use of manpower and material resources' would be achieved. Indeed, the writers explained, 'There is no limit to the economies of manpower'.

A Shansi colliery offered another example.[76] The 1971 workforce of 1,246 had been cut in 1972 by twelve per cent, yet the output of raw coal had increased by thirty-two per cent, labour productivity by forty-three per cent, and profits by a princely 347 per cent. Furthermore, major economies had been made. In one chilling claim, the writers boasted that 'the consumption of (pit) props declined by forty-two per cent'; presumably Mao's thoughts would hold up the roof of the mine shaft. The recent performance was not new. The original construction plan for the colliery had demanded 200 men working for two years at a cost of RMB 700,000. In practice, however, only seventy-seven men had been employed, and had completed the construction 'in several months' at a cost of RMB 190,000. Either the original planners were incompetent, or the claims exaggerated, or the construction unsafe.

Again, the Shansi pit had its number of malcontents. A cadre examined the poor production performance of the Number 3 tunnelling team: 'When he found that some young miners went down the shaft late and came out early and were lax in discipline, he thought of the problem of labour management.' He found, as one might guess, that 'a few young workers were influenced by bourgeois ideology and this was the principal cause of laxity of discipline'. However, education and 'mobilizing the masses' did the trick, so that the team labour force could be cut by thirty-one per cent in 1972 (the writers do not say whether those sacked included the young workers of 'lax discipline'). The production targets were met four months ahead of schedule.

The report from Shansi, like many other similar accounts, is a paean to what Western managers call 'man-management'. Indeed, with a toning-down of some of the more absurd claims, and phrases like 'improving communication with the shop floor' or 'taking the workers into the confidence of management' substituted for 'mobilizing the masses' and 'practising Mao Tse-tung thought', such articles would not be out of place in a Western progress-chaser's bulletin. Like the capital-ists before them, the cadres have discovered that 'the masses of people have boundless creative power', provided they are firmly disciplined. If the cadres only follow Mao, 'we can bring the creative power of the masses into full play, and save more manpower to do more things'. In the Shansi colliery, as a result, 'most miners have vigorously striven to raise the utilization rate of working hours, with one doing the work of two or even three'.[77] One year later, on the occasion of the 1974 British miners' strike, Chinese miners were told that 'British workers are get-ting more and more impoverished . . . the coal miners, at the bottom of British society, are suffering the most relentless exploitation by mono-poly capital'.[78]

If the lay-offs were as extensive as the Chinese press suggested, where did the unemployed go? The régime resumed its efforts to 'send down' workers and students from the cities, and cadres from clerical to manual occupations, partly in the last case to provide supervision 'on the pro-duction front' for the speed-up. Individual workers in 'non-productive' jobs – e.g. teachers, public health officials, administrative workers, physical training instructors – were prime candidates for transfer to manual agricultural jobs. Other workers perhaps secured jobs in the 'unorganized' sector of city industry – plants employing under one hundred workers, and not covered by the existing social insurance system.

(i) Lenin and 'Subbotniks'

The Chinese authorities were not slow to create an appropriate ideo-logical rationale for a general speed-up in production combined with constant or declining earnings and size of workforce. This was the model of 'Subbotniks'. Railway workers on the Moscow–Kazan line volunteered in the hard days of May 1919 to work five extra hours with-out extra pay (on Saturdays, the Sabbath or *Subbota*) as an increased contribution to the passage of railway freight and so the survival of the beleaguered Soviet State. In a famous speech, 'A Great Beginning', Lenin greeted this contribution as one of 'the young shoots of communism', a rejection of 'bourgeois right' (i.e. the principle that pay should be related to work done) and as an exemplary 'display [of the] class consciousness and voluntary initiative of the workers in developing the productivity of labour'.[79] The Subbotniks of China were to be Mao's 'new sprouts of communism' (Mao's quotation from the Russian loses some of its poetry in the English translation).

Even if we accept Lenin's formulation – and the retreat into the New Economic Policy suggests he might later have thought his speech premature – does it apply to China? First, Russia was in condition of grave collapse in which extraordinary measures were required to secure survival until the German revolution brought real support. In China, however, the extraordinary is presented as the norm for the long haul of national primitive accumulation. Secondly, in the Soviet Union, the efforts were expected primarily of the Communists rather than the whole labour force. Thirdly, the increase in productivity was in the long term to be based, not on the physical exertion of workers lacking basic equipment – building workers, for example, digging a well with spades, relying on their muscle power and disregarding safety – but on the organization of a technically advanced industry. Lenin criticized those who thought all could equally attain the same level of productivity: 'The assumption that all the "toilers" are equally capable of doing this work would be an empty phrase, or the illusion of an antediluvian, pre-Marxian socialist; for this ability does not come of itself, but grows historically and grows only out of the material conditions of large-scale capitalist production.' It is true that 'Communism is the higher productivity of labour – compared with capitalist productivity of labour' – but enhanced productivity comes not from more physical labour but the 'voluntary, class-conscious united workers, *employing advanced technique*'.[80] The Chinese emphasis on hard physical labour as itself the mark of socialism is contrasted with the Bolshevik aim of the *abolition* of hard physical labour.

What happened to the return to labour in conditions of speed-up? There has been no general wage reform of the kind seen in 1956 and therefore the wage *structure* today corresponds in essentials to the 1956 pattern. In so far as revolutions involve changes in the structure, none has occurred. Real effort was directed up to 1976, however, at ending payments made over and above the eight grade system, an effort which, in the case of bonuses, began in 1950. Cadres have attempted to end overtime pay and similar ancillary awards for extra work (for example, issuing meal tickets for overtime work), while retaining the same work

121

load. Estimates from the mid-1960s put the contribution of bonus and overtime to earnings at between five and seventeen per cent, a not inconsiderable element, given the low level of Chinese wages. Some visitors report that small pay increases were awarded to workers to induce them to give up overtime pay, and there were minor adjustments in prices to reduce the impact of reduced earnings. However, these cannot have been significant, given the scale of labour disputes in 1974 and 1975.

The justification for these changes was an attack on 'material incentives'. According to the régime, 'material incentives' were 'the magic weapons used by Khrushchev and Brezhnev for restoring capitalism'.[81] They still had 'a powerful hold on the minds of some people', not because incomes were low and conditions austere, but 'because of bourgeois ideas and the force of old habits . . . some of the selfish people are likely . . . to go so far as to turn "to each according to his work" into "work according to pay"'.[82] For some writers, it was necessary to detach work from pay altogether: 'the money wage received by a labourer represents a part of the total output of society used for individual consumption; this part corresponds to the amount and quality of each worker's labour, to his social contribution'. How did it 'correspond'? Clearly not in terms of a worker's output since workers were extraordinarily productive. How were income differences to be assessed? Mao divulged no more than that the current wage system was 'scarcely different from [that] in the old society'.[83]

By official acknowledgement: 'Wages are low and the living standard is not high. We only just get enough clothing and a full stomach. To develop the economy, this situation must be maintained for some time to come.'[84] The efficiency in the distribution of labour between jobs must be poor also, given the efforts made to reduce the size of the bureaucracy whose task it is to direct workers to the right job. As a result, pay must still be used as the primary means of getting people to work, to work harder and to move between jobs so that their skills are used to best advantage.

The contradiction between the two aims – to minimize the loss to accumulation from wages, and to induce people to work and learn skills – is the source of the confusion. As always, this is then attributed to the current enemy: 'swindlers of the Liu Shao-ch'i type consistently opposed Chairman Mao's revolutionary line and politics. In the countryside, they sometimes put "wage points in command" and give "material incentives", and at other times, practice "egalitarianism", violating the socialist principle of distribution and creating confusion.'[85] Liu Shao-ch'i's contradictory responses are the mirror image of the party leadership's own contradictory position. In the mid-1950s,

122

'egalitarianism' was a petty bourgeois deviation that 'thwarted the enthusiasm of the masses' for work. Now it appears it contributes to the restoration of capitalism, a system apparently identified by great inequality of income!

Understanding the reasons for inconsistency did not help the cadres to meet production targets. In tight spots, working against the clock, they were obliged to contradict one element in policy to achieve another (meeting the target). For example, in a Shansi factory, 'in the fourth quarter when time was pressing, the tasks were heavy and pressure was great, some people forgot the previous lesson and decided to pay the workers overtime'.[86] When there are people eager to replace the cadre, it is a dangerous tactic: 'After comrades of Number 14 work group of Number 5 workshop wrote an article, "Do we work hard to make greater contributions or to earn more money?", they were greatly educated and enlightened ideologically.' The writer does not say whether the education was sound enough to deduct the overtime pay from the workers' next wage packet. In another factory, workers pressed for overtime pay and were finally given it; whereupon a wall newspaper appeared, denouncing this 'bribery'; the party committee, under such an embarrassing threat (with the local party leadership watching), eventually reversed itself once more.[87]

There are many other forms of reward besides straight payment from the wage fund – ranging from preferential treatment in the supply of housing to promotion, titles, invitations to star events, medals, banners, holidays, and travel privileges. Travellers in a north-eastern industrial city in 1976 reported that workers were sometimes awarded goods (cups, basins), sometimes a monthly bonus of five yuan, and sometimes some of China's fiery liquor, maotai.[88]

The party did not honour its promise of increased pay, made in the heat of the moment in late 1966, although small increases for lower wage grades were announced in 1971 and somewhat larger ones in 1977. More characteristic of the party in these eleven years was the sustained effort to lower labour costs per unit of output. This does not mean that household incomes have not continued to improve since the Cultural Revolution. Due to the rapid expansion in industrial output perhaps, more household members could get jobs and so raise household incomes. As *Red Flag* reminded workers: 'In the past, a worker had to support his whole family. Now his dependants take part in work. So, the aggregate income of a worker's family is greatly increased.'[89] But the jobs in organized industry cannot have increased very much since 1969; the expansion in output has come from increasing the use of existing industrial capacity rather than adding to it. Perhaps more jobs have been created in unorganized industry, units employing less than one hundred workers. Wages and conditions are much inferior here, and not governed by the eight grade wage system. There are also 'a small number of labourers working on their own in the towns',[90] presumably day labourers and petty artisans providing miscellaneous services. The number of those employed outside the organized sector is not clear, nor how stable their income is (some seem to work on a wage point system as in agriculture). Visitors have listed a wide variety of jobs – from subcontracting work for big factories, the manufacture of consumer goods (household utensils, plastic flowers, paper goods) and petty services.

Since the Cultural Revolution, more has been done to encourage cooperative health insurance schemes among unorganized sector workers, and there seems to have been some neglect of the organized sector. Such schemes are financed out of the meagre wages of the workers concerned, and, as a result, provide no cover for old age or disability. The State's assistance has been limited to the provision of small items of equipment and reductions in the price of basic medicines.[91] It is, however, very remote from any kind of 'welfare State'.

(ii) Workers' control

It could be argued that the 'low wage' policy is essentially socialist, not because low wages are the mark of socialism (which would make nineteenth-century capitalism largely socialist!), but because the working class of China voluntarily imposes this policy upon itself as an act of conscious and collective self-discipline. The Cultural Revolution is seen as the time when China's working class established its power in the State, transforming social relations within society and winning popular control at the base. In sum, there was created workers' control in the workplaces and workers' power in the State.

The subject of 'workers' control' is often confused. Some socialists have regarded it as an anarcho-syndicalist aim which would obstruct the realization of the collective interests of the working class, exercised through the State. Others have seen it as no more than the final stage of 'participation' by the majority in making important decisions; every increase in participation would then be a step towards the final goal of democracy.

The Bolsheviks came to a different conception. For Lenin, workers' control was a necessary element in a working-class struggle for power, the tangible expression of class rule at the point of production and the precondition for an effectively planned workers' State. Participation, by contrast, was the method employers chose to sap the independent class power of workers, to bind them to the purposes of capital. Real power came only through *independent* workers' organizations, pursuing their own class interests, whether in the factory or in society.

The Bolsheviks accordingly *opposed* the proposals of the Provisional Government to create a system of workers' consultation committees in April 1917. Instead, Lenin argued that 'the workers must demand the immediate establishment of *genuine* control to be exercised by *the workers themselves*'.[92] The Mensheviks in the Provisional Government argued – as the Chinese Communists did in the 1950s – that the revolution of February 1917 (or 1949 in China) was not a socialist revolution, so the workers should not take over production. They offered participation to ameliorate the wage system without infringing managerial prerogatives. Russian workers themselves provided the answer. In August 1917, a conference of factory committees demanded power to control the composition, the hiring and firing of management, and the internal rules governing factories (hours worked, wages, hiring and firing). The Provisional Government could not concede such demands without jeopardizing its own power, based upon the employers. It denounced 'acts of coercion' by the workers as crimes. The Soviets themselves, then under Menshevik influence, urged the workers to restrain themselves; but the 'excesses' continued.

For the Bolsheviks, and particularly those workers active on the factory committees, it became clear that the struggle for workers' control was the necessary complement of the struggle for State power, not some alternative or diversion. Indeed, State power without workers' control would be no more than a minority seizing the old State machine and trying, without mass initiative, to implement reforms from above. Nationalization of industry by the State was not sufficient: 'The important thing will not be even the confiscation of the capitalists' property, but country-wide, all-embracing workers' control over the capitalists and their peasant supporters. Confiscation leads nowhere, as it does not contain the element of organization, of accounting for proper distribution.'[93]

In China, the new government did not undertake immediate nationalization, and was careful to protect managerial and private business authority. However, as part of the reorganization of labour, it encouraged measures of consultation through Joint Production Committees and Worker and Staff Representative Committees in the public sector, and Labour–Capital Consultation Committees in the private; public sector committees were not permitted to discuss wage and welfare issues.[94]

However, the priorities of planning soon overtook any functions these committees might perform; everything was subordinated to targets and timing. There were complaints of authoritarianism, but nonetheless, in 1956, the Central Committee affirmed that managers were fully responsible, under the direction of the party committee. In 1957, there was much talk of decentralization (that is, vesting more power in the local party committees). Events in Budapest showed the leadership some of the dangers of permitting the gap between cadres and workers to widen too far. Worker Representative conferences were reorganized, and, for a time, it was claimed they supervised the execution of plant plans (the committees included managers and party cadres). In a much publicized case, the Peking Tram Company set up an administrative committee of nineteen, including workers, managers, technicians, cadres, trade union and Young Communist representatives, empowered apparently to elect managers and supervise the implementation of the plan. Other attempts were made elsewhere, but the government stressed that management was fully responsible for meeting the targets, whatever other committees existed. Little was heard subsequently of these efforts, and, it seems, managers and cadres retained their full authority. The committees became, on one account, 'a mere vehicle for management and the party cadre to make speeches'.[95] In the Great Leap Forward, as we have seen, the cadres assumed managerial authority, and rules of operation (of which these committees were part) were only restored in the troubles of 1959.

Managerial authority again came under attack during the Cultural Revolution. There was once more a drive to scrap internal distinctions and what are known as 'unreasonable rules and regulations', or, in Britain, 'restrictive practices'. After the first upheaval, revolutionary committees were set up to unite the managers, representatives of the PLA, the party and the Red Rebels. Under the leadership of the PLA, these committees endeavoured to restore discipline, complaining of workers who 'in the name of rebellion and opposing slavishness . . . in reality stir up anarchism'.[96]

By 1971, factory rules and managerial cadres were once more supreme, but the memory of the hopes of the Cultural Revolution perhaps lingered on. The *People's Daily* continued to attack those who 'under the influence of the theory that "systems are useless", said that, since the Cultural Revolution had raised the consciousness of the masses, production could be stimulated without systems and rules so that the question of their revival was irrelevant'.[97] Forms of consultation continued in many factories, usually through a consultative body – 'worker-management groups' and 'Three-in-One' economic management groups (including cadres, managers and workers). Occasional mass meetings were organized by the cadres. Although this does not in itself constitute 'consultation', managers participated in manual labour. Some factories claimed that workers were involved in the election of managers, but it is not clear whether this was just a verbal change in the normal pattern of nomination from above. In a Shanghai watch and clock factory in 1975, 'a number of workers have been *selected* to assume leading positions and take part in management work';[98] as the report later explains, the selection was made by the factory committee.

This is very far from Lenin's conception of workers' control; in one sense, it is its opposite. It is also remote from the party's own claims that 'the rank and file take part in all aspects of management', a formulation which in any case preserves the idea of management as an authoritative élite. There are in fact no institutions whereby a collective workers' interest could be expressed, in contradistinction to the interests of management or local party committee. But even if there were, would it constitute workers' power? The right to control or participate (and the two are very different) in the direction of a factory is only a stable possibility if simultaneously the working class controls the State. For, in China, the national and provincial governments determine the level of wages, the numbers employed, the price of factory output, the allocation of raw materials and skilled labour, and the raw materials and equipment moving between provinces: that is, all the key items that determine what happens *inside* the factory. An individual worker may well be 'self-governing' at home, involving all members of his or her household in deciding what to do; but the alternatives open to the household depend on factors outside the home, and usually outside the household's control – how many have jobs, what the level of pay is, the conditions and hours of work.

However, this is not the end of the question, for there is another area of 'workers' control', the struggle for the control of the workplace quite independent of management and cadres, which has been impressively represented in China in recent years: the strike.

(iii) Strikes

The periods of known industrial disputes and strikes have already been mentioned – 1955–7, 1966–8 and 1974–6. From the Chinese press and radio, it is possible to reconstruct some of the disputes.

Forms of worker resistance range from resisting pay cuts or deterioration in conditions, refusing work discipline, disobeying the law or factory regulations (including changing jobs or place of residence without permission) through to direct resistance, the go-slow, outright strikes, refusals to work, to accept direction or transfer, and even attacks on the factory or managers. The sanctions similarly range from the mild – reprimands, public criticism by the cadres through wall posters or mass meetings, backed up by fines deducted from pay, loss of seniority or demotion, to the more severe: being transferred to a rural area and 're-education'. In some cases, workers were sent to prison; for example, in July 1957, the three leaders of a demonstration outside the manager's office at the Chungking Machine Tool factory were arrested as 'counter-revolutionaries'. In the 1950s, labour correctional camps were created to 're-educate' rebel workers. In extreme cases, even the death penalty was used; at the Kweilin Building Company, cadres were beaten up during a strike, and the two strike leaders were tried and sentenced to death, others being given terms of imprisonment.[99]

Was the situation qualitatively transformed by the Cultural Revolution? Certainly, the new constitution for the first time acknowledged that strikes took place and legalized them, but in practice how were things changed? The campaign in 1973 and 1974 to end all payments above the eight grade wage system produced a rash of opposition (perhaps difficulties were exacerbated by shortages of foodstuffs). Reports of disorder, go-slows and absenteeism occurred through 1974 and 1975, particularly in the mines, the steel industry and railways, and in a number of cities (Shanghai, Anshan, Hsuchow, Nanch'ang, Canton and Wuhan; in Kwantung, Liaoning, Kiangsi, Heilungkiang and Shensi).[100] Indeed, some foreign observers attributed the 1975 drop in steel output to labour resistance to the abolition of overtime pay. In Heilungkiang, the radio reported that 'factionalism has greatly disrupted and undermined our revolution and production'; the militia was required to protect cadres in some areas from those who 'misled' the people. Troops were sent to Hsuchow (Kiangsi) and also to the Tahuangshan coal mines.

However, Hangchow (Chekiang province) was the place that received most publicity in 1975, perhaps because it was the location of Mao's summer retreat. The factories there were apparently disturbed from early 1974. Late in the year, an expanded provincial militia was introduced into the city to police a sort of martial law on the streets. However, the militia itself is said to have divided into warring groups, and the troubles were sufficiently severe for train drivers to refuse to pass through the city (the line through Hangchow connects Shanghai to the south). As a result, there were severe delays of freight which were not overcome until May 1975.

In the spring, the new Vice-chairman of the party, Wang Hung-wen, who is credited with taming the Shanghai workers in the Cultural

128

Revolution, was despatched to the city but without success. Chekiang troops were then moved in and public security squads from north China were drafted in to patrol the streets. The leading deputy Prime Minister, Teng Hsiao-p'ing, also visited the city, and perhaps was instrumental in framing the Central Committee and Standing Council resolution on the situation: 'a handful of counter-revolutionary revisionist elements and newly emergent bourgeois elements sneaking into the party and the army and headed by sworn adherents of Lin Piao and Liu Shao-ch'i in Chekiang, vainly attempted to subvert the dictatorship of the proletariat in collaboration with the landlords, the rich, the counter-revolutionaries, the bad and the rightists ... [and] stirred up anarchism, factionalism and an evil wind of economism; conducted armed struggles; made trouble; interrupted the supplies of electricity and running water; disrupted production and transport; made a sally against troops; and blasted public security departments.'[101] The resolution concluded that 'chief plotters shall be severely punished according to the law. As to the masses, we should re-educate them and let bygones be bygones.'

The resolution was perhaps the signal for the final effort – over 10,000 PLA troups moved into the city to take over the thirteen leading factories. The municipal authority was reorganized, three leading officials replaced, and the local party put in order. Officially, the troops were necessary because the workers of Hangchow were 'unable to increase production under the pernicious influence of the counter-revolutionary revisionist line and bourgeois factionalism and due to the sabotage activities of a handful of class enemies'.[102]

Officially, the PLA – and later, air force and naval units – undertook 'participation in manual labour', or peacemaking. From 12 July, when PLA unit 1815 took over a car component manufacturing plant, there was a stream of reports of particular units taking particular factories – textile mills on 19 July, a textile printing and dyeing plant on 21 July, and a wool textile mill. The 7th PLA company worked at the cement warehouses where 'they completed one day's work in two hours and were praised by the workers'.[103] Air force units were sent into factories manufacturing heavy machinery, oxygen equipment, steam turbines, boilers and glass works. 'They all took the initiative in carrying forward the same vigour ... and worked continuously, fearing neither heat nor fatigue.' Commander Li Chi-ming 'set a good example to the fighters by arduously working for a few hours ... deputy commander Ni Chungsheng ... actively took the lead in unloading coal. He never uttered a word despite the blisters on his hands ... In one day, ten cadres and fighters unloaded fifty tons of cement, and none of them complained of being tired.' The workers must have been impressed at this temporary display of a fortitude they were expected to show month in month out.

Successive mass meetings were held to pull the local cadres into line – for example, 8,000 provincial cadres assembled on 22 July, and 15,000 on the 24th. Similar meetings were held in the main factories, to 'vigorously denounce Liu Shao-ch'i and Lin Piao'. As a result, reports said, everyone agreed to work harder – even 'cooks in the cafetaria strove to increase the variety of dishes. They provide the workers with steamed bread and hot vegetable soup.' Bus drivers, after finishing their regular runs in the daytime, 'returned in the evening to drive the night shift'; there were presumably no safety regulations to limit the number of hours of driving. The cadres 'have made use of their holidays and days off to do manual labour and have taken the lead in tackling the most difficult jobs'.

(iv) Theory and practice

In study classes at three factories in Chengchow, Honan, the cadre leadership raised the then fashionable, but curious, question, twenty-six years after the seizure of power in 1949, and eight or nine years after what was called a 'proletarian seizure of power' in the Cultural Revolution: 'Should the leaders of an enterprise put the workers in the position of the masters, trust and rely on them and ceaselessly strengthen their position in enterprise management, or regard them simply as hired labour and squeeze them out of management and supervision of the enterprise?' The implication escaped the cadres – he who has the power to choose the master is himself the master.

That curious quality is repeated in numerous statements of the party. The workers must be told that the factories belong to them, since there is no way that they will discover this in their daily experience. It was, according to the party's accusations, Liu Shao-ch'i, like those early anticapitalist dreamers of the socialist movement, who urged that labour should be paid more, or should be paid even the whole value of their labour. The writer's indignation at such an idea leads him to employ the same metaphor as would be used in the West – if workers consume all they produce, they will kill 'the goose that lays the golden egg'; there will be nothing with which to 'build socialism'.[104]

For nearly twenty years, the régime continued to pay annual profits of five per cent on capital to China's former capitalists. It was at the same time striving to hold down wages, increase output, cut the permanent labour force and dilute it with temporary and contract workers. None of the central leadership questioned this procedure. Labour was treated as an important factor of production, the goose that laid the golden eggs, and it was production which was the régime's continuing obsession. Labour was treated throughout, despite the rhetoric expended on 'the working class', as essentially passive, a commodity. If workers objected, they were accused of being the creatures of just those capitalists, so richly rewarded and protected by the régime. Workers reacted on the scale they did not because they were being manipulated nor because bad thoughts somehow persisted in their heads, but because of the onerous disciplines imposed upon them by the régime's pursuit of production.

Is the position of workers in the People's Republic qualitatively different from that in other societies? In objective terms it is the same, even if the propaganda is different. By no serious standard can the Communist party in the period since 1949 – or since 1968 – be seen as the leadership or representative of the Chinese working class. Chinese workers have been the object, not the subject, of modern Chinese history.

10

PEASANTS IN THE PEOPLE'S REPUBLIC

Before we examine the provisions and implementation of the Agrarian Reform Law of 30 June 1950, it may be useful to outline what the 'peasant revolution' meant in the Russia of 1917.

The inequality in landholding under Tsarism was much more extreme than in China. In the late nineteenth century, some 28,000 landowners had holdings 202 times that of the average peasant,[105] whereas in China, landlord holdings were between five and fourteen times the average. The holding of land was the economic basis of the Tsarist aristocracy, the social foundation of Tsarism itself; in China, the social foundation of power was an oligarchic combination of relatively small landlords, merchants and capitalists (land had been freely bought and sold in China for some two thousand years). It followed that, in Russia, the peasant seizure of the land was a decisive factor in destroying the old order, but in China it could not play the same role; destruction of the old order needed to encompass land, trade and industry. It also followed that a land revolution in China could not provide even the temporary material basis for an alternative form of production, self-sufficient small-holdings; the need for industrialization, for the provision of work outside agriculture, was much greater than in Soviet Russia.

Under the impact of the February revolution, sporadic peasant assaults on the holdings of the landowners took place through the spring of 1917. Some of the owners tried to sell out in panic. As a result, the first demand of the local peasant committees was for a ban on land sales. The Provisional Government urged the peasants to be patient and await the termination of the World War for a proper land settlement: 'The land question cannot be resolved by any means of seizures. Violence and robbery are the worst and most dangerous expedients in the realm of economic relations . . . The land question must be resolved by means of law, passed by the representatives of the people. Proper consideration and passage of a land law is impossible without serious preparatory work:

the collection of materials, the registration of land reserves, [the determination of] the distribution of land property, and the conditions and forms of land utilization.'[106] The Provisional Government was determined to keep control in its own hands: 'A great disaster threatens our native land should the local population take upon itself the reorganization of the land system without waiting for the decision of the constituent assembly. Such general arbitrary actions carry the threat of general ruin.'[107] The Mensheviks and Social Revolutionaries (the main radical peasant party) in the government stressed the same point – the need to defend existing production and retain control in the hands of the government. 'Do not confuse the socialization of land', a Social Revolutionary Congress adjured the peasants, 'with its arbitrary seizure for personal gain!', a notion to become in China 'economism'.

The advice could scarcely be heard in the din. The peasants, mobilized and stimulated by their mutinous soldier sons, began in some areas to seize the land, to burn down the manor houses of their hated overlords, to seize the stocks of grain, equipment and animals in the lord's outbuildings. In other areas, they unilaterally cut rents and seized uncultivated land. Within the Social Revolutionary party, a schism opened between the 'responsible' national leadership and the village committees.

The Bolsheviks did not lead, organize or actively promote the peasant revolution, although they recognized the decisive importance of this 'peasant war' for the workers' struggle. As early as 1905, Lenin had expressed the precondition for this war: 'There is only one way to make the agrarian reform, which is unavoidable in present-day Russia, play a revolutionary role: it must be effected on the revolutionary initiative of the peasants themselves, despite the landlords and the bureaucracy, and despite the State, i.e. it must be effected by revolutionary means.'[108] The position was repeated after the February fall of Tsarism in April 1917. As to the Provisional Government's advice to the peasants to wait, advice backed by troops driving the squatters off the land, the Bolsheviks were intransigent: 'As to the land', Lenin mimicked the government, 'wait until the constituent assembly. As to the constituent assembly, wait until the end of the war. As to the end of the war, wait until complete victory. That is what it comes to. The capitalists and landowners, having a majority in the government, are plainly mocking the peasantry.'[109] The Tsar might have been overthrown, but the social foundation of Tsarism, large landed estates, had survived intact. Only the immediate seizure of land, whatever the dangers in the ongoing war, would settle the question.

The party adopted en bloc the programme of the national Congress of Peasant Soviets (19 August 1917) as its own – for the abolition of the private ownership of all land without compensation, confiscation of livestock and equipment, a ban on all waged labour, an equal and periodically readjusted distribution of land among all peasant households. It was not a programme formulated by the party – indeed, Lenin argued it would not work; but it was the programme of the peasantry, and must be wholeheartedly embraced by the party if the workers' revolution was to succeed.

(i) Agrarian reform in China

Up to 1949 the position of the Chinese Communist party corresponded roughly to that of the Provisional Government in Russia – the maintenance of rural production to support the war first with Japan and then with the Kuomintang was the dominant preoccupation of the party. The programme was designed to achieve this while 'maintaining the enthusiasm' of the peasants and the collaboration of all landed classes, including the landlords and the 'patriotic gentry'. To this end, the cadres were required to prevent any spontaneous initiative by the mass of cultivators to settle the land question, to undercut the social foundations of Kuomintang power on the countryside. The party did not depend on the peasants except as cultivators and army recruits.

With State power, the party moved quickly to change land relations, both to go some way towards honouring its promises, and to eliminating Kuomintang, warlord and bandit power in the countryside. The Agrarian Reform Bill laid down that the land, equipment, animals and surplus houses of landlords, of temples, of industrialists and merchants, be either confiscated or requisitioned for redistribution. The land and properties of rich and middle peasants (including well-to-do middle peasants) were to be protected, although land rented by rich peasants might in certain circumstances be requisitioned.[110]

It was, on the face of it, a clean sweep of landlord power. But the 'cleanness' depended upon the application of the classification used in the bill – landlord, rich and middle peasants. It was not at all clear to whom these labels properly attached unless the mass of the peasants were given the right to say which peasant households in their village belonged to which class (but then they would not need the bill except to ratify their decisions after the event). The peasants were firmly refused the right. It was the party cadre who had to make the key decisions. An elaborate code was laid down to guide him, but no code could encompass the complexity of China's rural social structure, could eliminate the arbitrary and discretionary factor.[111] Even so the code included strange anomalies. The same family, for example, could include members of different classes: 'The status of those members who take part in labour, if their position in the family is not a dominant one but a subordinate one, should be appropriately determined as labouring people in order to distinguish them in status from other family members who do not participate in labour.'[112]

For those unfortunate enough to be classed as 'landlord', there were escape routes. In due course, they could secure reclassification. Their urban and non-agricultural properties were protected. In the 1930s, landlord merchant activities had been important – between a fifth and a third of landlords in some provinces were said to be engaged in trade as their main occupation.[113]

The one certain thing was that the peasants should not be permitted to settle these questions themselves. Reform must not be undertaken at all if there were insufficient numbers of trained cadres available to control it. 'It is necessary that the party cadres for land reform are, both in quantity and quality, capable of grasping local reform work without letting the masses indulge in spontaneous activities'[114]; or again: 'Spontaneous struggles by the peasants must be firmly prevented in agrarian reform . . . Pending the arrival of an agrarian reform work team, no official action is permitted and only policy, publicity and preparatory work are permitted.'[115] To cope with the demand, the party had to be vastly expanded, and, wherever possible, backed by military or public security forces lest the bitterness of decades explode and engulf the party in a 'peasant war'. William Hinton in his vivid account of Fanshen, explains why the poor peasants were not permitted to 'make a revolution': 'The military potential, the productive capacity and the political genius of the peasants had to be cultivated, mobilized and organized, not simply "liberated" . . . Without the Communist party, the poor peasants could easily have carried the Revolution so far to the Left as to convert it into its opposite, a restoration from the Right. Without the Communist party, the poor peasants might well have divided everything right down to the last bowls and chopsticks on the farmsteads . . . and in so doing would have destroyed the only productive base on which they had to build . . . such mistakes would only have broken the peasant population into factions, based on kinship, religious affiliation, personal influence and gang loyalty.'[116]

Implementing the law

The implementation of the 1950 law depended on the strength of the local party and the reaction of the landlords. Landlords and rich

135

peasants produced the marketable surplus of foodstuffs that kept the cities, and the party, alive. Yet the surplus was produced on relatively small holdings – to seize all the landlords' and rich peasants' land would eliminate the surplus without giving the mass of cultivators land adequate to support all. To take over all the land would be to break the fundamental link between the cultivator and his patch of soil, to destroy the incentive to cultivate altogether, resulting in national calamity – even if the party could have mobilized sufficient manpower to carry out such a policy. Party tactics were concerned with preserving the surplus rather than meeting the interests of the poor and landless. For this reason, different measures had to be employed in different localities, spread over a period of time, as the party advanced, then retreated when the surplus was threatened, then advanced again, edging slowly towards the elimination of the landlords. In Kiangsu, for example, the East China Military Administration varied its tactics in different districts – from rent and interest reduction to confiscation – the tactics being determined by the need to sustain peasant incentives, especially in the sowing and harvesting seasons.[117] The Administration was also concerned not to disturb trade and industry, so the draught animals, tools and buildings used by landlords for handicraft or trading activities were excluded from confiscation. Nonetheless, there was landlord opposition, expressed in the slaughter of livestock, destruction of equipment, concealment of arms and assaults on the peasants; in some cases, work brigades were bribed to ignore such activities, and rents secretly continued to be collected. At such stages, the Administration was obliged either to intervene to put down landlord opposition, or to retreat. In south Kiangsu, the regulations were diluted to mollify the landlords – the land brought into cultivation since 1948 was excluded; landlords were compensated for work already done in preparing the land; the land allowance for 'non-agricultural' activities of landlords was made more generous, even though this reduced the stock available for redistribution. As one official document recorded: 'This is against the interests of the peasants. However, in order to avoid confusion it is better to allow the landlords to keep their properties and enable them to invest in production.'[118]

The difficulties were severe, not merely because of the obligation to maintain tight party control. The amount of land available for redistribution was limited. Nationally, it was claimed that 700 million *mou* of land were redistributed to 300 million peasants, an average of two and one third *mou* per head, or a little over a third of an acre.[119] The variation between provinces was great – from ten *mou* in mountainous Shensi, to between one and three *mou* in south Shensi, Hunan, Hupeh and

136

Honan, and between 0.7 and three *mou* in east China (Shantung, Kiangsu, Chekiang, Anwhei).[120] The average per head in south Kiangsu was about 1.15 *mou*, or about a sixth of an acre. Since the middle peasants also received land – on average, 1.1 *mou*, in comparison to the 1.2 *mou* received by the poor and landless – the effect was to strengthen the middle peasants without making available to the poor enough land to secure an adequate livelihood. The middle peasants (and, depending on the favour of the local cadres, some of the 'rich'classified as 'middle') retained substantially more and better land, better supplies of water, fertilizer, draft animals and tools, giving them, on average, yields thirty per cent above the poor peasants. The average rich peasant holding in south Kiangsu remained on average twice the size of the average in the given locality, and its yield of grain, ninety-five per cent above that of middle peasant holdings.[121]

It was the party's estimate of what was objectively possible, not the interests of the poor and landless, which remained the guiding imperative. The chairman of the East China Military administration, paraphrasing those countless statements in the party's earlier history, expressed it thus: 'We must constantly keep in mind the interests of farm labourers, look after their livelihood and . . . raise their political consciousness and cultural standard. On the other hand, we must patiently educate the farm labourers to prevent "leftist" sentiment and deviation. No demand must go beyond the scope permitted by the present economic situation. If they exceed the scope, nobody will employ farm labourers.'[122] As so often, the exploited must support the exploiters if the continued basis of their exploitation is to be preserved!

The surprisingly conservative nature of the land reform perhaps partly explains the relative mildness of the opposition. In relationship to the size of the rural population, the numbers of 'bandits' were well within the scope of the party's armed power. But still, in some areas, collisions were bitter – in 1951, the Minister of Public Security complained, for example, of continued 'banditry' in south-west Kiangsi, claiming that 7,210 cadres and others had been murdered, 26,600 houses burned down and 200,000 cattle stolen. When cadres attempted to collect grain procurements, they were sometimes violent,[123] and this evoked strong resistance; according to Finanace Minister Po I-po; 'more than 3,000 cadres sacrificed their lives in the cause of collecting public grain'.[124] Mao later claimed that 2.3 million people had been 'killed, locked up and controlled' up to 1956.[125]

The victory of the Communist party in China had brought order and security to the squalor, violence and corruption of rural China under the Kuomintang. Supplies were at long last becoming available, and as the distribution network developed, the danger of local famine was brought increasingly under control. The depredations of the landlords had been ended, and elementary reforms in the village begun. Yet conditions remained harsh. With only marginally more land, rent and interest payments were now replaced by public procurements in the hands of arbitrary cadres, themselves harried by a remote national authority. A complex of taxes – on salt and foodstuffs, on slaughtering animals – increased the burdens. As a result of the civil war, in the early years there was a dearth of industrial goods and considerable price inflation. The local granaries and sources of credit, formerly under the tight but tangible control of the landlord, were now directed by an impersonal and distant State. Public grain distribution was less flexible than under the old order. In the case of credit, the State's inability to meet and police local demands obliged it to permit a resumption of private lending at whatever rates of interest the market would bear.[126] The strong mixture of revolution had become very dilute by the time it reached the villages.

(ii) Co-operativization

Land reform was, as the Act stated, a method of 'setting free the rural productive forces, developing agricultural production and so [paving] the way for New China's industrialization'. Yet to accomplish this, the scarcity of land, equipment and animals had to be overcome or neutralized. For this, a massive programme of investment in the land would have been required. But the new government was devoted to expanding industry first, and there was little investment left for agriculture. Instead, the peasants were urged to pool their resources in co-operatives. At first, this meant no more than traditional forms of co-operation – Mutual Aid Teams (covering three to five households for teams created for particular seasons, and between six or seven up to twenty for year-round co-operation). From there, the party raised its sights to the 'lower level' co-operatives, covering about 100 households, where the principle of pay was based, not on the amount of land contributed, but on the labour provided in the year. Co-operatives went some way to centralize activities and render more effective State supervision and access to the agricultural goods (provided the State assumed monopoly control of agricultural trading which it did from 1953). By the end of 1952, the government claimed that forty per cent of the farm population worked in Mutual Aid Teams, and the cadres moved on (although at different speeds in different localities) to promoting 'producer co-operatives'.

In the main, these changes still did not go beyond the traditional forms

138

of co-operation. The producer co-operatives came closest to changing the basic structure, and evoked much opposition (which the party attributed to the rich peasants being unwilling to pool their resources). In 1953, the government retreated in order that procurements should not suffer; about a third of the co-operatives by then established were dissolved. In the autumn, a further attempt was made, and the party's aim was to be 100 per cent 'high-level' co-operativization by 1960. The cadres However, opposition again led to a slackening of the pace in the spring of 1955. It was then that Mao accelerated the whole process. The target was to be 100 per cent high-level' co-operativization by 1960. The cadres were to brook no resistance; all opposition was now denounced as 'Rightist'; furthermore, 'semi-socialist' co-operatives were superseded by the aim of full collectivization. By March 1956, the government claimed eighty-five per cent of rural households worked in 'semi-socialist' co-operatives, and by the end of the year ninety-six per cent. Agriculture no longer waited on industrialization to achieve 'socialization'; its organization was being transformed in advance.

There were other forces at work on the countryside. The ink was barely dry on the new land deeds before the fluctuation in the agricultural economy and the high demand for foodstuffs from the cities as a result of the drive to industrialization began to drive the poor marginal cultivators out of production, and concentrate an increasing share of land, equipment and animals in the hands of the new, euphemistically styled 'middle peasants'. Each rural downturn as well as the need to make special expenditures forced the marginal cultivator to borrow, to mortgage his land, animals and equipment, and usually to do so when interest rates were high and agricultural selling prices low. A report from five villages in a former 'old Liberated Area' in Shansi concluded that: 'Since land reform, ninety-six peasant families in the five villages have sold a total of 284.11 *mou* of land to pay for wedding and funeral expenses, and the like. Ninety-nine peasant families bought land. Private ownership of land, natural calamities, and other inevitable misfortunes have caused a small portion of the peasantry to lose labour and land and become once more impoverished. On the other hand, another small portion of the peasantry has risen in status. This is the reason for emergent rural class distinctions.'[127] In north China, the chairman of the Administrative Committee complained that 'a considerable number of peasants sold their land and became impoverished shortly after land reform'.[128]

The cadres were no protection against the resurgence of rural capitalism. Many were already rich peasants on joining the party, or used their power and influence to become so. The party centre might forbid the rural cadres to hire labour, rent out land or lend money, but to no avail. In 1952, one of the party leaders warned: 'If no active steps are taken . . . to lead the peasant towards the path of co-operative economy rather than to the rich peasant economy, then rural village government is sure to deteriorate into a rich peasant régime. If the Communist party members all hire labour and give loans at usurious rates, then the party will become a rich peasant party.'[129] Three years later, Mao himself complained that 'new rich peasants spring up everywhere', while 'many poor peasants still live in poverty for lack of sufficient means of production, with some in debt and others selling or renting land'.[130] It was not surprising that there was a flight of peasants to the cities.

The 'new rich' peasants produced the marketable surplus, and strongly resisted the increase in controls as the State strove to secure a stable grain supply for industrialization. Their response was to lower production or divert an increasing share of it from the fixed price State procurements to the free or black market. The floods of 1954–5 illustrated the problem. Output declined as procurements, in the interest of the industrial plan, increased. One leading party member estimated procurements at fifty-two million tons (or thirty per cent of the harvest), a considerable increase on the twenty-five to thirty million tons taken in rent by the landlords.[131] The peasants hoarded their grain, as Mao acknowledged. They followed the 'dead cattle' policy of slaughtering their livestock, both to save grain used as fodder and to prevent the co-operatives acquiring them. Between July 1954 and July 1955, the national stock of pigs fell from 102 million to eighty-eight million, and by July 1958 (when purchase prices were raised) to eighty-four million.[132] Mao blamed the landlords and rich peasants, not co-operativization and State procurements. In Kiangsi, he said, the people who complained were cadres, a third of whom were really 'well-to-do peasants, or formerly poor and lower middle peasants who had become well-to-do peasants'.[133]

The disturbances led to no slackening in the pace of accumulation, but Mao henceforth stressed the need to watch peasant welfare. The peasants must be looked after, then 'the mouth of the bourgeoisie will have been stopped up'. 'Like us, the peasants have to eat and be clothed. They are paying for many things with coupons alone. This will not do. They will still conceal their grain and not sell it.'[134] In the aftermath of the Great Leap Forward, he put it more cynically: 'tackling production without tackling living would definitely result in tens of thousands of dropsy cases.'[135] In the short term, procurement prices were raised, more effort devoted to increasing rural employment, and the 'three fixed' policies proclaimed (fixed production, purchase and sale of grain), setting the total volume of procured grain at 43.25 million tons.

None of this, however, did much to alleviate the burden on the peasants. Nineteen fifty-six saw another tide of complaints against food shortages, the privileged position of the cities, the petty tyranny of the cadres and the depredations involved in co-operativization. The government rejected the charges, claiming that in 1956 the average consumption per person was of the value of RMB 180 for workers and RMB 81 for peasants, a doubling of the prewar average. Yet the eloquent language of the stomach confounded the statistics. The government was obliged, because of the shortages, to cut the grain and cloth ration. It also relaxed some of the constraints on private rural markets and the drive to form co-operatives; some 100,00 peasant households are said to have left Kwantung's co-operatives as a result. The prices paid for animals and equipment taken over by the co-operatives were also increased. Furthermore, the size of the co-operatives was reduced, making the village production team or brigade the effective level. The One Hundred Flowers movement – and a rectification campaign against 'commandism' by the cadres – were tokens of the government's goodwill.

(iii) After the Great Leap Forward

The pessimism of the early 1960s prompted a reassessment of the situation. The rural masses now became, not an advantage because they were 'poor and blank' and could be directed to any end the leadership chose, but 'a big problem': 'The population of the rural areas is a big problem, if we are to do away with an excess of population. To solve this, we must develop production rapidly . . . Year in and year out, they labour without getting enough to eat.'[136] Peasant attitudes could be changed only slowly and *after* industrialization: 'When the system of ownership by the basic commune has been put into effect, private property has been nationalized; new cities and big industries dot the whole country, communes and transport have been modernized, and economic conditions have been completely changed, the world outlook of the peasants will change little by little until the process is complete.'[137]

The 'rich peasant economy' reappeared. But there was no Great Leap to reverse the restoration. The party henceforth was more cautious and conservative, lest it inflict upon itself a repetition of the 'three hard years'. By comparison with the Great Leap Forward, the Socialist Education Movement was small in its impact on the rural population. Nor did the Cultural Revolution have any dramatic effect. The veto on worker and peasant participation could not be upheld in the cities in the heady days of 1966 and 1967, but in the countryside, the mass of the peasantry could be excluded. A number of cultivators took the opportunity to go to the cities with their children; and some of the Big Character posters listed their grievances – high interest rates on loans, poor selling prices, compulsory procurements, low wages (ten to twenty yuan per month) and poor supplies of meat. Some villages held meetings, and the local capitalist roaders received a drubbing. But in general, the mass of the rural population remained onlookers, the recipients of reforms (such as improved rural medical services) rather than the initiators.

(iv) After the Cultural Revolution

The short swing to the 'Right' from 1969 produced an affirmation that private agriculture, the right to raise livestock and practise 'sideline' activities (handicrafts, trade, peddling) were inviolable rights of the rural population. Indeed, the first two were explicitly dissociated from any 'capitalist road', and praised for damping down inflation and the black market.[138] However, in the subsequent swing 'Left' there were complaints that private agriculture and other activities were becoming excessive, that the extension of private rural markets was going too far, that too much rural labour was involved in private trade and commodity speculation, and that party cadres were involved in all these activities and were guilty of secret contracting of labour.[139]

However, when some cadres drew the logical conclusion and proposed to abolish private plots and markets, they were reminded that such activities were a 'supplementary part of the socialist economy', and that abolition 'would dampen the masses' enthusiasm for socialism and undermine the development of the forces of production'.[140] It was the same as the problem of wage differentials. Maintaining the 'masses' enthusiasm for socialism' required practices which the party said led directly to the contradiction of socialism!

How important were these activities? Rural 'sidelines' were supposedly marginal to the village economy, yet some reports suggest this was not always the case. In one instance, the rural cadres express unease at the profitability of their enterprise: 'the production and marketing of our transformer switches are not included in the State plan. We have travelled far to look for and sign marketing contracts; we have produced the raw materials for transformer switches ourselves. We have also processed some products for others. This, of course, has an impact on the State plan. We should consider whether such a way of sideline production is socialist or capitalist.'[141]

Most of the practices condemned benefited only the richer teams, brigades and households. For the poor, and especially those in persistent deficit (that is, their consumption was regularly above their income), matters were not improved in either the 'Right' or 'Left' phase. In late 1975, letters of appeal for loans from poor villages in Kwantung reached relatives in Hong Kong, alleging that they were subject to a drive by the rural cadres to foreclose on debts. One letter complained that: 'Those who are unable to do so [meet their debts] must sell their bicycles, watches, sewing machines, valuable household items and even their piglets to pay off their debts. Under the leadership of the cadres, this movement is a vigorous one and nobody dares to oppose it.'[142]

For the régime, the peasants were the scapegoats of China. In the years after the Cultural Revolution the press regularly cited Mao in support of the proposition that the peasants were to blame for the country's difficulties. In particular, they repeated a 1963 quotation: 'as small owners, they are individualistic and, what is more important, limited by their working conditions and methods and their use of outdated means of production; they are scattered, narrow-minded and ill-informed'.[143]

Such abuse affected rural life very little. The condition of the average household was hard, despite the improvements over the years. Although, from time to time, the modest 'sideline' activities of the majority, so important for rural incomes, might come under attack because they competed with the State's demand for land, labour and fertilizers, it does not seem to have affected the rural areas greatly.[144] The main problems remained – keeping up production, securing adequate supplies of inputs, coping with the still recurrent floods and droughts, absorbing and feeding urban inmigrants. For the majority, living in poor areas, particularly barren upland communes, 'self-reliance' continued to mean both austerity and occasional disaster.

The drive to work was unremitting. For example, an article in the *People's Daily* in 1975 stressed the need for family planning so that women are not 'bogged down by their children and household chores'.[145] With family planning, 'the attendance rate of the women labour force has been raised from the sixty per cent in the past to ninety-three per cent'. What kind of work did the women do when relieved of 'household chores'? In Nanking county: 'Within the army of more than 70,000 diggers of ditches, there were more than 60,000 women. Fearing neither hardships nor fatigue, they worked arduously for fifty days together with men, and had shifted 3,670,000 cubic metres of earth and completed the task of building 140 *li* of ditches ten days ahead of schedule.'

(v) Retrospect

What was the effect of the transformation of China's land? For the average

143

peasant, the ending of the perpetual wars, of gangsterism and banditry, of epidemic, and the worst severities of flood and sporadic famine, were tangible enough benefits. His children might now hope to secure an education, and his family some degree of medical care. The landlord had gone. The cultivator's crop received a stable return and, with time, he could afford to make improvements to raise output. Industry made avilable other comforts to rural existence. Yet, important as these improvements were, they did not demonstrate that the Chinese Communist party was the party of the Chinese peasantry.

It seems reasonably clear from the record of the Communist party during the years of the People's Republic that its leadership felt no particular commitment to the peasantry, no obligation to 'represent' it as a class. On the contrary, the government made sporadic efforts to eliminate the peasantry, to convert it into a tightly administered labour force, tied to the land more closely than ever before. The poverty of China, its intensive agriculture, the weakness of the administrative structure made it impossible to persist in this course for very long. The peasants refused to relinquish the products of the soil. Then State policy went into reverse, permitting the restoration of the 'rich peasant economy'. When that threatened the rural authority, the State swung back towards stricter administration, and so on, an endless series of zigzags to escape from the imperatives of backwardness and build a powerful national economy.

The drive to increase rural output – which did not rule out a slow and modest improvement in rural living standards – did not flow from any 'ideological preference'. On the contrary, the ideological formulations flowed from the efforts to sustain capital accumulation in peculiarly obdurate circumstances. For the majority there was little 'emancipation' in this. The 'emancipation' was, as Mao put it in the early years of the People's Republic, of the 'productive forces'.

It would appear, then, that the Communist party of China did not embody the *class* interests of either the working class or the peasantry. Its general political direction appears fully consistent throughout the period from the 1930s to the present, even if its immediate tactical responses vary. That direction of course represented interests that, it could be claimed, all classes shared – national unity, order, stability and the possibility of improving living standards – but no class interests specific to the exploited. On the other hand, the party did not represent the other two major classes – capitalists and landlords. Although it was indulgent towards landlord interests in the 1940s and capitalist interests in the 1940s and 1950s, it ultimately liquidated both as classes. It did so for material reasons, rather than ideological preferences. The landlords represented Kuomintang and warlord power on the land and were therefore a threat to the party in the rural areas (but not in the cities) and would be an obstacle to centralizing authority over the rural population; the capitalists encroached upon the public sector and jeopardized State control of the urban labour force, thus affecting the party's main priority, accumulation, the basis for building a powerful national State.

On the argument so far, it would seem that Marx, Lenin and the Marxists generally were wrong in the estimate that a political party has automatically an organic relationship with one or another major class. Here was a party apparently without a class basis. However, before we take up this theme, we need to look at another argument. A number of claims have been made about the People's Republic – that in the 1950s, by its reorganization of Chinese society, it was able to conquer the problem of economic backwardness with qualitatively more success than other countries; that because of the transformation, the party created a society moving steadily towards complete equality and fundamental democracy. If all three contentions are correct, it becomes clear that the Marxists were wrong in another way – in their estimation that *only* the industrial working class could achieve these purposes in the modern world.

NOTES

1. *Kuang-ming JP*, 28 Aug. 1953
2. *JMJP*; 14 Jul. 1954, *SCMP* 859, cited Gluckstein, *op. cit.*, p. 216
3. For details and Chinese sources, cf. Martin King Whyte, Corrective Labour Camps in China, *Asian Survey*, Mar. 1973, pp. 255–6
4. *Hsin-hua JP*, 22 Jul. 1953
5. *Kung-jen JP*, 3 Jun. 1953
6. *JMJP* 12 Dec. 1954. See also *JMJP* 30 Mar., 6 Jun., 20 Aug. 1954
7. *JMJP* 22 Oct. 1954, *SCMP* 922
8. *Chang-chiang JP*, Hangkow, 11 Aug. 1952
9. Quoted, *Seventh Congress ACFTU*, ACFTU, Peking, 1953, p. 56
10. See, for example, four family members in Tientsin No. 1 Dyeing and Weaving Mill, cited by Liu Pang-chieh, Family Emulation Drive, *China Reconstructs*, Oct. 1961, pp. 17–18
11. *JMJP*, 1 Jan. 1954, cited Howe, *Wage patterns, op. cit.*, p. 131
12. *Kung-jen JP*, 19 Apr. 1951
13. GAC (Committee for People's Supervision), Circular on labour accidents, 18 Sep. 1952, NCNA Peking, 17 Sep. 1952, *SCMP* 446
14. *Kung-jen JP*, 27 May 1955, *SCMP* 1076
15. *Kung-jen JP*, 20 Feb. 1955, *SCMP* 1024
16. *JMJP*, 12 Mar. 1961
17. *JMJP*, 13 Dec. 1954, *SCMP* 709

18. Report on the work of the government, *First National People's Congress,* first session, 23 Sep. 1954, p. 27; cf. also 'The incompatability of socialism and egalitarianism', *JMJP* 14 Sep. 1952, *SCMP* 472

19. GAC, Directive on the year-end double pay and bonus in public and private enterprises, 8 Dec. 1951, NCNA Peking, 8 Dec. 1951

20. Gluckstein, *op. cit.,* p. 253

21. Chin Lin, *Lao-tung* No. 3, 6 Mar. 1956, cited by Charles Hoffman, *Work incentive practices and policies in the People's Republic of China, 1953–1965,* New York, 1967, p. 85

22. Hu Shang, Speaking of the Government Issue System, *JMJP* 13 Nov. 1958, cited Hoffman, *Work Incentives, op. cit.,* pp. 96–7; cf. also Li Fu-chun, 'Report on the draft economic plan for 1960', *JMJP* 31 Mar. 1960

23. Wang Yu-ch'ang, 'Attend to the livelihood of workers', *JMJP,* May 1960, cited Hoffman, *op. cit.,* p. 105

24. *JMJP,* 3 Nov. 1955

25. Po I-po: '217,500 rooms were built to accommodate about one million people' in 1952 – NCNA Peking, 20 Feb. 1953

26. *Hsin-hua JP,* 12 Jan. 1952, cited *Far Eastern Economic Review,* 30 Oct. 1952

27. Report of a visitor to Taching, 'Forming Maoist Man', *Financial Times,* London, 2 Dec. 1976

28. NCNA Peking, 23 Oct. 1954

29. For examples and Chinese sources, cf. Howe, *Wage Patterns, op. cit.,* p. 126

30. Living standards of Chinese workers rise, NCNA Lanchow, 11 May 1972

31. Calculations for China by Barry M. Richman after an extensive visit to China, average wage assumed, 60 yuan per month; cf. *Industrial Society in Communist China,* New York, 1969, pp. 808–9; British wage assumed, £65.00 per week.

32. Li Fu-ch'un, cited by Wang Ya-nan, *K'o hsueh ch'u pan-she,* Peking, 1956, cited Hoffman, *The Chinese Worker,* Albany (New York), 1974 p. 50.

33. *Takung Pao,* Peking, 3 Jun. 1957, SCMP, 24 Jun. 1957, p. 23

34. Tan Chen-lin, cited in *Red Flag of Science and Technology,* 6 Mar. 1967, and by Deleyne, *op. cit.,* p. 58

35. This is a much simplified account of the debate; for a description, cf. R. V. Daniels, *The Conscience of the Revolution,* Cambridge, Mass., 1960, Ch. 5, pp. 119–36

36. The trade unions, the present situation and the mistakes of comrade Trotsky, Dec. 1920, speech to 8th Congress of Soviet Trade Unions, *SW* 9(1937), p. 9

37. Strikes in the State sector affected 192,000 workers (1922); 165,000 (1923) when 1,592,800 were in dispute; 43,000 (1924); 34,000 (1925); 32,900 (1926); 8,900 (first half of 1928) – from *Wage Labour in Russia,* Moscow (in Russian), 1924, p. 160, and *Trade Unions in the USSR, 1926–28,* Moscow (in Russian), 1928, p. 358, cited by T. Cliff, *Russia: A Marxist Analysis,* London, n.d., pp. 20–21

38. *Trade Union law of the PRC,* Peking, 1950, p. 5

39. Speech, 8th meeting, Central People's Council, 28 Jun. 1950, included *ibid,* p. 22

40. Teng Tzu-hui, vice-chairman, Southern-Central Military and Administrative Committee, *Chung Kuo Kung Jen*, Peking, 4 Aug. 1950

41. Resolution on ACFTU work, summarized in *Kung-jen JP*, 11 Feb. 1953

42. *Kung-jen JP*, 9 May 1957, *SCMP* 1535, p. 12

43. Li Hsiu-jen, in *JMJP*, 4 Aug. 1957, *SCMP* 1551, pp. 10–13

44. Lo Yü-wen, 'Distressing contradictions', *JMJP*, 21 May 1957, *SCMP* 1551, p. 21–22

45. Report on the railways in *T'ieh-lu Kung-jen*, Canton, 4 May 1957, p. 2, cited by Paul Harper, The party and the unions in Communist China, *CQ* 37, Jan.–Mar. 1969, p. 111

46. Trade Unions open debate on two lines, NCNA Peking, 28 Nov. 1957, *SCMP* 1665, pp. 40–42

47. In the course of criticizing Soviet trade unions for paying too much attention to the welfare problems of workers – in *Miscellany* II, p. 274

48. Ta-lien-wei, *JMJP*, 27 May 1968, *SCMP* 10 Jul. 1968, p. 5

49. *Wen Hui Pao*, Shanghai, 6 Jan. 1967, *SCMP* Supplement 64, 28 Feb. 1967, p. 3

50. For references, cf. Howe, *Wage Patterns, op. cit.*, pp. 107, 127

51. *Kung-lu*, 20 Apr. 1965, pp. 7–9, cited in *Current Scene*, VI/5, 15 Mar. 1968

52. *Kung-lu* 4, cited Hoffman, *The Chinese Worker, op. cit.*, p. 72

53. How the worker-peasant labour system is tried out in highway maintenance work, *Kung-lu* 12, 20 Dec. 1965, *SCMM* 4, 21 Feb. 1966, p. 23; see also 'The labour system of industrial and farming work in rotation is actively tried out', NCNA Peking, 27 Dec. 1965

54. The worker-peasant labour system in Finance and Trade Departments: Chang Ho-wei, *Hsin-chun-she*, Nos. 1–2, 20 Feb. 1966, in *SCMM* 534, 25 Jul. 1966

55. *JMJP*, 28 Dec. 1965, cited *Current Scene, op. cit.*, p. 5

56. *Current Scene, op. cit.*; see also *Hung Wei Pao*, 30 Sep. 1966 and NCNA Changchun, 11 Aug. 1966

57. 'Temporary and contract workers, rise up and rebel', *Shou-tu-hung-wei-lun*, 13 Sep. 1966

58. Posted 4 Jan. 1967, cited *Current Scene, op. cit.*

59. *Hung-kung Chan-pao*, 6 Feb. 1967, *SCMP* 177, 19 Apr. 1967, p. 18

60. *Wen Hui Pao*, 6 Jan. 1967, *SCMP* Supplement 164, 28 Feb. 1967, p. 31

61. *JMJP*, 16 Jan. 1967; see also joint editorial, *JMJP-Hung-ch'i*, NCNA, 11 Jan. 1967 on 'economism'

62. *JMJP*, 31 Jan. 1967, and *Wen Hui Pao*, 12 Feb. 1967

63. Notice on questions of temporary workers, contract workers, rotation workers and external workers, reported *Wen Hui Pao*, 28 Feb. 1967

64. *SWB* FE/2404/B/35; see also *Wen Hui Pao*, 28 Feb. 1967, *SCMP* 174, 10 Apr. 1967, p. 6

65. Cited *Current Scene, op. cit.*, p. 17

66. *Wen Hui Pao*, 3 May 1967

67. 13 Sep. 1967

68. NCNA Peking, 28 Dec. 1974, *SCMP* 5770, 10 Jan. 1974

69. 'To idle and not to idle', Hsiao Tung, PLA, *JMJP*, 13 Jan. 1969, *SCMP* 4350, Jan. 1969

70. 'North-east heavy industrial workers go all out to produce more', NCNA

Shenyang, 1 May 1973

71. NCNA Peking, 7 Apr. 1975, *SCMP* 5834, 17 Apr. 1975

72. 'Grasp well education in the line, arousing revolutionary spirit', from No. 2 work section, Tientsin Municipal No. 2 Building Construction Company, *JMJP*, 18 Sep. 1973, *SCMP* 5469, 1–5 Oct. 1973, pp. 159–60

73. *JMJP*, 25 Jan. 1974, *SCMP* 553, 14 Feb. 1974

74. *JMJP* 28 Oct. 1972, *SCMP* 5254, 13–17 Nov. 1972, p. 8

75. 'Economize on manpower wherever possible', *Hung-ch'i* II, 1 Nov. 1972, *SCMM* 741-2, 27, 4 Dec. 1972, p. 30

76. Chiangchiawan Colliery, Tat'ung Municipality, Shansi, in *Hung-ch'i* 3, 3 Mar. 1973, *SCMM* 749–50, 26 Mar.–2 Apr. 1973, p. 55

77. Chiangchiawan Colliery, *op. cit.*

78. NCNA Peking, 15 Feb. 1974

79. *SW* 9(1937), pp. 423–45

80. *Ibid*, p. 439; stress added

81. *Kuang-ming JP*, 27 Apr. 1975

82. *JMJP*, 15 May 1975, *SCMP* 75–24, 9–13 Jun. 1975

83. *PR*, 28 Feb. 1975, p. 5

84. Teng Hsiao-p'ing, 2 Oct. 1974, interviewed by Professor Fan Lan, cited Carl Riskin, 'Workers' incentives in Chinese industry', in *China: A Reassessment of the Economy*, Joint Economic Committee of the US Congress, Washington, 1975, p. 201

85. 'Perseveringly put politics in command, do a good job of reckoning wages of labour', Lin An, *JMJP*, 12 Aug. 1972, *SCMP* 5199–5203, 21–25 Aug. 1972, p. 186. The criticism continues: 'They vigorously practise "egalitarianism" for the purpose of sabotaging the policy of more pay for more work and equal pay for equal work, thwarting the enthusiasm of the masses in production, undermining the development of the productive forces, disintegrating the collective economy and restoring capitalism'

86. Sian radio, Shensi, 11 Mar. 1975, *SWB* FE/4860/BII, p. 20

87. Report, *China News Summary*, 555, 19 Feb. 1975

88. Reported, *Far Eastern Economic Review* 94/40, 1 Oct. 1976, pp. 89–90

89. 'The essential distinction between two systems of distribution', *Hung-ch'i* 7, 1 Jul. 1972, *SCMM* 733–4, 3 Jul.–8 Aug. 1972, p. 56

90. *Kuang-ming JP*, 19 May 1975, *SCMP* 75–23, 2–6 Jun. 1975

91. For details, see 'Some basic facts about China: ten questions and answers', in *China Reconstructs*, Supplement, Jan. 1974, p. 91; for further details after a visit, cf. Joyce Kallgren, *Welfare and Chinese industrial workers: Post-Cultural Revolution Prospects and Problems*, unpublished paper, Aug. 1976

92. 17 May 1917, *CW* 24, p. 428; Lenin stress

93. *CW* 26, pp. 107–8

94. 'Strictly implement Joint Production Committees', *Ch'ang Chiang JP*, 29 May 1951

95. L'i Ch'un, 'Why is it necessary to broaden the management of our enterprises?' *Chung-Kuo kung-jen*, 6, 27 Mar. 1957, cited by Choh-ming Li, Chinese Industry, *CQ* 17, Jan.–Mar. 1964, pp. 26–7

96. *JMJP*, 15 Jul. 1969

97. 'Grasp ideology systems and technique', *JMJP*, 8 Oct. 1971

98. *SWB* 4964/BII/9, 25 Jul. 1975; stress added

99. Hoffman, *The Chinese Worker, op. cit.*, Table 5:1, pp. 146–7

100. Reports, *China News Summary*, Nos. 577–8, Aug. 1975; on Shensi, *SWB* 4971/BII/8

101. Central Committee and State Council, Resolutions concerning the problem of Chekiang province, 24 Jul. 1975, translated and published, *Issues and Studies*, Jun. 1976, pp. 102–5

102. Hangchow radio, 21, 22 Jul., *SWB* 4965i and 4, 26 Jul. 1975

103. NCNA 2 Aug. 1975, in *SWB* 4976/BII/5–6, 8 Aug. 1975

104. *The essential distinction, op. cit.* (note 89), p. 59

105. Lenin, 'The agrarian question in Russia', *CW* (4th Russian) 15, pp. 57–8, cited Gluckstein, *op. cit.*, p. 83

106. Provisional Government, statement, 19 Mar. 1917, cited Cliff, *Lenin, op. cit.*, II, p. 208

107. *Ibid*, 21 Apr. 1917, cited *ibid*, p. 209

108. *CW* 9, p. 315

109. *CW* 25, p. 227

110 *The agrarian reform law of the PRC*, Peking 1951, pp. 2–4

111. On the difficulties and anomalies, cf. Gluckstein, *op.cit.*, pp. 88–90

112. *Agrarian reform law, op. cit.*, p. 22

113. Chen Han-seng estimates 22% of large landlords of south Kiangsu were mainly engaged in trade in 1930 – *The present agrarian problem in China*, Shanghai, 1933, p. 19; J. L. Buck estimates 31% of Szechuan landlords were also merchants – *An agricultural survey of Szechuan province*, (mimeo), Chungking, 1943, p. 13, cited Gluckstein, p. 89

114. Hsin Kuan Ch'a, Peking, 10 Dec. 1950, *CB* 63

115. *General Report*, Peking Municipal People's Government on Agrarian Reform in the Peking Suburban Areas, 21 Nov. 1950, *CB* 72

116. *Fanshen, A document of revolution in a Chinese village*, New York, 1966, pp. 605–6

117. See Robert Ash's reconstruction of events and documentation, 'Economic aspects of land reform in Kiangsu, 1949–52', Pts. I & II, *CQ* 66 and 67, Jun. and Sep. 1976

118. 'Methods of implementing land reform in south Kiangsu', People's Administration of Southern Kiangsu, 28 Nov. 1950, Ash, *ibid*, I, p. 289

119. *New China's Economic Achievements, 1949–1952*, Peking, 1952, p. 194

120. From I-nien-lai t'u kai-ko yün-tung ti ch'eng-chu, *Hsinhua JP*, 2 Jul. 1951, p. 3, and *Hsinhua JP*, 1 Dec. 1951, p. 2, cited Ash, *op. cit.*, II, pp. 521–2

121. *Su-nan JP*, Wusih, 1 Jan. 1952, Ash, *ibid*, II, p. 531

122. Shanghai, 14 Jul. 1950, *CB* 10, 29 Sep. 1950

123. 'The practices of indiscriminate beating, scolding, punishment, threats, arrests, etc., are frequently employed in promoting the work of collection' – Secretary, North East Bureau, 20 May 1951, *Nang Fang JP*, 9 Jun. 1952, *CB* 158

124. *New China's Economic Achievements, op. cit.*, p. 90

125. April 1956, *Miscellany* I, p. 34; and 8 Dec. 1956, *ibid*, p. 41

126. GAC, Directive on the issuance of farm credit, 7 Jul. 1953, NCNA Peking, 1 Sept. 1953, *SCMP* 645

127. 'Report on an investigation of conditions in five villages in an old Liberated Area in Shansi province', *JMJP*, 11 Nov. 1951, *CB* 143

128. Liu Lan-t'ao, *JMJP*, 14 Mar. 1953, *SCMP* 535

129. Kao K'ang, 'Overcome the corrosion of bourgeois ideology: oppose the rightist trend in the Party', *JMJP*, 24 Jan. 1952, *CB* 163, 5 Mar. 1952

130. *On agricultural co-operation, op. cit.*, pp. 18–19

131. Chen Yun, NCNA Peking, 21 Jun. 1955; volume of rent formerly paid, in NCNA 18 Sep. 1952; cf. also Chen Han-seng, *China Reconstructs*, Jan.–Feb. 1953

132. Chen Yun, NCNA Peking, 10 Mar. 1957; cf. also: 'cattle slaughtered this year [1955] has shown an increase of more than seventy per cent compared with same period last year, and calves constitute a very large portion of the animals slaughtered' – *Ta Kung Pao*, Tientsin, 21 Dec. 1955, *SCMP* 1200

133. 8th Party Congress, 17 May 1958, in *Miscellany* I, p. 102, and II, p. 237

134. Sixth Plenum, Sep. 1955, *Miscellany* I, p. 15

135. Feb 1959, in *Miscellany* I. p. 157

136. 1959, in *Miscellany* II, p. 313

137. *Ibid*, p. 253

138. *JMJP*, 22 Oct. 1971

139. Radio broadcasts, Hupeh 11, 24 Feb. and 2 Mar. 1975, Kansu, 16 Feb. 1975, Kiangsu, 16 Feb. 1975, in *Current Scene* XIII, 3–4, Mar.–Apr. 1975

140. Secretary of a County Party Committee, cited Changchun radio (Kirin), 28 Jul. 1975, *SWB* 4973/BII/8

141. Liu Cheng-sung, of Niulantaotzu production brigade, Wuchiang County, Hopei, Shihchiachuang radio, Hopei, 18 Aug. 1975, *SWB* 4989/BII/10, 23 Aug. 1975

142. *Ming Pau*, 23 Dec. 1975, in *Translations of PRC* 299, JPRS 63125, 21 Jan. 1976, pp. 9–10

143. 13 Dec. 1963, in *Mao Papers*, p. 88; cf. also *Miscellany* II, p. 252

144. A point made by *Kuang-ming JP*, 17 Apr. 1975, *SCMP* 5845, 5 May 1975; cf. also Shih Ta, *JMJP*, 3 Apr. 1975, *SCMP* 5844, 2 May 1975, and *Kuang-ming JP*, 19 May 1975, *SCMP* 75–23, 2–6 Jan. 1976

145. *JMJP*, 14 Apr. 1975, *SCMP* 5841, 29 Apr. 1975

PART IV

EQUALITY, DEMOCRACY AND NATIONAL INDEPENDENCE

11

EQUALITY

The French revolution of 1789 – for Marx the most spectacular example of the 'bourgeois revolution' – was fought under the banner, 'Liberty, Equality and Fraternity' (a device still borne on the coat of arms of the French Republic). The same themes echo through the nineteenth-century revolutions of national independence. But in the twentieth century there is a different slogan. Equality remains, but liberty and fraternity have been replaced by national independence and democracy. The terms have changed but some of the content persists – for example, 'democracy' often means much the same today as 'fraternity' meant to the French revolutionaries. If the 'nation' is embodied in the State, then 'national independence' secures the liberty of the State in relationship to other States.

However, none of these aims is achieved by a single act of national emancipation. National independence is not simply an abstraction, it requires a basis in economic power, and the capacity to defend national interests and frontiers. In short, 'national independence' requires 'economic development'. It is not a matter of a country *choosing* to develop; it is obliged to do so in so far as it wishes to sustain its national independence. The necessity flows from a world order dominated by competing capitalist States. This imposes the need for continuous armed preparedness, which in turn demands industrialization.

It was the growing sense of vulnerability in the Soviet Union, the fear of what was called 'capitalist encirclement', which drove the Russian leadership to undertake the first Five Year Plan, to lurch into the collectivization of agriculture, and to pursue blitzkrieg industrialization in the ensuing years, with all the toll of social deprivation involved. When, as early as 1931, there were calls for a slackening in the pace, Stalin replied: 'No, comrades . . . the pace must not be slackened. On the contrary, we must quicken it as much as is within our power and possibilities. We are fifty or one hundred years behind the advanced

153

countries. We must make good this lag in ten years. Either we do it, or they will crush us.'[1]

The rivalries which dominate the world system exercise a compulsion over all the national participants. The compulsion is extreme for States that have started in the race late, are 'economically backward', and particularly so, the more dedicated they are to *national* independence. But if the quest for independence compels a nation to industrialize, industrialization, if successful, transforms the material basis of the national State, and so, all the components of social life. The aims of equality and democracy cannot but be affected. In the Soviet Union, the history of events since the first Five Year Plan illustrates some effects of this transformation.

(i) Equality

What for Marx is the cause of the inequality of incomes? In early capitalism, it is rooted in inequality in the production process, an unequal access to the means of production and the social division of labour. In the process of 'primitive accumulation', great inequalities in the return from work are required to sustain accumulation – capitalists in expanding sectors of production get higher profits than those in declining sectors; industrial profits are higher than the returns to agriculture; skilled workers receive more than unskilled; and so on. The differentials are supposed to distribute capital and labour so that accumulation is maximized. It is accumulation in conditions of material scarcity – scarcity of investable resources, of the educated and skilled – which sustains the main lines of inequality.

Marx contrasts this situation with that in advanced capitalism where accumulation is well established and skills are more abundant: society already has within its grasp the conquest of scarcity. Here inequality persists, because of the domination of a ruling class, using its social and political power to sustain a privileged position; the capitalists, once the precondition for social progress, have become now a 'fetter on production', a parasitic formation no longer required to maintain production. Resources are now available, skills spread throughout the labour force (or capable of easy acquisition) or rendered unnecessary by the refinement of technology: the foundations of scarcity that made capitalism objectively necessary have disappeared.

On Marx's analysis, then, one would expect that in a backward economy, starting the process of rapid capital accumulation would increase the differences of income as the social division of labour was established. The gaps – between the controllers or owners of capital and those

154

with nothing to sell but their labour, between the contradictions Mao identifies as the 'Three Great Differences' (between town and country, mental and manual labour, managers and workers) – would all widen. A government which tried to prevent an increase in inequality at the same time as it pushed forward accumulation would be caught in a contradiction: either accumulation would be sacrificed to preventing inequality, or vice versa. Of course, it would be difficult to check which had occurred, for those controlling the means of production would conceal what was morally reprehensible, the increase in their returns; skilled workers, in demand because of the pace of industrialization, would change jobs to defeat controlled wages, or receive an expanding range of non-cash 'perks' to make up their income to a higher level, and so on. Furthermore, to control incomes would require a massive bureaucracy, intervening in detail to prevent evasion and ensure an efficient distribution of capital and labour; but then the bureaucracy becomes a separate social formation, consuming an increasing share of the surplus and so defeating the whole purpose.

In the twentieth century, matters are complicated by the fact that technology is now so refined that industrial *output* can be increased more rapidly than the number of jobs. This produces in backward countries a common picture of 'dualism' – a highly productive but tiny industrial workforce alongside a vast mass of low productivity workers in town and country, an ever more stark 'division of labour'. It becomes possible to secure industrial power without a general social transformation. In such circumstances, differences *within* the industrial workforce become less important than the differences between the mass and the minority.

(ii) The Soviet Union

In Russia, we can see the effect on income differentials of the State undertaking rapid capital accumulation, beginning in the first Five Year Plan (1928–33). In 1917, the new régime laid down clear guidelines; the State should move towards equality of incomes so that 'all citizens are transformed into salaried employees of the State, which consists of armed workers ... All that is required is that they should work equally – do their proper share of work – and get paid equally.'[2] So far as the State itself was concerned: 'the salaries of all officials, who are to be elected and subject to recall at any time, (should) not exceed the average wage of a competent worker'.[3] A few months after the October revolution, the aim was reaffirmed as the 'gradual equalization of all wages and salaries in all professions and categories'.[4]

155

The Bolsheviks recognized the problem. In conditions of material scarcity, war and civil war, 'socialism' was out of the question. Scarce skills would have to be paid more, even if less than under the old régime. A Tsarist expert, it was said, received twenty times the average worker's wage, but in the early years of the Soviet Union, an expert received no more than five times the average.

The retreat of the New Economic Policy – a partial revival of private capitalism and trade – produced more marked inequality, particularly between the now uncontrolled private sector and the public. But still, the absence of any sustained drive towards capital accumulation rendered the pressures controllable. The new unified seventeen grade scale of wages introduced in 1921–2 to cover the *entire* workforce envisaged a basic span between top and bottom of 1:3.5 (but some specialists could earn up to eight times the lowest paid worker). Party members were forbidden to receive salaries at the level awarded non-party specialists; the general rule up to the time of the first Plan was that party members could earn no more than the average wage of skilled workers (so that the two-thirds of directors of enterprises who were party members could legally earn no more than their leading workers). By March 1926, one study reports, the average wage for all workers was between fifty-eight and sixty-four *chervonet* roubles, and for factory directors who were also party members, 187.8 (a span of roughly 1:3.5), and non-party directors, 309.5 (a span of roughly 1:5).[5] Officially, the average annual income of manual workers was 465 *pre-war* roubles; the maximum salary permitted to specialists was 1,811 (a span of 1:4); some 114,000 people received this maximum salary, or 0.3 per cent of all earners.[6]

The impact of the first Plan and the continuing efforts to increase output transformed both the aims of the régime and actual differentials. Now equality of income became, not a key target, but a serious obstacle to what was called 'building socialism'. Stalin attacked *uravnilovka* ('crude levelling', an abusive term for egalitarianism) as 'the peasant outlook, the psychology of equal division of all goods, the psychology of primitive peasant "communism". *Uravnilovka* has nothing in common with Marxian socialism'.[7] Molotov went further and demanded that egalitarians be rooted out as class enemies: 'Bolshevik policy demands a resolute struggle against egalitarians as accomplices of the class enemy, as hostile to socialism'.[8]

The restraints on income differences and on the earnings of party members were dropped, and the practice of publishing income figures – other than averages for all workers and employees – ended. However, fragmentary information still appeared, indicating that income differentials (as opposed to the distribution of owned wealth) now became even more extreme than in the private capitalist countries. In 1937, for example, plant engineers were said to be receiving 1,500 roubles per month, directors 2,000, skilled workers 200–300; the minimum wage for piece workers at that time was 110 roubles, and for time workers, 115.[9] Managers also had access to special bonuses for fulfilling or exceeding plan targets.

This distribution of income was only *within* the factory. For the social distribution, we must add, at one end, those employed outside the factory sectors (in services and in agriculture), at the other, the ranked hierarchies of the State. Again the information is fragmentary. For example, in 1938, it was announced that the President and vice-President of the Council of Union and the Council of Nationalities were to be paid salaries of 25,000 roubles per month each, and deputies of the Supreme Soviet, 1,000 roubles per month, with an additional 150 roubles per day when the Soviet was in session.[10] To take another example, during the Second World War, it was reported that privates in the Soviet army received ten roubles per month; lieutenants 1,000; and colonels, 2,400, a range of 1:240. By comparison, in the United States army, rates for the same ranks were $50, $150 and $333, or a span of about 1:6.7.[11]

These extreme differences were the result both of deliberate government policy and the process of rapid capital accumulation in conditions of national isolation to which that policy was a response. Once the process was basically achieved, the supply of educated and skilled manpower became relatively abundant; differentials began to narrow, just as they had done in the industrialized countries of the West. But the narrowing was obstructed by the politically privileged order. Nonetheless the wage reforms of 1956–60 acknowledged the narrowing process but endeavoured to restrict it to wages alone. In industry the variations now are not wide. One study of engineering, for example, shows the differential between average wage earnings and the salaries of technical and office staff between the early 1930s and the 1960s as follows:

Technical staff	Office staff
(average manual wage earnings: 1)	
1932	1:2.6	1:1.5
1945	1:2.3	1:1.0
1966	1:1.4	1:0.8[12]

Another study gives the rate for skill grades as a ratio of the basic rate for different industries as follows: 1:3.75 (underground coal mining); 1:3.2 (ferrous ore mining); 1:3.2 (ferrous metallurgy); 1:2.85 (nonferrous metals mining); 1:2.4 (cement); 1:2.3 (chemicals); 1:2.0 (construction); 1:2.0 (oil refining); 1:1.8 (food preparation).[13]

The figures tell us nothing about the variation between industries, between industry and agriculture, between workers and all other occupations. For example, unskilled Leningrad engineering workers in the late 1960s were said to receive an average monthly wage of 97.5 roubles; skilled workers up to 120; foremen 173. But a government minister received about 1,050 roubles per month, or nine times the average wage. Furthermore, the top income figures contain no allowance for extra provisions like cars, holidays, houses, special shops and schools, all of which widens the gap between workers and top government officials to possibly 1:25–30.

(iii) Policy in China

Unlike the Soviet Union, China had no introductory phase in which official policy was dedicated to the achievement of equality. Officially, the régime always adhered to Stalin's proposition that egalitarianism is, in Chou En-lai's words, 'a type of petty bourgeois outlook which encourages backwardness and hinders progress. It has nothing in common with Marxism and a socialist system.'[14] On the other hand, in contrast to Stalin, the régime always expressed anxiety lest income differentials, particularly among workers, grew too wide; for example, in 1958, Mao argued that wage differentials were too wide and should be narrowed, although not eliminated.[15] Yet Mao also tolerated with equanimity – as we have seen – the high rewards given to capitalists, and when their properties were purchased or absorbed by the State, the continued payment to them of a rate of interest of five per cent on the capital.

In sum, this position has remained reasonably constant, although different elements have been stressed at different times. For example, we find Mao in 1964 arguing: 'The system of high salaries for a small number of people should never be applied. The gap between the incomes of working personnel of the Party, the Government, the enterprises and the people's communes, on the one hand, and the incomes of the mass of the people on the other, should be rationally and gradually narrowed and not widened.'[16] During the Cultural Revolution and afterwards, similar statements were regularly made by party leaders, although no one raised the question of changing the existing income *structure*. That structure, laid down in 1956, appeared to have been retained intact throughout all the different emphases of policy.

The approach to pay straddled a contradiction. On the one hand, capital accumulation in conditions of backwardness necessitated income differences – hence the opposition to egalitarianism. On the other, industrial jobs did not expand fast enough to make available to an increasing proportion of people some access to higher incomes. As a result, the potential for resentment at the income results of accumulation could become extreme (unlike the situation in the Soviet Union in the 1930s). The government stressed three different aims (which were often confused with each other) – narrowing income differences, not permitting income differences to become more extreme, and not allowing income differences to be expressed in marked differences in living standards and life style. The third received most attention, the second slightly less, and the first, in practice (that is, the wage structure) the least.

The official justification for the policies was curiously un-Marxist. It was argued that a relatively high living standard was the basis for the foundation of a bourgeoisie, a constant threat despite the achievement of 'socialism'. Thus, different levels of consumption are not the *result* of the existence of classes, they are the cause of the existence of classes. This turns Marx on his head.

However, in China, Marx and Lenin are cited in support of the case that permitting 'bourgeois right' (the temporary expedient of paying people according to their work, made necessary in an immediate post-revolutionary situation) can of itself re-create capitalism. The moral and the economic seem to coincide: 'If a Communist party member has no sober understanding of bourgeois right, and if he lets the concept of bourgeois right clog up his mind, thinks about narrow personal gains and losses, refuses to work half an hour more than the others or to receive less remuneration than the others, seeks fame, gain, enjoyment and privileges, and operates his own comfortable quarters . . . he would mark time on the road of continued revolution.'[17] The basis for increasing consumption is not, then, related to the ordering of the production process, but to the psychology of the individual concerned. Curbing the tendency of the cadre to indulge his appetite does not take the form of control of his income (nor the rationing of all consumer goods) but strengthening his self-discipline. Higher incomes are associated with lower work efforts: 'The kind of style of work that should be maintained and fostered is a major aspect of the struggle between the proletariat and the bourgeoisie'.[18] But if the proletarian is defined as no more than abstemious and hard-working, and the bourgeoisie as greedy or lazy, nothing ties such terms to any objective social structure. I may be proletarian today, bourgeois tomorrow and proletarian the day afterwards; the 'class struggle' comes to mean no more than the effort to prevent someone having phases of bourgeois tiredness between the times of proletarian hard work!

How does this conception of 'bourgeois right' compare with Marx's? For Marx, 'abolition of the wages system' is 'the revolutionary watchword'.[19] It is the most important mark of the post-revolutionary order, let alone of socialism. Workers now control production and the State, and have thus abolished the need to sell their labour as the sole means of material survival. However, all cannot immediately be paid equally since skills are still in short supply. Only over a longer period of time can the resistance of the old ruling class and the problems of immediate scarcity be overcome. Only then can the distinction between skilled and unskilled, between mental and manual labour, between town and country, finally be dissolved. It is material abundance – and what flows from this, *high incomes for all* – which dissolves the yoke of the social division of labour and 'bourgeois right', not an effort of will or a moral striving for abstemiousness, or government edict. Marx puts it in this form: 'In a higher phase of Communist society, after the enslaving subordination of individuals under the division of labour, and therefore also the antithesis between mental and physical labour, has vanished; after labour has become not merely a means to live but has become itself the primary necessity of life; after the productive forces have also increased with the all-round development of the individual, and all the springs of co-operative wealth flow more abundantly – only then can the narrow horizon of bourgeois right be fully left behind and society inscribe on its banners: From each according to his ability, to each according to his needs.'[20]

Is China on the threshold of such a situation? At the 1975 Fourth National People's Congress, Chou En-lai set as the national aim the 'comprehensive modernization of agriculture, industry, national defence and science and technology before the end of the century'. In Marx's terms, this means, not the abolition of the existing division of labour, but its establishment; not the ending of 'bourgeois right', but on the contrary, its most rigorous enforcement. The level of consumption is very low, reflecting great material scarcity. If a moral campaign by the State can achieve what Marx called communism, then Marx and his materialism are nonsense; in which case, the concept of communism as he presented it is equally false.

Does the reality of income differentials in China demonstrate the absurdity of Marx's materialism?

(iv) Income differentials in China

The basic income structure that governs China today was established in the late 1950s. The overwhelming majority of people – possibly 300–350 million earners – are governed by the wage point system in agriculture. The minority outside agriculture – some fifty to seventy million earners – can be divided into four groups:

1   *Workers and staff in State administration, welfare and educational organizations*, covered by a thirty grade pay system. In 1955–6, the rates (as opposed to earnings) were said to cover a range of 1:31 (and 1:19 in local government). This is said to have been reduced to a span of 1:20 (another estimate says 1:25.2) in 1958, but thereafter may have widened again to reach roughly the same span in 1972.[21] The PLA, whose pay structure is not known, ought also to be included in this category.

2   *Technicians and technical staff*, governed by an eighteen to twenty-four grade pay system with a rate span said to be of 1:10 in the late 1950s.

3   *Workers and staff in public sector economic undertakings* (employing 100 workers or more), governed by an eight grade wage system, at various times said to span a range of rates, 1:2–3.

4   *Workers and staff in enterprises with less than 100 workers*, contract and temporary workers, rural non-agricultural workers etc. The size of this group is not clear, but its pay seems to be the same as in agriculture, on a work-point basis rather than a grading system.

Having several overlapping scales makes it difficult to assess the overall span of incomes. The individual Chinese tends to assess income differentials solely in his workplace, rather than on a national scale. Furthermore, the government publishes no estimates of the numbers in each group or grade, so it becomes impossible to compare income inequality in China with that in other countries. Nonetheless, let us examine the fragmentary information on each of the five groups:

1   *The State administration*. The thirty grade pay structure had, in 1975, a top rate of RMB 400 which, according to Teng Hsiao-p'ing, was being received by some 100 people in the whole of China. The figure is misleading, for it includes no estimate of other privileges attached to high office. For example, Red Guard newspapers in January 1968 alleged that senior ministers received special allowances of up to fifty per cent of their pay for working away from home; there is no evidence that this practice has been discontinued. It is also misleading because it does not include all the top earners of China. Thus, in 1975, Tan Fu-ying, head of the Peking Opera troupe in Shanghai, and Chou Hsin-kao, one of the principal singers, were reported to have volunteered to cut their monthly salary from RMB 1,000 to RMB 300.[22] How many people,

receiving incomes above RMB 400 in China, did not volunteer for a cut is not known. Nor is it clear whether interest payments to capitalists are still made; this produced enormous incomes in the early 1960s (the end of such payments is assumed, but has not been officially announced). Presumably, the cumulative wealth of the capitalists was disposed of in some way, whether by buying State bonds or financing petty activities, and now produces an income outside the grading system. Writers presumably also continue to draw royalties on their works; Red Guard publications documented some of these payments, one of which brought an income of RMB 200,000 to the novelist, Pa Chin.[23] Foreign specialists employed by the government of China were said, in 1972, to receive incomes between RMB 300 and 800.[24]

Below the RMB 400 mark, there are a scatter of incomes, accruing to high State officials: for example, the Chief Astronomer of the Nanking Observatory is said to receive RMB 330 per month. Older professors in the universities are said to get between RMB 300 and 360, as opposed to the starting rate for university teachers which is close to the average industrial wage, RMB 50–60, a range of 1:6 which is wider than the official salary scales in, for example, British universities (roughly 1:4).[25] Particular ministers may get higher figures; a 1966 study reports a minister receiving nearly RMB 400; his bureau chiefs 200 to 250; divisional chiefs, 150 to 200; section chiefs 45; a span in this one ministry at the *national* level of roughly 1:10.[26] The editor of the *People's Daily* is said to receive RMB 200, and ordinary journalists, RMB 80 (a span of 1:2.5).

Edgar Snow reported in the late 1960s that in the PLA 'the present scale of pay ranges from US $2.50 per month for a private to US $192–236 for a full general', a span of 1:77–94.[27] In the excitable climate of the Cultural Revolution, such enormous pay differentials must have provoked much resentment. However, Mao's complaint was not against the differential itself, but against the resentful. 'There are people instigating the soldiers to oppose their superiors', he said in 1967, 'and saying that while you are making only six yuan a month, the officers are making much more and enjoying the luxury of riding in cars'.[28] Perhaps the differentials were narrowed as a result of the Cultural Revolution, but they remain extreme if Snow's figures are correct. Possibly such resentments lay behind the 1965 abolition of marks of rank in the PLA; rank itself was not abolished, but expressed in new forms (the number of pens in the top pocket or the number of pockets has been mentioned) and through social privileges (for example, gaberdine rather than cotton uniforms; first-class travel on the railways, air or car travel, as opposed to the 'hard class' on trains, or truck and bicycle transport).

Mao showed no concern with income differentials in the PLA, only with the need to have a common style *regardless of income*. A national newspaper expressed it in 1975: 'The officers and soldiers are all equal politically. They only differ in the division of work and official duties, and there is no distinction between high and low.'[29] This is as disingenuous as the phrase 'all equal before the law', or its ancestor, 'all equal in the eyes of God'.

The additional privileges of upper income groups are not included in the income figures, nor can they be easily quantified. They include the use of cars with chauffeurs, rail and air travel, servants, places in sanatoria, housing, access to special services and goods, banquets and so on. In the 1950s and 1960s, there were – as in Russia – special shops for high ranking cadres, denounced as 'little treasure pagodas' by the Red Guards (whether or not they have been ended is unclear). Housing is an important index of status for these holding high rank. The 1966 report on a Peking ministry mentions that about sixty per cent of the staff lived in State-run housing; the minister and his vice-ministers received individual houses; the assistants to the minister and bureau chiefs lived in apartments in a special modern block; and the rest of the staff in three dormitory blocks. Party members appeared to be consistently favoured in the allocation. In the PLA, senior officers have similar access to special services – for example, special military hospitals.

With such differentials, the children of the high ranking are inevitably favoured. After the Cultural Revolution, the press continued to complain that senior cadres used their influence to ensure their children gained access to university, avoided manual labour, and received the best jobs after graduation.[30] As we have seen, in 1971 Lin Piao's son had the remarkable distinction of being a senior officer in the Air Force at the age of twenty-four. In 1973, the press reported a scandal when a son refused to allow his father, a Long March veteran and senior PLA officer, to get him transferred from a rural area to enter university. The press cannot tell us of the cases where sons or daughters did not refuse such parental assistance.

Lower down the hierarchy, the administrative grade system becomes more complicated, with some eleven regional variations (with a forty per cent range between them) and graded living expense subsidies. Before the Cultural Revolution, the maximum addition to the basic pay was ninety-three to ninety-seven per cent. A grade 1 driver in Mangya, Tsaidam Basin, received RMB 196 per month, and in Shansi, RMB 70.[31]

Although the overall picture is not clear, the differences in official incomes appear so marked (even if their effect is curbed by the rationing

163

system, shortages and the stigma attached to conspicuous consumption) that a few voluntary pay cuts do not affect the situation. In the absence of a new wage and salary structure on one scale, published so that all the people of China can see it, one must assume that the basic structure of 1956 has remained intact.

2   *Technicians and engineers* are on a national scale that covers a wide variety of plants and enterprises. Visitors to Chinese factories since the Cultural Revolution report a range between a maximum comparable to the administrative top grade, and a minimum below the average industrial wage (RMB 50–60). Meisner reported from one plant a range between RMB 230 and RMB 34, or a span of 1:6–7.[32] Other reports confirm top rates of between RMB 200 and RMB 250. Little seems to have happened to the structure since before the Cultural Revolution. However, in 1977 it was reported that senior technicians were to receive pay increases from 1 October (whether achieved by an increase in the pay received in a particular grade or promotion between grades was not clear).

3   *Industrial workers* have a narrower span of wage grades than the two preceding groups, include more people, and are markedly in advance of the rest of the working class and much of the rural population. The span depends upon the skills involved and the priority attached to the plant and industry concerned. The average wage is RMB 50 to 60, and the span covers a range of 1:3, or RMB 36 to 108. Dockers' wages in Shanghai average RMB 70.[33] Apprentices do not figure on this wage scale. In some factories they receive RMB 18–20; in another in Peking, RMB 30.

In 1977, the government announced pay increases affecting some forty-six per cent of workers employed in the organized sector of industry. This was achieved, not by changing the grading structure, but by the promotion of workers in the two bottom grades to higher grades, the average increase being between RMB 7 and 18. Other workers also received increases, although no workers paid over RMB 100 were affected. The change excluded apprentices, workers in agriculture and workers paid on a work point system. At the time of writing, economists – stimulated by Hua's statement at the 11th Party Congress that wages should be linked to productivity – are debating the best form for productivity bonuses.

In the past, industrial workers have also received incentive bonuses and overtime pay, as well as welfare benefits, housing, recreation facilities, and pensions (financed out of the wage fund).

4   *Other non-agricultural employment.* There is a vast range of labour outside the grading system, from petty services and handicrafts to small-

scale factories. There seems to be a trend towards expanding this sector at the expense of modern 'organized' industry, but there is little evidence of the numbers involved. From the reports of visitors to a small selection of plants – presumably among the very best, since otherwise foreigners would be unlikely to receive permission to inspect them – it appears pay levels are strictly related to output, and are roughly half the average in the modern sector (or RMB 20–30 per month). Small-scale industry seems to draw heavily on the labour of housewives organized by neighbourhood committees. One visitor to the Yun Chun Lane Residents' Committee in Shanghai found that unemployed women were organized in factory piece work, in work at home for outside buyers (a 'putting-out' system) or in small neighbourhood workshops. They were paid RMB 26 per month, or slightly less than an apprentice in the organized sector, a level of pay which would be tolerable only in a household where there were other earners.[34]

5   *The majority* of the Chinese labour force is not paid on a grading system at all, but in relationship to the collective profits made annually by an agricultural team or brigade after meeting certain set obligations (taxes, accumulation and welfare fund costs). This income may be supplemented by 'sideline' activities (handicrafts, peddling, petty trade, cobbling, cutting grass for heating and fodder, as well as small industrial enterprises); by the sale of private agricultural output (including the raising of livestock); and remittances from household members working elsewhere (in the city or abroad, important for Kwantung villagers). The picture is therefore extremely varied – between brigades or teams working in intensive farming, horticulture or export crops, in well-watered fertile areas on the outskirts of a big city (with a large market), with outside work easily available for some family members or for cultivators in the 'off season'; and villages in the barren hill areas, remote from the cities, with little trade and no important local markets. The range is between incomes well above those received by the mass of the city population and pay on the verge of, or below, subsistence level.

The majority of Chinese cultivators receive incomes well below the average for the cities, and this makes for the sizeable gap between town and country. There are no recent figures available on the size of the gap, but in the 1950s estimates were made of the difference in *real consumption per head* in comparison with the 1930s:

	Workers and employees (RMB)	Peasants (RMB)	Peasants as percentage of workers and employees
1936	130	61	46.9
1956	179.6	81	45.1[35]

165

The figures show a surprising stability. However, the 'workers and employees' figure is raised by the high income of top urban wage earners; otherwise the gap between the mass of the urban and rural population would be less extreme. In the 1950s, the ratio was about 1:2. In terms of official *income* (as opposed to consumption; it costs less to live in rural areas), the gap between the average permanent employed worker in the city and the agricultural worker is wider – in 1960, RMB 560 as opposed to RMB 140 (or 1:4).[36] For rough comparison, the ratio between *all* city incomes and the rural average in two Latin American countries in the 1960s was: 1:2.5 in Venezuela, and 1:2.3 in Mexico.[37]

The figures are misleading because the variation in rural incomes is great. For example, the Westlake Commune, growing tea near Hangchow, claimed that its top teams received average monthly earnings of RMB 86, which does not include the proceeds from private cultivation; while a Hopei Commune, reported by NCNA in 1972, claimed that its annual product per head was 99.45 yuan which, if the income of its members took all the product, would have produced monthly earnings of only RMB 8.3.[38] Without employing the entire rural labour force on a standard wage grading system which in the main ignored the enormous regional differences in productivity, there is little possibility of doing much about such differences. Such a task is beyond the resources of the Chinese State, whether this means the resources to meet the wage bill or the administrative structure to supervise it.

Numerous visitors over the past ten years have been able to visit communes, but inevitably it is a small selection. What are the differences noted? Burki in a 1964 study of thirteen communes estimated the variation in annual family incomes as covering a range from RMB 405 to RMB 1,392 (or RMB 34 to RMB 116 per month), and for individual workers, from RMB 166 to RMB 568 (or RMB 14 to RMB 48 per month). The variation in agricultural wages per month was between RMB 17 in a Chekiang commune and RMB 47.22 in an Inner Mongolian commune, with an average in monthly wages from collective agricultural work of RMB 30.1.[39] Buchanan in a study of eighteen communes two years later calculated the average agricultural pay per month as RMB 23.9. The incomes of the communes he visited varied over a range of 1:4; of the teams in the communes, by 1:2; and of the members of the team, by 1:3.[40]

To the income received from agricultural labour on public land must be added the income from 'sideline' activities. Here the variation between households is extreme, depending upon the availability of a market. Burki estimates such work adds another twenty per cent to

166

rural incomes; Deleyne argues that private agricultural activity adds on average fifteen per cent with a maximum of thirty per cent.[41] In sum, a reasonable guess would be that the span of rural incomes covers a range of about 1:12.

There is little guide as to the condition of the poor. Some things are cheaper in the countryside, and foodstuffs from private plots safeguard rural families to a greater degree than urban; the income figures perhaps thus exaggerate the gap. The Hopei commune claimed that its richest families consumed 305 kilograms of grain per head per year, and the poor, 207 kilograms, a figure well above the urban ration of 175 kilograms. Nonetheless, families in the commune presumably had to borrow to make up their food and clothing. There is no information on the extent of rural borrowing apart from the fact of occasional campaigns to recover outstanding debts.[42]

Other inequalities persist. Women apparently can earn no more than seven to eight points per day, no matter how hard they work, whereas men can reach nine to ten. This entrenches a 'division of labour' that is not counted among Mao's Three Great Differences. There seems to be more equality between men and women in urban areas but, as in so many countries, women tend to be concentrated in the low-paying jobs – down to the notorious example once raised in the Chinese press (and then forgotten), the old women night soil cleaners of Peking. The differential work point system is justified on the grounds that women are physically less strong than men, a stock rationalization in most societies, and one contradicted in China by the use of women in heavy manual occupations.

While the vast rural sector remains outside a standard national pay structure, any aspiration to greater income equality is clearly utopian. The government does not raise the question. Its concern at most is with the urban minority, and even then it is with preventing people *expressing* their different incomes in different consumption standards rather than changing the differentials themselves. Nevertheless, the differences are expressed – between the cadre with leather shoes and tailored clothes, living in an apartment with a private kitchen, bathroom and running water, and those with cloth shoes, crammed in dormitories; between the city technician with a steel bicycle, a radio, a fountain pen, smoking Red Lantern cigarettes, and the worker who owns none of these things and smokes '10,000 Li' cigarettes.[43] Prices are low, but incomes are very low. A visitor reports, for example, that in one factory, monthly wages ranged between RMB 36 and RMB 53; a twenty-five-year-old could expect to earn about RMB 40, of which RMB 6 would go on rent and electricity, the remainder being divided between food (two meals a day in the factory canteen cost RMB 10 a month), clothing and cigarettes; almost everyone smoked, and an average-priced packet of cigarettes would take more than a quarter of the monthly wage.[44]

In the countryside, some families can afford new and better housing, can spend open-handedly on festivals, weddings and durables (bicycles, watches, radios, sewing machines); they eat white rice at all meals and, quite often, meat; their sons are able to continue in education, and easily find brides. Yet other families do not earn enough work points to buy their grain ration, persistently fall into debt (which, over a year, can accumulate to several hundred yuan); they eat congee, not white rice and, in some villages, depend on public relief grain.[45] The policy of local 'self-reliance', meeting local needs from local resources, exaggerates such problems; the rich areas no doubt would be happy to be left alone to be 'self-reliant' while devil take the poor.

Given the surprising degree of inequality evident in the official income figures, how is it that the general impression is of such relative equality? The secret lies partly in the stigma attached to conspicuous consumption, partly in the lack of typical Western signs of inequality and in the insensitivity of foreign visitors to the language of social status in China, but above all in the rationing system and the limited supply of goods available for purchase. Rationing imposes a certain equality of basic consumption – as it did in Russia in the 1930s and in Britain during the Second World War – and the limited supply of consumer durables resulting from the State's concentration on heavy industry makes it difficult for the better-off to express higher incomes fully.

There are many other components in consumption which cannot be quantified. Services and housing – where available – are relatively cheap, and so raise the real value of urban incomes. But on the other hand, there is no income tax, and the State's tax revenue comes entirely from indirect taxation, particularly on consumer durables. The availability of services must be a continuing problem, despite the great improvements made since 1949. For example, the number of hospital beds has increased dramatically since that year and may now have reached one million – or roughly one bed to every 800–900 people, compared to average figures in Europe of one bed to every 46–180 people.

There are reports in recent years of a narrowing of differentials, of pay cuts at the top, and of a bunching of workers in the middle grades of the eight grade system. But, as should now be clear, such changes – even if there were firm and comprehensive information – would barely change the national picture of differentials, and might indeed only increase the gap between top pay and the middle wage grades, or between the élite and the mass of urban and rural poor. China has to go a long way to reach the degree of equality in the Russia of the New Economic Policy, let alone anything the 1917 Bolshevik leadership would have regarded as 'socialism'. The overall picture is of great stability and considerable differences.

12

DEMOCRACY

The subject of 'democracy' is more confused than any so far discussed. There are few régimes in the world which do not call themselves 'democratic', regardless of local institutions. As a result, it is tempting to make a clean sweep and argue that 'democratic' means nothing of any importance. Yet to do that is to abandon what Marx saw as the essence of the struggle for socialism: freedom, the self-emancipation of the majority.

The Marxists indicted the form of 'democracy' practised in the representative institutions of capitalism as parliamentarianism. Parliament was a 'talking shop', a decorative façade for the 'dictatorship of the bourgeoisie'. Real power was exercised behind the scenes in the offices of the State and the boardrooms of great companies. Here, the decisions were made which determined the material conditions of the majority; they were not exposed to public debate, which was restricted to the superficial questions of what bourgeois democracy called 'politics'.

The critique of parliament, however, was not a rejection of democracy itself. Lenin wrote: 'The way out of parliamentarianism is not, of course, the abolition of representative institutions and the electoral principle, but the conversion of the representative institutions from mere "talking shops" into working bodies.'[46] For, Lenin continues: 'We cannot imagine democracy, not even proletarian democracy, without representative institutions, but we can and *must* think of democracy without parliamentarianism.'[47] The task was two-fold: to fuse real power with the assembly so that it became an executive, so that the execution of policy was directly related to those who elected the members of the assembly; and to establish open elections to the assembly on a free debate of the real issues. Such a procedure would indeed be rejected both by the bourgeoisie and by those on the Left who believed socialism was incapable of winning majority support in an open contest and must therefore be imposed by a minority.

But what was the 'real power' the assembly must direct?

(i) The State
The State is the instrument of power of a ruling class. Its existence, according to Engels, 'is the admission that this society has become entangled in an insoluble contradiction with itself, that it is cleft into irreconcilable antagonism which it is powerless to dispel'.

How does it subordinate society? Through its legal monopoly of the use of physical power, what Lenin calls 'armed bodies of men' – the army, the police, the secret police, the prisons, backed by the law and the courts. This is the ultimate line of defence of the ruling class and its answer to the 'irreconcilable class antagonisms'.

Many socialists agreed with this argument in the late nineteenth century. One group then went on to propose that, where open elections and the right to form a government existed, socialists should contest in order to capture power *within* the existing institutions. Once in control of the 'armed bodies of men', they could be used to advance the purposes of the working class as easily as they had previously been used to defend the ruling class. Gradually, the balance of class power could be shifted by successive waves of reforms without open violence of civil war, because now the workers controlled the State's army and police.

It would have been an excellent course of action if practicable. But it was absurd to suppose the State, constructed and designed to achieve one set of purposes, could be transformed into its opposite just by the addition of a group of different directors. The State was not a machine, depending for its direction on whoever sat in the driving seat. It was a set of men and women, themselves dedicated to the purposes for which the State had been created. Adding a few socialists to the existing State was not a method of changing its direction; it was a method by which the existing State colonized the socialists.

The only possibility of a real revolution came, not through endeavouring to redirect the existing State, but, in the words of Marx, Engels and Lenin, *smashing* it. It followed that, in the struggle for power, the socialists could not make themselves dependent upon the existing State for their power without entirely losing their purpose. They must base themselves upon the working class, keeping working-class institutions firmly independent of the existing State and rooted, not in the existing army and police, but in the workers' control of production, control of the very surplus upon which the existing State depended.

That was not the end of the question. Destroying the old State machine did not destroy its social foundations, the bourgeoisie. They would endeavour to mobilize armed force to reconquer power. To prevent such a reconquest, the workers would need a new apparatus of State power, itself the product of the 'irreconcilable class antagonisms'. On this question, Engels' logic was implacable: 'As before, the State is only a transitional institution which is used in the struggle, in the revolution, in order to hold down one's adversaries by force. *It is pure nonsense to speak of a free people's State*: so long as the proletariat needs the State, it does not need it in the interests of freedom but in order to hold down its adversaries, and as soon as it becomes possible to speak of freedom, the State as such ceases to exist.'[48]

But to create a new State, whether described as 'workers' or not, would surely be to perpetutate the oppression that the revolution was supposedly designed to end? Would not the new State simply degenerate once more into a force oppressing the majority? Such a state of affairs could not be prevented if the State became independent of its social basis, the working class. The bourgeoisie had succeeded in keeping *its* State subordinate to its purposes. How could the working class achieve the same alignment of the State and its own interests?

Marx used the Paris Commune – in his view, the first historical example of the 'dictatorship of the proletariat' – as the model for this relationship. Having suppressed the standing army of the old régime (the first decree of the Commune), workers' militia became the armed forces defending the Commune; all officials in the militia were to be elected, and subject to recall by their electors; all workers were at some stage to participate in the militia. The Commune itself was composed of delegates, a majority of them working men and women, elected on universal suffrage, subject to recall and replacement by the electors at any time, and remunerated by pay no higher than that received by an ordinary worker (with no special or additional privileges). Furthermore, the officials of the Commune were also to be elected, subject to recall and replacement by the electors, and to be supervised by the majority; all were expected in due course to serve as officials of the Commune. Finally, the Commune delegates were not elected to *comment* on policy (or such aspects of policy as the government was pleased to divulge to them), but to formulate and implement it, to be 'responsible' directly for carrying out the wishes of the majority.

There was one necessary precondition for such a system to work. All the main items of Commune policy, practice and finance must be public, accessible to majority consideration and discussion. Otherwise, knowledge itself became the secret power of the bureacracy, and the majority could no longer make a responsible decision on what its State should do. The exercise of power had to be dragged into the light of public discussion, so that the officials were distinguished solely by temporary task, not by knowledge, privilege or power.

Whatever else the Commune achieved, it laid down a set of criteria by which 'democracy' can be judged in any country. Such a system offered the promise of something else, the dissolution of the State itself – as Lenin put it: 'Democracy, introduced as fully and consistently as is generally conceivable, is transformed from bourgeois democracy into proletarian democracy; from the State [i.e. a special force for the suppression of a particular class] into something which is no longer really a State.'[49]

(ii) The Soviet Republic

The Bolsheviks refused to seize power until they had won a majority in the elected institutions of the working class, the Soviets. Their slogan was not, 'Replace the Provisional Government' (that is, taking over the existing State machine), but 'All power to the Soviets'. The Soviets already consisted of working men and women, elected and subject to recall, and around it there already existed workers' militia, an alternative to the established army. Once in power, the new government laid it down that all army commanders were to be elected; all ranks, titles, decorations and special privileges in the officer corps were to be abolished.

The moment was brief. The tight hold of civil war closed in on the infant republic, threatening to strangle Moscow. The struggle of the new government to survive imposed a different logic. For example, too few men volunteered for the armed forces to fight the White armies; either the régime reconciled itself to defeat and destruction, or it had to introduce conscription. Again, there was a shortage of military experience and competence; the White armies left no time for the new worker soldiers to learn how to fight. With great reluctance, the new government began to recruit former Tsarist officers. But such recruits were not elected by the troops in their units; they had to be appointed from above, with a special commissar attached to watch their every move, lest, in the exercise of power, they betray the purpose of the revolution. Yet the régime did not pretend that this was 'socialism'; it was a temporary expedient, made necessary only by the most urgent threat to the survival of Soviet power; a popular militia in which all participated remained the aim.

Given the backwardness of Russia and the failure of the revolution in industrialized Europe, the temporary slowly became the permanent, the 'retreat' became rationalized as an advance. The spirit of the régime's 'armed bodies of men' changed, and whether the commanders were former workers or Tsarist officers, their minds were slowly reshaped to accord to their real social life, that of an élite. One old Bolshevik recalls: 'They [the Red Army commanders] became members of the new officers' group, and no agitation whatsoever, nor beautiful speeches about the necessity of contact with the masses, would be of any avail. The conditions of existence are stronger than kind wishes.'[50] The political commissars appointed to represent the supervision of the working class over the commanders in due course succumbed, and were colonized by the commanders. The real changes were faster than those in the symbols; distinctive and pretentious uniforms, medals, epaulettes, gold braid, the elaborate hierarchy of rank, these came later. By the Second World War, the process was fully accomplished; commanders now, far from being elected, were vested with virtually absolute power over the troops. Indeed, even friendliness between men and officers was frowned upon. As one general put it: 'The hail-fellow-well-met spirit in the relationships between a commander and a subordinate can have no place in the Red Army. Discussion of any kind is absolutely prohibited among subordinates.'[51]

The transformation of the 'armed bodies of men' was only one symptom of social change in Russia. It could not take place in isolation; the changes were impelled by factors which had similar effects on the most important index of democracy, the Soviets, the assemblies of worker, soldier and peasant delegates.

The congress of Soviets met five times in 1918 and, thereafter, once a year until 1922. The USSR was formally declared in 1923, and the Congress met in 1924 and 1925, then every two years up to 1931. By then it was already clear that all the major decisions of the government were taken independently of the sessions of the Soviet. The members were no longer subject to recall; nor were they bound to receive no more than the average pay of working men; nor did they implement policy. The Central Executive Committee, which was supposedly the 'supreme organ of the Soviet Republic', met for only about ten days a year, a period quite insufficient even to appraise government policy, let alone initiate it. After Stalin's purges, its decisions were invariably unanimous. None of the major changes of policy were discussed before they were implemented, and usually the government's budget was ratified only long after it had come into effect.

Whether through the Soviet or the party, it was impossible for the majority of the citizens of the Soviet Union to exercise power. The sheer information needed to decide the main issues of policy – investment, defence, welfare, wages – was not publicly available, even supposing the institutions to express majority opinion had existed. There was – and is today – no way of removing or changing the Russian leadership except through a purge or a coup, an operation which can only be carried out *within* the bureaucracy.

Such a system does not prevent the national leadership from criticizing its subordinates, indeed *blaming* them for actions which prompt more than usual popular resentment. Stalin often attacked 'commandism', 'arrogance' by the cadres, bureaucratism, and occasionally purged large numbers of the party. His criticism was of a bad *style* of leadership, not of the structure of power. When he anathematized 'bureaucracy' he was not attacking the State of which he stood at the apex. Nor was he attacking the central decisions that compelled the cadres to behave in the way they did.

The changes in the Soviet Union muddled the key concepts, just as the evolution of representative institutions in Western capitalist countries had done. Now 'democracy' became, not the rule of the majority, but a government that, whatever its policy, 'represented' the people. In practice, at best it consulted them. Criticism of the style of the officials of the State was substituted for the critique of the existence of the State itself. The existence of 'armed bodies of men' came to be not the expression of 'irreconcilable class antagonisms' but the 'democratic' instrument of – what for Marx and Lenin was a contradiction in terms – a 'classless State' of the 'People'.

(iii) The Chinese Communist leadership and democracy

The Chinese Communist party's view of democracy was taken from the Russia of the 1930s. Democracy is a *style* of relationship between cadres and non-cadres, between party leaders and cadres, not the subordination of power to the majority. In this sense 'democracy' is not directly about power at all.

Mao, for example, argues: 'All leading members within the Party must promote democracy and let people speak out. What are the limits? One is that we must observe Party discipline, the minority must obey the majority, and the whole Party should obey the Centre.'[52] The majority here is ambiguous. In practice, it means the leadership's decision, since there is no mechanism available to identify what the majority of party members want. In the PLA Mao also calls for democracy, and explains what he means: [the leadership] 'must have a democratic style of work when something comes up, they must consult the comrades, give full deliberation to matters, and absolutely listen to the various views. Opposition views must be presented. Do not practise, "what I say counts".'[53]

The same applies to the relationship between cadres and non-cadres: 'An overwhelming majority of these people must be made to attend

175

meetings and air their views. Only thus can opposition views be established, contradictions exposed, the truth uncovered and the movement unfolded.'[54] Of course, in the original conception of democracy, it did not depend upon the leadership 'practising' it: majority control ensured that the leadership had no alternative.

At no stage has it been suggested that the officials of the State should be elected, subject to recall, paid no more than average wages. The bureaucracy of the Chinese State is appointed, works in secrecy, and is privileged by income and status. Mao objects not to the existence of such a bureaucracy, but to the style inevitably engendered by its monopoly of power: 'The overlord style, the three bad styles of work, the five undesirable airs, and the contempt for the common labourer'. The theme recurred throughout the history of the People's Republic. Yet at no stage did Mao propose the classical solution, manifested in the Paris Commune – elections. The most he offered was 'consultation', which in no way bound the leadership: 'We consult the people, the workers, the peasants, the capitalists, the petty bourgeoisie and the democratic parties, on whatever we plan to do. You can call us the consulting government. We do not put on a stern face and lecture the people. We do not give anyone a stunning blow if his opinions are not sound.'[55] It was disingenuous, since those who received 'stunning blows' were classified as 'counter-revolutionaries', not part of the 'people'. For example, in the Hundred Flowers campaign, Mao recalled later: 'After the events in Hungary, we allowed scattered free expression of opinion and tens of thousands of little Hungaries appeared . . . over 400,000 rightists had to be purged.'[56]

Because Mao regarded the preservation of the State and its bureaucracy as an absolute priority he could not urge the building of an alternative basis of popular power with which to supervise the bureaucracy. For the Chairman, the aim was always: 'We should get rid of the enemy. Rigid bureaucrats should be reformed into creative bureaucrats. If after a long time they can't be creative then we should get rid of them.'[57] Leaders are required to change, not their objective position of superior power and income, but simply their subjective attitude – they 'must *adopt an attitude* of genuine equality towards the cadres and masses, and *make people feel* that relationships among men are truly equal . . . No matter how high one's position, one must *appear* among people as an ordinary worker. One must not assume airs; one must get rid of bureaucratism.'[58]

As in the West, it is all a matter of projecting the right image. If democratic control actually existed, it would be unnecessary to deliver such homilies, for mass power would establish both equality of income (so that there would be no trouble about curbing conspicuous consumption) and a style of leadership appropriate to the task.

Mao has rarely shown any interest in establishing elections as a mechanism of control. Perhaps, in the heady days of 1966, he was persuaded to adopt the electoral principle, for clause 9 of his famous Sixteen Points did argue that 'it is necessary to introduce a system of general elections like that of the Paris Commune, for electing members to the Cultural Revolution Committees and Groups and delegates to the Cultural Revolution Congresses'. *Red Flag* went further: 'All leaders must be elected by the people; the elected must be servants of the people and be submitted to their supervision; the electors have the right to recall at any time.'

The moment was brief. More characteristically, Mao says, 'As far as I am concerned, election is merely a fancy word, and I do not feel that there is any genuine election.'[59] The press duly supports the Chairman in one of his characteristically misleading tags: 'Blind faith in elections is also a form of conservative thinking.'[60] Indeed it is, but that is not an argument against having elections, any more than the critique of parliamentarianism is an argument against *any* form of democracy! That however is the conclusion Mao draws – for example, in his discussion with President Pompidou over the instability of government under the Fourth Republic: 'Napoleon's methods were best. He dissolved all the assemblies, and he himself chose the people to govern with.'[61] How can he praise the *method* of counter-revolution independently of its purpose?

The confusion of 'participation' with 'majority control' affects each issue. For example, on occasions Mao has espoused the decentralization of power. At other times, he cites an aphorism from Lenin: 'Absolute centralization and the strictest discipline of the proletariat constitutes one of the fundamental conditions for victory over the bourgeoisie.' The contradiction is only resolved when we examine Mao's definition of 'decentralization': 'Concentrate important powers in one hand;/Diffuse less important ones.'[62]

The relationship between cadres and mass 'is comparable to that between fish and water'. It is clearly absurd to suggest that the water should control, direct or supervise the fish. Its role is merely to supply a medium for the fish, to support the qualitatively different élite; no matter how hard the water tries, it can never become a fish. If any are so misguided as to try, they promptly become 'rightists' and 'counter-revolutionaries'. Indeed, the masses are dangerous in such circumstances – 'Once the masses are aroused, they become blind' – and being blind, no longer supply that passive water which supports the fish, which swims in

177

it to power. As always, embedded in the Populism is élitism.

But perhaps Mao's conception of democracy is not borne out in practice? Perhaps the actual institutional structure of modern China goes much further than the Chairman was prepared to put into words. What is the record?

(iv) Democracy in China

When the Communist party came to power, as we have seen, it did not 'smash' the old State, nor dissolve the Kuomintang's 'armed bodies of men'. The new government took over the existing State machine and absorbed the Kuomintang armies into the PLA. There were no workers or peasant delegate bodies which played other than a purely supporting role in the conquest of power. In most of China, the PLA administered without supervision.

However, four years after coming to power, the government set about creating some basis for its own legitimacy by setting up the National People's Congress (NPC). So far as Mao was concerned, 'the Soviet of the Soviet Union and the People's Congress are both representative assemblies. Only in name are they different.'[63] In origin, however, the institutions were completely different. The NPC did not exist in 1949. It played no role as an independent power contesting with the Kuomintang government for national authority. It was invented by the new government under the electoral law of March 1953, and invested with no more than a puppet's life. The Soviet had to be emasculated by the party leadership. No such problem arose in China.

The membership of the Congress was to be elected by a series of electoral colleges at different administrative levels, based finally upon the universal suffrage of all adults over eighteen. There was no provision for the recall of the elected (indeed, the system of intervening electoral colleges made it impossible to establish any relationship between a representative and a section of the voters), nor for them to be paid an average working man's wage. The Congress was to be elected every four years, and to meet in annual session. One of its tasks was to elect the Head of State and his deputy, the Prime Minister and the State Council, the ministers of the government.

The first round of elections created some five million representatives at the lowest levels, who then proceeded to vote for 16,806 deputies to meet at the provincial and city level. These then elected 1,141 deputies to attend the first NPC, which was held between 15 and 28 September 1954. The Congress created a Standing Committee to meet twice a month when the Congress was not in session, to supervise the government, protect the constitution and decide on the sacking and appointment of ministers.

In practice, however, the first NPC did not meet annually; it met only twice (in 1954 and 1956). Elections were held for the Second NPC and it met six months behind the constitutional schedule, in April 1959. The second, like the first, managed only one other session (in 1960). However, the Third Congress was nearly two years late (meeting from 21 December 1964 to 4 January 1965), and was not preceded by any lower level elections. The number of deputies had been increased to about 3,000 (with 1,000 observers). So far as can be seen, the Third NPC had no subsequent sessions. The Fourth NPC did not meet for another *eleven* years. When it did meet, in January 1975, the 2,864 deputies were required to ratify, seven years after the event, the removal of the Head of State (Liu Shao-ch'i) and the Defence Minister (Lin Piao), and the decimation of much of the government. The Fifth NPC – scheduled for 1978 – was to be composed, according to Hua, of 'outstanding people from various fields of work, and representative personages . . . elected deputies . . . through full discussion and democratic consultations'.

Since the NPC meets for a fortnight at most even when it is summoned, there is no question of it supervising the government or changing the leadership. Its position is, if possible, even more insignificant than that of the Supreme Soviet in Russia (which has, however, a slightly better record in meeting). The NPC is part of the decorative façade of the State; indeed, it is more an empty 'talking shop' than those parliaments in Western countries criticized by Lenin. The major items of policy – the Korean War, the agrarian reform, the first Five Year Plan, the Great Leap Forward, the break with the Soviet Union, the Cultural Revolution, the détente with the United States, all took place without the participation of the NPC.

Perhaps the party Congress provides an alternative mechanism for popular control? Under the 1945 party constitution (passed at the Seventh Congress), the Congress was to meet annually, the delegates being elected by lower party congresses every five years. But the Eighth party Congress did not meet for eleven years, until 1956, and there was only one other session, in 1958. The Congress sessions lasted less than two weeks, so that it could scarcely do more than react, after the event, to a fraction of the work of its instrument, the Central Committee. The Eighth Congress ended its official term of life in 1961, but the Ninth Congress did not meet until 1969, again eleven years after its predecessor. At the Ninth Congress, it was acknowledged that the 'delegates' were not elected by lower party congresses, but, in the euphemism of the text, 'through democratic consultation'. The Ninth Congress had long

179

been rumoured but, given the turmoil of the Cultural Revolution, apparently could not be called with a secure majority for the leadership. When General Hsueh Fu-chih, head of the Peking Municipal Revolutionary Committee, announced the Ninth Congress to the Red Guards in October 1968, he promised it would be reorganized from the top so that the party old guard would not dominate it, and that the 'delegates' would be increased from 1,000 to 10,000. By the time of the Ninth Congress, however, the Red Guards had been defeated, and there was no need for such a concession.

The Ninth Congress was required to ratify the removal of the party Chairman's deputy, Liu Shao-ch'i, the general secretary, Teng Hsiao-p'ing, and a majority of the Central Committee. It was also required to ratify a new second-in-command to Mao, Lin Piao, whose elevation had occurred two years earlier. It was only four years to the Tenth Congress (the first time a Congress had been held on time since 1945) and the removal of Lin Piao and his associates in August 1973.

The Congress had the official task of electing a Central Committee to represent the Congress between sessions. The Central Committee numbered about seventy-seven members and alternates in 1945, 170 in 1956 (twenty-five more alternates were added at the second session in 1958) and 279 in 1969. The Central Committee was required to meet at least twice per year under the 1956 constitution. In fact, it met only twelve times in the thirteen years (1956–69) between the Eighth and Ninth Congresses. Furthermore, its Eleventh Plenum (August 1966) permitted the attendance of an unknown number of unelected Red Guards, responsible to no one except the party Chairman. At the Twelfth Plenum in October 1968, when Liu Shao-ch'i was officially denounced, non-members are said to have been granted voting rights, thus disenfranchising the supposed electors, the delegates to the party Congress.

Power was no more vested in the party Congress than it was in the NPC. Nor was it located in the Central Committee. Central Committee membership, like membership of the Standing Committee of the NPC, was merely a high honour. It was the Political Bureau of the Central Committee which came closer to power. Within the Politburo, its Standing Committee was, at various times, the key institution. However, in the Cultural Revolution, even that was not enough, and an entirely new body, the Cultural Revolution Group, was created, without a semblance of democratic legitimacy, to transmit 'Mao Tse-tung thought'. In the final analysis, only Mao himself represented the majority; what he thought was, by definition, the will of the majority, and no actual majority at any level of Chinese society was summoned to give a real verdict. In the unions, as we have seen, there was no mechanism for electing a representative leadership. On the revolutionary committees set up during the Cultural Revolution, 'established', as the party said, 'not by elections but by relying upon action by the broad revolutionary masses', mediated by the 'leadership of the PLA' at all levels, there was similarly no method for even formulating, let alone expressing, a majority will.[64] All such bodies were 'transmission belts', not for the controlling power of the majority over the leadership of China, but for the party centre over the majority. All the machinery of mass assemblies, criticism and self-criticism, cadre participation in manual labour, big character posters, popular education, are necessary precisely because democracy in any serious sense does not exist.

Even if the institutions existed, the basic information upon which the majority could make a responsible decision is not available. The Chinese State adopted from Russia the machinery of censorship and information control. No continuous sets of figures on the major sectors of the economy, on the course of popular consumption or any other matter of importance have been published since 1959. Finding out what has happened requires full-time specialized work for anyone not in the inner circle of leadership, a task certainly beyond the majority of Chinese. Mao has supported that control of information. Not only has he not raised the question, on some occasions he has positively increased the controls. For example, in 1956 he instructed the party centre to circulate Khrushchev's secret speech criticizing Stalin at the Twentieth Congress of the Soviet Communist party only to local and county party committee secretaries; it must not be discussed in the press or 'among the masses'.[65] Again, he urged the cadres to unite to protect 'the secrets of the State' in the turmoil of the Cultural Revolution. Neither the budget figures nor the Five Year Plans are publicly available. As one sympathetic observer remarked of the Second Plan: 'For the first time in a socialist régime, a whole people was ordered to embark on a Five Year Plan without being informed of the targets.'[66]

The cadres of the party have a better chance of being informed. For example, at some levels they have access to a daily reference bulletin, *Tsan Kao Hsiao Hsi*, and to reprints of foreign newspaper articles, while senior PLA officers have a confidential internal publication. But such privileged information in no way represents democracy in China, even if it is a precondition for the party leadership carrying the support of its immediate followers. Nor does it mean the cadres do not get confused by the shifts and changes of policy. One of the official commentators on the Tenth Party Congress reproved those cadres who believed the leadership struggle was too complicated to understand. 'In fact', he pronounced, 'this involves the long-standing question of whether or not the two-line struggle can be known . . . Those who believe in the incomprehensibility of the two-line struggle are completely wrong.'[67] After all the newspaper words and radio diatribes, *still* it was a 'long-standing question', even for party cadres! How much more 'incomprehensible' was it to those many millions who did not have access to the privileged information of the cadre?

The key institutions of the Chinese State, its 'armed bodies of men', its police force, its bureaucracy with its privileges and secrets, all survived the Cultural Revolution intact. It had been no part of Mao's intention that they should not survive even if particular individuals were removed (and many of those, only temporarily). Whether before the Cultural Revolution or afterwards, none of China's institutions accorded with the basic criteria of 'proletarian democracy' as outlined by Marx and Lenin. They do not even accord with the weak criteria of 'bourgeois democracy'. Nor can they, when the régime is dedicated to capital accumulation as the condition of its national survival. The few who did take Lenin's criteria seriously, like Sheng-wu-lien and Li Yi-che, were hounded as 'counter-revolutionaries' just as they would have been in the Soviet Union for that matter.

Neither in terms of 'equality', let alone 'democracy', it seems, is China distinguished qualitatively from many of the other States of the world. What of the central purpose of the party's leadership since 1949, the strengthening of China's national independence?

13

NATIONAL INDEPENDENCE

National independence – the ability of a State to secure and defend its territory, to deter potential threats and safeguard its future in conditions of competition between the world's dominant powers – requires a level of military preparedness commensurate with the nature of the threat. But the conditions of warfare are laid down by the existing level of development of the world defence industries. Even in the late nineteenth century, the development of defence industries required the transformation of economies. Engels noted this in the 1890s: 'From the moment warfare became a branch of the *grande industrie* (iron clad ships, rifled artillery, quickfiring and repeating cannons, repeating rifles, steel covered bullets, smokeless powder, etc.), *la grande industrie*, without which all these things cannot be made, became a political necessity. All these things cannot be had without a highly developed metal manufacture. And that manufacture cannot be had without a corresponding development in all other branches of manufacture, especially textiles.'[68] In sum, national independence requires 'economic development'.

The Chinese leadership were fully aware of this. Indeed, the justification of the 1949 revolution was that it 'set free the productive forces' to provide the basis for national independence'. Mao was even prepared to put a figure on the required target: 'During the transition period, it is necessary "to enable the productive forces to obtain a guarantee of the development required by a socialist victory". In so far as China is concerned, we require at least about 100 million to 200 million tons of steel [production annually]. Prior to this year [1959?], what we did was principally to clear the way for the development of our productive forces. The development of the socialist productive forces of our country actually has just begun.'[69] Steel alone was not enough; the whole range of modern output was required as soon as possible, all the components of contemporary national power, including the most advanced weapons:

183

'Yes, we must have them . . . no matter what country, no matter what missiles, atomic bombs, hydrogen bombs, we must surpass them. I have said before, when the atomic bomb is exploded, even if one half of mankind perishes, there will still be one half left.'[70]

(i) Economic development

In Marx's terms, 'economic development' is a long process whereby capital is accumulated in the competition between capitalists – the productivity of labour is continuously raised and a mainly low-productivity, agricultural society transformed into an urban industrial one. The capital is derived from the surplus of unpaid labour appropriated by the employers from those 'with nothing to sell but their labour power', and from the ransacking of agriculture and colonies. In the process, production, population, power, ownership and control are centralized on an unprecedented scale.

The accumulation of capital imposes upon society a division of labour which is quite new – between those who personify capital, whose social function is to accumulate and to organize society in order that accumulation should take place, and those whose surplus is the basis for accumulation. The two social roles cannot exist without each other – on the one hand, 'an independent social power, i.e. as the power of a part of society, it maintains itself and increases by exchange for direct living labour power. The existence of a class which possesses nothing but its capacity for labour is a necessary prerequisite of capital.'[71] The whole of society is, then, organized around this central division. All other divisions – among them, Mao's Three Great Differences – are subsidiary to this core in so far as the capitalists are successful in establishing their discipline over society as a whole.

(ii) The State

However, what happens where the dynamic of domestic competition between private capitalists does not exist, where the driving force – the struggle of each individual capital to secure its survival – does not operate? If a society could completely isolate itself, State ownership of the means of production would end the dynamic of competition and so the drive to accumulate. What would this mean in a backward economy? A return to *pre-industrial* stagnation in which the consumption needs of the ruling class would determine the level of output, not the drive for supremacy of the capitalists. The same situation would occur if the whole world economic system were directed from one centre: it would spell the end of what Marx calls 'capitalism' in so far as competition ceased.

However, neither state of affairs is a practical possibility in the contemporary world without a major political transformation. The competition of private capitals *within* one country is replaced, where the State owns the entire national economy, by the competition between the world's national capitals, States. The 'capitalist economy' today does not refer to a national, but to a global, system, subordinating each national capital as formerly the national market subordinated each private firm. It is for this reason that each economically backward State is compelled, as the condition of its survival, to industrialize, to accumulate capital.

Can a different 'ideology' defeat this logic? Only in the sense that a private employer can defeat the logic of the market. Very large capitalists can to some extent attain greater autonomy, provided they are protected by the local State. The richest world powers can, when the system booms, similarly afford greater leeway. The poorer an economy – the smaller and more dependent a firm – the more its reactions become predetermined by external forces. Of course, every ruling class justifies its existence on the grounds that it can control events, it can master its environment. Its power, it says, is not dependent upon the surplus it can extract from the people but on its capacity to embody the wishes of the people. If it were possible, simply by willing, for a régime to transform objective circumstances, then the axioms of Marx's materialism would become false – ideas, not the material basis of society, would determine events. But surely, it might be argued, this means there are no alternatives to capitalism, regardless of local fashions? That is the case if we restrict ourselves to *national* power, just as it would have been the case if someone in the nineteenth century had talked of 'organizing socialism' in a single firm, as if it could escape the discipline of the market in which it operated. We will return to the question in Part VI.

Competition between States differs from that between firms. Each State must be capable of defending itself but military competition is not the sole influence on a domestic State-owned economy. The need to finance imports, whether of foodstuffs – as in the case of the Soviet Union's massive imports of grain in 1974 – or industrial equipment and components of advanced technical quality is another form of discipline imposed by the world system upon all its parts. The 1974–8 slump illustrates this. Soviet borrowing from advanced capitalist countries to finance its imports has become in recent years, with rising interest rates and a growing trade deficit, an important factor in Russian domestic planning.[72] World market prices govern its external trade even with its

185

Eastern Bloc partners. The trade agreements utilize world prices, and transactions are increasingly settled in Western currencies in order to help the Soviet Union overcome its difficulties with the West.

The more backward an economy, the less it depends on external forces for immediate economic survival, but the more it depends upon them to overcome domestic backwardness, to promote modernization. Since all the State-owned economies are devoted to industrialization,[73] the dependence of the smaller and more backward countries on external assistance to achieve domestic transformation is great.*

Involvement in world trade, in capitalism itself, assists domestic growth and development when the system booms. But in slump, it imposes contraction on the national economy, whether the means of production are owned by the State or not. National planning can offset some of the effects of the crisis, but basically it must also transmit the external disciplines of the 'law of value', rather than frustrate them.

Despite the difficulties, the Societ Union did accomplish the process of domestic transformation in the 1930s and 1940s, and did so despite, for much of the time, a world slump of unprecedented severity. Can every country repeat that process? The conditions have changed. The advanced capitalist powers dominate the world market more than ever before. In all fields, the production of the advanced concentrations of capital defeat smaller rivals in any open contest. The early stages of industrializaton are jeopardized unless a backward State can exclude competition; but excluding competition shuts off the sources of technology and advanced inputs, so that the process becomes more costly, inefficient and long-drawn-out.

Furthermore, the technology has changed. Not only does it cost more, it produces relatively few jobs. It also produces a faster stream of output. This is the source of the contemporary paradox: the mass of backward countries have increased their industrial output more rapidly than did the European powers in the nineteenth century, but with

* Take, for example, the two richest of the backward countries of the Eastern Bloc, Cuba and North Korea. Both suffered more severely in the current crisis than the Soviet Union, but for the same reasons. Despite continued Russian assistance, Cuba was obliged to reshape its programme of economic development for 1976, to slow down drastically its future growth, as a result of what Fidel Castro calls 'the worse [slump] since the 1930s'; all this, despite a loan of £115 million by two hundred international banks in October 1975; for the Cubans, the subordination of their economy to the world crisis is most vividly demonstrated by a cut in the coffee ration from forty-three to thirty grammes a week.[74] In the case of North Korea, the scale of its current debts (primarily to banks in Japan and eight other Western countries) – about US $430 million – as well its severe balance of payments difficulties has forced it to default on its loan servicing payments, not to mention forcing its diplomats abroad to use their position for smuggling.[75] Vietnam, far poorer and terribly ravaged by war, is, at the time of writing, appealing for foreign private capital.[76]

186

decreasing success in employing the existing labour force. Enclaves of high productivity industry, colonies of advanced production, coexist in a sea of urban and rural poor. The ruling class certainly secures an industrial basis for its power, but without being able to implement the 'historic task of the bourgeoisie': the tranformation of society or what Marx called the 'socialization of the labour force'.

Some of the statistics illustrate the nature of the problem. For example, between 1925 and 1960, the countries of Latin America experienced a *decline* in employment in manufacturing industry (as a proportion of the non-agricultural labour force) – from 35.4 to 27.1 per cent. In the period of most rapid industrial growth, from 1950 to 1965, employment in manufacturing industry (as a proportion of the total labour force) declined, albeit at a slower rate, from 14.2 to 13.8 per cent. Latin America is the most advanced of the backward continents. Nonetheless, the overall picture is not impressive. Between 1920 and 1950, the proportion of the total labour force employed in manufacturing in all the backward countries together showed a slight decline, from 8.5 to 7.6 per cent, and then a slight increase up to 1960 (to 8.9 per cent).[77] Yet this has been the period of the most rapid growth in history. The next quarter of a century looks unlikely to repeat the performance of the last. World capitalism falters long before it has touched the lives of the majority of the world's population.

Thus, if China – one of the poorest countries of the world – can provide a different model of economic development, can steadily narrow the gap between backward and advanced, and transform the real material conditions of the majority of Chinese, it would be a staggering achievement. The Chinese Communist party would have shown itself to be a totally new force, capable of defeating the imperatives of backwardness in the peculiarly obdurate circumstances of the second half of the twentieth century. To do so on an isolated national basis, denied access to the accumulated resources of the world economy held by the advanced powers, would be a triumph indeed.

(iii) A different 'model'?

There is little evidence for the existence of a different model of development in the statements of China's leadership. Consistently they have measured their success by Stalin's central criterion – the growth of heavy industry, and in particular of steel. Such a policy imposes the maximum rate of accumulation, but, on the theory, promises the most rapid process of transformation. What distinguishes China from Russia is not so much the chosen strategy of development, but the different conditions imposed on that strategy by the greater backwardness of China – the growth of heavy industry is continually restrained by the incapacity of intensive agriculture to feed the population without receiving a greater share of investment. Within heavy industry, the régime, like Stalin, has been single-mindedly dedicated to raising labour productivity and the profit rate, at the expense of employment and consumption.

Mao has been one of the chief architects of this approach, and his writings and speeches give no indication of a 'different model', only of the necessity to make greater tactical concessions. During the first plan, Mao made steel the key to China's performance: 'Our country is poor, very poor. This year, steel production amounts to only 4.5 million tons . . . Japan's production is seven million tons.'[78] By 1975, China's steel output had reached around twenty-five million tons, a very creditable achievement in view of the difficulties, but far below Japan's 102 million tons (let alone the United States' 106 million and the Soviet Union's 141 million tons).

Steel and heavy industry could only expand if the population was being fed. Mao continued to stress the need to ensure an adequate harvest – then there would be food for the people, raw materials for light industry, a market for heavy industry, exports to earn foreign exchange with which to purchase imports for heavy industry, and funds for accumulation:[79] 'While developing industry, *especially heavy industry*, we must at the same time give agriculture a certain status by adopting correct policies for agricultural taxation and for pricing industrial and agricultural products.'[80] The emphasis is the same in the first plan and in the Great Leap Forward – the two key targets were for steel (Mao hoped for 100–120 million tons by 1962) and grain.

The setbacks of 1960–62 led to a temporary shift of emphasis towards agriculture and light industry. But the change was justified, for Mao, as a method of *assisting heavy industry*. Thus: 'The experience of the Soviet Union and our country show that if agriculture and light industry are not developed, it will be harmful to the development of heavy industry.'[81] There was no question, despite the disasters, of giving up the struggle for accumulation and increased production: 'The accumulated capital of the Soviet Union constitutes approximately one-fourth of the national income [per annum]. The ratio of our country's accumulated capital to national income was twenty-seven per cent in 1957, thirty-six per cent in 1958, and forty-two per cent in 1959. It appears likely that the ratio of our accumulated capital to national income henceforth can be maintained at over thirty-nine per cent or higher. The most important question is the rapid development of production.'[82] This was a staggering scale of accumulation for a poor country, particularly at a time when there was evidence of famine.

Quite a number of people in China and outside interpreted the retreat to a greater stress on agriculture as an agriculturally based strategy of development, whereby industry was subordinated to the demands of agriculture. If this had been the case, the régime would indeed have sacrificed the growth of the material foundation of its power to the immediate welfare of the majority. Two writers in 1962 made this mistake (or were covertly arguing for a different policy): 'As the foundation of the national economy, agriculture demands that all production departments, including those of industry, all construction departments and all cultural and educational undertakings develop themselves with the actual conditions of agricultural production as the starting point and give due consideration to the quantities of commodity grain and industrial raw materials and to the sizes of the market and the labour force which agriculture can supply . . . National economic plans should be formulated in the order of agriculture, light industry and heavy industry'.[83] Another urged that investment in agriculture should be higher than that in industry: 'the accumulation used for agriculture will increase at a faster rate than that used for industry . . . The State must plan the emphasis of its economic work on agriculture and invest heavily in agriculture and give it massive material support.'[84]

The national leadership was not so easily seduced from its self-appointed historic task. The most it would concede to these demands was the singularly obscure phrase, 'agriculture as the foundation and industry as the leading sector'. It did not publish its investment figures to indicate what the phrase meant, and, so far as can be seen, there seems to have been no sudden increase in investment in agriculture, although pricing policies left a little more income in the hands of those peasants with a marketable surplus. What it did was seek to cut urban consumption by reducing the urban population, consigning these extra mouths to the countryside to be fed by the peasants instead of from State procurements; this required a further increase in labour productivity in industry so that output did not fall with the smaller workforce.

Despite the verbal concession, heavy industry expanded at a faster rate than any other sector through the 1960s and into the 1970s. The régime avoided publicizing any strategy as to what it was doing, beyond repeating old phrases, until 1969. Then an authoritative article re-stated the strategy of the 1950s anew. Quoting Mao of 1957: 'It must be affirmed that heavy industry is the core of China's economic construction. At the same time, full attention must be paid to the development of agriculture and light industry', the writers elaborated: 'The

189

realization of socialist industrialization requires priority development of heavy industry. With heavy industry developed and the growth of the means of production enjoying priority, we shall be able to realize socially expanded reproduction, provide advanced techniques and equipment for the technical reform of agriculture and for the development of light and heavy industry and bring into play the leading role of industry in the national economy.'[85]

The thread throughout the years remains the same. But agriculture's capacity to support the main priority changes. Mao expressed it in the early 1960s in this way: 'How do we plan for our annual harvest? It will be determined by the assumption that in five years, there will be one year of good harvest, two years of ordinary harvest, and two years of poor harvest.'[86] Only massive investment by the State, diverting the surplus from industrial investment to agriculture, would have slowly flattened this variation and provided some measure of security in the supply of foodstuffs. Yet this the State would not do since it would jeopardize its national power and, thus, China's national independence. Given the drive to build heavy industry – and, as we shall see, the results have been impressive – all other items became negotiable.

(iv) The Chinese economy in the 1970s

Accumulation can only take place if there is a surplus, and it can be appropriated. How is this done in China? Primarily through the State's control of wages and prices, exercised through State-owned enterprises (including trading monopolies in agricultural commodities). The central government determines the level of pay, the numbers employed, the allocation of raw materials and equipment for the larger units in modern industry which produce the largest share of national industrial output. Other things being equal, these controls determine the level of enterprise profits which the State appropriates. The State controls the supply of bank credit and the interest charged to borrowing enterprises. The control mechanism is the party, its cadres in factory management, banks and local administration. In addition, the State procures compulsorily a certain proportion of agricultural goods from the communes at relatively low fixed prices and sells it at higher prices, as well as taxing the movement of goods between provinces through its control of trade. Finally, it levies indirect taxes on a number of goods – cigarettes, liquor, and a fifty to sixty per cent rate on goods such as bicycles, sewing machines, radios, etc.

The government claims that the taxation of industry is high and of agriculture low, but it does not divulge any figures. Its revenue, it says (and it is not clear whether this applies to only the central government, or includes provincial and lower authorities), takes about six per cent of farm incomes in comparison to thirteen per cent in the early 1950s. About ninety per cent of State revenue comes from State-owned enterprises.

If the government's view is accepted, it appears that in the 1960s the bulk of State revenue was derived from the surplus product of industrial workers. Even then, however, the régime was dissatisfied with the size of urban consumption (which reduced the available surplus). Hence the dilution of the urban labour force with temporary and contract workers and the expansion of enterprises outside the large-scale modern sector. Hence also the consistent efforts made to reduce labour costs. In the model project of Taching, for example, there was apparently no provision made for housing and other services when the new township was begun in the bare plains (with winter temperatures reaching −30°C). Workers were required to build their own dwellings after work, with 'pounded earthen walls' (kan-ta-lei). Foodstuffs were similarly to be grown locally by workers in their spare time, a practice which the authorities have attempted to generalize to all enterprises. A hundred years ago in Germany, Engels identified the economic meaning of obliging workers to grow their own food: 'Since, for the most part, the worker in domestic industry carries on his little bit of agriculture, it becomes possible to depress wages in a fashion unequalled elsewhere. What formerly constituted the happiness of the small man, the combination of agriculture and industry, now becomes the most powerful means of capitalist exploitation. The potato patch, the cow, the little bit of agriculture make it possible for labour power to be sold below its price: they oblige this to be so by tying the worker to his piece of land, which yet only partially supports him.'[87] In Taching, in the 1950s, workers were initially given higher than average pay to compensate for the lack of social investment, but it seems this was removed in the 1960s (although one visitor reports the average monthly wage of under RMB 60 is still supplemented by an RMB 5 allowance). Workers are expected to complete all work outstanding without overtime pay. No wonder this oilfield was held up as the régime's proudest achievement; its output is reported to have increased by thirty per cent per year, yielding a ten-fold return to the State's investment; labour productivity and the surplus appropriated by the State has increased two and a half times over.[88]

The campaign for everyone to grow their own foodstuffs can similarly be seen as a method of relieving the pressure on State procurements, even though it must be expensive in terms of the labour time of workers. The policy of 'self-reliance' in the villages protects the State's industrial sector from peasant demand and forces the villagers to use their own savings or go without.

The result of this overall strategy is, in productivity terms, a more marked dualism than in most countries – between a carefully segregated high productivity, capital-intensive enclave and a sea of low productivity, labour-intensive agriculture. The 'socially necessary labour-time' in the industrial sector has been reduced to the barest minimum, so that the rate of exploitation must be extraordinarily high. As a result, the State has apparently been able to maintain a very high level of accumulation. It may not be as high as Mao suggested in the early 1960s – thirty-nine per cent of national income – but it still must be exceptional.

·In terms of national power, the first call on the government's revenue must be defence. In turn, heavy industry provides backing for defence as well as inputs to all other sectors. Expenditure must be considerable, given the size of the defence sector – three and a half million men and women under arms (supported by possibly ten million in ancillary production and construction brigades, and many millions more, most of them in the part-time militia), as well as the hugely expensive nuclear and missile establishment. Since the first nuclear test in 1964, there have been over twenty by 1977, and Western estimates suggest China now possesses a growing stock of medium-range missiles, some experimentally based in submarines. If we compare China's resources and the size of the nuclear programme with other countries undertaking such an exercise, we can guess that possibly one-half of modern national investment goes in part or whole to defence (officially, a quarter of the national budget's *current* – as opposed to capital – expenditure was devoted to defence in 1956), and possibly a fifth of total industrial output. The proportions change relative to the government's estimate of the threat – US sources provide evidence, for example, of a sharp increase in defence spending following the armed clashes with Russia in 1969, and then a falling-off in 1973–5 as the threat receded.[89] By 1976, China's defence spending was equivalent to some eight to ten per cent of the gross national product, a much higher level than, for example, the United States, with a gross national product some ten times larger than China's (China's GNP is estimated as US $300 billion; the United States as US $1.8 trillion). Whatever the exact figures, China's defence spending represents a substantial diversion of resources from accumulation.

There are other leakages from accumulation, of which the most important must be the consumption of the bureaucracy. There are no estimates of this component. The régime has shown itself aware of the problem – it must maintain a bureaucracy to supervise the extraction of

192

the surplus, yet the bureaucracy itself absorbs a large share. The campaigns to cut bureaucracy, to transfer 'non-productive' labour and administrative cadres to the 'production front', show the efforts made to reduce consumption, yet the drive is constrained by the need to maintain control and supervision. If the bureaucracy is too much reduced, the régime could be threatened by a loss of control, even a major revolt.

What has been the performance of the two main sectors, industry and agriculture, as a result of these policies?

(v) Industry

The growth rate of China's industrial output has been very rapid, if inconsistent. In the period of the first Plan (1952–7), output grew by a fifth on average every year, a remarkable performance. Growth in the 1960s was slower – in the first half, about six to seven per year, and in the second half, between eleven and fourteen per cent;[90] in the first half of the 1970s, the average rate was about eight per cent per year, fluctuating between twelve per cent (1972 and 1973) and four to five per cent (1974).

Heavy industry has grown much more rapidly. The share of 'producer goods' industries in terms of value of output increased from twenty-eight per cent in 1949 to fifty-two per cent in 1957, and an estimated seventy-nine to eighty-three per cent in 1971.[91] Manufactured consumer goods – for example, bicycles, radios, sewing machines – represented about seven per cent of machinery output in 1956, and declined to three per cent by 1971 (of course, the absolute increase in the output of these goods would be large).

What of Mao's key link industry, steel? Output was 4.5 million tons in 1955, and rose to thirteen million tons during the Great Leap Forward and the following year. This fell back to eight million tons in 1961, before reaching twelve million tons in 1968, twenty-one million tons in 1970, and the record figure of 25.5 million tons in 1974; it fell by about three million tons in 1975–6. In the main the output comes from large and very large plants – a quarter of it from Anshan, seventeen per cent from Shanghai and about thirty-four per cent from other one to two million ton plants. The rapid expansion of output in the late 1960s led to technical difficulties as well as the labour problems mentioned earlier. The rest of industry has expanded, and as a result there is a continuing shortage of steel despite the increase in output. This obliged the régime to make large steel imports in 1974 and 1975 – over 3 million tons in 1975, equivalent to fifteen per cent of steel consumption. About a fifth of the imports were seamless pipes, probably for the oil industry; other imports included steel scrap, pig iron, iron ore, showing that domestic supplies of these items were inadequate. The steel shortage has also been a factor in prompting the government to make major purchases of steel plant abroad – for example, the US $550 million rolling and treatment complex at Wuhan, built and supplied by a West German consortium under Demag, and a sixteen-company Japanese consortium led by Nippon Steel (the plant is expected to begin production in 1978).

Industrial expansion makes heavy demands on energy supplies. Although the oil industry has experienced a remarkable expansion in recent years – officially, 680 per cent between 1965 and 1975 – it is severely restricted by the lack of pipes and refinery capacity. As a result, the coal industry still supplies about four-fifths of industry's energy consumption. Like steel, coal output has expanded rapidly – from 290 million tons in 1959 (with an estimated 210 million tons in 1968) to 430 million tons in 1975. Coal output fell in 1974 because of labour troubles, say foreign observers. Like steel, coal is a bottleneck, partly because of wasteful methods of preparing coal for use. Coal depends on the railways for movement, and occasional labour difficulties in the 1970s impeded its use. The government again turned to imports of coal machinery to expand production quickly.

Other heavy industries have perfomed well. For example, the machine building industry has officially expanded in the 1960s by fifteen per cent per year. The railway network, limited in 1949, has been considerably expanded. The 50,000 miles of highway that existed in 1949 had, by 1976, become half a million miles, and the NCNA claimed that by then eighty-three per cent of all communes could be reached by road. With the considerable imports of motor vehicles and China's own trucking capacity, this is an important advance.

The expansion has come in the main from modern large-scale industry through increases in the use of capacity and labour productivity rather than increasing jobs. Western estimates of, for example, the producer goods industries put the value of output in 1952 at 10.7 billion yuan, and in 1971 at 246.5 billion yuan, or a twenty-four times increase; whereas employment in the same industries increased between fifty-nine and 182 per cent, or by a half to one and three-quarters.[92] The government has deliberately invested heavily in machinery while trying to curb or reduce the size of the labour force. As part of this process, the electronics industry has received strong official support, and some visitors report that Chinese industry is relatively advanced in the use of automated techniques. For example, a 1974 visitor reported that over half the horizontal knitting looms in Shanghai's textile mills are electronically controlled; and a major part of the woollen knitwear mills are in part or whole automated, as is part of the mining industry.[93]

194

Combined with the use of low-paid temporary and contract labour, this makes for spectacular increases in labour productivity and the surplus accruing to the State.

(vi) Agriculture

Agriculture is at the opposite extreme. With half as much cultivated acreage as the Soviet Union or the United States but four times the number of mouths to feed, with a preceding century of neglect, it would have been extraordinary if agricultural output had been capable of rapid expansion.

It is the relative stagnation of agriculture which pulls down all the national statistics. Thus, despite the rapid increase in industrial output in the 1950s, the gross domestic product per head in 1957 was still only twenty per cent above the 1933 level,[94] and consumption per head about the same.[95]

The major part of China's agricultural output is grain, and the long-term increase in production has been fairly consistent – about two to three per cent per year.[96] There are disagreements in detail, but this rate of growth has brought total output from about 110 million tonnes in 1949 to 286 million tonnes in the 1970s, a one and a half times increase in twenty-seven years. It is not clear how reliable these figures are, but they give a picture of the trend. The increases must have stemmed from a few provinces, since the overall picture is more patchy. Officially, only nine provinces and municipalities out of twenty-five had, by 1976, met the 1967 targets of the National Programme of Agricultural Development. six provinces (Shensi, Kansu, Chinghai, Shansi, Liaoning and Ninghsia) were only 'self-sufficient in the main'; that is, they were on occasions obliged to import; presumably, the remaining ten were permanently in deficit.[97]

In the early 1970s, Chou En-lai said that China's population was growing at 'around two per cent' (the urban population, it seems, is increasing more slowly). Grain output is increasing at a similar rate on average, so that the major part of agriculture can make little or no contribution to accumulation – even if, given the difficulties in an intensively farmed country, we assume that the régime could actually appropriate the surplus. The availability of grain per head of the population has been roughly constant since the early 1950s – at most it has increased twelve to eighteen kilograms over the 295 kilograms available in 1957.[98] If the supply of other foodstuffs, livestock etc., has increased more rapidly than grain output, this relative stagnation can be accompanied by an improvement in the average diet, although that will be

195

limited ultimately by the grain supply (for example the supply of fodder for livestock).

The grain situation has eased surprisingly little over the past quarter of a century, despite massive and sustained efforts through multiple cropping, water conservation, irrigation, improved tools, use of fertilizers, hybrid seeds and pesticides. Fertilizer availability is particularly important here since the use of new hybrid seeds and multiple cropping of the land depend on a large increase in water supplies and fertilizer application. Virtually no chemical fertilizers were manufactured in the early 1950s, but since then there has been a considerable increase, apparently in the main financed by commune savings. There is now said to be roughly seventy kilograms of fertilizer available on average per hectare, roughly two-thirds of it manufactured in small plants (compared to 300 kilograms or more in, for example, South Korea and Japan). The government has imported both fertilizer and large-scale chemical fertilizer plant, and this may raise the fertilizer availability per hectare to 100 kilograms. Not all observers agree that this will raise yields. Some agronomists have argued that the poor long-term performance is because the soil is relatively exhausted, afflicted by salination and alkalinization as the result of intensive cropping of a small cultivated area for many hundreds of years. Others have been impressed by the use of organic fertilizer which raises the total fertilizer applied per hectare closer to the South Korean figure, but also means that output is already near the maximum to be expected under present conditions.

Imports have been used to ease scarcities of grain, raw cotton, fertilizers and equipment. In the bad years of 1960–63, some sixteen million tonnes of grain were imported; and 6 to 7.5 million tonnes were imported annually in 1972–4 (falling to 4.4 million tonnes in 1975, and 1.7 million tonnes in 1976, the lowest level of imports since 1966). In the early 1970s, grain imports made up between thirteen and sixteen per cent of the total import bill. After two poor years for grain, 1975 and 1976, China's imports for 1977 – 11.8 million tonnes – were at the highest level since 1961. Raw cotton has regularly been imported, and the import volume has grown by about fifty per cent since 1964 (with a rough value of US $360 million annually). To China's domestic output of about twenty-five million tonnes of chemical fertilizer, imports have added 6 to 7 million tonnes annually. Furthermore, the régime has imported thirteen fertilizer plants (mainly from the US and Holland, but also from France and Japan), which should begin production in 1977–8.

The poor performance so far has not dissuaded the government from raising its sights. At an important agricultural conference in October 1974 and in the fifth Five Year Plan (which began in January 1976), a set of long-term targets was laid down, apparently for the first time since the 1950s. The stated aim was to achieve a total grain output of 360–400 million tonnes by 1980, to secure the mechanization of agriculture, and to follow the model of the Tachai Brigade (the agricultural equivalent of Taching). The last long-range plan, supposedly in operation from 1956 to 1967, disappeared in the Great Leap Forward and its aftermath, so that the formulation of a plan gives no assurance as to how practical it is. Perhaps at long last the government is to devote a larger share of national investment to agriculture, and it is on this basis that the targets have been drawn up. Otherwise, to achieve the stated grain target after twenty years of roughly two to three per cent annual growth would require agriculture to increase grain output by between five and seven per cent annually up to 1980. Without massive imports, it would seem an unlikely achievement. Indeed, on the past record, the government would have reason to congratulate itself if it could achieve a consistent three per cent annual increase (to reach 330 million tonnes by 1980).

(vii) Foreign Trade

Imports – whether for use in agricultural or industrial production – are an important precondition for releasing China's capacity for economic growth. When the economy has grown rapidly, the government has permitted rapid increases in imports, curbed by the available reserves and China's export earnings. Imports – estimated from the accounts of countries which trade with China – increased by eighteen per cent in 1970, were cut back in 1971, presumably to protect the reserves; expanded in 1973 at a rate higher than at any time in the history of the régime, and then were cut drastically in 1974, before expanding more gradually in 1975, and again falling (by ten per cent) in 1976.

What does China import? Grain, raw cotton, fertilizers have been mentioned, but there are other foodstuffs, for example, soya-beans and soya-oil. But the recent major expansion in imports has been in the industrial field, with imports either to relieve domestic bottlenecks or to gain access to advanced technology. Between 1971 and 1976, China imported or ordered a great deal of steel (US $800–1, 200 millions worth annually); 30,000 trucks; 3,000 cars and buses; 170 locomotives and seventy ships. From the United States it imported an RCA Global Communications Satellite earth ship, and ten Boeing aircraft. It contracted for ammonia plants, power shovels, car gear and axle making machines, twenty blow-out preventer stacks (to control oil-well bore pressure), magnetic recording equipment, oil-well boring pumps, photographic and optical equipment, and data processing equipment. It signed agreements for supply with many of the major multinational corporations, including Kellogg, Bucyrus-Erie, Sohio, Amoco, Toyo Engineering, Mitsui Toatsu. Negotiations in 1975 led to an agreement with Rolls-Royce to build a Spey jet-engine plant in central Sian (at an estimated cost of US $182 million; presumably with United States approval since such a project is banned under the North Atlantic Treaty Organisation). Talks were under way for the purchase of twelve Japanese patrol aircraft, four Sanwa Group nylon fibre plants, three petroleum refineries and three large computers. In late 1975, an agreement was signed for the purchase of a 100,000-ton Japanese oil tanker.

The list illustrates both what the Chinese leadership sees as the main weaknesses in China's economy, and the fact that in practice, regardless of domestic propaganda or the state of the leadership faction fight, China's imports were kept high. The total trade – about US $15,200 million in 1976 – imposed a deficit on China with the advanced capitalist nations of about US $2,700 million.

How are the imports paid for? China's exports in 1973–4 included soya-beans, oilseeds, tea, bristles, feathers, rice, wolfram, antimony, tobacco, silk, tinned pork, mutton, rabbit, cotton goods, wild cat coats, antiquities and some light industrial goods (bulbs, wigs, vacuum flasks); about a quarter of these exports go to Hong Kong. These exports, concentrated in the areas of raw materials or foodstuffs, yield a poor return, and in the mid-1970s were sorely afflicted by the world slump – prices fell while the prices of industrial imports rose under the impact of inflation in the advanced countries. Oil exports, which doubled in 1975 to US $1,000 million and mainly went to Japan, Philippines, Hong Kong, Thailand and Romania, helped balance the trade deficit. But to increase oil exports requires more imports of pipes, refinery and tanker capacity, as well as measures to improve the peculiar quality of Chinese crude oil. Trade earnings are supplemented by the profits of China's enterprises operating in Hong Kong and cash sent from overseas Chinese families. But even so, the reserves are small in relationship to the scale of current imports (US sources estimate them at RMB 7 billion or US $3,560 million).

In the autumn of 1974, all these factors united to cause a severe and unexpected balance of payments crisis (estimated at US $1,000 million). The régime cancelled orders for grain and foodstuff imports, and to cut the deficit expanded oil exports. The government needs to keep up the level of imports for future growth, but thereby incurs a new range of burdens. In recent years, it has moved into borrowing abroad to sustain import purchases – first, using short-term commercial credit from its suppliers, then medium-terms loans from the Japanese Exim Bank (starting in 1972), reaching deferred payments agreements (twenty per cent payment down, and the rest over five to seven years at six per cent rate of interest), and accepting foreign currency deposits at competitive interest rates in the offices of its banks abroad. At the same time, it sold abroad an estimated 12 to 24 tonnes of gold in late 1975 and early 1976. In early 1977, some 80 tonnes of gold were sold (worth $206 million). For 1976, China's cumulative foreign debt was estimated to be US $1.3 billion, or twenty-three per cent of hard currency exports.

In sum, the rate of growth of industrial output has been rapid, possibly as rapid as that of the Soviet Union in the first two Five Year Plans (1928–38) – ten to fourteen per cent per year. In the 1970s, it has been less impressive but still substantial – although below rates achieved, for example, in Taiwan, Thailand, South Korea and Malaysia. Over the whole period since 1949, the structure of China's product has been shifted so that perhaps half or more of China's national product (in value terms) now comes from industry. The effort has been sustained over a quarter of a century, a period comparable to that in the Soviet Union between 1928 and 1951.

But the social transformation of the Soviet Union that took place in those years has scarcely begun in China. By the criterion of employment – as opposed to value of output – matters have not changed radically since 1952. Then as now, about seventy-five per cent of the labour force was employed in agriculture, in the main at very low levels of productivity and austere living standards. The effects of the dramatic growth in industrial output has been only slight on the rural majority, even though much improvement has undoubtedly taken place.

At the Fourth NPC in January 1975, Chou En-lai revived Mao's 1964 perspective (at the Third NPC): 'to build an independent, relatively comprehensive industrial and economic system . . . before the 1980s; and 'to accomplish the comprehensive modernization of agriculture, industry, national defence and science and technology before the end of the century so that our national economy will be advancing in the front ranks of the world'.[99]

Can it be done? Clearly it is within the capacity of the world economy to achieve this result. If China can continue to expand its imports and world capitalism resumes rapid and sustained expansion, so that the demand for China's exports increases and China can borrow at relatively low interest rates (all of which assumes world peace and no serious domestic disorder in China), it is a possible target. All provided the Chinese working class continues loyally to deliver up its massive surplus to the régime. But even if the output target could be achieved, could China's masses be incorporated in such a short time, could the 'dual economy' be overcome? The assumptions are all in doubt – world expansion, the continued philanthropy of the Chinese working classes and, above all, the possibility of transforming China while it retains its national isolation.

For many people, China is a splendid triumph because its people are more equal, it is democratic, and the country has made the breakthrough to sustained economic development. Poor it may be now, but its government has the wisdom to make those continued efforts which will ensure that the people of China will in due course 'close the gap' with the advanced powers and come to enjoy all that is most valuable in terms of human progress in this century.

This chapter has attempted to assess whether these claims are correct. There is, on the face of it, greater equality in China than in most other countries, but it has been achieved through the rationing system and the basic scarcity of unrationed goods rather than equality of income. In terms of the official income scales, the degree of inequality is striking, nor is there a detectable trend towards more equality in Chinese society as a whole (even if, as some argue, there are efforts to increase the equality of income solely within the eight grade wage system). The reasons for the inequality seem less to do with any government preferences, more with the basic material conditions of the society and the commitment of the régime to accumulation. By any rigorous standard of democracy, there is none in China, although the régime gives the impression of being popular and consulting widely. In terms of the economy, China has experienced a relatively high rate of industrial growth, achieved by tenacious efforts to increase labour productivity. What distinguishes China from most other backward countries is not the material quality of life, but the structure of control which ensures that, for example, all are fed and clothed. The urban–rural gap and income differentials remain sizeable, but the rationing system – and its maintenance against the corrosive forces at work on the countryside – has ensured that the mass of the population has received tangible benefits. In terms of the productivity of labour, the gap between the permanent industrial labour force and the mass of cultivators is possibly more extreme than in most backward countries, and this – a function of China's intensive agriculture and its resistance to central supervision – has been to the benefit of the rural population.

China's future depends not simply on its internal resources, but on the international context in which it exists. The government and the party can secure through external activities both protection and assistance for the tasks it has undertaken. The politics it proclaims are internationalist. How far has the party been able to elicit international support? This is the theme of the following section.

NOTES

1. Speech to managers, Feb. 1931, cited by Isaac Deutscher, *Stalin*, London (Penguin edition), 1966, p. 328

2. Lenin, *State and Revolution*, *SW* 7, p. 92

3. Lenin, Tasks of the Proletariat in the Present Revolution ('April Theses'), *SW* 6, p. 23

4. Lenin, *CW* 27 (Russian), p. 132, cited Tony Cliff, *Stalinist Russia*, London, 1955, p. 53

5. S. Zagorsky, *Wages and regulation of conditions of labour in the USSR*, Geneva, 1930, pp. 176–8, cited *ibid*, p. 55

6. *Statistical Handbook of the USSR*, Moscow, 1926, cited *ibid*, p. 56

7. Cited by Z. M. Chernilovsky, *History of State and Law*, Moscow, 1949, cited *ibid*, p. 56

8. Cited by D. I. Chernomordik, *The economic policies of the USSR*, Moscow, 1936, p. 240, cited *ibid*, p. 56

9. Cited Cliff, *Stalinist Russia, op. cit.*, p. 57

10. Annual figures given in *Stenographic Report*, First Session, Supreme Soviet of the USSR, Moscow, 1948, pp. 124, 205, cited *ibid*, p. 60

11. *New York Times*, 23 Aug. 1943

12. Extracted from Janet Chapman, *Wage variations in Soviet industry: the impact of the 1956–60 wage reform*, Santa Monica, 1970, p. 26

13. From figures supplied by Alastair McAuley, Essex University, cited by Malcolm Crawford, 'Pay: has Russia a better answer?', *Sunday Times*, London, 3 Oct. 1976

14. *Report on the work of the government*, First session, First National People's Congress, 23 Sep. 1954, Peking 1954, p. 27

15. Talks with directors of various co-operative areas, Nov.–Dec. 1958, in *Miscellany* I, p. 134

16. *JMJP*, 14 Jul. 1964

17. *Kuang-ming JP*, 22 Apr. 1975, *SCMP* 75–22, 27–30 May 1975

18. *JMJP* 28 Mar. 1975, *SCMP* 5846, 6 May 1975

19. *Value, Price and Profit*, in *SW* I, p. 337

20. *Critique of the Gotha Programme*, in *SW* II. p. 566

21. Estimates by Howe, *Wage patterns, op. cit.*, pp. 40–41, for whom see official Chinese sources. Another estimate states a span of 1:28, cited from *Chung-yang Ts'ai-cheng fakui hui-pen*, in *Collection of the 1956 Central Financial Regulations*, Peking, 1957, pp. 228–9, by M. K. Whyte, 'Inequality and Stratification in China', *CQ* 64, Dec. 1975, p. 684

22. *SWB* 4949/BII/8 May 1975

23. Cited by Whyte, *op. cit.*, p. 732

24. Report, *New York Times*, 17 Mar. 1972, p. 10

25. Report of a visit, Jules Nadeau, *Far Eastern Economic Review*, 21 Nov. 1975, p. 47; see also Ross Terrill, *800,000: the Real China*, Boston,

1972, pp. 127, 130

26. Reported by A. Doak Barnett, *CQ* 28, Oct.–Dec. 1966, p. 8

27. *The other side of the river, op. cit.*, p. 289

28. Jul.–Sep. 1967, in *Miscellany* II, p. 465

29. *Kuang-ming JP*, 5 Jan. 1975, *SCMP* 5771, 21 Jan. 1975

30. JMJP, 14 Sep. 1973, and *Hung-ch'i* 4, 1974, pp. 35–42

31. Cited Hoffman, *The Chinese Worker, op. cit.*, p. 101 (for which, see Chinese sources)

32. Maurice Meisner, 'The Shenyang Transformer Factory', *CQ* 52, 1972, p. 731

33. Nadeau, *op. cit.*

34. William Shawcross, *Far Eastern Economic Review*, 12 Dec. 1975, pp. 30–31

35. At 1952 prices: State Statistical Bureau, 1957; T'ien Lin, in *Hsin-hua pan-yüeh-kán*, 1957, p. 158, cited Whyte, *op. cit.*, p. 686

36. JMJP, 3 May 1962, cited Hoffman, *Work incentives, op. cit.*, p. 13

37. Table 8, *Income distribution in Latin America*, United Nations (ECLA), New York, 1971, p. 105

38. Report *Far Eastern Economic Review*, 19 Feb. 1973

39. Table 11, Shahid Javed Burki, 'A Study of Chinese Communes' in Kuan–I Chen and Joginder S. Uppal, *India and China, Studies in Comparative Development*, New York, 1971, p. 181. (Extract from *A study of China's Communes, 1965*, Cambr. Mass., 1969, pp. 8-32)

40. *The Transformation of the Chinese Earth*, London, 1970, p. 136

41. Deleyne, *op. cit.*, p. 73

42. Document of the Central Committee, *Chung-fa* 1971, 82, translated in *Studies on Chinese Communism*, 6/6, Sep. 1972

43. The example comes from Nadeau, *op. cit.*

44. See letter from Shanghai, *Far Eastern Economic Review*, 18 Mar. 1977, p. 110

45. The example comes from Whyte, *op. cit.*

46. State and Revolution, *SW* 7, p. 44

47. *Ibid.* p. 46

48. Letter to Bebel, 18–28 Mar. 1875, in *Selected Correspondence*, Moscow, 1955, p. 294; stress added

49. State and Revolution, *op. cit.*, p. 41

50. Petrovskii, cited by D. H. White, *The growth of the Red Army*, Princeton, 1944, pp. 63–4

51. V. Ulrich, in *Soviet Army Daily (Krasnaya Zvezda)* 22 Apr. 1940, cited Cliff, *Stalinist Russia, op. cit.*, pp. 89–90

52. In *Mao Unrehearsed*, p. 183

53. Jan. 1964, in *Miscellany* II, p. 364

54. Letter to cadres, Mar. 1959, in *Miscellany* I, p. 172

55. Dec. 1956, in *Miscellany* I, p. 41

56. Jan. 1961, in *Miscellany* II, p. 238

57. Jan. 1961, *ibid*, II, p. 240

58. In *Mao Papers*, p. 68; stress added

59. May 1967, in *Miscellany* II, p. 460

60. *Hung-ch'i* 4, 1968

61. Conversation with Mao by the President of France, Georges Pompidou,

1973, published extract in English, *Sunday Times*, London, 24 Oct. 1976, p. 56

62. Rule 28, from Sixty Points on Working Methods, 1958, in *Mao Papers*, p. 68

63. Dec. 1964, in *Miscellany* II, p. 417

64. *PR* 43, 1968, p. 7

65. April 1956, in *Miscellany* I, p. 35

66. Deleyne, *op. cit.*, p. 29

67. Su Hsi, *JMJP*, 11 Jan. 1974, *SCMP* 5547, 6 Feb. 1974

68. Engels to Danielson, Sep. 1892, *Selected Correspondence, ibid*, p. 498

69. Commenting on a Soviet work, 'Political Economy', 1961–2, in *Miscellany* II, p. 248

70. Jan. 1965, in *Miscellany* II, p. 445

71. Marx, *Wage, Labour and Capital*, in *SW* II, pp. 265–6

72. On the Russian debts in 1976, cf. Alec Nove and Dubravko Matko, 'USSR labours under a huge trade deficit with the West', *The Times*, London, 22 Jul. 1976; Mary Campbell and David Lascelles, 'What eastern Europe owes the capitalists', *Financial Times*, 29 Jul. 1976; and 'Concern as East steps up borrowing', Supplement on Anglo-Soviet Trade, *The Times* 21 Oct. 1976

73. For a discussion of the theoretical basis of this section, see Chapter 8 of T. Cliff, *Russia: A Marxist Analysis*, London, n.d.

74. On the rescheduling of the Cuban plan, cf. 'Dr Castro reveals the extent of Cuba's economic difficulties', Agence-France Press report, *The Times*, London, 6 Oct. 1976

75. *Far Eastern Economic Review*, 6 Jun. and 19 Dec. 1975, and 8 Oct. 1976, p. 42

76. On the occasion of the visit to Europe of vice-minister for foreign affairs, Nguyen Co Tach, cf. 'Hanoi wants foreign capital for Five Year Plan', report *Sunday Times*, London, 7 Nov. 1976

77. P. Bairoch and J. N. Limber, 'Changes in the industrial distribution of the world labour force by regions, 1880–1960', *International Labour Review*, ILO, Geneva, 98/4, 1968

78. Dec. 1956, *Miscellany* I, p. 38

79. Jan. 1957, *ibid*, p. 61

80. April 1956, in *Mao Unrehearsed*, p. 64; stress added

81. 1961–2, in *Miscellany* II, p. 280

82. *Ibid*, p. 293; the translation of Mao's terminology is poor – the phrase, 'the accumulated capital' should be 'the rate of capital accumulation'

83. Lu Hsu'n and Li Yün, 'On the practice of economy', *JMJP*, 21 Aug. 1962, *SCMP* 2817, 1962

84. Onyang Ch'eng, 'Concerning the question of harmony or disharmony in the proportional relationship between industry and agriculture', *Ta Kung Pao*, 22 Oct. 1962, *SCMP* 2863, 1962

85. Writing Group, Peking Municipal Revolutionary Committee, 'The road to China's Socialist Industrialization', *Hung-ch'i* 10, 30 Sep. 1969, p. 11, *SCMM* 666, 31 Oct. 1969

86. 1961–2, in *Miscellany*, II, p. 353

87. Letter to Bebel, Dec. 1884, in *Selected Correspondence, ibid*, p. 432

88. 'Report of a visitor, Forming Maoist Man (The Taching Oilfield)', *Financial Times*, London, 2 Dec. 1976, p. 2; see also 'Ta-ch'ing: A Model

Industrial Community in the People's Republic of China', David D. Buck, *The China Geographer*, Spring 1977

89. Sydney H. James, 'The Chinese Defense Burden, 1965–74', in *China: A Reassessment of the Economy*, Joint Economic Committee, Congress of the United States, Washington, 10 Jul. 1975, pp. 459–66

90. The figures span a range of foreign estimates, based on different assumptions about the official information available; for figures and sources, see Table 6, Thomas Rawski, 'The growth of producer industries, 1900–1971', in D. H. Perkins (ed.), *China's Modern Economy in Historical Perspective*, Stanford, 1975, p. 222: cf. also R. M. Field, 'Civilian industrial production in the PRC, 1949–74', in *China: A Reassessment, op. cit.*; also, *ibid*, Rawski, pp. 175–98, and 'Recent trends in the Chinese economy', *CQ* 53, Jan.–Mar. 1973, p. 3 ff.; and Alexander Eckstein, 'Economic growth and change in China: a twenty year perspective', *CQ* 54, Apr.–Jun. 1973, pp. 221–41, and, with Walter Galenson and Tachung Liu (eds.), *Economic Trends in Communist China*, Chicago, 1968, p. 7 *passim*

91. Table 5, Rawski, in Perkins, *op. cit.*, p. 222

92. Rawski, in Perkins, *op. cit.* pp. 222–3

93. Report, *Far Eastern Economic Review*, Dec. 1974

94. Table 3, D. H. Perkins, 'Growth and changing structure of China's economy', in D. H. Perkins, *op. cit.*, p. 122

95. 'However the estimates are made, there is no way one can make them show a substantial rise in average per capita consumption expenditures between the 1930s and 1950s' – *ibid*, pp. 125–6

96. For the official figures, 1952–72, cf. Table, Production of foodgrains, in 'The economic development of India and China', in my *India-China: Underdevelopment and Revolution*, Delhi, 1974, p. 286; husked grain output for 1973 is put at 213.8 million tonnes (264 million unhusked); for 1974, 228 million (275 unhusked – given by Yang Li-kung, Deputy Minister of Agriculture at the UN Food Conference, Rome, Nov. 1975); 1975, 228 million unhusked; guesses for 1976, 286–92 million unhusked. Figures for the last three years have been challenged on the grounds that soya-bean, formerly counted separately, has now been included in the figures; if this is not so, the rate of growth 1970–76 is raised to nineteen per cent, or 3.6 per cent per year; allowing for the soya-bean inclusion, the growth is thirteen per cent, or 2.4 per cent per year

97. NCNA Peking, 29 Jun. 1976

98. Giving an average per head per day of 2,280 calories – cf. D. H. Perkins, Supplement on China, *Far Eastern Economic Review*, 1 Oct. 1976, pp 50–3

99. Report on the work of the government, 4th NPC, *JMJP*, 21 Jan. 1975, in *PR* 4, 24 Jan. 1975

PART V

PROLETARIAN INTERNATIONALISM

14

THE THEORY

The Bolsheviks came to power on the assumption that the events of October 1917 would be the signal for the seizure of power by the workers of Western Europe. They did not see themselves as a separate national group, awaiting the action of workers in other countries, but, by historical accident, the temporary leaders of an international movement. It was the duty of the Bolsheviks to ferment revolution in the rest of Europe by all the means in their power. Since, in their opinion, the revolution in Europe was the political and material condition of their own survival, it was understandable that they poured their energies into the new international workers' party, the Communist International. This was the key to the paradox: a workers' revolution in a country where the working class was a minority and the material conditions backward.

Nonetheless, the new State had also to ensure its own survival. That required opening up relations, particularly trade relations, with existing States. The 'international bourgeoisie', with sections ruling each of the constituent units of the advanced world, was riven with internal rivalries (just as each country was riven with the rivalries between individual firms). It was the rivalry between the Austro German and the Anglo-French-American 'imperialist predators' which permitted the Soviet Union its temporary lease on life. It permitted the treaty of Brest-Litovsk with Germany whereby Russia ended its involvement in the First World War.

The treaty evoked considerable opposition within the party, and Lenin spent much time explaining why it was necessary: 'The outcome might have seemed something like a bloc between the first Socialist Republic and German imperialism, against another imperialism [Anglo-French-American imperialism]. However, we did not conclude a bloc or defame the socialist state; we simply took advantage of the conflict between the two imperialisms in such a way that both were ultimately the losers. Germany obtained nothing from the Brest peace except several million poods of grain, but she *brought the disintegrating force of Bolshevism into the country*. We, however, gained time, in the course of which the formation of the Red Army began.'[1] The treaty cost Russia the Ukraine. 'In the case of the Brest-Litovsk peace, we sacrificed Russia's interests, as understood in the patriotic sense, which were in fact secondary from the socialist point of view.' The Bolsheviks *sacrificed* the national interest in order to spread disaffection among the Kaiser's armies and mobilize support for German workers in the task of overthrowing the Kaiser. The policy was the reverse of what came later, the sacrifice of the international purpose for the defence of the Russian State.

In the aftermath of the treaty, the Bolsheviks were preoccupied with fighting the civil war at home and supporting the revolution abroad. By 1920, as we have seen, the party and the country were exhausted; the revolutionary assault of 1919 in Western Europe had been beaten off. The need now was to retreat, to bind up the wounds, to prepare for a future assault. While the International endeavoured to consolidate its membership round the world, the Russian State needed to pursue policies which, as far as was possible given Soviet material weakness, would sustain the rivalries between its enemies (so preserving some measure of security for its own survival) and restore the Russian economy, the material base of world revolution.

'To restore the economy . . . is more difficult than fighting . . . victory will not depend on enthusiasm, dash or self-sacrifice, but on day-to-day, monotonous, petty and workaday effort. That is undoubtedly a more difficult matter. Where are we to procure the means of production we need?' Russia had too little gold to buy the means to rehabilitate the economy; it could not pay in raw materials because the urgent need was to feed the population. It must offer 'foreign concessions', quasi-colonial rights over some of the raw materials unexploited in Russia's vast territories.

Such a proposal evoked considerable unease, indeed alarm, in the party ranks. With characteristic bluntness, Lenin laid down the priorities: 'For Kamchatka, we shall pay in terms of 100,000 poods of oil, taking only two per cent for ourselves. If we do not pay up, we shall not even get two poods. This is an exorbitant price, but while capitalism exists, we cannot expect a fair price from it. Yet the advantages are beyond doubt.'[2]

Surely this was to sacrifice the fruits of the revolution for the sake of a pittance? It was not, for the primary justification was not Russia's survival, but that it gave the Russian State the means to exacerbate the

208

rivalries between its enemies. Not all rivalries were involved: 'We must take political advantage of the differences among our opponents, but only of major differences *that are due to profound economic causes*. If we try to exploit minor and fortuitous differences, we shall be behaving like petty politicians and cheap diplomats.'³ For only major differences exhibited the structure of world power, the drift of conflict. In the case of Kamchatka, Japan eyed it as part of its sphere of influence. The United States was offered the concessions, and the by-product was the means of material survival for Russia. But the conflict of the United States and Japan which, according to Lenin, would sooner or later produce an open war should not induce the Soviet Union to side with one or the other: 'To support one of these countries against the other would be a crime against communism; we Communists have to play one off against the other.'

The Brest peace and the foreign concessions raised different issues. The justification of Brest was that it made possible Bolshevik survival and intervention in Germany; in the case of foreign concessions, when the revolutionary movement abroad was in temporary decline, it exacerbated rivalries in the enemy camp and assisted the survival of Russia.

The Soviet Union extended aid to Ataturk in Turkey, to the Shah of Iran and to Sun Yat-sen in China. Yet in certain circumstances, such aid could make it more difficult for local Communist parties to lead a revolution against these rulers. The Russian leadership endeavoured to prevent the agreement between the Soviet Union and Weimar Germany being construed as political support for the German ruling class, the target of the German Communist party. Without such a distinction, the policies of the Russian State directly obstructed the aims of the Communist International.

In the case of the backward countries, the possibility of confusion was much greater. For the alliance between the Western proletariat and the 'oppressed nations' could with ease be construed as support for the ruling classes of the backward countries. Then working-class internationalism faded into something else, the 'internationalism of nations', the fraternity of ruling classes. Lenin had no doubt what this meant: 'Petty bourgeois nationalism calls the mere recognition of the equality of nations internationalism, and (disregarding the purely verbal character of such recognition) considers national egoism inviolable. Proletarian internationalism on the other hand demands: (1) subordination of the interests of proletarian struggle in one country to the interests of the struggle on a world scale; (2) that the nation which achieves victory over the bourgeoisie shall display the capacity and readiness to make the greatest national sacrifices in order to overthrow international capitalism.'[4]

The Bolshevik view, then, was that the October revolution was a temporary victory; its justification was that thereby Russia could 'make the greatest national sacrifices' for the overthrow of the world order. State relations were subordinate not to abstract principles but to temporary survival while the revolutionary movement was built to *overthrow*, with Bolshevik material aid, the States with which Russia had relations. Russian State relations must not be such that they could be construed as political support for a ruling class. Similarly, the Russian State could not extend material aid to a foreign State even if it was effective as a bribe for certain purposes or exacerbated the rivalries between States, if that aid could be used to repress a domestic revolt, to eliminate the possibility of revolution. Above all, State relations must at no stage prevent or inhibit local Communists making independent propaganda against the local ruling class and endeavouring to build a workers' alternative. If that did occur, then the interests of the Russian State had taken priority over those of world revolution.

(i) The Chinese Communist party

How far do these elementary principles apply to the external activities of the Chinese Communists and the State they direct? The most striking observation is that there is no International, no instrument of a world working class and no strategy for creating a 'world proletarian alliance'. Up to the 1960s, it might have been argued that the Chinese party accepted the leadership of the Soviet Union in external affairs and was unwilling to challenge Moscow by the creation of a new International (the Comintern was ended in 1943 as a Russian gesture of Allied solidarity to its British and American partners in the Second World War; its successor, the Cominform, included only nine governing and two non-governing parties – it did not include the Chinese – and lasted from 1947 to 1956). But in all the polemics between Moscow and Peking, the Chinese party never reproached the Soviet Communist party with scrapping the Comintern or failing to create a new International. Indeed, it opposed any such proposal since it saw an International solely as a method of Russian domination of China. After the Sino-Soviet break, the Chinese party took no serious initiative in the matter. It is thus reduced to being a passive spectator in most domestic confrontations; it has no instrument for changing the world, and is confined to the role of commentator, distributing praise and blame but without active involvement. Supporters of China explain this anomaly as flowing from the weakness of the world movement. This presents a paradox, for, on the one hand, the Chinese Communists proclaim that the world situation is 'excellent'; on the other, the proletarian forces are weaker than in the 1860s when the first International was formed!

The Chinese party has encouraged some of its supporters abroad. But so far as can be seen, it has never given such groups material aid. This is confirmed repeatedly by the Chinese leadership, and there is no reason, despite Western propaganda, to disbelieve it. Nor do such groups pursue any common strategy; 'national egoism', as Lenin called it, is all. China's material aid to 'unofficial forces' such as it is has been given, not to its declared supporters, but to other forces fighting foreign occupation – the National Liberation Front in Vietnam, FRELIMO in Mozambique, the FNLA in Angola, and, briefly, to the Palestine Liberation Organization in the Middle East.

The entirety of the Chinese Communist party's policies abroad is therefore directed through the official foreign policy of the People's Republic. State policy is thus no longer a minor tactic to secure temporary survival. 'Internationalism' must mean relations between States, between ruling classes, not a world class alliance. It must mean also that the Chinese State is bound to accept the States concerned, to accept the given order of the world; it is impossible to maintain State relations while simultaneously taking active steps to encourage revolt or even using Chinese diplomatic missions abroad to proclaim the need for revolution. The People's Republic recognized this convervatism in the principle of 'peaceful co-existence' (as did Stalin, who originally formulated the idea), which is espoused officially by China and, indeed, by all the States of the world – domestic revolt is solely a matter for the ruling class concerned, and no 'foreigner' has the right to interfere. Chinese Communists may sympathize, but they have no instrument other than the Chinese State with which to influence events.

The principles of Chinese Communist policies abroad have remained remarkably consistent, although tactically there have been different phases in their application. Whereas Lenin was concerned to secure the temporary survival of the Soviet Union *in order to prosecute world revolution* – and to 'utilize the contradictions' between rival powers to this end – the Chinese party has expended much energy in endeavouring to 'utilize the contradictions' solely for its own survival. What have been the phases in this effort?

1   Up to the Civil War, the party was primarily concerned to divide the Kuomintang from the United States. Much effort was devoted to wooing the US military mission in Chungking. So far as can be seen, no efforts were made to foster mutiny in the Japanese army or rebellion in Japan, the primary purpose of the relationship between the Bolsheviks

and Germany in 1917–18.

2　From 1949, the party accepted of necessity (particularly during the Korean War) the international leadership of the Soviet Union. The Cold and Korean Wars ended all relationships with the United States and drove China into an alliance with Russia. However, the Chinese party seems to have endeavoured to form a bloc of Communist parties under its leadership, committed to rural guerilla warfare (not necessarily without Soviet blessing). It was not accidental that such warfare broke out in 1947–8 in Burma, Malaya, the Philippines and Indonesia. The movements were contained by the established governments in all cases. China also extended, from 1949, considerable material aid to the Vietminh in Vietnam against the French attempt to re-establish its control.

3　With the ending of the Korean and the first phase of the Vietnam War, the People's Republic endeavoured to form a bloc of States, the 'Third World', under its leadership. The close relationship between China and Nehru's India, and Chou En-lai's role at the 1955 Bandung Conference, were the high points of this endeavour. China's position was somewhat ambiguous since the dominant theme at Bandung was 'non-alignment' between East and West, whereas China was aligned with the Soviet Union.

4　In the late 1950s, the relationship with the Soviet Union deteriorated rapidly over a range of issues, while the relationship with India began to decline from 1959 over the question of Tibet, finally being destroyed in the border clashes of 1962. China now sought to create a new bloc of States, more narrowly defined in ideological terms than in 1955 – North Korea, North Vietnam, Sukarno's Indonesia, Ben Bella's Algeria, Nkrumah's Ghana, and even, at one stage, Castro's Cuba. It was short-lived. North Korea and North Vietnam opted for neutrality in the Sino-Soviet dispute (both attended the 23rd Congress of the Soviet Communist party which the Chinese party boycotted) and for Russian material assistance. Cuba, in urgent need of Soviet aid, chose to try to create a rival International, the Havana Tricontinental Congress (January 1965), and ultimately opted for the link with Russia. Sukarno, Ben Bella and Nkrumah were all overthrown.

5　China simultaneously attempted to secure close relationships with the advanced States (other than the Soviet Union and the United States); an effort continued after the Cultural Revolution (when, very briefly, other policies were pursued, although in general the external activities of the People's Republic declined markedly). This brought material supplies to make up for the loss of Russian help or sales.

6　In the late 1960s, by a fortunate conjuncture of events, China was

212

able once more to achieve a relationship with the United States. After the armed clashes with Russian forces on the Chinese border in 1969, the threat of Russia increasingly came to dominate all the external policies of the People's Republic, including the fluctuating relationship with Washington. The American link permitted the People's Republic to gain entry to the United Nations, and this became a central forum for China's continuing efforts to create a bloc of backward States, the 'Third World'.

What is the theoretical underpinning of Chinese foreign policy? The Chinese party has revised Lenin's concept of imperialism in an interesting way. Imperialism now is not a world system dominated by the rivalries of the advanced powers, each advanced power being compelled to compete by the world system itself; it is a world of States, dominated in the 1950s by one 'superpower' (the US), in the 1960s by two 'superpowers', and increasingly in the 1970s again by one 'superpower' (now the Soviet Union). The word 'imperialism' refers not to a world order, but to the relationship between the 'superpowers' and pre-eminently the backward States (but latterly, as we shall see, the advanced capitalist powers other than the superpowers are also oppressed). In practice, such a view implies that the superpower has the most freedom to manoeuvre; it can *choose* whether or not to 'oppress'. In Lenin's view, the advanced capitalist States have very little choice but to compete, and thereby oppress.

What is the prize for the superpower? According to the Chinese, it is domination of the backward countries, not the defeat of other advanced powers (as it was for Lenin; competition *in* the backward countries was only the arena of struggle for the advanced). In 1945–6, when Stalin warned the Chinese party not to start a civil war lest the United States attack Russia in retaliation, Mao claimed that the United States was not interested in dominating the Soviet Union, only in the zone between Russia and America.[5] In Mao's terms, the 'principal contradiction' was not between the advanced rivals, but between the United States and all the other States of the world other than the Soviet Union. Thus in 1958 he saw the purpose of NATO not as competition with the Soviet Union's Warsaw Pact, but as 'an attack on nationalism and domestic communism (the emphasis is to attack the intermediate zone, Asia, Africa an Latin America)'.[6] In 1964, he described the aim of the United States eighteen years earlier as 'to invade the buffer zone and not to fight the Soviet Union. The anti-Soviet slogan was a smokescreen.'[7] By the mid-1960s, however, the situation had apparently become less clear, for Mao told Edgar Snow that he had not decided whether the 'principal contradiction' was between 'neo-colonialism' and 'the revolutionary peoples' or between the capitalist countries themselves.[8]

The contenders were States, national ruling classes, not international classes. It followed, as it had for Stalin, that the 'revolutionary peoples' included 'also the patriotic national bourgeoisie, and even certain kings and princes and aristocrats who are patriotic'.[9] The States were constant, but all the other terms – for example, 'superpower', 'intermediate or buffer zone' – could change according to temporary tactical needs. Thus in 1965 Mao startled a French parliamentary delegation with his use of the term 'the Third World': 'France itself, Germany, Italy, Great Britain – provided the latter stops being the courtier of the United States – Japan and we ourselves: there you have the third world.' The definition was of no particular importance since it was not part of a strategic orientation on an objective world situation (that was due, in Lenin's words, 'to profound economic causes'). Theory, concepts, were rationalizations after the tactics had been decided upon, not the basis for the tactics. It is this factor which gives Chinese politics such a timeless character. At any given moment, the situation is equally excellent, the revolution always rising, there are no defeats, all is ever onwards and upwards. For example, in 1958 Mao observed that 'The Western world is disintegrating. Currently, it is in the process of breaking up . . . Final disintegration is inevitable.'[10] And again: 'The enemy is in disarray, more and more so. We are getting better, better and better every day . . . the truly discouraged is imperialism. They are rotting, becoming disorderly, full of conflicts, splitting apart, experiencing a bad time. Their good days are over. Their good days were before they turned into imperialism, when they only had capitalism.'[11] This, at the height of a quarter of a century's unprecedented growth in world capitalism, well before the Vietnam war! Sixteen years later, the Chinese press was still repeating: 'The imperialist camp has split and disintegrated as a result of the daily decline of US imperialism. The socialist camp no longer exists as the Soviet revisionist renegade clique has restored capitalism and turned the socialist Soviet Union into social imperialism. Meanwhile, the third world flourishes with its ranks growing stronger and stronger, its political consciousness raised daily and its unity strengthened daily.'[12] Morale is all, truth nothing. There was, on this formulation, apparently nothing to be done except assume power in all countries.

The concepts were ambiguous to preserve tactical flexibility. However, the clashes affecting China's borders invariably prompt the régime to take a much firmer line than on other occasions (in contrast to Lenin's attitude to the Ukraine at the time of Brest-Litovsk). The bitterness of the relationship with the United States in the 1950s was provoked by the Korean War and the US defence of Taiwan. The relationship to India was completely reversed, regardless of all such classifications as the 'Third World' and 'oppressed peoples', by the 1962 Sino-Indian border clash. And the bitterness, at the time of writing, in full flood against the Soviet Union was sparked by the 1960 withdrawal of Russian experts, but heightened by the border clashes of 1969.

(ii) The mode of struggle

The aim of Chinese foreign policy is to win greater security for China. To achieve this, the People's Republic has endeavoured to win foreign ruling classes as allies against the 'superpowers'. To this end the Chinese leadership has never been so naïve as to rely on political argument and propaganda. They have used 'material incentives' – that is, aid and trading agreements. Overwhelmingly, this is the main part of China's assistance abroad, not aid to revolutionary organizations.

China began its foreign aid programme in the 1950s. Aid was used to secure certain relationships, to give sinew to diplomatic détente. After the Cultural Revolution – with the physical threat from the Soviet Union – China extended its aid programme in an effort to secure a seat in the United Nations and create a loose voting bloc within it. Between 1970 and 1974, cumulative Chinese aid was about US $2,400 million, more than double the total for the years between 1956 and 1969. From 1970 (when foreign estimates of cumulative Chinese grants, loans and credits put the figure at about US $1,200 million) the chief recipients have been Vietnam ($400 million) Romania ($200 million), Pakistan, Sri Lanka, Tanzania, Zambia, but have included Guyana, Chile, Malaya, Peru, Equatorial Guinea, Ethiopia, Mauretania, Somalia, Iraq and Burma.

Chinese aid has been heavily concentrated on Africa. By 1975, it was larger in cumulative total than Soviet aid, although China's total world aid is only sixteen per cent of all Eastern Bloc aid, of which the Soviet Union supplies seventy-seven per cent (Eastern Bloc aid in 1975 was US $1,715 million, compared to Western aid of US $26,000 million or more than the total cumulative Eastern Bloc aid in twenty-one years). Some twenty-three countries in Africa are in receipt of Chinese aid, but the largest expenditure has been on the Tanzam railway (completed in 1976). In Asia, seven countries have taken a quarter of all Chinese aid, and in the Middle East, five countries have been the chief beneficiaries. In South America, Peru has been the main recipient, although there is a wide scatter of other countries, some of whom were granted aid without according China diplomatic recognition (for example, Guyana).[13]

Aid seems to have been extended for two related purposes: to secure

215

entry to the United Nations, and to block Russian influence. Because Russian aid is roughly five times larger than Chinese, the contest is difficult. It is obligatory that Chinese terms are more favourable than those of its rivals. The political nature of the régime to which aid is extended has, with a few exceptions, never been an important calculation. For example, Pakistan in 1966 was the main military client State of the United States in south Asia (a member of the two American-sponsored pacts, CENTO and SEATO, and the location of the US spy base at Peshawar); it was also a conservative authoritarian régime in which the Communist party was banned; nonetheless, Chinese aid was extended to the government without obliging it to withdraw from the US relationship. Chinese aid was similarly advanced to the 'feudal' régime of Hailie Selassie, aid taken from the surplus product of Chinese workers and peasants was used to support a régime comparable, in Chinese terms, to the Ch'ing dynasty!

However, with regard to the first aim, under the benevolent neutrality of the United States, the policy worked. In October 1971 the People's Republic was admitted to the United Nations. China had hitherto rejected the United Nations, although not as 'the League of Imperialist Bandits' (Lenin's phrase for the United Nations' predecessor, the League of Nations). For example, it was full of praise when Sukarno's Indonesia walked out of the United Nations in the 1960s. Now the United Nations became an 'arena of struggle', a world court for the indictment of the superpowers. Pursing the same logic, China applied for entry to the International Monetary Fund and the World Bank, but subsequently withdrew its application when those bodies refused to expel Taiwan.

Is China using the United Nations to publicize its condemnation of the world order? It would be a poor way of achieving this purpose since the deliberations of that body have no popular following. The delegates are the audience and, by objective criteria, members of the world ruling class. Such tactical considerations have not guided China since it is dedicated to supporting the United Nations. It increased its contribution to the UN budget from four to seven per cent of the total in October 1972, so becoming the third largest contributor after the United States and the Soviet Union. China's declared policy is not to denounce the United Nations as a conspiracy of the 'imperialist bandits', an employers' confederation, but to 'uphold the principles of the United Nations Charter'. For example, on entering the United Nations, Vice-minister of Foreign Affairs, Ch'iao Kuan-hua, proclaimed: 'We hope that the spirit of the United Nations Charter will be really and truly carried out. We will stand together with all the countries and

216

peoples that love peace and uphold justice and work together with them for the defence of national independence and State sovereignty of various countries and for the cause of safeguarding international peace and promoting human progress.'[14] The United States delegate could not have put it better. Was the statement a subterfuge? It was published in China and around the world; there was no accompanying commentary which suggested any alternative strategy, of which this was only a tactical diversion. Nor does China go further than the conservative principles that govern the United Nations in its main interventions. For example, in August 1972, China vetoed the application of Bangladesh for membership on the grounds of 'defence of the principles of the United Nations Charter, the relevant resolutions of the UN General Assembly and Security Council, which gave expression to the will of the overwhelming majority of the countries of the world and the fundamental interests of the entire people'. If the United Nations in any sense represents the interests of the people of the world, clearly so do the national governments represented there – the world order, apart from a few anomalies, is the best possible!

15

FOREIGN POLICY

A detailed account of Chinese foreign policy is beyond the scope of this book, but some examples will illustrate the central thesis: that China's foreign policy is in no way different from that of other world powers.

(i) The Superpowers
The United States
The revision of Lenin's concept of imperialism did not originate with the Chinese, but with Stalin. He needed to portray a world in which the Soviet Union was not bound by an external logic, but could present whatever it did as freely chosen by a free society. He needed also a justification for distinguishing between the 'peace-loving democratic' imperialists who became his allies in the Second World War and the 'warmongering fascist' imperialists. For Mao also, some imperialist powers were 'aggressive', and others 'anti-war, anti-aggression, anti-Fascist'.[15] It seemed historical accident, or the function of the temperament of the leaders. Mao did not explain, as Lenin might have done, that the 'anti-war' ones were on top and holding down the 'pro-war' ones.

In the Chinese context, the distinction before 1949 meant an orientation on the main foreign power influential there, the United States. The policy had no ultimate success since American strategic interests changed when it was decided not to invade the north China coast.[16] The Cold War made this early lack of success into something of a principle. The prowess of Chinese arms in Korea perhaps also led the People's Republic to reassess its relative weakness. Nonetheless, American rivalry with the Soviet Union ruled out any rapid restoration of relations, even though China displayed great 'reasonableness' at the Geneva Talks in 1954. It became taken for granted that: 'The US is not dependable. She would give you something but not much . . . How could we expect imperialism to give us a full meal? It won't . . . Imperialism is stingy'[17] and that 'US imperialism is a very ferocious imperialism'.[18] Foreign minister Chen Yi was even so rash in 1965 as to formulate this tactical rift as a principle: 'Peaceful co-existence with US imperialism, which is pushing ahead its policies of aggression and war, is out of the question.'

It was rash because the late 1960s produced a reversal of this position. It was rash also since throughout these years, overshadowed by the US war in Vietnam, representatives of the United States and China held regular talks with each other – up to May 1971, there were 137 Sino-American discussions in Warsaw.[19] These talks, it was presumed abroad, stabilized China's relationship to Vietnam – the PLA would not intervene in Vietnam unless American troops crossed the seventeenth parallel dividing south and north. China was thereby enabled to undertake the Cultural Revolution without fear of US intervention. On the other hand, the United States was assured that China would not, for example, launch attacks on Taiwan (as occurred in 1954 and 1958) in order to divide American forces operating in Vietnam and so relieve the National Liberation Front; this was no idle threat, since in the Indo-Pakistan war of 1965 China had divided Indian forces by threatening India on the Sikkim border.

What caused the reversal in Chinese foreign policy? It was the change in the situation of the United States. President Nixon was faced with military stalemate in Vietnam and heavy American losses; the costs of the war were fuelling world inflation and jeopardizing the ability of American businessmen to compete abroad (a situation reflected in a steadily weakening dollar and increasing currency instability). Furthermore, opposition to the war was mounting in the United States. It was therefore urgent that the United States extricate itself from Vietnam, but without appearing to have been defeated. On the Chinese side, the Russian invasion of Czechoslovakia in 1968 (illustrating the willingness of Moscow to put down rebels within its own 'sphere of influence'), and armed clashes on the Sino-Soviet border in 1969, sharply brought home China's relative isolation. China needed allies and entry to the United Nations, particularly after having allowed external relations to decay during the Cultural Revolution.

Contrary to Chen Yi's promise in 1965, China did not require an end to American 'policies of aggression and war'. Mao had, at the height of the Cold War, laid down the correct line: 'Our policy is that we will not invite him [US Secretary of State John Foster Dulles] as a guest, but if he should knock on our door, we would entertain him.'[20] In 1969, Nixon instructed his Secretary of State, Henry Kissinger, to 'knock on Mao's door', perhaps calculating that the Soviet threat would induce Mao to open it, despite the continuation of the war in Vietnam. In December

1970, Snow interviewed Mao, who invited Nixon to visit Peking. The following spring, an American table tennis team visited Peking; the US government relaxed its embargo on trade with China, and ordered the mining of North Vietnam's harbours (China protested when two *Chinese* ships were damaged). The US announced that it had dropped 6.2 million tons of bombs in Vietnam, or 262 pounds per head of the Indo-Chinese population. In June, China condemned the United States for having extended its bombing raids in Vietnam right up to the Chinese border, but when Kissinger visited Peking the same month, he was received with 'extraordinary courtesy'. In July, the United States had some 100,000 troops in Vietnam, and again extended the massive bombing of the North; President Nixon, it was announced, would make a State visit to China. The Hanoi daily, *Nhan Dan*, attacked Nixon – for 'dividing the socialist countries' (19 July 1971).

Publicly, the attacks on Nixon and US government policy – 'Nixon's fascist atrocities', as Mao put it in 1970, 'have kindled the raging flames of the revolutionary mass movement in the United States' – ceased, although not the atrocities themselves. The crowds turned out in their millions to cheer the American architect of Vietnam's destruction. Nixon was received by Mao, and duly secured his release from Vietnam (in return, China gained entry to the United Nations, and was permitted access to the US market – it purchased ten Boeing aircraft in September 1972). Who was using whom? The United States could claim with more substance that it had 'exploited the contradictions' between China and the Soviet Union – to the loss of Vietnam.

Mao's support did not, to his regret, save Nixon from the consequences of his appalling record. The Watergate scandals forced him from office. They were a dramatic revelation of the corruption of the most powerful State in the world, yet they were not reported in the Chinese press. Furthermore, in the autumn of 1975, Mao personally invited the ex-President, then the least popular American in the world, to make a further visit to China, despatching an aircraft to California to collect him, and greeting him as 'one of the greatest leaders of our time'. Presumably, the Chinese Communist party were not concerned about the effect of this quixotic behaviour on their supporters in the United States. The suggested explanation – the possibility of embarrassing the new President, Ford, just entering his first election campaign, and so forcing him to make greater concessions on the question of Taiwan – was of greater significance.

China had too little weight in the world system to influence the major powers in conditions of relative peace. It might complain bitterly that Ford had dispensed with the services of a leading anti-Communist,

James Schlesinger (who was promptly invited to China to inspect the Chinese defence preparations); that the West was appeasing a Hitlerite Soviet Union; that the Helsinki agreement was a second Munich, with Kissinger playing the role of Neville Chamberlain and anti-Communist Senator Jackson that of Winston Churchill; but it did not influence US policy.[21]

The Soviet Union

The relationship between the Chinese party and Moscow was, as we have seen, full of difficulties, but Chinese self-restraint ensured that these did not become public. The Cold War prevented any independent initiatives on the part of China and although the PLA performance in the Korean War was highly creditable, outside its own 'sphere of influence' in east Asia China remained dependent upon Soviet nuclear and military power.

However, as China's strength grew, its tolerance decreased. The Russians were more concerned with their rivalry with the United States and with competing for allies in the 'non-aligned' world, than with helping China to build an industrial economy (for example, Soviet aid in 1959 to Iraq was 78 roubles per head of the population; to Egypt, 154 roubles; and to China, 9 roubles).[22] The Russians were more worried about the danger of world war than helping China to regain Taiwan; the launching of the first sputnik in 1957 gave the Soviet Union a military lead over the United States, and China inferred from this that the threat of US attack need no longer intimidate the Eastern bloc. The Russians refused to help during the Great Leap Forward and afterwards; and supported India in the Sino-Indian dispute which began in 1959. Finally, the Russians unilaterally withdrew all aid from China in 1960, the onset of the most severe crisis in the history of the People's Republic.

To that date, however, the Chinese leadership made no public criticism of Russia. They apparently accepted the nature of Soviet power in Russia and East Europe. The beginning of a workers' revolution in Hungary in 1957 found the Chinese party insisting 'on the taking of all necessary measures to smash the counter-revolutionary rebellion in Hungary', and attempting to stiffen the resolve of Moscow when it 'intended to adopt a policy of capitulation and abandonment of socialist Hungary'.[23]

Twelve years later, an identical action by the Russians in Czechoslovakia evoked a completely contrary response from China – fierce protests at the denial of the Czech right of national self-determination.

In the early 1960s, the Chinese view was still expressed as irritation.

221

The fierce attacks were reserved for Yugoslavia, the surrogate for Russia, just as Albania became the whipping-horse for China. All those inside the semi-secret debate knew the code – China's delegate to the Sixth East German party (SED) Congress in January 1963 was howled down for criticizing the 'Tito clique'. The only people left in the dark were the mass of the population in Russia and China. However, the split was open by 1962 but not until 1964 did Mao suddenly announce: 'The Soviet Union today is the dictatorship of the bourgeoisie, a dictatorship of the grand bourgeoisie, a fascist German dictatorship, and a Hitlerite dictatorship. They are a bunch of rascals.'[24] In the ensuing years, this startling reassessment was explained in more detail – a 'monopoly bourgeoisie', presumably lurking in the Soviet Union through the years of Stalin's rule, had seized power by a coup between 1953 and 1956 under the leadership of N. S. Khrushchev, and 'restored capitalism'.

We have some idea of the massive social upheaval required in Weimar Germany and Italy to bring the fascists to power – and in particular, the role of a major threat from working-class parties. There is no evidence of such an upheaval in Russia, nor of the appearance of a new class, a 'monopoly bourgeoisie', qualitatively distinct from the ruling order of Stalin's years. The changes in the Soviet Union of the 1950s were trivial in comparison to those of the 1920s and 1930s. The Chinese press might proclaim that, 'Fascist white terror reigns in Soviet society today', but to all appearances, there were *fewer* political prisoners, arbitrary arrests, sudden disappearances than in the 1930s. To make any sense, Mao would have had to examine the years of Stalin's rule; but if he had done that, not only would he have jeopardized the apostolic succession he claimed, he would have challenged a social order based on the imperative to accumulate, an order he was seeking to duplicate in China: State capitalism.

Mao's 'analysis' was no more than an expression of extreme irritation *after* the Sino-Soviet break, not the theoretical justification for the break itself. It was not a new use of the term 'fascist'. Stalin identified Tito as a fascist at the time of the break between Russia and Yugoslavia: 'The bourgeois nationalist Tito clique in Yugoslavia, having taken the anti-Soviet, anti-Marxist path, has reached the logical end of its anti-Communism – fascism.'[25] The Chinese shared this view, but it did not prevent them giving a hero's welcome to Marshal Tito on a State visit to China in August 1977. As we shall see, the term 'fascism' describes only the attitude of the State concerned to either the Soviet Union or China; it denotes nothing about the domestic order.

The Chinese party set out to split Communist parties round the world and organize a counterforce loyal to its own position on the questions in dispute with the Soviet Union. They did not pursue their goal with great zeal or publicity, so that results were meagre. The only major party to accept Chinese leadership was the Indonesian, the PKI. Others moved towards a position of neutrality.

Although the private polemics against the Soviet Union were sharp, publicly China was still restrained. What changed the situation was the increasing military competition of the mid-1960s (the Soviet Union placed forty to fifty divisions along the 6,850-mile Sino-Russian border) and the events of 1969. Now, China's 'sacred territory' was at stake. The United States was defeated in Vietnam, and, in any case, had begun a withdrawal from south-east Asia (a withdrawal partly contingent upon its new capacity to fly American troops to most parts of the world at short notice, without the need for fixed bases; partly to force US allies to provide their own troops). It was further constrained by domestic political difficulties, and again defeated, politically if not militarily, in Angola. China was vulnerable, and began to identify the Soviet Union as the main threat to the world: 'This superpower is even more greedy and more cruel than old-line imperialism in its plunder and exploitation of the third world.'[26]

The United States, fresh from the ruins and terrible death toll in Vietnam, became a friendly neighbourhood imperialism. There was no coherent argument, merely the assertion that the Soviet Union was in an 'expansionary phase' and the United States in decline, as if somehow national souls, the rise and decay of civilizations, so beloved of conservative historians, were at stake.

Characterizing Tito as 'fascist' did not prevent the Soviet Union from once more embracing its old ally, Yugoslavia, and the same is true of China. Since the 'theory' is only a rationalization of short-term tactics, it can be reversed by a change in the tactical situation. At which stage, the Soviet Union will become a secondary 'superpower', perhaps another 'superpower' will appear (Japan or West Germany), the Chinese press will switch off its ferocious anti-Russian propaganda, and a few of China's supporters round the world will be shed.

(ii) The Intermediate Zone
At one stage, the 'intermediate zone' was composed of all the powers between the United States and the Soviet Union. Today, however, there is a hierarchy in which the 'first' world is not the Western industrialized bloc (as opposed to the 'second' world, the Eastern Bloc, and the 'third' world, the economically backward countries) but simply the two superpowers. The 'second' world, the new 'intermediate zone', becomes the

advanced industrialized countries other than the two superpowers, a kind of world middle-class between the two ruling powers and the proletarian-peasant masses of the backward countries.[27] The structure is pure fantasy in Marxist terms since the participants are not world classes but national States; the States are not peoples but national ruling orders.

The 'intermediate zone' is identified solely by its relationship to the 'superpowers'. It therefore has no independent competitive role; American fear of competition from Japan and the European Common Market is thus merely private foolishness. On the analogy of the 'middle class', China's role is to show the régimes of the intermediate zone that they are oppressed by monopoly capital (alias the two superpowers) and ought to ally with the proletariat (alias the third world), under the leadership of China. As Teng Hsiao-p'ing described the task to the audience of the United Nations in 1974: 'The developed countries in between the two superpowers . . . are in varying degrees controlled, threatened or bullied by the one superpower or the other . . . all these countries have the desire to shake off superpower enslavement or control and safeguard their national independence and the integrity of their society'. The industrialized powers of Europe are invited to demand their right of national self-determination, their right to break up the international economic system which grants them power and wealth. In the 1960s, this meant the encouragement of France under De Gaulle in its challenge to NATO, and Romania in asserting its independence from the Soviet Union. Indeed, China went so far as to denounce East Germany's demand to be recognized as an independent power, and champion West Germany's 'right of national self-determination' – that is, the unification of Germany under the West Germans.[28]

However, once the Soviet Union became the main threat, the disunity of the Europeans, their continued maintenance of elements of national autonomy, became a factor of vulnerability. China began to urge unification in the Common Market, which, in practice, now means the acceptance of West German hegemony. Chou described the official position in 1973: 'The cause of European unity, if it is carried out well, will contribute to the improvement of the situation in Europe and the whole world.' The fact that much of the European Left regards the European Economic Community as a rationalization of 'monopoly capital' – and some even see it as a plan by the United States to create a large market for its industries – is of no significance for Peking in comparison to the Russian threat to China.

This produces curious paradoxes. Elements of European and American domination of the world become favoured by China – from the Commonwealth military security arrangements for south-east Asia to that traditional object of the Left's opposition, NATO. The NCNA published in the *People's Daily* extracts from the British Conservative Government's Defence White Paper on the need to increase military spending and to strengthen NATO against the Russian threat.[29] It is the most anti-Communist Right-wing politicians who are received with most warmth in Peking – the Cold War warriors of the United States, the Conservative politicians of Europe – Heath of Britain, Franz Joseph Strauss (of the CSU, the right wing of the Christian Democratic party) of West Germany, Tanaka of Japan, Frazer (rather than Whitlam of the Labour party) of Australia, and Muldoon of New Zealand (who had for twenty years opposed the diplomatic recognition of China).

The paradoxes are more extreme. In February 1974, the British Conservative government was overthrown by a miners' strike. In the union, the leader of one of the most militant sections was a Communist, Mick McGahey, president of the Scottish miners. China invited the leader of the Conservative party, and, although now only an ex-Prime Minister, he was accorded a reception appropriate to a head of State – a guard of honour, gun-salute, military band playing 'God Save the Queen', and a personal interview with Mao. The new Labour Prime Minister was not invited. But the miners' union had been invited to send a delegation, and appointed McGahey as its leader. While Heath, the man the miners had defeated, was fêted in China, McGahey, one of the miners' leaders, was refused a visa as leader of the delegation (the British Communist party was pro-Moscow).

China's relationship to *Japan* illustrates the predominance of tactical questions in Chinese foreign policy. In the 1960s, Peking criticized the Liberal Democratic government for being instruments of American imperialism. In the late 1960s when negotiations were under way with the Soviet Union for Japanese exploitation of raw materials in Siberia, the attacks became sharper. The *People's Daily* put the official view confidently in 1971: 'Look at the past of Japanese imperialism, and you can tell its present; look at its past and present, and you can tell its future'.[30] What was its future?

'Japanese monopoly capitalism is sure to protect its colonial interests by armed force and scramble for spheres of influence. An "economic power" is bound to become a "military power", and economic expansion definitely leads to military expansion. This is the inexorable law of development of Japanese militarism ... What Japan should take is another road, the road of independence, democracy, peace and neutrality. That is to say, Japan must free herself from US imperialist control, dismantle US military bases and achieve national independence; she must renounce fascist dictatorship.'[31] The advice might seem a little irrelevant, given the 'inexorable law' which indicated that Japan *must* become a 'military power'. In fact, it turned out to be quite unnecessary for Japan to follow China's advice in order to buck the 'inexorable law'. It required only a visit by Prime Minister Tanaka (a millionaire, subsequently imprisoned for implication in the Lockheed scandal). He met Mao, and the 'inexorable law' disappeared. The joint declaration provided a brilliant explanation: 'China and Japan are neighbouring countries separated by a strip of water, and there was a long history of traditional friendship between them. The two peoples ardently wish to end the abnormal state of affairs that has hitherto existed between the two countries.' Chou En-lai, with admirable discretion over the record of Japanese pillage of China in the preceding one hundred years, welcomed the agreement with a country, 'with whom government relations had not been good since 1894 . . . The new relationship was not directed against third parties. Neither was seeking hegemony in the Pacific region, and both were opposed to those who were.'[32] Those alarmed at the possibility of Japanese expansion were no doubt reassured; that is, until new irritations re-created the instant theory of Japan's inexorable imperialism.

Spain has a special place in the history of the European labour movement. When Franco led the forces of Spanish fascism to overthrow the elected government in the 1930s, an international brigade of volunteers fought alongside the Spaniards to save the republic. The bitterness of their defeat, compounded by Franco's collaboration with Nazi Germany and fascist Italy during the civil war and the Second World War, made Spain and Franco outcasts even in establishment circles in Europe. The Soviet Union did not restore diplomatic relations with Spain until February 1977.

In 1973, Franco's Prime Minister, Admiral Carrero Blanco, was assassinated, no doubt to the moderate delight of the clandestine Spanish Left and those in the European labour movement who remembered the past. But China's response was to despatch its Prime Minister to Sr Jaime de Ojeda to express condolences to the Spanish chargé d'affaires in Peking, an event solemnly publicized in China.[33] Two years later, the admiral's master declined in health, but held off death for an extended period. A group of socialist dockers in east London endeavoured to hasten Franco's departure by despatching him a telegram, 'Die, you bastard, die!' (it was sadly refused by the telegraph authorities).

When Franco's end finally came, there was much opposition in the British government to sending a representative to his funeral; Labour MPs boycotted the House of Commons in protest at the government's decision to despatch a Cabinet minister. They might have quoted

Byron's comment on the burial of George the Third:

> 'It seem'd the mockery of hell to fold
> The rottenness of eighty years in gold.'[34]

Of the European powers, only Monaco sent its head of State; in Latin America, only Generals Banzer (of Bolivia) and Pinochet (of Chile) attended.

The People's Republic did not send its head of State (the post had been vacant since the fall of Liu Shao-ch'i), but, as the Chinese press reported to the masses of China: 'Chairman of the NPC Standing Committee, Chu Teh, mourns the death of Spanish Chief of State Franco.' Wreaths were sent from Chu Teh, premier Chou, and the foreign minister; and the following day Chu Teh sent the official congratulations of the People's Republic to King Juan Carlos on his coronation.[35]

Such niceties are the trivia of relations between States, but China claims to be something other than an ordinary State. In the case of Spain, it might – wrongly – have been thought to be committed to the forces fighting to overthrow Franco and his heir, the King.

(iii) The Third World
Asia

(a) South-east Asia. Only in China's traditional 'sphere of influence' has the People's Republic given consistent material support to powers abroad – to North Korea and North Vietnam – and verbal support to movements against governments with which it has friendly diplomatic relations.

In the case of *Vietnam*, China extended recognition and material aid before the Soviet Union, and its artillery was an important factor in the final siege of Dien Bien Phu. However, at the Geneva Peace Talks in 1954, both the Soviet Union and China tried their utmost to persuade the Vietminh to accept partition and not to sweep the French out of Vietnam.[36] It was not clear whether this flowed from the same fear of extending the war as guided Stalin in his efforts to force the Chinese Communists to make concessions to the Kuomintang in the 1930s. However, the Vietnam problem remained unsolved and broke out in a much more massive form in the 1960s.

As we have seen, China's role in the second war in Vietnam involved both an expanded flow of aid and a careful stabilization of its role with the United States. The détente with Nixon provoked a reaction in Hanoi, but perhaps the Vietnamese simply wished to keep both its powerful patrons at arm's length. The new united State took over the claims of its southern half, including the Paracel (Hsisha) and Spratly

(Nansha) islands in the South China Sea, both of them also claimed by the People's Republic. It is said there may be oil reserves beneath the islands, and also that China fears the establishment of a Soviet base in the area which would dominate the far eastern shipping lanes. Whatever the reasons, China stated her position unequivocally: 'All islands belonging to China must certainly return to the bosom of the motherland', and 'The archipelagos of the South Sea are our sacred territory and we have a responsibility to defend them.'[37]

Perhaps this territorial issue became as sharp as it did because of the estimate of the Soviet threat, which also caused China to revise her attitude towards four countries hitherto seen as US clients – Thailand, Malaysia, the Philippines and Singapore.

In 1971, *Thailand*, in the view of the People's Republic, was ruled by the 'Thanom clique' of American puppets. However, the first contacts between the two régimes were made in that year. They agreed to end hostile radio propaganda and open up trade. The Thai Prime Minister, Pramoj Kukrit, made a State visit, and signed an agreement with China, Article 8 of which instructed Chinese nationals in Thailand to 'abide by the law of the Kingdom of Thailand, respect the customs and habits of the Thai people and live in amity with them'[38]; that is, not to 'make revolution'. Mao, according to Kukrit, denied that any aid was given to insurgents in Thailand or to the clandestine Voice of the Thai People radio; he advised Kukrit not to be troubled by the insurgents of the Thai Communist Party – 'since it is small, it should not be dangerous'. No protest was made when the Thai civilian régime was once more overthrown with great bloodshed in the autumn of 1976.

In the *Philippines* President Marcos was engaged in a four-year programme of establishing a civilian dictatorship, destroying all opposition, including both supporters of Mao Tse-tung thought (operating for twenty years as partisans in the Central Luzon province) and a Muslim rebellion in the south. In September 1974, Marcos' wife, Imelda, was invited to China where she met Mao and was offered Chinese crude oil in a trading agreement. In June the following year, her husband followed her on a State visit. Marcos was overwhelmed by the hospitality, referring to China as the 'natural leader of the Third World' (Chou reassured him that no material aid went to the Communist rebels in Luzon), and adopting the slogan of 'self-reliance'. Indeed, the President, one of the closest allies of the United States in the east Pacific, despatched a stream of missions to China to learn how to copy certain institutions, and even set up a 'Commune' in Leyte, Manila.

Malaysia made the same transition. In 1970, the NCNA reported that the Rahman-Razak clique' was terrified by the guerillas of the Malaysian Communist Party and its power was crumbling.[39] Nonetheless, diplomatic relations were announced in 1974, and half of the 'clique', Tun Abdul Rahman, duly made the pilgrimage to Peking. He was assured no material aid was being given by the Chinese to the Malaysian guerillas. Later, in April 1975, the Prime Minister was upset by the Chinese Communist party's greetings to the Malaysian party on the occasion of its forty-fifth foundation anniversary (the actual message was critical of the warring factions of the party, and urged it to stay away from the urban areas). No doubt the Chinese ambassador reassured the Malaysian Prime Minister that the message had no real significance. However, it could be used as a bargaining counter on some future occasion, much as Stalin tried to use the Chinese Communist party in bargaining with Chiang Kai-shek.

Singapore's opposition has been successively repressed by the régime of Lee Kuan Yew. On his State visit in 1976, Prime Minister Hua Kuo-feng assured him that Singapore's treatment of rebels would evoke no protest from China (an assurance published in the Singapore press but not in the Chinese).

What were the contradictions the People's Republic sought to exploit in these four cases? They were not utilizing any 'major contradictions' at all, nor were they trying to compete with the United States, which was no longer seen as an enemy. It was a simple territorial security exercise, an exercise that in all but open expression consigned the domestic rebels to insignificance and permitted the régimes concerned to claim that they had Chairman Mao in their support.

Indonesia remained, at the time of writing, the last country of the area (apart from Singapore) without diplomatic relations with the People's Republic. The régime under General Suharto originally came to power through a military coup in 1965. Up to that time, Indonesia was governed by President Sukarno, basing himself latterly on the Indonesian Communist Party (PKI) and the army. The PKI had followed a policy of creating a United Front, but without independent territories or armed forces. In practice, this meant sacrificing its radical policies – for example, land reform – to maintaining the alliance with forces that, in some cases, represented those liable to suffer in any land reform. It meant also that the PKI offered entirely uncritical support for Sukarno, calling for a strengthening of his government (his so-called 'Guided Democracy'). Sukarno, on the other hand, needed a civilian counterweight to the powerful army, which the PKI provided. Sukarno therefore protected the party from the army and advanced its position in the government (although never in the decisive agencies governing the defence forces). Under Sukarno's patronage the party became the largest Communist party outside the Eastern Bloc, with a claimed membership of three million, and between eight and ten million in party front organizations. But it was captive to Sukarno's purposes, for it could raise radical demands for domestic change only at the cost of its position in the Indonesian government.

China gave strong support both to the PKI and to Sukarno, even though the PKI's policy was one of united front *without* armed struggle. It was impossible to have the one with the other; had the PKI tried to create its own military forces, the army would have seized power.

In September 1965, a section of the palace guard launched a coup against the main leadership of the army. The army counter-attacked, alleging that the conspiracy was hatched by the PKI and China; it was further alleged that China had flown arms in to the leading air force base for use in the coup. The military rapidly won control, and there followed one of the most appalling massacres in modern history. More than half a million people were slaughtered by the army and its supporters; 200,000 PKI members lost their lives, including forty-five of the fifty central committee members. Many hundreds of thousands of others were gaoled.

China did not comment publicly at the time of the coup, nor has any balance sheet of lessons drawn from the catastrophe appeared since. For the ordinary Chinese newspaper reader, revolutionary Indonesia simply disappeared, in due course surfacing as fascist Indonesia. The People's Republic continued its aid programme to the new military régime and did not break off diplomatic relations until an attack was launched on the Chinese embassy in April 1966. The Russians behaved in a similar fashion. *Pravda* published no protest at the destruction of the PKI, and the 700 Soviet advisers in Indonesia continued at work. But the political role of the Russians in Indonesia is not as important as that of the Chinese, who form a large minority in control of much business and commercial activity. The attack on the PKI and China could therefore draw on anti-capitalist sentiments.

In these circumstances, the restoration of diplomatic relations is more of a problem than elsewhere in south-east Asia. However, it will almost certainly come. Then China's criticism of Indonesia's repression of the Freitlin struggle for national independence in East Timor will disappear in time for the arrival of General Suharto (or his successor) in Peking. The fate of the survivors of the PKI, the insurgents lying low in Central Java, is of less importance to Peking.

(b) **South Asia.** Asia was China's main area of operations in the 1950s.

India was an important ally, and given that, after China, it was the most populated country in the world, what the Indians called 'Hindi-Chinni bhai bhai' included over half the population of the 'third world'. However, the two countries had a common border and were also competitors. At various times India attempted to dabble in China's 'sphere of influence' in Tibet. Yet in terms of its domestic régime, India seemed to be a natural candidate for the title of 'progressive State'; it was republican, secular, and operated a planned economy within 'a socialistic framework'. It was also 'non-aligned' between the two major blocs, a position it reached in advance of China.

Such details, however, were irrelevant compared to the imperatives of the defence of Chinese territory. After the much publicized clash of 1962, India was excluded from the grand design. Mao put it thus: 'We have an anti-imperialist task. We have the task of supporting national liberation movements, that is, we must support the broad masses of the people in Asia, Africa and Latin America, including workers, peasants, the revolutionary national bourgeoisie, and the revolutionary intellectuals . . . But they do not include the reactionary national bourgeoisie like Nehru.'[40] Why did the commitment exclude Nehru, but not Emperor Hailie Selassie of Ethiopia or General Ayub Khan of Pakistan? Supporters of China later argued that India's close relationship to the Soviet Union was the reason. However, at the time when strains began, 1959–60, it was China who was the close ally of the Soviet Union and the recipient of Russian aid. Since Mao did not discover that the Soviet Union was 'fascist' until 1964, Nehru was perhaps to be forgiven for not having discovered earlier. What, for Mao, determined the character of India's domestic order was not the Soviet relationship, but the actions of Indian troops in Ladakh.

The break with India led to the rapid promotion in Peking's eyes of *Pakistan*, up to that time considered the closest ally of the United States in south Asia. An equally important factor, however, was the attempt by the Soviet Union to establish its influence in Pakistan (Russia assumed the role of mediator in the Indo-Pakistan war of 1965, and instigated the agreement signed between the two countries in Tashkent). China's promotion of General Ayub Khan from 'American puppet' to 'anti-imperialist force' was not an idle commitment, since, as earlier mentioned, Chinese intervention in the 1965 war on Pakistan's side divided the Indian forces. China's role placed its sympathizers in India in an extraordinarily difficult position, only exceeded by that of its supporters in Pakistan. In the case of Maulana Bashani, one of the leaders of the Pakistani Left, he was induced – after a visit to Peking – to give 'critical support' to the quasi-military dictatorship, and to its role in

231

exploiting the Maulana's own province, East Pakistan. It was also China's interests which led the East Pakistan Left to oppose the demand for Bengali independence, so giving the movement up to Sheikh Mujibur Rahman's Awami League and to Indian influence.

Between 1968 and 1971, both wings of Pakistan – East and West – were in revolt, culminating in the collapse of Ayub Khan's power and the demand from the Bengalis of the East for the 'right of national self-determination'. However, China's geopolitical considerations took priority in Peking over the national liberation of Bengalis. In June 1970 the Soviet Union received a State visit from Ayub Khan's successor, General Yahya Khan, who accepted a Russian offer of aid in constructing a heavy industrial sector. China could scarcely risk losing its most consistent ally in south Asia to 'social imperialism' for the sake of a handful of Bengalis. Accordingly, the Bengali revolt became a 'CIA-Soviet Union-Indian' plot to destroy the Pakistan nation. As the Pakistan army moved to crush the revolt in the East, China extended material and moral support to the Pakistan régime.[41] Maulana Bashani might appeal directly to Mao, but Chou En-lai congratulated General Yahya Khan on safeguarding 'national independence and State sovereignty'.[42] The Chinese people were given the General's speech justifying the repression, and the General in turn quoted China in explaining his action to the Pakistanis.

The repression produced an enormous flight of refugees to India. The Indian régime could not afford to neglect the opportunity. Only a few days after the repression began, the Indian high command began to formulate plans to achieve the central aim of Indian foreign policy since 1947, the destruction of the threat of Pakistan. Thus, Chinese policy both directly and through its influence over the Pakistani Left was instrumental in achieving the exact result it was supposed to be aimed to prevent; it opened the door to Indian intervention, and made it possible for the Indian government to establish a dominant position in the independent Bengali State of Mujibur Rahman. To compound the paradoxes, in August 1972, the Chinese delegate at the United Nations vetoed the entry of the new State of Bangladesh; and in May 1975, Pakistan reaffirmed its fundamental loyalty to CENTO at the Ankara meeting of the alliance.

Some supporters of China have attempted to protect Peking's honour by suggesting that officials in the Chinese foreign ministry were privately appalled by events in East Pakistan. No doubt in the high days of the US war in Vietnam, the State Department was full of officials grieving over the behaviour of American troops in Vietnam. Such private qualms may be face-saving, but they do not relieve the régimes concerned of their responsibility. Others have found retrospective justification in the corruption of the Bangladesh régime and the famine of 1974. Yet China was indirectly instrumental in permitting that régime to come to power; no alternative was offered by the Bangladesh Left. Forcing East Pakistan back into the authoritarian rule of Islamabad would in no way have prevented the famine. But none of this was acknowledged in Peking or in the Chinese press; no lessons were drawn, no explanations offered either to the Chinese people or China's supporters abroad.

For *Sri Lanka*, China has been an important ally since 1952. By 1975, China took eleven and a half per cent of the country's exports and supplied twelve and a half per cent of its imports. In 1972, China's financial aid covered three-quarters of Sri Lanka's budget deficit.

1971, however, was a difficult year. Mrs Bandaranaike's government, having done very little in its short time in office, provoked a Left-wing mass revolt in the rural areas.[43] Possibly three to four thousand young people were killed, and many thousands imprisoned. China – along with the United States, the Soviet Union, Britain, India and Yugoslavia – rallied to give moral and material help to Mrs Bandaranaike's government. The Sri Lanka press published an official letter from Chou En-lai, released by the Sri Lanka government (but not published in China), which offered a further long-term interest-free loan of £10.7 million (extended twice later in the year) and congratulated the government on defeating the insurgents – Chou was 'glad to see that the chaotic situation created by a handful of persons who style themselves as Guevarists ... has been brought under control'. On her State visit to China two months later, Mrs Bandaranaike was able to thank her hosts publicly for their support; in return, Chou thanked Sri Lanka for supporting China's application to enter the United Nations.

(c) **The Middle East.** China appears to have given some aid to the Palestinian Liberation Organization until King Hussein of Jordan endeavoured to destroy the movement; then China assisted the government of Syria (the main force seeking to destroy the PLO in Lebanon in 1975–6). But although Chinese propaganda made much of this aid at the time, it was the least important component in China's foreign policy in the area.

What raised the most difficulties for the supporters of China was the relationship between the People's Republic and the Imperial State of *Iran*. As a long-standing ally of the United States and a pillar of CENTO, the régime of the Shah was at once aligned with a superpower, internally repressive and 'feudal'. Yet in April 1971 when the

233

indefatigable Chou En-lai was busy congratulating General Yahya Khan of Pakistan and Mrs Bandaranaike of Sri Lanka, he also found time to receive Princess Ashraf Pahlevi, sister to the Shah, on an official visit to Peking. The Princess was received by Chairman Mao, and even accompanied him on the rostrum during the May 1st celebrations, no doubt to the delight of the parading masses. Simultaneously, the Shah's notorious secret police, SAVAK, were launching a widespread attack on all opposition in which thirteen urban guerillas were summarily executed. Chou praised the Shah's 'struggle against foreign aggression and for national construction', a phrase that possibly referred to Iran's massive military expenditure. In August, diplomatic representatives were exchanged, and the Chinese people informed that it had congratulated the Shah on his sterling work for his people.[44] The following year, the Shah himself and Empress Farah Diba 'were accorded a warm welcome by tens of thousands of people lining the streets' of Peking. In return, Chinese representatives graced the Shah's grotesque extravaganza, the Persepolis celebrations of 2,500 years of Persian 'feudalism'.

The Shah had joined the 'progressive forces'. The clandestine Iranian Left might denounce the corruption and repressive character of his régime, but this was an entirely marginal matter so far as China was concerned. The Left might deplore the continued arms drive of Iran and the use of Iran's oil revenue to finance Western arms manufacturers, but the People's Republic decreed otherwise: 'As an independent sovereign State, Iran has the right and every reason to ensure her self-defence by strengthening national defence. As to the kinds and number of weapons it intends to buy and from where it buys them, it is the internal affair of Iran and other countries have no right to intervene.' Whence came this 'right'? From Iran's 1,562 mile border with the Soviet Union.

Africa
The creation of national States on the African continent coincided with the development of an independent Chinese foreign policy. As a result, it was possible for China to be more effective in contest with other world powers which had not had time to consolidate positions. It is said that African guerillas were trained in China in the early 1950s. But by the late 1950s, it seems, diplomatic representatives of China were engaged in training militia and youth organizations in some African countries that received financial aid. Those financed included Ethiopia, the Batutsi government in the former Ruanda-Burundi, Algeria, Egypt, Ghana, Guinea, Mali, Somalia and Congo. However, a contradiction soon emerged; training youth organizations could only take place if there was no hint

234

of mobilizing an opposition to the established régime (the United States was prepared to manufacture such hints to secure influence among independent African States). Revolutionary propaganda opened the door to United States, and later Soviet, intervention. Thus the military government of Congo (B) was induced to disband the youth movement. In Mali, a military coup against President Modibo Keita ended the Chinese link. Chinese diplomats were expelled from Burundi, Dahomey and Central African Republic.

In 1964, a new diplomatic offensive took place, culminating in an African tour by Chou En-lai. Although a number of African States were irritated by Chou's declaration, 'Africa is ripe for revolution', the visit had solid achievements. Before his visit, seven countries recognized the People's Republic, and fifteen Taiwan; afterwards, fourteen recognized China, sixteen Taiwan and four remained neutral.

These efforts were slightly nullified by the neglect of external relations during the Cultural Revolution. However, immediately afterwards Peking began a new drive to win diplomatic recognition as the stepping stone to membership of the United Nations. Financial aid was expanded, but this time without any hint of organizing subversive youth groups. Aid went overwhelmingly to established governments, although some assistance is said to have been given to the liberation struggles in Mozambique and Guinea-Bissau (and possibly some, but very little, to the Zimbabwe guerillas in Rhodesia). The largest share went to Zambia for the building of the Tanzam railway. President Kaunda has divulged that, at one stage, Chinese representatives did distribute propaganda in Zambia, but withdrew it and apologized when he complained. China's aid tends to contradict its stress on 'self-reliance', and possibly raises problems at home. During the negotiations for the Tanzam railway, it was rumoured that there was opposition to the project in Peking because it would considerably delay China's own railway programme, and would do so for a country, Zambia, where the per capita income was double that of China.

To Hailie Selassie of *Ethiopia*, China was a generous patron from the mid-1950s, despite the presence of US military bases in the country. The Emperor made numerous State visits to Peking. Chou, in October 1973, toasted the aged scoundrel: 'We admire the Emperor of Ethiopia, Hailie Selassie . . . I raise my glass to commemorate his struggle against colonialism, racialism, and slavery.' Chinese loyalty was in no way deflected by the protracted war of national liberation forces in the province of Eritrea, a revolt the heroic Emperor endeavoured to root out. Nor was China more than embarrassed by the student movement in Addis Ababa which precipitated a general strike and the collapse of the imperial régime in 1974. The Chinese people were told nothing of these events. Peking rapidly recognized the new military rulers, extended financial aid to the Emperor's successors and refrained from comment on the escalation of the war against the Eritreans and the savage persecution of the Ethiopian trade unions and Left.

Nineteen seventy-one was a year of embarrassment for the People's Republic not only in Asia. In July, a section of the Sudanese army, with the support of the pro-Moscow Communist party, carried out a short-lived coup against the régime of President Nimeiri. The President reacted in force with a severe repression of the Communists. In Peking, the China-Sudan Friendship Society organized demonstrations in support of Nimeiri.[45] Officially, the People's Republic congratulated the President on his victory and offered him a grant equivalent to US $45 million. Meanwhile, the Soviet Union and North Vietnam made strong protests at the slaughter. China saw the events in the Sudan not as they affected the Sudanese, but only as they affected its competititon with the Soviet Union (an attitude shared in Moscow and Washington).

However, it was in the south that Chinese foreign policy received its greatest humiliation in Africa. The disunity of the liberation forces in the former Portuguese possession of *Angola* provided an opportunity for both Soviet and South African influence there, which in its turn divided the loyalties of the African States. Zambia, already immersed in a détente with South Africa, called for no more than an end to foreign intervention. Nyerere of Tanzania, the recipient of much Chinese aid, and Machel of the recently victorious Mozambique, led the majority of the Organization of African Unity in support of the MPLA, Russian and Cuban assistance or not, and against the South African-backed UNITA and the Zaïre-backed FNLA (the two subsequently allied).

Zaïre, a corrupt and brutal Right-wing régime under General Mobotu, financed the FNLA, a force based upon the old tribal kingdom of the Bakongo. The leader of the FNLA was Holden Roberto, the ex-king of the Bakongo, and a successful businessman in Kinshasa, the Zaïre capital. Like his father-in-law, General Mobotu, Roberto is reputedly strongly anti-Communist. By contrast, the MPLA had a much less defined tribal base, had a major following among the urban working class of Luanda (the Angolan capital) and was explicitly opposed to private capitalism and foreign domination of an independent Angola. However, General Mobotu has received financial aid from China for a number of years (as well as military assistance from the United States). In December 1974 the General made the customary State visit to Peking. Both the MPLA and the FNLA sent representatives to Peking to secure aid.[46] However, China, presumably on the grounds that the

Russians were assisting the MPLA, chose to support the weaker of the two, the FNLA. Roberto himself claimed in May 1974 that 200 Chinese instructors were in Zaïre to train his troops. As a result, China found itself supporting a front, the FNLA–UNITA, which was not only defeated, but was supported by South Africa and the United States, a factor sufficient to shift the loyalty of virtually all the African States to the MPLA. It was an ignominious disaster.

China will live down the exposure, and the tides of rhetoric will once more cover the credibility gap. Yet the case illustrates the relative weakness of China's foreign policy as an instrument of change. China lacks the material power to be as effective as its rivals. As a result, it has too often been compelled to fall in with purposes it has previously condemned, simply in order to retain influence. For example, China condemned all talk of détente between the independent African States and South Africa, but by 1975 it was obliged to accept this if it wished to retain its influence in Zambia.[47] Again, despite having fostered a long relationship with Ethiopia, China was displaced by the Soviet Union in 1977 with the onset of war with Somalia; China could not match Russia's arms supplies.

Latin America

Latin America, most advanced of the three backward continents and most penetrated by foreign capital, was the least suitable for Chinese preoccupations. For no amount of argument could have persuaded the Left there that the threat of the Soviet Union was greater than that of the United States. In any case, there was a home-grown revolution, that of Cuba (in 1959) which more clearly epitomized the conditions of the continent for the Left (and without the obfuscation of Peking's jargon). Fidel Castro in the 1950s opposed forming a 'united front' with the 'national bourgeoisie' of Cuba in order to create 'new democracy'. Guerilla struggle, its class basis unspecified at the time, led straight to 'socialism'. Peking might ritually intone in 1960 that 'the tide of national and democratic revolution in Latin America is surging to unprecedented heights', but Fidelismo blocked any real influence. For a time it looked as though the two might collaborate, but the importance of Russian aid for Cuban survival (despite the Soviet defeat in the 1962 missile crisis) finally proved decisive.

China turned to 'material incentives' for established governments. Peru, governed by a military régime but with the largest Chinese minority in the continent (estimated at 60,000) became the main recipient of Chinese aid. A Sino-Peruvian trade agreement was signed in June 1971, shortly after the signing of a Soviet-Peruvian treaty.

In the case of *Chile*, China warmly supported the Allende government of Popular Unity, despite the fact that it was not the result of a revolutionary seizure of power and despite the warning of the Indonesian disaster. One week after the Sovet Union offered Allende a loan of US $150 million, China capped it with an interest-free loan of US $65 million. By 1972, China had become the fourth largest buyer of Chile's copper. The Chinese press described Chile as a revolution, without qualification or warning. The coup by General Pinochet might have been an embarrassment, except that coups were by now a frequent occurrence among China's associates abroad. The embassy of the People's Republic was one of the three foreign legations in Santiago (the others were the British and the French) that refused to offer refuge to the hunted supporters of the government, and China was the first country in the Eastern Bloc to recognize the new régime. No official statement was published in China on the question of how another progressive force had slipped through the interstices of history, although in the United Nations delegate Huang Hua expressed regret at the murder of Allende and the attack on the Cuban embassy as 'in violation of international practice'. Subsequently, China extended the financial aid made to Allende to Pinochet. The régime was grateful; under-secretary of foreign affairs, Cmdr Claudio Collados specifically praised the People's Republic as one of the few countries which had not tried to isolate Chile.[48] The opportunity to scoop the Soviet Union by securing privileged access to the new régime proved a temptation too great to be resisted.

Hypocrisy is the stock-in-trade in relations between States, each flattering the other while arming. What is surprising is not that China conforms to this rule but that so many people should be able to disregard the evidence and believe that China's activities abroad reflect the cause of world revolution. The consistency of Chinese policy is impressive; its principles have remained constant throughout the period. What has changed, unfortunately for Peking, is the world. That is not China's fault, but it is the source of the 'mistakes'. Policy is tested not by its rhetoric in times of stability. It is in crisis that the test comes. Unswervingly, each crisis finds the People's Republic 'failing' by the criteria laid out in the opening section of this chapter.

The current changes in the world signify the onset of a long-drawn-out crisis, and herald a new opportunity for revolution. If China were devoted to world revolution in anything other than a rhetorical sense, now would be the time for a radical change of gear and the creation of an International. Foreign policy would be subordinated to building mass movements dedicated to the overthrow of the States with which the People's Republic has relations. Yet the Chinese State has consistently sacrificed that purpose to the maintenance of its competition with the Soviet Union. Its material support to national liberation struggles has been too marginal to affect the domination of the major powers. Its border conflicts, the defence of its 'sacred territory', has been the primary concern of its foreign policy: which is why the Soviet Union, still economically far weaker than the advanced capitalist bloc, is offered as the main threat. As a result, China is more often used by the other powers of the world than it is able to use them; it is China which is dragooned behind the United States or Holden Roberto.

Many of China's supporters abroad do not examine the record closely. They claim that the People's Republic has policies superior to those of other States, not that it practises something different, 'proletarian internationalism'. Then the fact that the terms of Chinese aid are better than those of its rivals, and its rhetoric borrows on a tradition of using the word 'revolution', becomes the substance of the case. The evidence proves otherwise.

16

MAO TSE-TUNG THOUGHT ABROAD

Chinese foreign policy is only one aspect of the influence of Mao Tse-tung thought. Supporters of the Chinese Communist party would argue, indeed, that it is only a minor aspect. Is it possible that this wider influence could stimulate revolution in the world, independently of China's official activities?

Before the Sino-Soviet split, the Left was crippled by its identification with the notorious tyranny of the Soviet Union. Every challenge forced socialists on the defensive, and it was Western capitalism that was able to lay claim to 'freedom'. For the Communists, only an immense intellectual evasion could keep their faith alive. Indeed, theory became a faith, an opaque scholasticism no longer accessible to any except the most dedicated student. For workers, 'the Party' remained for many years the most consistent defender of their immediate shop-floor interests, but the link between those interests and the conquest of political power became so tortuous few could identify it. For politics in the Party had now become identified with the interests of the Russian State, not the struggle for workers' power. The material basis of 'Marxism-Leninism' – the defence of the national interests of the Russian ruling class – was in contradiction to its supposed principles, the international emancipation of the oppressed.

Without the Sino-Soviet split, it is possible, for example, that the new Left in the United States in the 1960s would ultimately have gravitated towards Moscow. As it was, the idealism of the student radicals spread outwards to embrace a wealth of doctrines, from anarchism, experiments in new ways of life and new religions, to the orthodoxies. In the short term, the unity of a common cause, rooted in the interests of the Soviet Union, was irrevocably weakened, but in the longer term, the change compelled socialists to rethink the tired formulae of Moscow, and rediscover what the struggle for freedom was supposed to mean.

The pace of the process of intellectual emancipation is not, however, determined politically by cogitation, but by events, by the crises which test the relevance of the responses inherited from the past. Events are determined independently of the Left, and most frequently without socialists playing even a slight role. Socialists who will not or cannot be involved sometimes conceal their unimportance by pinning labels over events, by trying to colonize them intellectually, and thereby reconcile rectitude with impotence. The real need, however, is not labelling but to reshape thought and action so that the socialists become relevant, become able to learn anew the tasks required to shape revolt so that it is aligned with the principle of universal emancipation. Does Mao Tse-tung thought assist this process?

There is an immediate problem. The practice of the Chinese Communist party in its ascent to power was only indirectly related to the theory it claimed to follow. The party's basic aim was to create a strong national State, not to precipitate a world movement of self-emancipation (although its supporters would argue that the first was a step towards the second). The material basis of power was not the party's relationship to China's working class or peasantry, but its command of an independent army and territory. The Japanese invasion gave the party its opportunity to champion Chinese nationalism, not workers' internationalism.

However, these material factors play little role in Mao Tse-tung thought. There, it is suggested that revolution flows, not from material factors, but from 'ideology'.

The party has, in Marx's terms, an 'esoteric wisdom', sustained independently of the perception of workers. The wisdom does not contribute to the struggle of workers, except in the sense of giving it a style of rhetorical extremism. The party is united by doctrine, not by its relationship to a class, and it is doctrine which identifies all other parties, not their class. The party thus conforms to Marx's criterion of a sect: 'The sect sees the justification for its existence and its "point of honour" not in what it has in *common* with the class movement but in the *particular* shibboleth which distinguishes it from it.'[49]

The party grows by inducing people to accept its ideology, and this accounts for the stress laid on 'education' and psychological transformation. Theory does not explain the perceptions *workers* derive from their own experience. Rather, faith provides a spiritual consolation and direction independent of those perceptions. The faith has sometimes echoes of non-conformist Christianity, for it embodies a moral attitude rather than a scientific theory that relates the experience of a class to society as a whole. Part of the faith may be an abstract emphasis on science. For example, the Australian Marxist-Leninists say of Mao

Tst-tung thought that 'it teaches us to study actual conditions and respect the facts', a proposition sadly not implemented in their publications.[50]

A faith requires enemy doctrines to give it definition and unity. The differences are *doctrinal*, not about the appropriateness of the theory to an independent material reality. Since doctrine is all, the greatest animosity is directed at those doctrinally closest – whether Communists or Trotskyists. These are traitors, not to be argued with or shown the error of their beliefs, but anathematized. Above all, the true believers are always threatened with the virus of 'revisionism'.

The word 'revisionism' sums up the confusion. For the word is rarely defined, and therefore disagreements can never be specified and argument directed at a particular question. Yet the word has become the small change of Left-wing circles today. It carries the connotation of corruption among the true believers, arising from the combination of greed and bribery by the enemies of the party. This implies that what is 'true belief' is clear, and not revisionist. Yet it is precisely that which is in dispute.

The word was not unclear when it began its life. At the turn of the century, a group of thinkers in the social democratic movement argued that some of Marx's important predictions were wrong and, furthermore, that Marxism was a science of economic analysis, showing the inevitability of socialist revolution, without indicating why anyone should do anything about it. It lacked, they said, a moral imperative to inspire workers to revolution. Some of them later formulated such an imperative, drawn from the work of the philosopher, Immanuel Kant, and employed much ingenuity in trying to graft it onto Marxism. The issue is complicated, and the criticisms depended for much of their force on the peculiar character of the 'Marxism' presented by the leading theoretician of social democracy, Karl Kautsky.

'Revisionism' in this form was the point of re-entry for philosophic Idealism, for a re-emphasis upon morality, moralizing and voluntarism. Marxism was misconstrued as a bourgeois science, and then a bourgeois ethic brought in to 'restore the balance'. It had the effect of asserting the decisive role of those who could understand what it was all about, the intellectuals. Ideas in the hands of those most adept at manipulating them were made the primary force, rather than the material reality facing the majority.

The issues in dispute died with the creation of the Communist International (the revisionists went with the Socialist International and social democracy), but not the need of intellectuals to expropriate workers intellectually within the workers' movement. The impact of Stalinism was to achieve just this result. After Stalin, it took extraordinary intellectual dexterity to master what had become sacred texts, to smooth the contradictory twists and turns of Soviet policy into one continuum. The Sino-Soviet dispute removed what is required to sustain an orthodoxy an international authority defining what is orthodox. China has established no new defining authority, so the field is open to all with the ambition to perform that role. Neo-Kantian ethics could now emerge in the guise of the 'correct Marxist-Leninist leadership'. But the sheer diversity of correct lines jeopardizes the authority of each; for one group, all other 'correct lines' are 'revisionism'.

'Revisionism' is apparently not reformism – the argument that socialism can be achieved gradually through the accepted institutions of existing society. Nor does it mean revising certain propositions advanced by Marx, for Mao has done as much of that as anyone. It is an individual error and can be overcome simply by changing loyalties.

If 'revisionism' is a dividing line between socialists, separating the true from the false, there is a similar supposed division between ruling classes. Much of the literature argues that a ruling class is wrong because it is greedy, corrupt, arrogant, the implication being that if it were not these things, it would be acceptable. *Bad* ruling classes are the problem, not ruling classes *per se*, much as in China, as we have seen, bad bureaucrats are a problem, not bureaucrats in general. The literature of Maoist groups employs the word 'fascist' to denote bad ruling classes. Thus, in recent years, in the eyes of many supporters of China, almost the entire capitalist world is governed by fascists – Presidents Nixon and Ford, Mrs Gandhi, Edward Heath, Mr Frazer of Australia – all have been at times 'fascist' or 'semi-fascist'. Governments can become fascist, and then stop being fascist, as we have seen in Peking's view of Japan. There is no objective structure which defines the term, only subjective responses.

The term has another function. It provides the rationale for 'stages'. All 'democratic' classes, including the 'patriotic' part of the ruling class, must be united under the leadership of the party to overthrow 'fascism' and create 'new democracy'. There is thus apparently an interest common to all classes in the existing national State. Once the party secures power, the workers are supposed gradually to establish their 'dictatorship' through a series of peaceful reforms, culminating in socialism. Thus, revolution through class collaboration is followed by a gradualist and reformist stage. The effect is to displace workers' interests as the primary force in revolution (except in so far as workers are part of the 'nation'). The politics of class alliance entail that the workers must restrain their instincts to the pace of development of their 'ally', the national bourgeoisie; the exploiters determine the tolerable degree of activity of the exploited. The party is, above all, the supreme mediator balancing between contradictory class interests. An almost identical set of propositions is embraced by pro-Moscow Communists.

Supporters of Mao give legitimacy to these propositions with citations from a tradition. But the quotations are not seen as responses to concrete problems at a particular time, but as abstract principles, universally applicable as are religious principles. The writings of Lenin, for example, become reduced to a set of abstractions, and since Lenin said many things which are contradictory when taken out of context, there is a vast field for doctrinal disputation. Furthermore, the Lenin of *What is to be done?* becomes the manual of party organization, not the *practice* of Lenin's party organization between 1905 and 1917.

In this way the 'ultra-leftist' slogans of the Comintern's Third Period (1928–33) can, in Maoist publications, be sumultaneously conjoined with their contradiction, the Right-wing directives of the Comintern's Seventh Congress (1935). It will be recalled that the Comintern introduced its Third Period by arguing that the world was about to enter a phase of unprecedented revolutionary activity. It was therefore no longer necessary to have defensive collaboration with other working-class parties, the united front. On the contrary, such parties were an obstacle to radicalizing the workers; the largest of these parties, the Social Democrats, was described as 'social fascist' to emphasize the point. Communists must now prepare for armed insurrection for an immediate seizure of power. By contrast, the Seventh Congress relinquished all intention of revolution. It was argued that the world was about to be swamped by fascism, and the Soviet Union might be embroiled in devastating war with Nazi Germany. Defence of the Soviet Union became the overriding priority, and Communists must take action to unify *all* national forces opposed to fascism and secure an alliance between their own State and the Soviet Union. Regardless of the validity of either strategy, they were based on quite opposite assessments of the immediate future. Yet, as we have seen, Mao's estimate of the two key elements in the Chinese party's experience are armed struggle (armed insurrection) and the united front.

The effect of this combination is paradoxical – a refusal by Maoist groups to collaborate with other working-class parties, a rejection of efforts to unite the class, and a willingness to collaborate with parties of the bourgeoisie. The result is nationalism with a left sectarian rhetoric. Because the strategy is founded upon 'principles', mere experience cannot invalidate it. That Spain was lost to Franco, Indonesia to Suharto or Chile to Pinochet are not relevant to testing the validity of the united front. In fact, there are apparently no circumstances where success is not possible. The prairie is always equally dry and needs only the spark of 'Marxism-Leninism' to ignite it. It is this abstract activism in some Maoist groups that gives it the flavour of anarchism: In the Beginning was The Deed.

However, identifying the doctrine does not allow us to comprehend the sheer diversity among the supporters of Mao Tse-tung thought. All do not conform equally to the scheme. Some are drawn to Third Period slogans (to the point of acts of isolated violence), some to the more comfortable patriotism of the Seventh Congress; some to the doctrine of psychological change, with few political implications (but embodying a quasi-Christian ethic of 'Serve the People'); others are fascinated by a version of the culture of China, quite independent of the reality facing the majority of Chinese. Around such groups there is an even wider range of thought that seems particularly powerful among the European and American professional classes. A claim to support the Great Helmsman thus does not indicate any predictable political behaviour.

Usually the organized supporters of Mao Tse-tung thought are not tested by the demands of practice. As a result, the most serious questions concern ideological differences that may in no way be related to what the group does. However, in relationship to China's foreign policy, there are tests few can escape. For example, if the countries of the 'intermediate strata' are part of China's progressive world alliance against the superpowers, is it justifiable to pursue revolution in one of those countries? If it were successful, it might jeopardize the security of the People's Republic and permit the intervention of 'social imperialism'. Yet if China's foreign policy takes priority in this equation, the group concerned has no other function than to defend the existing ruling class.

China offers little guidance to its supporters abroad. In the early 1960s, it was rumoured that the Chinese party intended to create a new authoritative body to define tactics – a small conference of its supporters was said to have met in Auckland in 1964 – but nothing came of it. China's leadership has preferred to remain neutral, or at least intervene only to the extent that some are invited to visit Peking, some not. A closer identification might embarrass State-to-State relationships (as has happened in south-east Asia, for example). The obverse of this neutrality is that movements can develop under the banners of Mao Tse-tung thought which are actually inconsistent with it.

Below, three examples are examined to illustrate some of these points.

(i) The Naxalbari Movement in India

In the mid-1960s, India was already in crisis. The optimism which accompanied the early years of independence had faded. Economic development seemed to be permanently jeopardized by the incapacity of agriculture to support industrialization, and of the external balance to support the required volume of industrial imports.

In the last half of the 1960s, real factory wages declined by seven per cent. The central government cut public investment radically, and this afflicted most severely heavy industry and India's 'Ruhr', the eastern region centred in Calcutta. Between 1965 and 1969, some 100,000 people were sacked in the registered factory sector of the Calcutta Metropolitan District (and, on the trend line of 1951 to 1965, 326,000 jobs were lost). Inflation accelerated and there was a sporadic but severe crisis in basic food supplies.[51]

This is the background to the rapid escalation in class warfare. In the State of West Bengal (of which Calcutta is the capital), the number of workers in dispute as a percentage of all workers in registered factories rose from an average of fourteen to fifteen in the 1950s, to eighteen in 1966, thirty-two in 1967 and 1968, and fully eighty-five in 1969. The figures illustrate imperfectly the persistent militancy of workers in eastern India. For example, at the giant Durgapur steel works there were in 1969 517 *gheraos* (in a *gherao*, the workers 'lock-in' the management until they concede), or many more than one per working day.

The economic crisis and the class battles placed an intolerable strain on India's fragile political order. The dominant national party, Congress, split in 1969. The Communist party – with its leading stronghold in Calcutta – had divided into a pro-Moscow party (the Communist Party of India, CPI) and a supposedly pro-Peking party (the Communist Party of India (Marxist), CPM) in 1964–5. The events of 1967–9 again split the CPM, the dominant party in West Bengal, into a majority that retained the name, and a new overtly pro-Mao Tse-tung thought party, the Communist Party of India (Marxist-Leninist), CPML. The CPML embarked on a course of action designed to achieve power by revolution.

The split in the CPM was impelled by the party's participation in the State government of West Bengal. In 1967, the CPM was a coalition partner (with the CPI and twelve others) in a short-lived administration. It fell in late 1968, and after a short period of central administration (President's rule), new elections in February 1969 produced a CPM-led coalition. This survived until March 1970 (when another period of President's rule ensued).

In early 1967, a group of CPM cadres, without the authority of the

246

party leadership, began an agitation for the peasant seizure of land in a district of north Bengal, Naxalbari. Peking identified the 'Naxalite' movement as led by 'a revolutionary group in the Indian Communist party' (it refused to distinguish between the CPI and the CPM). It was full of praise for the movement, and affirmed confidently that: 'So long as the Indian proletarian revolutionaries adhere to the revolutionary line of Marxism-Leninism-Mao Tse-tung thought and rely on their great ally, the peasants, it is entirely possible for them to establish one advanced revolutionary rural base after another in the huge backward rural areas and build a people's army of a new type'.[52] Peking gave no evidence that the revolutionaries *were* proletarian, nor whether bases could be established in modern India; nor did it report a number of other peasant agitations parallel to that in Naxalbari since they were directed by an 'unrecognized' leadership (for example, under the Naga Reddy group in Andhra Pradesh). By its praise of the Naxalites and by its criticism of individual 'CPI leaders' (for example, the chiefs of the CPM, E.M.S. Namboodiripad and Jyoti Basu), Peking distanced itself from the CPM. However, in general there was little coverage of India in Chinese publications, particularly in 1968 when, apparently, the Indian revolution announced in 1967 disappeared from view. In 1968, the West Bengal State government with its strong CPM contingent (and Jyoti Basu as Home Minister, in charge of police) was obliged to launch a police counter-attack on the Naxalites.

Naxalite publications continued through 1968 to report the spread of the movement far beyond Naxalbari. Indeed, the relative weakening of the movement in Naxalbari was explained by the leadership as the result of the lack of a strong party organization. In November, the first steps were taken to set up a new party and make a formal break with the CPM (but the new organization contained only a small minority of the groups identified as followers of Mao in India). Charu Mazumdar, a former CPI district secretary, became the new leader of the organization. He proclaimed that the 'main contradiction' in India was between the peasantry and feudalism. Armed struggle was the priority for the cadres as a method of inciting the peasants to seize the land and crops of landlords. Finally, in March 1969, at an open rally in Calcutta (not in Naxalbari), the CPML was inaugurated.

The new party had, apparently, no programme or constitution. It was to be clandestine, rural-based and armed. Peking gave unstinted public support to the party in general and Charu Mazumdar in particular, even attributing a new agitation in Andhra Pradesh (in the Srikakulam district) to his personal leadership. The Andhra movement, it was said, now included 300 villages, administered by revolutionary councils and

247

committees.[53] An attentive reader in Peking must have been astonished at the speed with which so much had been accomplished.

In fact, the CPML had had some success in maintaining small armed groups in various areas, but had not succeeded in inciting the participation of the peasants in any significant numbers. The cadres remained overwhelmingly Calcutta students. The illegality of the party's activities obliged it to work in conditions of extreme secrecy which had the effect of blurring the distinction between the party and ordinary bandit gangs, so limiting its appeal to an uncommitted rural population. Police and military units became increasingly successful in pursuing and infiltrating the partisan units, and the party was obliged to be even more secretive. This was no Chingkang mountain region, but densely settled areas, within easy access of district towns; peasant informers, whether eager for police favour or simply to defend themselves and their villages from reprisals, were everywhere. Mazumdar finally concluded that any 'open' organization would lead to the domination of the party by rich peasants and 'revisionism', so that all must be secret. Only a completely clandestine group could lead the landless! Apparently the politics of the party and the landless were too weak to withstand revisionism. When the party had secured areas against class enemies, it would become possible to create mass organizations. Peking apparently expressed no disapproval of this change of emphasis.

Later, after the defeat of the CPML, it was argued that Mazumdar's change of emphasis constituted 'neglect of mass organization' and a deviation from Mao Tse-tung thought. Is this correct? As we have seen, in the early days of partisan warfare in China, 'mass organizations' were not formed until *after* the party had secured a stable administration. Indeed, Mao went much further in 1930, suggesting that the party must hold cities before mass mobilization was possible: 'Only after wiping out comparatively large enemy units and occupying the cities can we arouse the masses on a large scale and build up a unified political power over a number of adjoining counties. Only thus can we arouse the attention of people far and wide.'[54] The needs of military survival rendered any alternative approach in areas close to enemy-occupied towns wilfully 'irresponsible'.

If there is a criticism of Mazumdar's orthodoxy, it is that – unlike Mao – he pursued a 'poor peasant line'. He set the party to incite land seizure against the rich peasantry. By contrast, Mao urged an *alliance* with the rich peasantry and, during the second United Front period, with the 'patriotic landlords and gentry'. Mao's alliance was to be directed against Japanese imperialism, but Mazumdar had already defined the 'main contradiction' as between peasant and landlord.

Presumably, Mazumdar would have had to identify foreign capital in India as the main enemy, and endeavour to build a class coalition against it (but that would have made CPML politics indistinguishable in this respect from those of the CPI and CPM).

Peking made no effort to point this out. It continued to offer public support. In late 1969, Mazumdar announced that the party was on the verge of forming a People's Liberation Army to begin full-scale civil war. By early 1971, the PLA would have begun its triumphal march across the plains of Bengal.

So far as tactics were concerned, Mazumdar and his associates did not restore the earlier emphasis on mass organizations. On the contrary, they moved in the opposite direction: to the 'annihilation tactic'. Now it was not so much self-reliant mobile guerilla groups, inciting the peasants to seize land, but individual cadres assassinating particular landlords in the hope that this would set off peasant revolution (February 1969). Peking voiced no criticism, but, on the contrary, stressed that the CPML had 'unswervingly taken the correct road of seizing political power by armed force'. Now, *Peking Review* reported, 100 square miles of Andhra Pradesh were under guerilla control as well as areas in six other States (West Bengal, Bihar, Uttar Pradesh, Orissa, Punjab, Kerala). The Indian government was 'tottering'.[55]

In mid-1969, a major change took place. Mazumdar directed the CPML cadres to return to Calcutta. There, the CPM-led government, it was claimed, were imposing a reign of white terror (presumably the CPM had become fascist). Only red terror could defeat it. It is not clear why this change took place: whether it reflected the party's relative lack of success and increasing police harassment in the rural areas, or the need to replenish the ranks of the cadres from Calcutta. However, the result was open street warfare between the two parties. The CPML proclaimed a small-scale 'Cultural Revolution' in educational institutions. Mazumdar described it as the students destroying the superstructure of bourgeois culture while the peasants destroyed the base.

Peking presumably disapproved of the change since it lapsed into silence. For the ordinary Chinese reader, the heroic Indian revolution disappeared without explanation. But in Calcutta, the war between the CPM and CPML gave the national government the opportunity to intervene with military power. Most of the cadres of the CPML and many of those of the CPM were killed or imprisoned (Charu Mazumdar died or was killed in captivity).

It is said that, in November 1970, Peking did privately inform Mazumdar of certain criticisms, and extracts from this letter have been published in a source sympathetic to the CPML.[56] The excerpts make a

249

number of points of which the most important is that the CPML misunderstood the concept of the United Front and neglected 'mass struggle'. Both, it said, must be created in the course of the conquest of power, not afterwards. As noted earlier, this is not true of 'mass organizations' in China. The Chinese party stressed the need for unity between the exploiter and the exploited [those exploiters who are not the main target of the revolution]. The characterization of the bourgeoisie as a whole [as] comprador is wrong.' The letter did not divulge whether this was also true of landlords, nor what political force in India would play the role of the Kuomintang in China in the United Front. The logic of the case, if not the realities, suggested the CPML should ally with the Congress (the line pursued by the pro-Moscow CPI!).

However, our central interest is not the personal role of Mazumdar and the CPML leadership but rather whether the party followed the line of Mao Tse-tung thought in essentials. In that respect, the Chinese party confirmed: 'The general orientation of the CPML is correct, but its policy is wrong.' Amid the ruins of the party, there were few to ask how the 'general orientation' could be correct and yet invoke such a terrible defeat. Nor did anyone draw political conclusions from the fact that Calcutta's working class had been through a movement of revolt more massive than that seen in the rural areas, but without the self-proclaimed 'proletarian leadership'. India in 1970 was not China in 1930 or 1937 or 1947. There was no Japanese invasion that paralysed the Kuomintang government and permitted the building of the Yenan base. Indian forces in 1970 could reach almost all parts of the country speedily in a way the Kuomintang could not, even before the Japanese invasion. There were no local warlords jeopardizing the power of the national government. Even if there had been a foreign invasion, it seems unlikely that a stable rural base could have been created in areas with a potential for material and political survival. In this scheme of misjudgements, Mazumdar's errors were of relatively minor significance.

Peking published no lessons. Mrs Gandhi had been given a unique opportunity to re-establish central power in West Bengal, to purge a stronghold of the Left; thousands of the most idealistic and self-sacrificing young people of India had been thrown to destruction for no useful purpose at all; the CPM was defeated for six years. Yet Peking felt no need to correct any errors. The Indian revolution merely disappeared from the pages of *Peking Review*.

(ii) Portugal in revolution
The fascist régime of Portugal collapsed in April 1974 after more than

forty years in power. General Spinola inherited office and was obliged to take steps to restore representative institutions and a free press. Almost immediately, there was an upsurge of popular agitation against what remained of the old order, in particular the secret police. Sections of the army were radicalized and Spinola fell. The creation of militant trade unions, together with massive strikes and demonstrations, pushed politics rapidly to the Left. The Communist party which emerged in April with the largest following among workers found itself holding the centre, with the Socialists and Social Democrats on the Right and a scatter of organizations the Communists called 'ultra-left' on the other flank. The party's aim was to use its worker following as a bargaining counter to secure a firm position among the junior officers of the army, the Armed Forces Movement, which held the balance of power.

The Right, with substantial foreign help (particularly from West Germany, Britain and the United States), reorganized. There were physical attacks on the Communist party and some infiltration of the Socialists. However, the Right's opportunity to reverse the tide came with an ill-judged and abortive coup by left-wing officers and men in November 1975.

Mao Tse-tung thought was important on the Left, whether as a form of vague emancipatory populism, a formal doctrine of 'armed struggle', or the inspiration of an organization. There were four groups of significance: the Portuguese Communist Party (Marxist-Leninist), PCP(ML) or AOC (Workers' and Peasants' Alliance), publishing a paper, *Voz de Operaia*; the MRPP, with a paper, *Luta Popular*; FEC(ML); and the UDP (Popular Democratic Union). All four organizations in one form or another accepted the idea of stages: the first task was to build a broad class alliance to carry the country through a 'democratic stage', not a workers' mass organization for the conquest of power. The MRPP was initially the most extreme – its cadres courted imprisonment and denounced the Left's stronghold in the army, COPCON, as simply the old fascist secret police. However, as the Communist party advanced its influence in the Armed Forces Movement, China's foreign policy concerns overshadowed both the PCP(ML) and the MRPP – a restoration of fascism became relatively less important than the threat of 'social fascism' that is, the pro-Moscow Communists.

In 1975 the situation was highly unstable. The Western powers used their influence to discredit the Communists and, by implication, those further Left. In such circumstances, the PCP(ML) allied with the Socialist party and parties further to the Right (building the United Front), denouncing the rest of the Left as creatures of 'social fascism'. There were even reports that members of the PCP(ML) participated in the armed attacks on Communist headquarters in the north. The MRPP described these attacks as the peasantry rising up against 'social fascism'. When the luckless Communist cadres at Leiria endeavoured to defend themselves, the party was accused of 'shooting down peasants'.

Both organizations adjusted their politics to defeat the Communist party. The PCP(ML) supported the right-wing programme of Major Antunes in the Armed Forces Movement, and the MRPP supported the candidate of the Right, General Eanes, for the presidency. The MRPP worked closely with the Socialist party to split the Communist-controlled trade union federation, the Intersyndical, and organized demonstrations against the general strikes of August and 24 November. Both groups supported the FNLA in Angola.

Both the PCP(ML) and the MRPP were loyal to the thought of Mao Tse-tung, and, as a result, were consistently on the Right of Portuguese politics. They added a tone of left-wing rhetoric to the efforts being made to stifle a revolution. The Communists were not concerned to make a revolution in Portugal, but the attack upon them was designed to make a revolution impossible, and, although neither organization had great influence, the two groups added their weight to the counter-revolutionary movement.

FEC(ML) was a federation of groups that argued that any struggle for power was utopian until the party had been built. They were thus able to combine extremist rhetoric with conservative and cautious practice. In the great events of the time, they chose to abstain. The UDP, on the other hand, the largest of the organizations, diverged from Mao Tse-tung thought when this collided with the movement of the Left as a whole. Thus their paper stressed the dangers of 'social fascism' but treated the threat of Russian and American domination as equally dangerous (where in fact the United States had a much more powerful position in Portugal). The UDP collaborated with other groups on the Left, but not with the Communists.

In China, Mao Tse-tung thought summarized retrospectively some of the tactics the party was obliged to pursue for survival; the tactics were 'flexible' because the party had an independent military base. But in Portugal this historical residue became a straightjacket, inhibiting even the tactics appropriate to survival. The Right might, in certain extreme circumstances, have tried to use the followers of Mao as a disguise for its advance to power; once in power, the followers of Mao would have been annihilated along with the rest of the Left. The only defence for the Left was to build a basis of independent power in a mass workers' movement, and that was only possible if the politics of winning State power were fused with the real material interests of workers. No mere party, even with clandestine military units, could substitute for this. The FEC and the UDP diverged from the logic of Mao, and operated pragmatically, with resulting muddle and inconsistency.

In all cases, the doctrine of 'stages' was a means to insert a separate class interest, to make the party and its leadership the master, not the leader, of the workers. It was a utopian aim since Portuguese workers remained unconvinced that either 'stages' or 'protracted struggle' were necessary. To choose these was to opt for the victory of the Right.[57]

(iii) The 'Intermediate Zone'

In the industrialized countries, there has been no continuing upsurge in political activity. Mao Tse-tung thought has not been tested in practice as it has in India and Portugal. The followers of Mao, organized in a few clearly-defined groups within a broader current of opinion sympathetic to China, have therefore been largely restricted to doctrinal matters.

A recurrent problem is to define the class of country in which the group operates since this determines the 'main contradiction'. For Norway's AKP(ML), 'the most important contradiction in the world is between the peoples of the world and imperialism' – that is, between the two superpowers and the rest. Thus the task appropriate to Norway is to build a united front to eliminate American and Russian influence on the basis of 'independent national capitalism'.[58]

In Australia, the CPA(ML), a clandestine organization, identifies the country as part of the 'third world', struggling for its national independence. At first the struggle was primarily against American influence, but latterly it has been directed against the threat of Soviet aggression. The change produces a familiar paradox. In 1975 Frazer's conservative Liberal and Country party replaced Whitlam's Labour Government. The Frazer administration was more anti-Communist than that of Whitlam, so the 'threat of Soviet aggression' loomed larger in its preoccupations. A shift from Left to Right in the domestic scene produced a shift from Right to Left in foreign policy! *Vanguard*, weekly paper of the CPA(ML), praised Frazer's foreign policy, even though on other occasions it referred to him as 'the fascist Frazer': 'While the result of the coup [against Whitlam] is to have a more realistic foreign policy, it is also bound to lead to attacks upon the living standards and democratic rights of the people.'[59]

China's foreign policy imposed a comparable paradox on the pro-China KPD and KPD(ML) (the initials of the pro-Moscow German Communist Party are DKP) in West Germany. When China welcomed

253

West Germany into the comity of progressive opposition to the super-powers – receiving with particular hospitality the leader of the German parliamentary Right, Franz Josef Strauss – the supporters of Mao loyally demonstrated for a strengthening of NATO. Indeed, it is said that the KPD(ML) tried to sue the Bundesrepublik Defence Minister, Georg Leber, for neglecting Germany's military preparedness in the face of the threat of Russian aggression.

The contradiction between external and domestic policy in Maoist eyes was duplicated in France. General de Gaulle's reassertion of French nationalism abroad was approved while growing 'fascization' was detected at home. Attempts to prevent 'fascism' in France might have included the agitation of the United Socialist Party (PSU) and other socialist organizations for trade union rights in the French army in 1975. However, supporters of China did not see it in this light. They attacked 'subversive activity' in the army, attributing it to the intrigues of the 'social fascists' (the French Communist party) as part of Russia's grand scheme to suborn France.

Maoist groups are reasonably consistent in their orientation on local nationalism and building a coalition of classes. They are less consistent in their attitude to the working class. Some have orientated on the trade union movement – the Swedish KFML (now the Swedish Communist party, SKP), Norway's AKP(ML) and the Communist party of Britain (ML). But, for example, the Appel tendency (KAK) in Denmark and Sweden holds that the entire working class of the industrialized countries is a 'labour aristocracy', living off the exploitation of the backward countries. KAK's activity has therefore been restricted to charitable efforts to help particular backward countries. In the same way, the Danish KF(ML) operated for a long time to spread 'friendship' between Danes and China, as did the October League in the United States. Politics fade into a cultural identification with China, but a China charged with fantasy. This view of China is popular among sections of the intelligentsia, it is a kind of daydream, and in no way inconsistent with extreme hostility towards organized labour. The image of the selfless Guardians of the Chinese Communist party, a dedicated élite serving a grateful but untutored mass, has appeal in some professions, for example, medicine and teaching.

Perhaps another section of the professional middle class is drawn to the rhetorical extremism characteristic of *La Cause du Peuple* in France. In 1969 the paper promised the French bourgeoisie: 'And when we want to, all together, we'll kidnap you, we'll spit in your throats and hang you – first, by the feet, and if you don't understand then, by the neck.' The paper was banned in 1970 for advocating murder, theft, pillage and arson.

These side-curents – the one, the daydream of the professional classes, the other, its Nihilist nightmare – reflect social tensions and alienation, but not particularly Mao Tse-tung thought. It is the stage props of the united front, class collaboration, and loyalty to China's foreign policy which reveal that. Foreign policy was the only area of difficulty, the only point where reality could touch the doctrine. Some prided themselves on following China through thick and thin. *Humanité Rouge* wired its congratulations to Pakistan's General Yahya Khan on the slaughter of Bengalis in 1971. Australia's *Vanguard* pronounced in 1971 on events in Ceylon: 'The people of Ceylon have taken to arms against the great tea plantation owners, against exploitation . . . Their efforts to date have revealed the essential capitalist character of Mrs Bandaranaike.'

Shortly afterwards, Peking revealed that China was on the side of Mrs Bandaranaike and the 'great tea plantation owners'. *Vanguard* did not flinch: 'We have made a mistake. Chairman Mao has shown us the correct way again.'

The 'mistakes' are supremely unimportant, for the audience is tiny, the proclamations no more than shadow play. But the 'mistakes' show a method of approaching questions, the same servility to authority that Stalin bred among the Communists. The 'Marxist-Leninsts' have no independent criteria, no world view founded upon the material existence of a world class, no disciplines rooted in an objective social situation.

The impact of Mao Tse-tung thought on the world has been small by comparison with that of the October revolution. In general, established Communist parties have not been afflicted by severe splits. The greatest impact has been felt by the intelligentsia of the backward countries, particularly in Asia. In conditions of major social upheaval, Mao's ideas can be important. For example, in the 1973–6 revolt in Thailand, the workers of Bangkok fought alone; those who claimed to be revolutionaries were far away in the hills of the north-east, practising guerilla warfare with a perspective of surrounding Bangkok after twenty years' struggle, long after many of the workers on strike would have died of old age. Mao Tse-tung thought robbed the Thai movement of a leadership, and ensured Sino-Thai relations were not embarrassed.

The Sino-Soviet dispute did have a liberating effect, but if we restricted our attention to 'Marxist-Leninist' groups, the proposition would be doubtful. The supporters of Mao seem most often to have created

only new prisons of the mind, new 'esoteric wisdoms' to isolate themselves from workers. Not all Mao's supporters had the stomach to
pursue Peking's logic to its conclusion, the defence of local capitalism.
Their instincts rebelled against the transformation of revolution into its
opposite. But instincts, like common sense, sensible fellows in their own
sitting rooms, as Engels once put it, are not enough in the outside world.
In so far as supporters of Mao are loyal to his thought and Peking's
foreign policy, they are counter-revolutionary; in so far as they bend it to
fit their instincts as workers, they are confused. No collective self-
emancipation can result.

NOTES

1. Speech delivered at a meeting of activists of the Moscow Organization of
the RCP(B), 6 Dec. 1920, *CW* 31, p. 440 *passim*; stress added

2. *Ibid*, p. 457

3. *Ibid*, p. 442, stress added

4. Second Congress, Communist International, in *The Communist International 1919–1943* (edited by Jane Degras), London, 1971, I, p. 143

5. Cited by John Gittings, from *Wan Sui*, 1969, in *CQ* 60, Oct.–Dec. 1974,
p. 756

6. In *Miscellany* I, p. 136

7. *Ibid*, II, p. 364

8. 'Mao Speaks', in the *Sunday Times*, London, 14 Feb. 1965, p. 11

9. *A Proposal concerning the General Line of the International Communist
Movement*, Peking, Jun. 1963, p. 15

10. 25 Nov. 1958, in *Miscellany*, I, p. 123

11. Dec. 1958, *ibid*, p. 148

12. NCNA Peking, 22 Jan. 1974, *SCMP* 5545, 4 Feb. 1974

13. For further details, see Lynn Yamashita, *The Times*, 28 Sep. 1976 and *Far
Eastern Economic Review*, 30 Jul. 1976, pp. 45–6

14. *PR* 46, 1971

15. Edgar Snow, *Red Star over China*, London, 1937, p. 95

16. For details, cf. Gittings, in Horowitz, *op. cit.*, p. 182 *passim*

17. Mao, 8 Dec. 1956, in *Miscellany*, I, p. 37

18. Jun. 1964, *ibid*, II, p. 364

19. NCNA Peking, 19 May 1970, *SCMP* 4665, 27 May 1970; cf. also NCNA,
20 May 1970, *SCMP* 4666, 28 May 1970

20. May 1958, in *Miscellany* I, p. 115

21. Reported, *The Times*, London, 24 Oct. 1975

22. *Neue Zeit* No. 13, Moscow, 1961, p. 23, cited T. Cliff, 'China-Russia: the
monolith cracks', *International Socialism* 14, Autumn 1965, p. 6

23. 'The origins and the development of the differences between the leadership of the CPSU and ourselves', *JMJP*, 6 Sep. 1963

24. May 1964, in *Miscellany* II, p. 349, cited Joint Editorial, *JMJP
Hung-ch'i*, 1 Jan. 1970, and *PR* 17, 1970

25. *For a lasting peace, for a people's democracy* (journal of the Cominform), 1 Sep. 1949, cited by Ian H. Birchall, *Workers against the Monolith*, London, 1974, p. 49

26. Vice-minister of Foreign Trade, Chou Hua-min, United Nations Conference on trade and Development, Nairobi, 11 May 1976

27. A structure outlined by Teng Hsiao-p'ing to the United Nations, reported *PR* 15, 12 Apr. 1974

28. NCNA Peking, 7 Jul. 1974

29. *JMJP*, 27 Feb. 1973, reported by Peking correspondent, *The Times*, London, 1 Mar. 1973

30. *JMJP*, 18 Sep. 1971; see also, 'Down with revived Japanese Imperialism', *JMJP*, 3 Sep. 1970

31. *PR* 39, 1971

32. Interview, *The Times*, London, 27 Oct. 1972

33. NCNA Peking, 22 Dec. 1973, *SCMP* 5527, 4 Jan. 1974

34. The Vision of Judgement, in *Byron: Poetry and Prose*, Oxford, 1940, p. 111

35. NCNA Peking, 21, 22 and 23 Nov. 1975, SWB 3, FE/5066/i, 22 Nov. 1975

36. Chou En-lai: 'he had wrongly persuaded the Vietnamese to make concessions at Geneva in 1954 to get a settlement: he was wiser now than then' – Interview, *The Times*, London, 13 Jul. 1972

37. *Kuang-ming JP*, 24 Nov. 1974

38. *PR* 27, 4 Jul. 1975

39. NCNA Peking, 23 Apr. 1970, *SCMP* 4647, 1 May 1970; see also *ibid* 14 May 1975, *SCMP* 4662, 22 May 1975

40. Tenth Plenum (8th Central Committee), 24 Sep. 1962, in *Mao Unrehearsed*, p. 189

41. See 23 Mar. 1971 message of support, Chou En-lai to General Yahya Khan; NCNA 2 Apr. 1971, and *JMJP*, 11 May 1971 – 'The relevant measures taken by President Yahya Khan in connection with the present situation in Pakistan are the internal affairs of Pakistan in which no country should, or had the right to, interfere'

42. Bashani's telegram to Mao: 'The ideology of socialism is to fight oppression ... and if Mao refused to protect against the atrocities of the military junta, the world may think you are not the friend of the oppressed'

43. For details, cf. my: 'Ceylon 1971', *International Socialism* 48, Jun.–Jul. 1971

44. The NCNA statement reads: 'Today, under the direction of his Imperial Majesty, the Shah Mohammed Reza Pahlevi, the Government and the Iranian people work without cease to safeguard the sovereignty of the State, to protect national resources, to advance the programme of national culture and to educate the country, and has registered success in these aims. The Chinese Government and people congratulate them sincerely and applaud their efforts to achieve new victories in their march forward'

45. The *People's Daily* reported that the coup had been undertaken by 'some Sudanese officers' – *JMJP*, 27 Jul. 1971

46. MPLA's Augustinho Neto visited Peking in 1971; both organizations sent delegations there in June 1975 – cf. NCNA Peking, in *SCMP* 75–24, June 9–13 1975, and *Le Monde*, 6 Jun. 1975

47. Vice-premier Li Hsien-nien, at a banquet in honour of the secretary of the Zambian UNIP, 16 Sep. 1975, in *PR* 38, 19 Sep. 1975

48. Press statement, Santiago, 26 Jan. 1975, reported *The Times*, London, 27 Jan. 1975

49. Letter to Schweitzer, 13 Oct. 1868, in *Correspondence, op. cit.*, p. 251

50. *The Australian Communist*, No. 57, p. 48

51. For more detail, see Chapter 1, India: Capitalism and Revolution, in my *India-China: Underdevelopment and Revolution*, Delhi, 1974, pp. 3–41

52. *JMJP* editorial, 5 Jul. 1967, translated and republished in *PR* 29, 14 Jul. 1967

53. *PR* published *Liberation*'s article launching the new party, and also one by Charu Mazumdar – see *PR* 28, 11 Jul. 1969; 32, 6 Aug. 1969; 44, 31 Oct. 1969; also *PR* 1, 2 Jan. 1970

54. Jan. 1930, *SW* I, p. 123

55. See articles in *PR* 5, 30 Jan. 1970; 7, 13 Feb. 1970; 8, 20 Feb. 1970

56. *Frontier*, Calcutta, 4 Nov. 1972

57. See, for further details on Portugal, Tony Cliff, 'Portugal at the Crossroads', *International Socialism*. Nos 81–2, Sep. 1975, and Tony Cliff and Chris Harman, *Portugal: The lessons of the 25th November 1975* London, 1975 .

58. *Prinsipprogram*, Feb. 1973, II, p. 12

59. *Vanguard*, 29 Jan. 1976

PART VI

THE CHINESE COMMUNIST PARTY
AND MARXISM

17

MODERN CAPITALISM AND
THE BOURGEOIS REVOLUTION

At the risk of repetition, let us summarize the argument. On the evidence presented, it is reasonable to conclude that the Chinese Communist party does not embody the class interests of either the workers or the peasants of China. By no criterion can the People's Republic be seen as a 'Workers State', although at various times the régime has claimed to embody the 'dictatorship of the proletariat'. In 1978, as in 1949, the most important role of the workers of China was not the leadership of the country but as the primary source of the surplus which sustains the State and national accumulation. The mass of the peasants have been permitted to retain a larger share of their very much smaller product; but again, by no stretch of the imagination can they be seen as collectively directing the Chinese State. The reality is concealed by the party's consistent confusion of popular consultation with majority control, of mass support with mass initiative, of popular participation with democracy, of the emancipation of the State and 'the productive forces' with the self-emancipation of the majority.

On the other hand, when the Communists came to power, they did not embody the aims of the other two classes identified by the party – the capitalists and landlords. The new State demonstrated this when, having secured power, it eliminated both of them. The concessions to private business in the early years were not forced out of the State, but awarded to achieve increased production. The State was not a Buonapartist clique, balancing between classes. It had its own independent power, far greater than that of landlord and capitalist. It eliminated them in part to tighten its control of the other two classes for its own *independent* purpose – national accumulation.

In sum, then, it seems Marxism is wrong, invalid in the light of Chinese experience. Parties do not embody the interests of particular social classes, themselves the products of the social division of labour rooted in the material foundations of society. The State does not necessarily

261

embody a particular class (or survive only temporarily by playing one class off against another). The Chinese Communist party has consistently claimed to represent the *national* interest, over and above all 'sectional claims', whether of workers, peasants, capitalists or landlords. The party's definition of 'national interest' included *benefits* for the exploited (and, indeed, for the exploiters), but they did not include the abolition of exploitation, the 'wage system', nor the right of the exploited to fashion directly the new State. The rhetoric of the régime suggested the reverse but, in essence, the claims of the Chinese State are not dissimilar to the claims of Western capitalist régimes to 'represent the people'. Clearly, Marx's slogan, 'the emancipation of the working classes must be achieved by the act of the working classes themselves', was false in China.[1] It was equally false during the Cultural Revolution, launched and terminated by the party leadership, and in no way changing the structure of power (although it changed, even if temporarily, the position of some of the cadres). In 1949 the party did the 'emancipating' on behalf of the Chinese 'nation'. In the Cultural Revolution, if there was 'emancipation', it was largely the result of actions by Mao and his Cultural Revolution group.

If the party represents the 'national interest', how is it distinguished from ordinary bourgeois parties that make the same claim? Marxists have hitherto understood that the parties of the bourgeoisie always present the interests of the ruling class as the 'national interest'. But if the Chinese Communist party's claims are correct, there *is* a 'national interest' different from the interests of the constituent classes of a country. Then the critique of bourgeois parties becomes uncertain. In bourgeois democracy, the right of a party to claim to represent the 'national interest' in theory turns on its willingness to submit to elections to parliament, in competition with other parties; a majority vote supposedly vindicates what the winning party says the 'national interest' is. Not even that exists in China to validate the claims of the Communist party.

Clearly, Marxism is incapable of a coherent account of the Chinese revolution and of the People's Republic. The theoretical assumptions contradict the known reality. A 'non-class' force, representing the national interest, came to power in an isolated backward country (that is, before capitalism had created the material prerequisites for socialism). On the basis of its own independent consciousness, the Communist party then began to construct socialism. The material basis of China was apparently not a decisive obstacle to the socialist transformation. Charles Bettelheim, a distinguished defender of the Chinese order, puts it in this way: 'What has happened in China demonstrates in

262

effect that "the low stage of development of the productive forces" is not an obstacle to the socialist transformation of social relations and does not have the necessary result, arising from the process of primitive accumulation, of aggravating social inequality, etc.'[2] Provided only that there exists a 'proletarian party armed with revolutionary theory and playing a direct role', socialism can be built. In sum, the party can both conceive and implement a strategy to achieve socialism, independent of the society of which it is a product. The problem can only be resolved if we reconsider the context in which Chinese development has occurred.

(i) Modern Capitalism and the State

Competition between capitalists concentrates capital in a few hands and production in a few large-scale plants and in a few geographical areas. By Lenin's time, sectors of national production were already dominated by a few large companies, 'monopoly capital'. The maintenance of monopoly required the State to exclude or restrict competition from foreign rivals. The State became a major factor, working in alliance with the corporate giants, and negotiating with other States over the conditions of competition in the world market.

Competition was intensified in the world market as a result of the 'colonization' of each domestic market by the State. Thus, the centralization of capital was even further accelerated. Slump and war compelled each national bourgeoisie to subordinate its private activities to State direction as the condition of its own survival. Indeed, in time of war, the State converted itself into the board of directors of one gigantic national conglomerate, all the efforts of which were directed against the external enemy.

The change sapped the system's juridical foundations in private property. The mass of shareholders became passive pensioners of the system, not its directors. The State replaced them in many respects.[3] Ownership became decisive for wielding power only when it was massive; the professional managers in private companies depended upon the favour of the largest institutional owners of stock, not their own holdings. In the public sector, even these considerations did not apply. Indeed, the boundaries between public and private became so blurred as scarcely to exist – the State financed 'private' activities; taxes on business profits contributed to financing the State; businessmen directed segments of the public sector, and civil servants moved into private business. The growth of capitalism produced the steady attrition of the majority of those people previously identified as 'capitalists'.

The institutional transformation in no way changed the central drive,

263

accumulation as a condition of survival. But the survival at stake was not now simply that of the individual private capitalist, but of the collective capital of a national ruling class, competing with other ruling classes. The extension of the State to encompass all domestic activities in no way changed matters, as Engels long ago pointed out: 'The modern State, whatever its form, is an essentially capitalist machine; it is the State of the capitalists, the ideal collective body for all capitalists. The more productive forces it takes over, the more it becomes the real collective body of all the capitalists, the more citizens it exploits. The workers remain wage earners, proletarians. The capitalist relationship is not abolished; it is rather pushed to an extreme.'[4]

This 'statification' of the national parts of the world system was accelerated by the conditions of slump in the interwar years and the Second World War. It was an empirical response; few people endeavoured to lay out a plan for the reorganization of the advanced capitalist countries, to defend a particular country against its rivals.[5] The processes were only indirectly acknowledged in the bourgeois theories of society. Supposedly, the slow transformation was merely a marginal amendment to the idealization of nineteenth-century capitalism presented in the founding theories. Nonetheless, the process was general, whether, as in Britain and France, without major political upheaval; in the United States through the instrument of Roosevelt's New Deal programme; or in Germany through Nazism or Japan through its new order.[6] Almost every country stumbled in the same direction.

The State reorganized society to a greater or lesser degree on the model of its own instrument of power, the army. The militarization of Germany, the imposition of what was supposedly strict hierarchy, the direction of labour, the elimination of dissent as treason, the destruction of trade unions and political parties, all were designed to make every citizen a soldier. The largest private businessmen were guaranteed their profits provided they accepted the State's direction that all national efforts should be organized to compete abroad and not at home.[7]

Sections of the ruling class fought the trend fiercely. Those that would fail to inherit in the new order had to oppose it as the condition of their survival. Keynes might threaten the rentier with 'euthanasia', but something much slower was required to achieve orderly change; in practice, too many people, like Keynes himself, made a little something on the stock exchange, for the rentier to be completely wiped out. He survived the war, and even managed to make a modest, albeit carefully controlled, revival in the conditions of post-war boom. It required a radical break with old capitalism, a 'dialectical leap', to achieve the right State

264

structure. While private capitalism might evolve towards State capitalism, it could not reach it without a new social foundation; the old social relations of production impeded even the limited rationalization involved in State capitalism.

The demands of the Second World War accelerated the trend, which continued after the war although at a slower pace. By contrast with the interwar years, a long-term boom – quite unexpected for the ruling classes of the advanced countries – pushed the world economy into unprecedented growth from 1948. The elaborate State controls were dissolved under the acid of a revival in private capitalism; autarchy faded before a new 'liberalization'. But the State did not entirely relinquish its position in the civil economy. In the military sphere, in the face of greater rivalries than ever before, expansion reached new records in the effort to maintain a permanent preparation for war.

For those of the advanced countries in relative decline – in the 1960s, Britain and Italy – the role of the State in the civil economy continued to increase despite the boom. In Britain, 'centralization' proceeded with particular speed. In 1909, fifteen per cent of manufacturing net output was produced by the 100 largest firms; by 1930, twenty-five per cent; and by 1970, forty-five per cent. In the 1950s, under a supposedly pro-private-business government, the State employed nearly a quarter of the total labour force (a share which had risen to 29.1 per cent by 1975), invested forty per cent of gross national investment and took forty per cent of the gross national product (a share which had risen on one method of calculation to fifty-nine per cent by 1976; on another, fifty-two per cent). Between 1890 and 1955, the State's share of the gross national product had risen from four to thirty-seven per cent, a forty-seven-fold increase in money terms (and ten-fold in real terms).

The State had an even more important role in promoting future growth. In Britain, roughly three-quarters of research expenditure in the key technological industries (atomic energy, aircraft, electronics) has been advanced by the State in the past twenty years. In the United States, of the projected national expenditure on research and development for 1976–7 of US $38 billion, $21 billion was provided by the federal government (half of it for defence projects); while some two-thirds of academic research was financed by the State.

What can we infer about the nature of the system from these trends? First, that the most advanced productive forces had broken out of the shell of private ownership. Whatever the institutional forms – whether the State or some combination of the State and large private corporations – *ownership* per se was not a decisive question. The mass of private owners had become simple parasites, living off the proceeds of production as pensioners, but without any role or power to influence the process. Of course, the rentiers' loss was the gain of the largest owners; their power now drew together vast concentrations of capital.

Under the impact of world economic growth, the productive forces had broken out of the old mould in a different way. The largest private companies had in part escaped from the State itself. In Europe, the national ruling classes were obliged to try to recapture them by creating a 'common market', by setting up the political framework for a vastly increased scale of concentration, the standards of which were determined by the United States, a much larger unit than any single European State. That still did not snare the multinational corporations in conditions of boom; their activities encompassed the globe, using States as stepping stones in a world contest.

However, in neither case – whether the EEC or the multinationals – were such institutions able to mobilize the physical force required to defend their position in conditions of slump. Physical force remained the monopoly of the national State. The return of slump or long-term stagnation could thus produce both the disintegration of the Common Market, paralysed by the competing interests of its constituent national ruling classes (that is, assuming the most powerful of these, the West German, did not use physical force to subordinate its erstwhile partners), and the retreat of the multinationals behind the boundaries of national State protection. The tendency to the internationalization of the world's means of production conflicts directly with the political form of the social relations of production: the national State.

Much of the orthodox Left remained unable to draw the political conclusions. They remained preoccupied with the private nature of ownership. Indeed, for some, the decline of private ownership was seen as a step towards socialism. Yet it was capitalism itself which impelled State direction, ownership, financing and planning, the conditions of survival in the new phase of competition. European Social Democracy became one of the forces pressing for statification, for the strengthening of the national State against the declining segments of private capital.

Nationalization without workers' control, without a change in the balance of class *power*, represented no more than a rationalization of capitalism, a fortification of the position of the existing ruling class. Indeed, in so far as the future of the 'productive forces' was embodied in an international economy, this strengthening of the national State was essentially 'reactionary'. The key question – what happened to the wages system? – remained unasked. State planning had no automatic working-class character; it distinguished modern capitalism and the corporate managers from nineteenth-century capitalism and its mass of small capitalists, but in itself it did not advance the interests of workers. Indeed, nationalization and planning, without a change in class power, were the bourgeoisie's methods of increasing exploitation to compete more effectively with its foreign rivals. Only in the sense that, with increased centralization of power, the system became more vulnerable to attack, could such changes be seen as an advance for workers, and then the advance depended upon there being a revolutionary workers' movement to make the attack.

(ii) The Bourgeois Revolution
If the capitalist class was in decay, how could the capitalists seize power in relatively backward countries and perform its 'historical tasks': the accumulation of capital and the socialization of the labour force? In Tsarist Russia, the native employers were not a popular class of small local businessmen, rooted in the cities, towns and villages. Industrial development had been undertaken not by Russian capitalists but by the Tsarist State as the condition of its military survival. The Tsars undertook the development of the Donetz coal basin (later under private operation), the steel and engineering industries, built the trans-Siberian railway, expanded ports and telecommunications, all to defend the imperial frontiers. Private business was heavily concentrated in foreign hands. Thus, the class of indigenous private employers was tiny when the Russian working class was already large. The employers, even had they wished, could not have led all the classes of Russia against the Tsar.

By the 1890s, most European Marxists recognized that the bourgeoisie could no longer lead the majority. Furthermore, Russian employers would not dare to make the attempt lest they unleash the proletariat which would overwhelm both the Russian State and the employers together. The first Social Democratic manifesto of 1898 put it this way: 'The further east one goes [in Europe], the weaker, meaner and more cowardly in the political sense becomes the bourgeoisie.'

Yet Tsarist Russia was among the most advanced of the backward countries and, though dominated by foreign capital, at least had sufficient political independence to rank as imperialist. What of the other backward countries? There, the entrenched position of the great concentrations of world capital, backed often by direct political control through colonialism, meant that the bourgeois revolution was impossible unless it also established the political independence of the country concerned. Quite often, as in Russia, the native capitalists were anxious to secure a monopoly position, to exclude the competition of the advanced concentrations of foreign capital. They were thus drawn

267

to oppose foreign domination. Yet simultaneously, their weakness made them materially dependent upon foreign capital – they were economic extensions of the great world concentrations rather than indigenous growths. For the same reason, even in conditions of political independence (such as existed in Latin America), private business was incapable of repeating what the European capitalists had done in the nineteenth century, building independent capitalist economies; in special cases, a dependent development was possible, but in most cases not even that.

The confidence of the private employers also varied with their fortunes in the market. When the world system boomed, there were far greater chances of undertaking the political tasks (but less need to do so). In the interwar years of slump, the opportunities evaporated from fear that any political change would lead to disaster. The private employers in most backward countries could not create a bourgeois republic. Even in industrialized Germany, at an earlier stage, the private employers could not overthrow the Kaiser, let alone establish a stable republic. It took German workers to destroy the old imperial order, but then the highest achievement of the German bourgeoisie was the Weimar Republic, founded upon counter-revolution, tottering from one crisis to another, speared at every stage by the intransigent vengeance of its victorious neighbours, and finally tumbling helplessly into Nazism. In Japan in the 1920s, a similar exercise in weak bourgeois rule effectively became fascism under the impact of world slump. Now the barbarities of war became the only method of safeguarding the old order. In backward Italy, Poland, Romania, Hungary, Portugal and finally Spain, fascism became the sole means available to ensure, if not progress, at least the survival of the ruling class. In China, it was a comparable order under Chiang Kai-shek's Kuomintang. Yet even then, the territory of China could not be unified under the national government, nor could Nanking provide serious opposition to the depredations of Japan.

Such régimes emerged from defensive reactions to world crisis. But they went halfway to meet the needs of national survival, to securing national independence and the bourgeois revolution. They could go only halfway because of the decay of the world capitalist class, its dominant economic position and yet its social shallowness in the backward countries. The material basis for an effective national class of private employers had disappeared. The bourgeois revolution had become an archaic concept.

The growth of the great concentrations of capital in the hands of the industrialized powers and the resulting decay of capitalists in both advanced and backward countries made the tasks of the bourgeois revolution contradictory; the accumulation of capital, national independence and the socialization of the labour force became mutually inconsistent. Some of the backward countries opted for the first, some for the second; almost none were able to achieve the third. For those who opted for national independence, it became not, as in the case of the United States, a means of popular emancipation but the simple precondition of national survival.

In the twentieth century, the programme of popular freedom has all but disappeared in the face of the changed preconditions of some measure of national independence. The masses are offered improved welfare as a substitute for freedom. Sun Yat-sen, founder of the Kuomintang in China, or Nehru in India, the lineal descendants of Garibaldi, to a greater or lesser extent accommodated to the changed conditions in their demand for 'socialism' – a system in which the State assumed the dominant directing position in the economy. Most of the backward countries entering independence in our own times – Nasser's Egypt, Ben Bella's Algeria, Sukarno's Indonesia, Nkrumah's Ghana – have adopted strikingly similar formulae. But in terms of actual State power – as opposed to popular welfare – even the declared right-wing régimes, like Brazil, are drawn in the same direction.

The bourgeois revolution was founded upon the demand for the freedom of the majority. That demand fused the perceptions of different classes in a common social transformation, culminating in the conquest of the old State. But in the twentieth century, the material requirements of State power, of surviving against the now much stronger dominant powers, rule out the possibility of popular freedom. The revolutionaries of national independence have substituted 'social reform', a clumsy accommodation to the contradictory interests of different classes. Even so, many of the leaders were still frightened of the possibility of unleashing a popular revolution. They went only halfway to meet the need of the time, to the 'mixed economy' or 'democratic socialism' (which means an increase in State power while protecting private capitalism).

However, without a popular revolution, a 'peasant war', how were the revolutionaries to come to power? Only through the army or a comparably disciplined instrument, a mass party. If such instruments could be rendered independent of the interests of existing classes, there was no need to demand liberty. At the moment when history required it, a model was created.

18

THE SOVIET UNION AND THE RISE OF A NEW CLASS

The Marxists were supposedly engaged in a quite different undertaking – not the creation of a national bourgeoisie to withstand the impact of the advanced concentrations of capital, but the destruction of the bourgeoisie in the countries controlling the advanced concentrations of capital; not the tasks of national capital accumulation and the socialization of the labour force, but the creation of an international planned economy, founded upon the abolition of the wages system; not national liberation but the dissolution of the national State.

In Tsarist Russia, the two contradictory tasks, the national bourgeois revolution and the international proletarian revolution, coincided. By European standards, Tsarist Russia was backward, its working class small, and its private industry dominated by foreign interests. The material conditions permitted only a bourgeois revolution. Yet Russia's bourgeoisie was far too weak to undertake the task. According to the Bolsheviks, the only class which could overthrow the Tsar was the working class, provided the historic allies of the bourgeoisie, the peasantry, simultaneously seized the land and so destroyed the material basis of the aristocracy, the social foundation of Tsarism. The workers would in due course be ousted from power by a new alliance of the propertied, the land-owning peasants and the capitalists – unless Russia's bourgeois revolution proved the signal for the European proletarian revolution. Then the beleaguered Russian proletariat would receive the political and material help of advanced societies to placate the Russsian peasantry and ensure the survival of the workers' State.

The Bolsheviks were not at all concerned with the 'national liberation' of Russia. On the contrary, they identified this as the demand of the petty bourgeoisie, the 'revolutionary chauvinists'. For the Bolsheviks, the aim was the dissolution of the Russian State in an 'international Soviet Republic'. The new international workers' party, the Communist International, declared that it would 'fight by all available means, including armed struggle, for the overthrow of the international bourgeoisie and for the creation of an international Soviet Republic as a transitional stage to the complete abolition of the State'. Thus, the growing contradiction between the political structure of the world, a set of competing national States, and the unified international economic structure, embodied in the domination of Tsarist Russia by foreign capital, would be resolved by creating an international Republic.

The perspective failed. There was no German revolution, and the movements in other countries, substantial though they were, did not approach even the German level. There were massive defeats for the European working classes. As a result, the Bolsheviks entered a quite new situation. Two mutually exclusive sets of tasks faced them:

(i) to secure the survival of Russia as an independent national entity in a world dominated by the advanced concentrations of capital. For that, the Bolsheviks had to build the material basis of national independence, an independent economy. The historic tasks of the bourgeoisie, the accumulation of capital (by appropriating the surplus product of workers and peasants) and the socialization of the labour force (through the systematic transfer of workers from low productivity agriculture to high productivity industry) had to be accomplished.

(ii) to persist in the original task and subordinate the Russian economy to that of building an international working-class movement, the social foundation of an international republic; in this way, Russia's working class could escape, break out of the backward Russian ghetto and the disciplines backwardness threatened to impose on their ambitions to freedom.

In the years following Lenin's death, the leadership evaded a choice between fulfilling the tasks of a Russian national bourgeoisie or those of a world working class; or rather, the effect of the faction fight within the leadership and the temporary necessities of surviving in power prevented any clear choice. The régime stumbled between domestic needs of great urgency – for grain, for the rehabilitation and expansion of industry, for modern armed forces – and demands from abroad, for help in Germany, Bulgaria, China and Britain.

It was the peculiar historical task of Stalin and his followers to end the stalemate, to transmit the imperatives of national survival, imposed on Russia by the world economy, into the Communist party and the Soviet State. They were pushed – by the external threat of war and the internal threat of a catastrophic fall in the grain supply – into a choice, and they chose with increasing determination to transform backward Russia so that it was equipped to compete with, rather than overturn through revolution, the advanced concentrations of capital of the world economy. It was impossible to postpone the choice indefinitely. If Russia did not industrialize, the régime would sooner or later lose its basis of power and be overthrown through some combination of internal revolt and external threat. What of the other set of tasks? The prospects in Germany as the Nazis moved to power opened up again the possibility of revolution, but only if the Communists had been prepared, contrary to the tactics of the 'Third Period', to collaborate with the Social Democrats. In France, the potential independent force that was smothered in the Popular Front was another basis for breaking Russia's isolation. In Spain, the civil war need not have been lost if Stalin had not been so obsessed with driving Britain and France into the arms of Nazi Germany. But by then, these were empty hypotheses; history now seemed to have a 'necessary' character that flattened out all choice; the 'necessity' was in fact no more than the subordination of the world movement to the tasks of Russia's industrialization.

The party and its politics were not at all appropriate to the tasks the leadership chose. Its ranks of hardened cadres had fought, not to build national 'socialism', but to win a world. The old cadres had to be purged, and a new mass membership inducted. Waves of new recruits flowed into the party in the 1920s to tilt the balance. The leadership of 1920 was transformed by 1930, and that of 1930 had been decimated by 1939. By 1939, only 1.3 per cent of the members dated their membership from 1917, and 8.3 per cent from 1920. At the 18th Congress (1939) seventy per cent of the membership had joined since 1929.

The politics of the party had also to be transformed, its concepts rendered opaque and confusing, a confusion through which only the party leadership could be relied upon to guide the members. Now 'democratic centralism' was not a method of unifying one tendency in the working-class movement, but the principle of an authoritarian State. Now the 'dictatorship of the proletariat' meant not the Russian working class holding power, but the Communist party exercising a monopoly. Now the 'class struggle' became, not a conflict between workers and capitalists, but the collision of different national orders, the Russian and the American. Now 'building socialism' meant 'the accumulation of capital', emancipation 'submission to the Russian State'.

Stalin's success in mobilizing the Russian State for accumulation demonstrated that the new Communist party represented neither workers nor peasants, since these two classes were the primary victims of rising rates of exploitation. The party 'represented' no class. On the contrary, it endeavoured to constitute *itself* as a class, whose material basis

272

lay in its collective control of the means of production through its mastery of the State. In the history of industrial societies it was a novel phenomenon (although not new in relationship to many pre-industrial societies) that the hierarchy of a party should become a class, that its individual members should have no right of ownership over the means of production, no juridical right of inheritance (although its children in fact inherited power), no right to profit. The originality of the Russian solution to the problem of national independence was impelled by the decay of the world capitalist class; there was now no private capitalist solution to the problem of national backwardness.

Ironically, the Soviet Union carried to an extreme degree the trends of advanced capitalism, the statification of the economy, the militarization of society. In institutional terms, the Russian State leapt to a 'more advanced' stage than that achieved by the advanced concentrations of capital themselves, the creation of a gigantic national conglomerate under one board of directors, the Russian government. The Soviet Union could accomplish its innovation to this degree only because it had, in 1917, swept away all the old social forces of the past phase of Russian national development, the forces which, in the advanced countries, *held back* the drift to State capitalism.

Could the Soviet Union have accomplished the accumulation of capital while maintaining the advance to popular emancipation? This is clearly an absurd proposition. The accumulation of capital in conditions of national backwardness imposes a division of labour independently of the wishes of the participants, the more so, the more urgent the need to accumulate – in Russia's case, in order to 'catch up' with its foreign rivals. October 1917 was not premature for the agenda of world working-class revolution, for the working classes already formed a majority of the population in the advanced countries; but it was premature for backward Russia in isolation. Regardless of the aspirations of the new State, its behaviour would be shaped by the historically appropriate task – accumulation. Marx describes just such a process: 'If the proletariat destroys the political rule of the bourgeoisie, that will only be a temporary victory, only an element in the service of the *bourgeois revolution* itself, as in 1794, so long as in the course of history, in its 'movement', the material conditions are not yet created which make necessary the abolition of the bourgeois mode of production . . . Men do not build themselves a new world out of the fruits of the earth, as *vulgar* superstitition believes, but out of the historical accomplishments of their declining civilization. They must, in the course of their development, begin by themselves *producing* the *material* conditions of a new society, and no effort of mind or will can free them from this destiny.'[8]

For more than a generation, the most advanced sections of the working class in the advanced countries were tied politically to the needs of accumulation in the Soviet Union, unwilling to recognize that the new Russian ruling class in no way embodied the aspirations of 1917. It was the authority of the October revolution, the ambition of world working-class power, which sanctioned Stalin's betrayal of that ambition. It permitted the Russian State to bend each workers' movement it controlled to the needs of its foreign policy, to the territorial defence of the Soviet Union as a national power. Invariably that meant Russia stressed the weakness of the workers' movement, its incapacity to rely on its own independent power, its need therefore to depend on the local bourgeoisie. At every crisis, the Soviet Union compelled its supporters to collaborate with the local ruling class against what Russia saw as its main enemy. Whether it was the United Front in China in 1927, the Popular Front in France in 1935 and during the civil war in Spain, the Popular Unity in Chile, the 'historic compromise' with Christian Democracy in Italy today, or the absurd call of the British Communist party in 1945 for a coalition government with the Conservative party,[9] the working-class movement was persistently sacrificed to the defence of that 'bulwark of socialism', the Soviet Union.

The consistency of the record betrayed a strategic political position. Many years before, Rosa Luxemburg had confronted the same argument as Stalin's in the writings of Bernstein. She concluded that the argument that the working class was too weak to take power was, in reality, 'nothing more than *a general opposition to the aspirations of the proletariat* to possess itself of State power'.[10] The general opposition flowed from the particular opposition of the Russian State to working-class power in Russia and to the conditions of 'instability' that jeopardized its own existence.

None of this was of any significance to those struggling for national independence in the mass of backward countries. They were impressed rather more by the heroic repudiation of the control of the advanced centres of capital. Russia was anti-imperialist because it was dedicated to achieving *equality* with the leading centres. It was anti-capitalist because – to undertake accumulation – it utilized the State, not private businessmen with their manifold links with foreign capital. It was, at least according to propaganda, as rationally planned as the small firm was supposed to be in the early phases of accumulation. It seemed to have imposed a pattern of austere equality on Russia, eliminating the sordid extravagance of monopoly capital, ending the waste and duplication of the search for private profit. In the 1930s when the whole advanced bloc was smitten by a crisis some saw as fatal, Russia seemed to be the only embodiment of the pristine virtues of capitalism – discipline, order, energy and drive. Above all it was successful; it transformed Russia from a backward peasant society, from the *muzhik* world, to an advanced industrial power that could lob missiles into space and challenge the imperialists of the world, all within a quarter of a century.

The fact that the price of this remarkable progress was the barbarous exploitation of the Russian working class did not trouble ruling classes, actual or potential. It was the 'model' of a 'new civilization', an 'experiment' in Utopian social organization: the dogmas of planning exercised fascination over those who aspired to form new independent ruling classes. For many of those struggling for independence, it was the discipline of a mass party, the instruments of dictatorship, and Stalin's version of 'democratic centralism', that excited admiration. Socialism became not a society of collective self-emancipation but a 'model of economic development'.

The irony would have struck Marx forcefully – that the institutions of proletarian emancipation were converted by material backwardness into the mechanisms of intensified proletarian exploitation. The State which Marx and Lenin identified as the primary instrument of class rule had become supposedly the very essence of classlessness.

However, the abstract lessons of Soviet development are of no value in tackling national accumulation – and so securing national independence – unless there are social forces available and willing to implement the programme. Marxists had argued that in the final analysis only two classes dominated modern capitalism, workers and employers. The private capitalists in backward countries would not collectively undertake a process, no matter how much it was objectively required, which involved their own liquidation. Workers similarly would have no interest in creating a system for their own increased exploitation. There was thus apparently no force with sufficient autonomy to identify the needs of national survival and carry them out in the face of the opposition of the existing classes.

Social formations

The four classes identified by the Communist party and the Comintern in Kuomintang China did not exhaust the class spectrum. Indeed, by Marx's *broad* criteria, there were only three – capitalists, workers and 'petite bourgeoisie'. For Marx, 'petite bourgeoisie' covered a vast heterogeneous group – peasant small-holders and their landless dependants, shopkeepers, independent artisans, small businessmen in the cities, small-town merchants and capitalists. They had in common only an interest in the defence of small property or, in the case of the landless, an aspiration to own small property. It was a social position which stimulated an equal hostility to the large property owners and the demands of the concentrated propertyless, the working class. It was, for Marx, a doomed class. As capitalism developed, big business, through the logic of the market, would expropriate urban and rural small owners, driving the majority into the ranks of the proletariat. Nonetheless, before that occurred, political alternatives would be presented by this class, ones essentially reactionary – opposition to advanced capitalism and in defence of pre-capitalist, or at least early-capitalist, society.

Because the petite bourgeoisie was opposed to the growth of capitalism in the interests of its own survival, it could come to champion a number of demands of workers. This was particularly true in the approach to a bourgeois revolution. It was in this light that Marx warned workers in Germany, still at that time a backward country, to draw a sharp line between their class interests and those of the 'democratic petite bourgeoisie'. Since what he had to say is of much relevance to our theme, his words are quoted at some length:

> 'As far as the workers are concerned, it remains certain above all that [after the revolution] they are to remain wage workers as before; the democratic petty bourgeoisie only desire better wages and a secure existence for the workers and hope to achieve this through partial employment by the State and through charity measures, in short, they hope to bribe the workers by more or less concealed alms and to break their revolutionary force by making their position tolerable for the moment . . .
>
> 'While the democratic petty bourgeoisie wish to bring the revolution to a conclusion as quickly as possible and with the achievement of most of the above demands, it is our interest and our task to make the revolution permanent, until all more or less possessing classes have been displaced from domination, until the proletariat has conquered State power, and the association of proletarians, not only in one country but in all the dominant countries of the world, has advanced so far that competition among the proletarians of these countries has ceased and that at least the decisive productive forces are concentrated in the hands of the proletarians . . .
>
> 'At the present moment, when the democratic petty bourgeoisie are everywhere oppressed, they preach, in general, unity and reconciliation to the proletariat; they offer their hand and strive for the establishment of a large opposition party which will embrace all

276

shades of opinion in the Democratic Party, i.e. they strive to involve the workers in a party organization in which general Social Democratic phrases predominate behind which their special interests are concealed and in which the particular demands of the proletariat may not be brought forward for the sake of beloved peace. Such a union would turn out solely to their benefit and altogether to the disadvantage of the proletariat . . .

'As soon as the victory has been decided, [the democratic petty bourgeoisie will] take possession of it for themselves, call upon the workers to maintain tranquillity and return to their work, guard against so-called excesses and exclude the proletariat from the fruits of victory . .'[11]

The passage has an uncanny relevance to the ascent to power of the Chinese Communist party, even down to its opposition to 'excesses'. But it is not applicable directly since, for Marx, the 'democratic petty bourgeoisie' remained wedded to *private* property, even if they might make temporary concessions on the question of State ownership to induce worker support with the offer of public employment. The Chinese Communists were not at all wedded to the private ownership of the means of production.

The growth of large-scale concentrations of capital and of the State accompanied the attrition of the small owners of capital, and it was this that created the potential for a new social stratum. In the absence of workers' control, large-scale production and control produces bureaucracy, the layered hierarchy of managerial supervision, public or private. Furthermore, the maintenance of labour productivity at very high and rising levels required the creation of vast new sectors of 'white collar' employment – teachers, health and medical workers, technical and research staff. In the twentieth century, this stratum of employment has grown much more rapidly than manual occupations. In the period since the Second World War, most industrial countries have witnessed a relative decline in the proportion of the workforce in the strongholds of the old labour movement. The solitary master clerk with a handful of writers in the medium-sized business of a century ago has swollen into vast 'mass-production' clerical grades, symbolized in the tower blocks of central ministries and giant companies.

By its work, this new stratum is often collectively organized in large-scale units, unlike the petite bourgeoisie of the nineteenth century. Above all, it is propertyless; it has no more realistic opportunity to own part of the means of production than the manual working class. Objectively, it has nothing to sell but its labour power, although in some cases it has greater access to the *control* of part of the means of production. Objectively, such a stratum is part of the working class, but whether its members subjectively feel this depends upon the existence of a clear-cut working class alternative. Without that alternative, such a stratum is ambivalent, drawn towards, not private ownership, but the control of the means of production, an expansion in the role of the State, in its own employment and promotion. There is no difficulty in it being anti-capitalist, hostile to private ownership, but, on its own, it adopts the frontiers of the existing State as its own; it is nationalist.

Late Tsarist Russia represents a transitional phase between the nine-teenth-century picture and the present. On the one hand, there was a majority 'petty bourgeoisie' of the type Marx would have recognized – rural small-holders, merchants etc. On the other, the massive Tsarist bureaucracy represented a force far more powerful than anything comparable in Germany sixty years earlier. Before the revolution, the Bolsheviks had no need to distinguish the two. Together, they represented a force liable to pull the party towards compromise with national power and capitalism. Lenin identified the contradictory quality of the old petty bourgeoisie with characteristic ruthlessness: 'The petty bourgeoisie, i.e. the vast mass of the barely awakened population of Russia, is groping blindly in the wake of the bourgeoisie, a captive to nationalist prejudices on the one hand, prodded into the revolution by the unparalleled horror and misery of war, the high cost of living, impoverishment, ruin and starvation, but on the other, glancing *backward* at every step towards the idea of the defence of the fatherland, towards the idea of Russia's state integrity, or towards the idea of small peasant prosperity to be achieved through a victory over Tsarism and over Germany, but without a victory over capitalism.'[12]

Indeed, he identified the accommodation of the party leadership to the Provisional Government in the spring of 1917 as an accommodation to the interests of the petty bourgeoisie.

The failure of the revolution abroad, the destruction of the Russian working class in the civil war, and finally the urgent need for industrialization and rearmament in the late 1920s were the basis of Stalin's transformation. The State was mobilized for accumulation, the needs of which impelled those who commanded the State, the bureaucratic petty bourgeoisie, to liquidate small rural property. The historical clash which filled the minds of the Left, between the nationalist private capitalists and the internationalist workers, was refracted into a much narrower contest, between the small property owners (the 'NEPmen' and kulaks) and the bureaucratic stratum, between small capitalism and State capitalism.

Sustained industrialization appeared to validate the change. In Asia, the appeals of Communism attracted the same stratum, the propertyless middle class. The struggle to establish an independent State, to exclude foreigners from the competition for jobs in the civil service, loomed larger than talk of the small working classes emancipating the majority. Indeed, in its finished form, Stalinism was the most coherent expression of the most radical elements of the propertyless urban middle classes.

Stalinism could only secure a popular following in peculiar circumstances. First, it required that the working class proper present no political alternative; the transformation of the Comintern ensured that. Second, that the private employers, dominated by the giant concentrations of capital abroad, did not provide an alternative nationalist political focus (in general, private capitalism was far too weak to do this). Third, that the old petty bourgeoisie, the small property owners, were too weak or disunited to offer an alternative. In the majority of cases, the bureaucratic middle class could not mobilize sufficient independent power to establish its own unchallenged leadership. It was obliged to make concessions to entrenched interests, land, capital and small business, to prevent revolution. Thus it mortgaged its future power.

India provides an example of this loose coalition. Congress combined the interests of the old petite bourgeoisie, symbolized by the pre-eminent position of Gandhi. But it also gained support from Indian capitalists and landlords. Alongside these forces, the Congress Socialist party and, outside Congress, the Communist party competed to embody the interests of the bureaucratic middle class. The role of Pandit Nehru was to balance these competing forces, apparently in rhetoric leaning towards the bureaucratic class, but in behaviour never deviating from the central line laid down by Gandhi. From the 1930s, the debate in Congress was on the surface between 'socialism' and 'capitalism', but in practice it was between the majority segment of the petite bourgeoisie and the bureaucratic minority.[13]

Egypt provides a different case. There was no lack of government bureaucracy there; the overwhelming majority of educated Egyptians were employed by the State, and some forty-six per cent of government expenditure was allocated to salaries before Nasser came to power. The drive to 'emancipate the State' and thereby expel and keep at bay foreign powers (primarily the British) which had historically frustrated all domestic attempts to sustain accumulation, came from within the bureaucracy itself and, in particular, from its military section. Nasser was able to accomplish considerable changes in ownership, to go some way to creating a statified economy, before the combined effects of the war with Israel and the contracting world opportunities for accumulation closed in on the Egyptian economy.

Neither India nor Egypt escaped the logic of backwardness. The new State capitalists developed as much a taste for high consumption as the private capitalists had, absorbing an increasing part of the surplus through corruption. They were compelled in conditions of relative stagnation to reach a new accommodation with both the old entrenched classes at home and the dominant foreign powers abroad. They had no instrument of power, extending throughout the society, obedient to the imperatives of accumulation; Congress was tied by the existing social structure; military power in Egypt remained the prerogative of the old officer corps. Neither could raise the question of self-emancipation and create a popular force. The workers, lacking any class alternative, traded their political loyalty for 'alms' as Marx described it, measures of labour legislation and welfare for the minority of workers in large plants.

How does this discussion relate to China? The 'switching of the points' of history from the aspirations of 1917 to those of 1789 (as reshaped by capitalism in the twentieth century) afflicted the Communist party at just the moment when it found itself leading a genuine working-class movement, between 1925 and 1927. There was no time to make a smooth adjustment. The contradiction between the interests of the new Russian ruling class and those of the Chinese working class wrecked the party, uprooting it from the traditions of the October revolution. It was re-created, slowly and painfully, but only in isolation from the class it claimed to be leading. The task of the partisans would have been insupportable if they had been encumbered with the interests of an urban working-class movement. The partisans were no more rooted in the peasants of the localities in which they operated, although they were dependent upon them for food supplies and manpower. The party was *independent* of the entrenched classes of China, the embodiment of a future national ruling class appropriate to the demands of *national* survival today. The experience of the Soviet Union in the 1930s illustrated that, if the Chinese Communists could only secure power, they could create an independent State. But it was a very long process, a 'protracted struggle', because the party insisted upon its independence, insisted on not leading the independent initiative of the exploited of China lest that jeopardize its own *party* freedom. Indeed, without the Japanese invasion, there is no certainty that it would have come to power at all.

From the mid-1930s the leadership of the party oriented itself on the interests of the 'majority', what Mao called 'the middle class'. His attitude to it is in striking contrast to that of Marx to the 'democratic petite bourgeoisie' in Germany or that of Lenin to the Russian petite bourgeoisie: 'Chinese society is a society with two small heads and a large body; the proletariat and the big landlords and capitalists are minorities; and the broadest group is the middle class. If the policy of any political party does not look after the interests of the middle class, if the middle class does not gain its proper place ... affairs cannot be well-managed.'[14] The party was oriented in this direction, but not subordinated. On the contrary, the orientation secured that it did not compromise its independence.

Once in power, the party showed its ability to eliminate its erstwhile allies, the landlords, 'patriotic gentry' and capitalists, and to limit the activities of small property owners. Its main task – to accelerate accumulation – was triumphantly accomplished in the early years.

But China was more backward than Russia, and needed more time for development. It was not possible to eliminate the small property owners without jeopardizing the security of the State. Each acceleration in the pace of accumulation prompted counteraction from both workers and peasants. The régime went into reverse, permitting the reappearance of the 'rich peasant' economy, the old unregenerate small-holder. Indeed, in the rural areas the boundary between party and rich peasants tended to disappear. Then the party leadership, in alarm at the disintegration of its power, was compelled to purge or at least chastise the rural cadres, to try to reopen the gap between the bureaucratic and small propertied middle classes.

Throughout the shifts and zigzags of policy as the régime tried to propel China towards industrialization, none of the factions of the party challenged the need for rapid accumulation. The so-called 'Left' was distinguished by being ruthlessly devoted to accumulation, to the highest possible rate of exploitation. So far as Chinese workers were concerned, none of the factions raised the question of the 'abolition of the wages system', except as rhetorical play, much as Stalin promised one day 'the withering away of the State'.

Could this be seen as, in reality, 'building socialism'? Only by ignoring the material reality, and seeing only the ideology.

If Marxism is valid, if human thought is the product of material circumstances, Mao Tse-tung thought could not but reflect the material necessities of China, rather than independently reshaping China. It is claimed that Mao Tse-tung thought is no more than a contingent adjustment to Chinese circumstances, a 'Sinification of Marxism'. Yet if

281

this is so, the materialist determination of thought must be false. The next chapter examines this question.

19

MAO TSE–TUNG THOUGHT

It is the mark of both religion and bourgeois thought that they deal in abstract principles, applicable independently of time and place. Marxism is by contrast historically specific. It offers principles covering all societies solely in terms of methods of analysis. In Russia, the different tactics of different phases of Bolshevik history became translated in Stalin's time into general principles, as if they were all equally applicable at any given moment; the selection of the principles and their interpretation remained the prerogative of the leadership (which took care to purge the historical record, to rewrite or reinterpret episodes that might be embarrassing).

This was the 'Marxism' the Chinese party embraced. Given the standards of the Comintern, whatever the party did had to be described in terms of the orthodoxy, with appropriate quotations from the sacred literature. As a result, the originality of much of what the party did is not reflected in its 'theory', and its 'theory' provides little understanding of its practice. Practice is entirely determined by tactics – the tactics of the United Front, of armed struggle, of military conflict – and has no link with the claimed intellectual foundations. We can see the line between on the one hand Lenin's *Imperialism* and *State and Revolution* and Marx's *Capital* and, on the other, the specific tactics pursued immediately after the October revolution. No such sequence occurs in Mao's work. We do not need his modest foray into philosophy to understand party actions, and these works did not guide Mao's tactical responses; they offered a convenient rationalization after the event.

Why was a theory important for Marxists? Because a particular *class* was identified as the selfconscious agency of revolution. Capitalism was dynamic, continually changing itself, the working class and all relationships – today's truth became tomorrow's falsehood. Only through an account of the present position of a changing society, how it is changing, and its relationship to the rest of the world, does it become possible to identify the immediate interests of a class embracing millions of people, to predict how those interests are changing, and how they relate to the final aim of working-class power. Such an exercise is never final nor foolproof, but it is necessary in order to identify what should be done in a context where there are many alternatives being offered simultaneously, some of them appearing very like workers' programmes. The analysis makes possible a preliminary programme in which the interests of workers as they see them at that moment can be fused to the final aim; practice may show the identification to be wrong, 'lessons are learned', the programme adjusted and theory corrected. Science and struggle are interrelated, shaping each other.

However if a party does not base itself upon the working class, such concerns are irrelevant. It is not necessary to outline a perspective nor to draw lessons in order to correct it. Failures can be attributed not to flawed analysis (since none was prepared), but to poor morale or ideological deviation. The failure to draw lessons is one of the signs that the relationship between theory and practice has been broken. We have seen the most glaring examples of this in the Comintern's attitude to China between 1925 and 1927. In 1927, Bukharin, leader of the Comintern and expressing the views of the Soviet Communist party, marked the change to the 'Third Period' with a wildly inaccurate assessment: 'The period has also foreshadowed anew the greatest historical catastrophe. Between labour and capital, between the imperialist countries and the Soviet Union, there is about to be a tremendous struggle . . . a defiant resistance on worldwide scale by the oppressed masses of the people and the colonial areas. Such a great struggle is unprecedented in the history of mankind.'[15] Now most predictions are borne out (with a bit of skilful window-dressing) if we extend the time period long enough. The Second World War and the victory of the anti-colonial struggles would then vindicate Bukharin's prophecy. But he did not intend his prediction in that way. His prediction was the basis for *immediate* tactics of insurrection in the years 1927–31. In that light, he was wrong on all counts. Yet no one within the Comintern raised the question of this mistake for it was no longer possible to learn from it. The Comintern's perspectives were no longer grounded in a public analysis of the objective situation; they were a verbal reflex of the tactics pursued by the Russian leadership for purposes that could not be divulged lest they destroy the illusion of an international working-class movement. Analysis was now a decoration added after the tactics had been decided upon, or, in some cases, even carried out.

In China, the basis of the party's power was its independent military forces and territory. As a result, the leadership was preoccupied with the

284

tactics of survival against a militarily superior enemy. The programme deteriorated into public relations work among a heterogeneous population, instead of galvanizing a class into independent action which would discipline the party through its experience. Mao had no need to undertake the sort of theoretical work which Lenin accomplished. His survival did not depend on understanding China and the world, only on understanding the military potential of the districts in which the Red Army operated.

This experience, in conjunction with what was learned from Russia, is the origin of the peculiar élitism in the party's attitude. The people become no more than the water in which the Communist fish swim. 'Without a people's army, the people have nothing.' It is the source of the Idealism apparent in Mao Tse-tung thought – morale, élan, consciousness, so vital for the small partisan bands, are the decisive historical factors, not the contradiction between the productive forces and the social relations of production: 'men are not the slaves of objective reality. Provided only that man's consciousness be in conformity with the objective law of the development of things, the subjective activity of the popular masses can manifest itself in full measure, overcome all difficulties, create the necessary conditions, and carry forward the revolution. In this sense, the subjective creates the objective.'[16] The 'objective law' apparently lacks all necessity, because if it were necessary, it would be impossible *not* to act in conformity with it. In any case, what is it? Since no acknowledgement is made (as it is in Marx) that the degree of necessity varies with the degree of development of the material forces, we are left with an abstract principle – regardless of material circumstances, the subjective can 'create' the objective, the exact opposite of Marx's contention.

Mao pursued this logic to its conclusion – propaganda and education, methods of changing *consciousness*, not the material forces of production, are the key factors in revolution and economic development: 'First and foremost, create public opinion and seize power. Then resolve the question of ownership. Later, develop the productive forces to a large extent. This in general is the rule.'[17] But how are the educators to be educated? How does the 'correct Marxist-Leninist leadership' itself acquire its consciousness, so making itself independent of the society concerned, and how does it prevent that consciousness from reflecting the material reality of society?

If Marx turned Hegel on his head, Stalin and Mao reversed Marx's posture. There are paradoxical results. Lenin understood that it was easier for a minority to secure a following in a backward society than in an advanced one, easier to manipulate a dispersed peasantry than a concentrated working class; but backwardness meant also that the material base for a socialist society did not exist, so that socialism could not be achieved in an isolated Russia. But Mao reverses this: 'Lenin said: "The more backward the country, the more difficult its transition from capitalism to socialism". Now it seems that this way of speaking is incorrect. As a matter of fact, the more backward the economy, the easier, not the more difficult, the transition from capitalism to socialism. The poorer they are, the more people want revolution. After the revolution has borne fruit, boosting mechanization further should present no serious problems. The important question is remoulding of the people.'[18] Whereas for Lenin, the materialist, material backwardness was the most threatening obstacle to the realization of freedom, for Mao, the backwardness of *consciousness* made all things possible.

If objective reality is open to any changes consciousness determines, there is no necessary division of labour, determined by the degree of backwardness. The great differences within society – Mao's Three Differences – can be overcome if consciousness can be moulded appropriately. Compare Engels' assessment of class differences and the possibility of ending them: 'Only at a certain level of development of the productive forces of society, and even very high level for our modern conditions, does it become possible to raise production to such an extent that the abolition of class distinctions can be real progress, can be lasting without bringing about stagnation or even a decline in the mode of social production. But the productive forces have reached this level of development only in the hands of the bourgeoisie. The bourgeoisie therefore, in this respect, is just as necessary a precondition of the socialist revolution as the proletariat itself. Hence a man who will say that this revolution can be more easily carried out in a country, because *although* it has no proletariat, it has no bourgeoisie *either*, only proves that he has still to learn the ABC of socialism.'[19]

In the Cultural Revolution, Mao at no stage measured the aim, the abolition of the Three Great Differences, against the material conditions of China, nor would he have even seen the need to do so.

The division of labour, in Marx's writings, is impelled and sustained by the nature of production, and in turn provides the basis for objective social classes. But in Mao's work, the word 'classes' confuses class, strata, occupation, political attitudes, all dissolving into 'the people': 'Workers, peasants, urban petit bourgeois elements, patriotic intellectuals, patriotic capitalists, and other patriots, comprise more than 95% of the whole country's population. Under our people's democratic dictatorship, all of these come under the classification of the people.'[20]

Mao uses the terms 'proletariat', 'peasant', 'capitalist' in a similarly loose fashion. The terms do not refer to objective categories, to different relationships to the means of production, but to political attitudes, degrees of support for the Communist party (which is itself the 'proletariat'). Consider his casual identification of the class character of the Chinese State, and compare Lenin's careful description of the Russian State ('a workers' State with bureaucratic distortions') 'To practise democracy among the people and to practise dictatorship over the enemies, these two aspects are inseparable. When these two aspects are combined, this is then proletarian dictatorship, or it may be called people's dictatorship.'[21] The class character of the State is not determined by its relationship to class any more than the party's class character is; it is determined by the method of describing what it does. Thus, the 'dictatorship of the proletariat' can arrive in 1956, ending the 'New Democracy', somehow disappear along the way, and then become the prize in the Cultural Revolution (this time, arriving in the new constitution). Nothing happened in terms of the structure of *class* power, even if, by 1956, the juridical forms had been changed (i.e. private capitalism had been abolished, and agriculture co-operativized). The use of the terms was so careless it was clearly a matter of no great importance.

If classes are no longer defined by their relationship to the means of production, class struggle is not what participants in the production process do. Left to themselves, the producers are capable only of 'selfish, sectional' attitudes; given to 'excesses', to 'economism'. Only the party can see their 'long term interests', for ultimately only the party and, in a faction fight, only Mao's following is the proletariat. Class struggle is what the party does – whether in the revolution or, afterwards, in a purge. We have already noted an example of this in Mao's 1963 observation: 'We have not had a class struggle for ten years. We had one in 1952 and one in 1957, but these were just in the administrative organs and in the schools.'[22] Class struggle is something you 'have', like a bath or a drink – or a hobby: 'Man's social practice is not confined to activity in production, but takes many other forms – class struggle, political life, scientific and artistic pursuits.'[23] Since the workers cannot be won until after the revolution, the proletariat must be something other than workers; the class struggle in the Marxist sense (between workers and employers, poor peasants and landlords) is not the basis of the seizure of State power, it is at best a side issue. The main role of workers before the victory of the party is to volunteer to work in the Liberated Areas, to send supplies, to leave the workplace (where the class struggle in Marx's sense takes place). The party needs no organic link with workers; workers do not need to play a specific role in the

287

party; the party does not need a programme embodying the class interests of workers – it needs only military manpower and production to support it. This was the source of the party's programme for mild social reform before 1949. The party reserved the expropriation of capitalists or landlords not for structural change of Chinese society, but as a punishment for the 'unpatriotic'.

Because there is no objective basis for classes and class struggle in Mao's writing, the essence of the ideas of 'necessity' and 'contradiction' disappears. Contradictions are now no more than problems the government must *overcome*. In Marx, contradictions can be understood, but cannot be resolved without entirely *transforming the production base* from which the contradictions flow. But in Mao's case, workers, if left to themselves, become selfish because they get more money than peasants, so they have to be educated out of a situation where they might 'contradict' the long-term aims of the proletariat (alias the party). Mao, the legislator, *ordains* what is to be 'done about' contradictions: 'The contradiction between exploiter and exploited, which exists between the national bourgeoisie and the working class, is an antagonistic one. But, in the concrete conditions existing in China today, such an antagonistic contradiction, *if properly handled*, can be transformed into a non-antagonistic one and resolved in a peaceful way.'[24] Where classes exist without class struggle, and class struggle without classes, everything, even contradictions, are negotiable, a matter of the right public relations.

In party history, the past is not the result of the collisions in the material basis of Chinese society and how the party related to them, it is an account of the struggle between the correct line (source unspecified) and *ideological* deviations. The deviations are vaguely attributed to alien social forces, but the attribution is only an embellishment, not an explanation. The Kuomintang loses any specificity – at one time, respected ally ('authentic national revolutionary bourgeoisie'), at another, main enemy ('counter-revolutionary, comprador bourgeoisie'), and yet again, an ally ('learning lessons'). Apparently, only an erratic *moral* turpitude in Chiang Kai-shek separates the phases. The Kuomintang *is* the bourgeoisie when the alliance is secure, so its behaviour indicates what the 'bourgeoisie' believes, just as the Communist party's actions indicate what the 'proletariat' believes: the scrabble of political fragments has completely eliminated the social structure.

Just as the Communist party cannot explain why it exists, what its foundation in the peculiar material reality of China is, so it cannot explain the source of its 'ideology' which is what supposedly distinguishes it (since its class character does not distinguish it). Mao's

288

innocence in this respect is charming; he justifies Marxism in the following fashion: 'Since the feudal class has a feudal doctrine, the bourgeoisie a capitalist doctrine, the Buddhists Buddhism, the Christians Christianity and the peasants polytheism, and since in recent years some people have also advocated Kemalism, fascism, vitalism, the "doctrine of distribution according to labour" and what not, why then cannot the proletariat have its communism?'[25] After all, if other people have their eccentric notions it is only fair that we should have ours! In general, Mao does not seek to explain or justify his tactics; he decrees them, embellishing his account with such concepts as will put his proposals beyond dispute. Consider his account of the difference between Russian and Chinese revolutionary experience: 'the Chinese bourgeoisie differs from the bourgeoisie of old Tsarist Russia. Since Tsarist Russia was a military-feudal imperialism which carried on aggression against other countries, the Russian bourgeoisie was entirely lacking in revolutionary quality. There, the task of the proletariat was to oppose the bourgeoisie, not to unite with it. But China's national bourgeoisie has a revolutionary quality at certain periods and to a certain degree, because China is a colonial and semi-colonial country which is a victim of aggression. Here, the task of the proletariat is to form a united front with the national bourgeoisie against imperialism and the bureaucrat and warlord governments without overlooking its revolutionary quality.'[26] The case does not stand serious examination. The terms, 'military-feudal imperialism', 'colonial and semi-colonial' are there to block further examination, to seal off the case from questions as to why the Russian bourgeoisie showed this curiously different response to the Chinese. We are not meant to take the history seriously, only the tactical line. The history is false – the Russian bourgeoisie was possibly more 'revolutionary' than the Chinese – in the 1870's and in 1905. It could equally be argued that the Chinese bourgeoisie was weaker than the Russian and therefore *more* dependent upon foreign interests and easier to eliminate; it was *more* necessary to do so since, because of its relative weakness, it was more easily used as the tool of foreign powers.

In sum, Mao Tse-tung thought is a return to pre-Marxist doctrines of socialism and to philosophical Idealism. In the beginning was the Word, and the Word – the correct Marxist-Leninist line – was with the Communist party, or, in certain circumstances, with Mao alone. The élite, defined both by its possession of the Word and its exemplary spiritual character, will emanicipate the majority, lift them and enlighten them. All the problems are in the area of doctrine, arising from those who misinterpret or neglect the doctrine and thereby become the prey of other alien forces. Mao does not refashion Marxism, he merely uses the terminology to express something quite different, something which contradicts it. As a result, Mao Tse-tung thought can scarcely even count as a form of 'revisionism' since it does not 'revise', it ignores.

Pre-Marxist Socialism

Some of the key ideas of Mao Tse-tung thought take up much older themes than those of Marxism (indeed, Marx and Engels spent much time in refuting some of these ideas). Mao did not copy the pre-Marxists; there was no opportunity for him to acquire a knowledge of them; but a comparable material context reproduced similar ideas, especially given the loose theoretical approach of the Chinese party.

The *sans-culottes*, some of the most radical participants in the French revolution, argued for some of the same things as the Red Guards. They also aspired to equality of *consumption* without understanding the relationship of income to the organization of production. They also had no real sense of class divisions based upon the process of production. The People – 'a word which is neither defined nor analysed; it is as if the nation in its entirety had been moulded into one mythical person' – was identified not by a position within an objective social structure, but by an attitude of patriotism: 'Failing to define their place in society as a working population, the *sans-culottes* had no clear and precise idea of the nature of labour itself. They did not appreciate that it had a social function of its own; they only considered it in relationship to property.' To be a patriot, a republican, was not to occupy an objective class position, but to exhibit the right political responses and live, at least in externals, with austerity and humility: 'The *sans-culottes* could not endure pride or disdain, since these feelings were thought to be typically aristocratic and contrary to the spirit of fraternity which should reign among citizens equal in rights . . . such personal defects are frequently mentioned in the reports justifying the arrest of suspects.' Expropriation of property was a punishment for moral failure, not a method of changing the structure of society regardless of the moral status of the propertied. Furthermore, the *sans-culottes* never relinquished hope that the propertied might join the cause, regardless of what they owned: 'the frustration and resentment revealed by the *sans-culottes* at their failure to convert these citizens [the rich] for the revolutionary cause only emphasizes their sincere desire for unity, and their inability to grasp the true nature of class differences: *insouciants* were arrested not so much on account of their social standing, but as a result of their political behaviour . . . Their search for unity, transcending class barriers, underlines the utopian aspect of their political and social aspirations.'[27]

The economic interests and political aspirations of the revolutionaries diverged. In the winter of 1793–4, when the Revolutionary government failed to keep Paris adequately supplied with grain, there were strikes for increased wages. The local committees of the revolution declared such action illegal; in China, strikes against the abolition of overtime pay were 'economist'. The artisans could not, according to the régime, know their own true interests.

However, there are important differences between France in the late eighteenth century and present-day China. Then the pressure of the world was trivial in comparison to its unremitting influence today. The revolutionaries could afford, even if only briefly, the most extreme demands for freedom in all matters. No mass party encompassed France, balancing, as the Communist party in the Cultural Revolution, between the contradictory demands of defending State power and winning mass loyalty. The revolutionary leaders in France had less ability to control the movement, so that the revolution was much more given to 'excesses'. In the Terror, the guillotine cut swathes through the rich to feed and clothe the poor, establishing an image of revolution to disturb the sleep of the rich of Europe for decades to come. Some of the militants urged that the guillotine should not just stand on every street corner, it should accompany the army as it went about the countryside to persuade the farmers to sell their grain. In the autumn of 1793 the National Convention decreed that 'all that part [of Lyons] that was inhabited by the rich shall be demolished; only the houses of the poor and the homes of good patriots, those who have been murdered or outlawed (by the federalists) shall be left standing'.[28]

The leadership of the revolution – as in China – endeavoured to rouse and sustain support by *helping* the poor, but did not encourage them to help themselves, let alone run society. In France, when the only organized and armed force, the State, asserted itself, the *sans-culottes* were wiped out. The mass organizations, the Section Assemblies, were converted into the paid agents of the government. In the same way, the mass organizations of China in 1966–7 were absorbed into Revolutionary Committees, the backbone of which was the PLA, and then finally taken over by the rehabilitated party.

Through much of the nineteenth century, what Marx called 'Utopian Socialism' repeated themes which recur in contemporary China – the hostility to the cities (usually by members of the urban middle class), the demand that the urban working class should return to the land, forming self-sufficient agrarian-industrial communities which, it was thought, would prevent the growth of hierachical organization, bureaucracy and a specialized division of labour, and ensure all-round educational

291

development in manual labour. Marx regarded such ideas as fantasies, forms of reactionary opposition to the necessary centralization of capital and the development of a specialized division of labour, without which abundance would never occur and so the possibility of socialism. As Lenin put it: 'The separation of town from country, their opposition and the exploitation of the countryside by the town . . . [are] universal concomitants of developing capitalism . . . Only sentimental romantics can bewail this. Scientific theory, on the contrary, points to the progressive aspect given to this contradiction by large-scale industrial capital.'[29] For Marx, one advantage of capitalism was that it 'rescued a considerable part of the population from the idiocy of rural life'.

Equality could not be based for very long on a common sharing of poverty, a moral ideal of ascetic self-denial; only upon the full development of the means of production, ensuring all had access to abundance. For those however whose income is not in doubt, it becomes possible to play with ideas of socialism without troubling about the material base.

The Utopians were speculative, and while in some areas influential – for example, through Ebenezer Howard, on the traditions of town planning, and conceptions of garden cities and New Towns – they in no way deflected the development of capitalism. The same is true in China. While Mao was clearly excited during the Great Leap Forward and the Cultural Revolution, years of warfare and struggle grounded his final views in the bedrock of reality – the supreme need for accumulation. That determined the approach of tolerating the real inequality of income generated by the need for accumulation while sporadically attacking the symptoms of inequality. Utopian socialism was the decorative form of the process, not its essence.

Marxism did not, then, remain intact in an isolated backward China. It could only have done so if linked to an international class which sustained the theory. Confined to China and even there isolated from its claimed foundation, Chinese workers, it could not fail to become 'false consciousness', an ideological rationale concealing purposes other than those expressed in the rhetoric. It was fortunate, for Marxism in its original form would have been an insuperable obstacle to achieving what the party aimed for – a new and powerful Chinese State. Through the trappings of Marxist jargon, the essentials of nineteenth-century radical nationalism reappeared to justify the role of a new class.

The Chinese revolution was not 'betrayed'. The Communists in the 1930s did not propose the self-emancipation of the working class (or indeed of the peasantry). Mao did not set out with the aims of 1917, but with the target of national liberation. In the Comintern's original scheme, national liberation forces were to ally with the main force, the European proletariat, just as the Russian workers were to lead the peasants. The interests of each were different – for national liberation and an international workers' republic on the one hand; for nationalized property and small peasant private property on the other. Yet without an alliance, each force would lose. By Mao's time, the distinction between national and international liberation had been entirely lost; indeed, the first had entirely swallowed the second.

Nonetheless, national liberation was a great step forward for China, even if it was entirely different from the aims of the 1917 Russian revolution. Stalin's transformation of the purpose of the Russian Communist party, by contrast, was a major retreat from the ambitions of 1917. National independence was the precondition for the survival of China as a national society. Given the real alternatives in the 1930s in China, given the Comintern's destruction of any serious world workers' alternative, there was little option. Mao settled for the twentieth century's version of the 'bourgeois revolution', for the 'emancipation of the productive forces'.

The story is not done. For the survival of the Chinese Communist party now depends upon securing that continued process of accelerating capital accumulation which will build the material base appropriate to China's national independence. The effectiveness of the party depends upon its ability to transmit to China the imperatives of the present stage of the world's means of production, and to organize the Chinese people in the form most appropriate. Forty years ago, in the Soviet Union, with world capitalism in disarray around it, that meant full State ownership of the means of production, planning and the militarizaton of society – a far cry from what was appropriate in France in the late eighteenth century. The People's Republic has gone a considerable way to achieving as close a parallel as it can to this in the cities; the importance of the PLA as the model for Chinese society is much greater, indeed, than the Red Army was in the Soviet Union. But China's vast countryside remains outside, uncolonized. Accumulation has proceeded rapidly, but whereas in Russia this led to a steady decline in the rural and agricultural proportion of the population (although it still remains high by the standards of the industrialized countries), in China it has had in this respect only a slight effect. Accumulation is possible, but it does not now produce 'the socialization of the labour force'.

It appears that State ownership by itself is no longer enough to combat the power of the advanced concentrations of capital. The terms on which the competition are waged have changed. Indeed, it now seems that the aim of an independent developed national economy has beome utopian; the material basis for China's national independence can be no more than an industrial enclave.

In conditions of world growth, the problem is concealed. The backward countries, including China, were swept along, albeit at a relatively declining pace. But now, as the system enters stagnation, it becomes apparent that national power is the obstacle to the further growth of an international means of production, to feeding the mass of the world's population. The condition of China's national survival becomes an international revolution.

NOTES

1. Address and Provisional Rules of the Workingmen's International Association (the first International), 1864, in *SW* II, London, n.d., p. 442

2. Charles Bettelheim, *Les luttes de classe en URSS, Iere periode, 1917–1922*, Paris, 1974, p. 40

3. In the case of Britain, tax as a proportion of net company income increased between 1938 and 1956 from 14 to 39%; dividends and interest payments as a proportion of net company income fell between 1912 and 1949–50 from 67 to 23% – cited by Michael Kidron, 'Imperialism: Highest Stage But One', in *International Socialism* 9, Summer 1962, and reprinted, *Capitalism and Theory*, London, 1974, p. 129

4. Socialism: Utopian, *op. cit.*, p. 180

5. The nearest equivalent to such a conscious plan in Britain was Harold Macmillan's *The Middle Way : A Study of the Problem of Economic and Social Progress in a Free and Democratic Society*, London, 1938

6. For what is still the best outline of some of these tendencies, see Robert A. Brady, *Business as a system of power*, New York, 1943

7. In the case of British Conservatives, this is examined in Chapters 3 and 4 of my *Competition and the Corporate Society, British Conservatives, the State and Industry 1945–1964*, London, 1972, pp. 48–74. On the situation in the United States, see E. W. Hawley, *The New Deal and the Problem of Monopoly*, Princeton, 1966

8. Die moralisierende Kritik und die kritisierende Moral, *Deutscher-Brüsseler Zeitung*, 28 Oct.–2 Nov. 1847, in *Karl Marx: Selected Writings in Sociology and Social Philosophy*, edited by T. B. Bottomore and Maximilien Rubel, London, 1963, pp. 244–5. Stress in original.

9. *The Daily Worker* was calling, in April 1945, for the Labour Party to 'form a National Government, inviting others, including Tories like Churchill and Eden, to participate'; no doubt they had in mind Stalin's wish to exploit the peasant's old nag of Chiang Kai-shek – cf. above, Chapter 2(5)

10. *Social Reform or Revolution?* 1900, translated and published by the Young Socialists, Colombo, 1966, p. 56; Luxemburg stress

11. Address of the Central Council to the Communist League, 1850, in *SW* II, pp. 161–8

12. *CW* 21, p. 380; Lenin stress

13. Examined in my 'India: A first approximation', II, *International Socialism* 18, Autumn 1964; cf. also *India-China, op. cit.*, Part I

14. 22 Dec. 1941, Address to the Shensi-Kansu-Ninghsia Border Region Assembly, in *Mao's China: Party Reform Documents, op. cit.*, pp. 247–8

15. The Chinese revolution and the tasks of the Chinese Communists, *Communist International* (Political report to the 6th Congress of the CCP), Part I, translated in *Chinese Studies in History*, Summer 1970, III/4, p. 268

16. Wu Chiang, cited by S. R. Schram, *The Political Thought, op. cit.*, p. 80

17. *Miscellany* II, p. 269; see also:'Our revolution began with making propaganda for Marxism-Leninism. This was to create a new public opinion to push the revolution ahead. In the course of the revolution, only after the backward superstructure was overthrown was it possible to put an end to the old relations of production' – 1961–2 in *Miscellany* II, p. 259

18. *Ibid*, p.259; compare Che Guevara's argument: 'It is more difficult to prepare guerilla bands in those countries that have undergone a concentration of population in great centres and have a more developed light and medium industry, even though not anything like effective industrialization. The ideological influence of the cities inhibits guerilla struggles' – 'Cuba: An Exceptional Case?' *Monthly Review*, Jul.–Aug. 1961

19. On social relations in Russia, *SW* II, pp. 46–7

20. Jan. 1962, in *Mao Unrehearsed*, p. 169

21. *Ibid*, p. 167

22. May 1963, in *Miscellany* II, p.33

23. *SW* I, p.296

24. *On the correct handling of contradictions among the people*, Peking, 1964, p. 4

25. 'On new democracy', 1940, in *SW* II, pp. 361–2

26. *Ibid*, p. 348

27. All citations from: Albert Soboul, *The Parisian sans-culottes and the French Revolution*, Oxford, 1964, p. 5

28. Albert Soboul, *The French Revolution, 1787–1799*, vol. 2, London, 1974, p. 342

29. A characterization of economic romanticism, in *CW* 2, p. 229

RETROSPECT

We have endeavoured to trace the course of the 'class politics' of the Chinese Communist party during its period in power. We noted in its earlier history how a decisive change took place in the second half of the 1920s. The ensuing politics were the result of the interaction of the changed aims of the Communist International (a reflex of the changes taking place in the Soviet Union) and the needs of material survival imposed upon the party by operating as partisans in a backward rural area. In those years, a transition was made from Lenin's conception of an alliance between the proletariat of the advanced capitalist countries and the national liberation struggles of Asia, to the national liberation struggles as a complete substitute for the proletariat. The teeth of class war and internationalism were drawn.

Nonetheless, the party retained a tenacity, courage and honesty which, when the Japanese invaded China, enabled it to champion the immediate demands of Chinese national independence. It was thus as a nationalist party, not a working-class party, that it was able to win power. It was in the same vein that it established order and began the reconstruction of the Chinese economy. Its aim – the building of a powerful modern State – remained consistent throughout the years of the People's Republic, even though from time to time it was compelled by objective circumstances to meet some of the demands of the mass of the population, through whose exploitation the State was built. The Chinese revolution was a spectacular triumph; it represented not only a defeat for the corrupt ruling order of China and its foreign backers, but an opportunity to purge the country of the errors of the past and begin its social transformation. By the act of ending endemic famine, it was a major step forward for mankind.

It is by these criteria that the Chinese Communist party exercises political influence in the mass of the backward countries. There, the legacy of colonial domination continues even though its political forms

296

have changed. But the conditions which made possible the rise of the party to power in the 1930s – the destruction of a workers' alternative through the emasculation of the Comintern, the withdrawal of workers in the main from independent political action – are changing. The world is entering a new period, and already there is abundant evidence of a reassertion of working-class action. It is not the creation of those who call themselves socialist, but the by-product of a prolonged crisis in world capitalism. If the class struggle revives, the old issues of its relationship to national liberation will reappear.

For the mass of backward countries, only the establishment of an economically independent State can ward off the depredations of Western capitalism. In a similar way, the 'Peasant War' aimed to establish, not the common ownership of land, but the equal sharing of land. The Bolsheviks recognized that neither independent States nor the equal sharing of land could ultimately overcome the threat posed by world capitalism. Nonetheless, the workers' revolt in Russia needed a peasant war to succeed; and, it was argued, the world proletariat needed the struggle for national liberation to succeed. The *alliance* was not the union of those who agreed on the entirety of each other's programme, but simply those who agreed on the limited end of the overthrow of the system. The peoples of the backward countries, and the peasants of Russia, had the right to learn their own lessons. They could be compelled to adopt the Bolshevik standpoint only at the cost of the struggle for universal freedom.

Discrimination between the aims of different social forces became lost. National liberation and land reform came to mean socialism itself, not steps along the road towards it.

In the Chinese case, the change – from the aims of international workers' emancipation in the early 1920s to those of national liberation in the 1930s – was not a 'pragmatic' adjustment to a particular Chinese reality. That interpretation takes for granted that the basic reality is the nation, when the nation itself has been identified only by a world order. The change embodied a fundamental shift. Marx was turned on his head, just as he had claimed to put Hegel on his feet. Mao Tse-tung thought is a form of philosophical Idealism, not dialectical materialism. For the self-emancipation of the majority it substitutes a romantic conception of socialism, incapable of realization except through its contradiction, a bureaucratic nationalist State.

The change was not a mistake. It was the result of events, the changes in Russia and China. Mao awaited no theory: he made a revolution, knocking together a rationale as he proceeded, borrowing on the cultural flotsam of the Chinese and Western intelligentsia. He did not fight within the Communist International for an alternative strategy, for he had none. His path to power required the ideological symbols of the October revolution, so he employed the phrases – for example, 'the working class' – but emptied of all content. As he bent China's social reality to his task, so also he bent the 'ideology' into a shape appropriate. Men, not ideas, made his world.

The change would 'ordinarily' be of no more than pedantic interest. But as the world enters a new period of history, the old issues surface once more. Capitalism can no longer guarantee to meet the modest ambitions of the majority. Indeed, it can no longer keep alive a section of its slaves: famine will become an increasing threat. Workers in many countries have reacted on a scale not seen for decades. The central issue – of universal freedom, of using the massive productivity of the world system to meet the needs of all – again appears.

In such a context, the rhetoric of the Chinese Communist party becomes more than an eccentricity. It becomes a political alternative. But it is one of a peculiar kind, that simultaneously offers world revolution in words, but an accommodation to the world order in fact, achieved through local alliances with existing ruling classes against 'social fascism'. It sacrifices class parties to the creation of sects, armed or not. Mao Tse-tung thought plays an objective role, regardless of the subjective intentions of those who adhere to it: the strengthening of a world order, not the creation of an international alternative order.

Mao Tse-tung thought is tested, not by its quotations, but by reality – the reality of Hangchow in 1975 or Bangladesh in 1971. Faced with such a test, Peking invariably defends its interests as a national ruling class. It is, in its own parlance, 'reactionary', defending its place in a world order of national ruling classes, sacrificing the interest of the majority to the maintenance of its own position as a class.

The prospects of working people once more contesting for power against the system are now greater than at any time since the 1920s. Nowhere is this more true than in the oppressed nations, the economically backward countries. But the influence of the Chinese 'road to socialism' will again frustrate that revolutionary potential if it is permitted to do so. That would secure the world for imperialism once again. The freedom and, indeed, the feeding of the majority will then have been sacrificed to the safeguarding of the privileged interests of those who command the States of the world.

298

INDEX

absenteeism, 56, 98, 128
accumulation (of capital), 41, 47, 56, 60, 61, 62, 66, 95, 103, 114, 121, 122, 140, 144, 154 *passim*, 165, 182, 184, 187 *passim*, 192, 200, 261, 263–64, 267, 269–71, 272 *passim*, 292–93, rural rate of, 1958, 51; agricultural contribution to, 195
agrarian reform, 7, 18–19, 22, 25–26, 28, 40, 133, 179, 134–38 (*see also* land reform); Agrarian Reform Law, 1950, 132, 134–38
agriculture, 37–38, 44–47, 54, 56, 100, 109, 112, 115, 120, 124, 132–45, 153 *passim* (*see also* land); intensive, 37–38, 55, 188; exports from, 41, 45; private plots in, 73, 74, 77, 81, 99, 142, 167; mechanization of, 81; incomes to workers in, 160–61, 164, 165–69, 184; as the basis of development strategy, 188–90; taxes on, 190–92; performance of, 195–97, 199, 200; in India, 246; First Plan on, 40–41, 48, 50
aid (by China), 211, 215, 227, 230, 234 *passim*
Algeria, 212, 234, 269
alliance (of Kuomintang and Communist party), 4 *passim* (*see also* United Front); attitude of Mao, 20; after 1935, 21 *passim*, 27, 297
Angola, 211, 223, 236–37, 252
Anshan, 93, 94, 106, 117, 128, 193
Anwhei, 137
armed struggle, 18–20, 22, 129, 230, 247, 251, 271, 283 (*see also* guerilla, insurrection, partisans); in Cultural Revolution, 69, 70
Ataturk, Kemal, 209
Australia, 54, 225, 243; Marxist-Leninists of, 241, 253

'backyard furnaces', 52–53
balance of payments (1974 crisis), 198–99
Bandung, 212
Bangladesh, genesis of, 232–33, 290
Chinese veto on U.N. application, 217
Bhutto, Z. A., 78
Big Character Poster (campaign) 1958, 51; in Cultural Revolution, 62, 64, 114, 142, 181; 1974–75, 79
'bloc of four classes', 4 *passim*
Bolshevik, 4, 11, 13–14, 17, 39, 121, 124 *passim*; 133, 156, 169, 173, 174, 211, 270–71, 278, 283, 297; and internationalism, 207–10
Bolshevism, 208
bonus, 97, 98, 109, 112, 121–22, 164
Borodin, 5, 10
bourgeois, 117, 118, 187 (*see also* business, capitalists, employers); democracy, 5, 170, 182, 261; revolution, 14, 153, 260 *passim*; dictatorship of, 63–64, 78; ideology, 74, 79, 119; right, 121, 159, 161; factionalism, 129
bourgeoisie, 4, 11, 14, 21, 25, 28, 63, 70, 76, 80, 140, 159, 170, 171 (*see also* business, capitalists, employers); international, 207, 209, 271; bureaucratic, 69; Mao on, 43, 57; petty, 25, 43, 69, 92, 96, 123, 158, 176, 209, 270, 275, 276 *passim*; national, 214, 231, 237, 243, 244, 263 *passim*, 289; in Russia, 222; in France, 254
boycott (of British goods, 1925), 7
Brest–Litovsk, treaty of, 207–08, 209, 214
brigades (in agriculture), 52, 56, 58, 141, 142, 165
Britain, 3, 49, 126, 168, 214, 225, 233,

299

Po I-po, 137
Poland, 46
Portugal, 250–53, 268
private plots, *see* agriculture
private sector, 42 *passim*, 107; in Russia, 156
procurements, 45, 77, 99, 102, 137, 138, 139, 140, 142, 189, 190
profits, 42, 45, 53, 82, 113, 119, 130, 154, 165, 188, 273
proletariat, 5, 20, 38–39, 57, 79, 103, 104, 117, 159, 170, 171, 177, 207, 209, 224, 289 *passim*, 297; dictatorship of, 57, 63, 76, 129, 172, 261, 272–87
Provisional Government (in Russia), 14, 38, 125, 132–33, 134, 173, 276
public sector, 29–30, 40, 56, 156

rationing (grain), 44, 50, 102, 141, 164, 168, 202
  cards, 46
raw materials, 41, 42, 44–45, 54, 65, 127, 142, 188, 189, 190, 198, 208, 225
rebellion (1962), 55, 56, 126
rectification (of Party), 26, 51, 52, 57, 61, 62, 141; of army, 69
Red Army, 18, 19, 23, '285 (*see also* People's Liberation Army, Eighth Route, New Fourth); in Russia, 207, 293
Red Guards, 63, 64, 65–66, 70, 75, 78, 112, 113, 161, 162, 163, 180, 290
Red Rebels, 66 *passim*, 114, 126
reformism, 68, 69, 243
rent reduction (on land), 15, 27, 28, 136
rents, 198, 215, 224, 268
revisionism, 80, 107, 129, 242–43, 248, 290
revolution, 3, 9, 15, 16, 17, 18, 28, 29–30, 74, 81, 115, 121, 128, 132, 135, 159, 172, 173, 183, 208, 209, 211, 212, 228, 235, 238, 239, 240 *passim*, 252, 255, 256, 262, 285, 292, 296; world, 15, 208, 210, 211, 238; Russian, 3, 38, 125, 132, 155, 210, 278, 283, 293; in Germany, 121; Cultural, 60 *passim* (*see also* Cultural Revolution); French, 153 290–92; Cuban, 237; Sheng-wu-lien and, 69; People's, 40; socialist, 39, 79, 242; peasant, 18, 64, 133, 249; workers' 3, 134, 207; bourgeois, 14, 153, 261 *passim*, 267–69
revolutionary committees
  including Triple Alliance, 67, 68, 70, 107, 181, 291

Shanghai, 114
Peking, 180
in factories, 126,
Romania, 198, 215, 224, 268
Russia, 3, 13 *passim*, 21 (*see also* Soviet Union, USSR); in Manchuria, 26; State in, 1917, 38; Tsarist 17, 37, 267, 270, 268, 289; 41, 92, 98, 103, 121, 132–34; 1969 clash with China, 77; incomes in, 155–58; 168, 169, 173–79, 181, 187, 192, 207 *passim*; and Indonesia, 230; and Pakistan, 231; in Africa, 235–36, 240, 272, 283

schools, 47; in Cultural Revolution, 62, 67, 74; and *hsia fang*, 75, 82, 100, 158
'self-reliance', 100, 103, 143, 168, 191, 228, 235
'sending down', *see hsia fang*
Shanghai, 6–7, 8; 1926–27, 11–13, 16, 18, 22, 23, 28, 58, 61, 66, 67, 68, 74, *passim*, 96, 113 *passim*, 127, 128, 161, 164, 165, 193, 194
Shansi, 95, 119, 123, 139, 163, 195
Shantung, 5, 55, 137
Sheng-wu-lien, 68–69, 182
Singapore, 228
Sino-Soviet dispute, 54, 210, 212–13, 215, 225, 221–23, 240, 243, 255
slums, 99
Snow, Edgar, 22, 162, 213, 220
Social Revolutionaries (in Russia), 14, 133
socialism, 39, 54, 61, 63, 74, 121, 124, 130, 142, 156, 159, 160, 167, 170, 173, 243, 266, 269, 272, 275, 279, 281, 286, 287, 289; pre-Marxist, 290–92
Socialist Education Campaign (Movement), 55–59, 61; 64, 65, 141
South Africa, 236–37
Soviet China (Soviet Kiangsi), 7, 18–21, 22, 23
Soviet government, 3, 14, 41, 54
Soviet Republic, and democracy, 173–75
Soviet Union, 4, 8, 15, 21, 24, 26; compared to Chinese economy, 37; as model for PRC, 39, 41, 44, 48, 80, 95, 121, 132, 153–54; inequality in, 155–58, 159, 174, 179, 182, 185–86, 188, 195, 199; and Chinese foreign policy, 207–10, 212 *passim*, 221–23, 231–33, *passim*, 239, 240, 244, 270–82, 293, 296

soviets (in Russia), 173; decay of, 174, 178, 179

Spain, 226–27, 244, 268, 270, 274

Sri Lanka, 214, 233, 234, 255

'stages' (of revolution), 14, 243–44; in Portugal, 251, 253

Stalin, J. D., 8, 10, 12, 14, 17, 18, 21, 24, 26, 38, 54, 71, 92, 93, 104, 153, 156, 158, 174, 175, 181, 187–88, 211, 213, 214, 218, 222, 229, 242, 255, 271–72, 274, 275, 278, 281, 283, 285, 293

State, 37 *passim*; finance, 43; interests of, 6, 57; Tsarist 38–39, 66, 67 *passim*; 73, 80 *passim*; appropriations, 95, 100; control, 102; workers', 103–104, 124, 127, 160, 261 *passim*; capitalism and, 263–67; State, 265 *passim*; incomes of officials of, 161–64; in Russia, 157, 173–75; in revolutionary France, 291; and rural finance, 138; emancipation of, 153; and Marxism, 170, 171–73; and foreign policy, 207 *passim*; secrets of, 176, 181, 241, 242; and internationalism, 213–14; and industry, 183 *passim*; and economic development, 184–87

State Planning Council, 45, 102

steel

in Great Leap Forward, 49 *passim* (*see also* iron and steel); 53, 128, 183, 187 *passim*, 193–94; small-scale production, 50; strikes in, 1974, 128; imports of, 197

strikes

of early 1920s, 4; of 1925–26, 6 *passim*; Hong Kong, 4, 7–8; CPC policy late 1920s, 17; and Kuomintang, 24; CPC post-war attitude to, 29–30; in Cultural Revolution, 66; legalization of, 81, 92; in Russia, 104; after Cultural Revolution, 127–30

students, 3, 6, 12, 45; in Cultural Revolution, 62, 63 *passim*, 74, 114, 120

Subbotniks, 120–21

Sudan, 236

Sun Yat-sen, 3, 4, 5, 8, 209, 269; Three People's Principles of, 5, 10, 22

Szechuan, 56, 70, 94

Tachai, 58, 197

Taching, 99–100, 191

Taiwan, 37, 40, 105, 199, 214, 216, 219, 220, 221, 235

Taiyuan, 96, 99; experience, 58

Tanzania, 215, 236

team (production), 52, 58, 110, 138 *passim*, 142, 165

temporary and contract labour, *see* worker, temporary

Teng Hsiao-p'ing, 65, 73, 78; 2nd disgrace, 81, 82, 129, 161, 180, 224

Thailand, 40, 198, 199, 228, 255

Third Period (of Comintern policy), 16 *passim*, 18, 21, 244, 245, 284

Third World, 212–13; definition of, 214, 215, 223, 228; as proletariat, 224, 253, 272

'Three Great Differences', The, 50, 63, 110, 112, 155, 167, 184, 285

'three-in-one' (worker-management groups), 126

Tibet, 212, 231

Tito, 222, 223

town and country, 110, 111, 155, 160, 165–66, 292

trade, 37, 41, 132; and traders, 42 *passim*, 45, 136, 142; State, 44, 190; in Great Leap Forward, 50; in Russia, 156; US embargo on, 198, 207, 220

trade union, 6, 9, 11 *passim*, 17, 68, 92, 100–101, 103–107, 114, 126, 181; 'yellow', 16; in Nazi Germany, 263; Federation of (ACFTU), 91, 92 *passim*, 104, 106, 107

'triple alliance', 67, 69, 70 (*see also* revolutionary committees)

Trotsky, L. D., 10, 15, 16, 103

Tsarism, and agriculture, 132–33

Turkey, 209

Ukraine, loss of, 208

unemployment, 29; educated, 45, 46–47, 92, 96, 101–103, 120; rural, 46, 47; among women, 165

'united front', 17, 21–23, 26; after 1949, 39; in Indonesia, 228–29; Cuban opposition to, 237; Comintern and the end of, 244; India and, 248, 250; in Portugal, 251; in Norway, 253, 255, 274, 283, 295

United Nations

PRC entry, 213, 215, 216; attitude to, 216–27, 219, 220, 224; Bangladesh entry, 232, 235, 238

United States (US), 3, 24, 26, 37, 41, 54, 95–96; military assistance, 23; bases, 40; in Vietnam, 66; détente